The Ordeal of Desegregation

REED SARRATT

The Ordeal of
DESEGREGATION
The First Decade

HARPER & ROW, PUBLISHERS • NEW YORK AND LONDON

To the Board of Directors

of Southern Education Reporting Service

Contents

v

Preface

"Separate educational facilities are inherently unequal."

With these words the Supreme Court of the United States, on May 17, 1954, lit the fuse to a decade of explosive social change. The Court invalidated laws that required racial segregation in the public schools. For Negroes the decision unlocked the door to realization of their rights as citizens, and they pushed to open it wider and wider. Pushing against the other side, determined to keep the door closed, were those white Southerners to whom the decision was heresy, a threat to their way of life.

The school segregation barriers fell quickly and quietly in some places. Even where resistance was strong enough to delay change, desegregation began voluntarily and without incident in most instances. Ten years after the decision, however, fewer than one in fifty Negro pupils attended a desegregated school in the eleven states of the Confederacy.

Violence and disorder periodically marked the slow pace of change. Mobs gathered when Negroes entered some formerly white schools and colleges. Local and state police, National Guardsmen and federal marshals and troops occasionally were needed to bring rioting under control. The casualty lists included many injured and two shot to death. Schools, homes and churches were bombed and burned. Advocates of desegregation were the victims of economic reprisals, personal harassment and beatings. A few schools were closed to avoid admitting Negroes and whites together as students.

The resistance to desegregation was not entirely, or even primarily, physical. The battle raged in the legislative halls, in the courtrooms and at the ballot box. The struggle touched the lives of nearly everyone in the seventeen Southern and border states and the District of Columbia, where schools had been segregated by law. Many stood on the sidelines as spectators, but even among those who merely watched, few were impartial. Public opinion was a powerful mover and shaper of action.

The school desegregation story is one of people—of men and women and children, white and Negro, of every station and walk of life. It is a story of leadership and the absence of leadership, of kindness and cruelty, of heroism and cowardice, of human emotions rubbed raw by change and resistance to change.

For almost everyone, of whatever persuasion or race, the process of change was an ordeal. Negroes in the South suffered the frustration of being denied the right that the Supreme Court said was theirs, of having to fight to win and to keep one toehold after another. Southern whites who cherished the tradition of segregation tried desperately to protect it from the ravages of slow but steady erosion.

The Court's decision changed the law, but it did not change the thoughts and feelings of vast numbers of white Southerners. After the decision, Negro and white children in the South gradually began to attend the same classes. The shift was from segregation to desegregation—a removal of the legal compulsion to keep the races separated. Negroes entering formerly white schools usually found an attitude of toleration or hostility—seldom warm welcome or full acceptance.

This book is a journalistic account of desegregation in public education during the decade between the Supreme Court decision and passage of the Civil Rights Act of 1964. The focus is on the actions and words of the people directly and significantly involved. The approach to the tumultuous story is reportorial. No effort is made to pass judgment on what happened—to say whether it was good or bad, right or wrong, a success or a failure. Each reader is left to form his own opinions.

The book is written under the auspices of Southern Education Reporting Service. A group of Southern newspaper editors and educators, with the financial support of the Ford Foundation, established the agency in 1954 to collect and disseminate factual, objective information about developments in education arising from the United States Supreme Court decision declaring compulsory segregation in the public schools to be unconstitutional.

The author is grateful to the Board of Directors of SERS for their authorization and support of the book. Alexander Heard, chancellor of Vanderbilt University and chairman of an advisory committee of board members, has been especially helpful. Others on the committee are C. A. McKnight, editor of the Charlotte *Observer;* Thomas R. Waring, editor of the Charleston *News and Courier;* Stephen J. Wright, president of Fisk University; and Bert Struby, general manager of the Macon *Telegraph* and *News.*

Members of the SERS headquarters staff also contributed to the preparation of the manuscript. Mrs. Terry Cheek retyped the several drafts that were written. Mrs. Eleanor Phillips prepared the index. Others who contributed were Thomas A. Flake, James T. Leeson, Jr., and Mrs. R. C. Griffitts and Walter Schatz. A special research staff of graduate students was composed of Robert D. Smith, Hoyt Purvis, Robert B. Hyde, Salim Kublawi and Nafhat Nasr.

Chester Davis of the Winston-Salem, N.C., *Journal* and *Sentinel,* served as a writer on the special book staff. T. A. Smedley, of the

Vanderbilt University Law School faculty and director of *Race Relations Law Reporter,* read the manuscript for accuracy as to law.

The publications and library of Southern Education Reporting Service have provided the source material for this book. Principal reliance was placed on the monthly *Southern School News,* the periodic *Statistical Summary of School Segregation-Desegregation in the Southern and Border States,* and the quarterly *Race Relations Law Reporter.* The SERS policies of factual reporting, objectivity and non-advocacy apply to this book as well as to all other publications and programs of the agency.

Although many assisted in the process of producing the manuscript, the author assumes full responsibility for the content of the book.

R. S.

Atlanta, Georgia
April, 1966

1.
The Governors

"A court order can't suddenly change the way the people have thought and lived over centuries," Governor Herman Talmadge of Georgia said soon after the United States Supreme Court ruled that compulsory segregation in the public schools was unconstitutional. Most of the governors who held office in the former Confederate states at the time of the decision expressed confidence that the races would continue to attend separate schools.

As political leaders, the governors reflected the popular mood. In the spring of 1954 the people of the South showed no great concern about the Court's opinion. Governor Hugh L. White of Mississippi bluntly pronounced, "We're not going to pay any attention to the Supreme Court's decision. We don't think it will have any effect on us down here at all." Orval Faubus, a candidate for governor in Arkansas, recalled after his election that he had thought school desegregation would be the most important issue in the campaign but that he dropped it because interest was so slight. In Alabama, James E. Folsom, also running for governor, humorously remarked after winning his party's nomination, "All I can say is I told the good colored people of this state during my campaign that they wouldn't have to go to school with us white folks." Governor James F. Byrnes of South Carolina, himself a former justice of the Supreme Court, commented that his state would wait to "see the kind of decree that the Court will render," adding that it then would "be up to the legislature and the people of South Carolina—not to me—to determine South Carolina's course of action."

History gave the South ample reason for its generally calm reaction to the precedent-shattering decision. In 1896 the Court had enunciated the "separate but equal" doctrine, which was ignored with impunity. Schools and other public facilities were kept separate, but there was little pretense of making them equal.

In striking down the "separate but equal" principle, the Supreme Court justices displayed their awareness of the deep-rooted customs and traditions with which their decision conflicted. They asked for further arguments to assist them in formulating their implementation decree. Another year was to pass before the decree was issued. It was a year of grace—and a year for the preparation of defenses and the stiffening of resistance.

The Court's ruling in the *School Segregation Cases* became known as the *Brown* decision, because the first case listed was *Oliver Brown et al. v. Board of Education of Topeka, Shawnee County, Kansas.* The case that gave the decision its name came from a state where law permitted, but did not require, segregated schools. The Topeka schools were desegregated promptly, and received no further attention on this score.

The Border States

The states along the northern border of the old Confederacy, in common with the Southern states, had maintained separate white and Negro schools by force of law. In these states reactions to the

Brown decision were more nearly like Topeka's than the South's. With a few notable exceptions, school boards acted rather quickly to desegregate, and in none of the border states was school desegregation a major political issue.

Most of the governors in office in the border states in 1954 gave assurance that their states would comply with the Supreme Court decision. Governor J. Caleb Boggs of Delaware notified the State Board of Education by letter that it would be the policy of his administration "to work toward adjustment to the United States Constitutional requirements" and asked the board "to proceed toward this objective." In neighboring Maryland, Governor Theodore R. McKeldin said, "Maryland prides itself on being a law-abiding state, and I am sure our citizens and our officials will accept readily the United States Supreme Court's interpretation of our fundamental law." Governor William C. Marland of West Virginia expressed his state's intention "to abide by the Court's decision." Governor Lawrence Wetherby said that Kentucky would "do whatever is necessary to comply with the law."

Oklahoma offered the only exception to the general acceptance by the border states of the Court's decision. While Governor Johnston Murray said that his state would "obey the law of the land," he added, "I don't believe in forcing people to do something they don't want to do." His successor, Governor Raymond Gary, a year later indicated that some Oklahomans didn't want to desegregate their schools. "Many sections of Oklahoma can be desegregated easily with a minimum of preparation," he said. "In other places it will take longer both because of local attitudes and special local school problems." At the same time he warned school boards inclined to defy the mandate of the Court that they would "find themselves on their own."

First Reactions in the South

By contrast to the border-state governors, no governor who held office in any of the Southern states during the year between the 1954 *Brown* decision and the 1955 implementation decree advocated compliance. Some recognized the opinion as "the law." Some deplored it. Some denounced it. Some were defiant in their opposition.

Governor Frank G. Clement of Tennessee came nearer than any other state chief executive to supporting the Court. He said, "I must point out it is a decision handed down by a judicial body, which we, the American people, under our Constitution and law recognize as supreme in matters of interpreting the law of the land." Early in 1955 Clement vetoed two segregation bills that the state legislature passed. In his veto message, he said, "Segregation is not a political issue to be misused to the detriment of Tennessee and Tennesseans, but is a significant and far-reaching social issue, which demands statesmanlike consideration, prayerful thought and careful legal analysis."

The governor of North Carolina, William B. Umstead, died a few months after the 1954 decision, but the state followed the course toward which his initial statement pointed. "The Supreme Court of the United States has spoken," he said. "It has reversed itself and has declared segregation in the public schools unconstitutional. In my opinion its previous decision on this question was correct. This reversal of its former decisions is in my judgment a clear and serious invasion of the rights of the sovereign states. Nevertheless, this is now the latest interpretation of the Fourteenth Amendment."

Governor Folsom reminded the people of Alabama, "When the Supreme Court speaks, that's the law." In a state where segregationist sentiment was predominant, Folsom told the annual meeting of the Alabama Education Association, "Due to high court rulings of recent months, as well as more yet to come, there is a certain degree of anxiety existing in the educational field. I would like to remind you that we always hear more noise from those who are guided by blinded prejudice and bigotry than is ever the case with those who try to think through and be fair in their approach. If there ever was a time on the American educational front when we needed wisdom and tolerance and objective thinking it is certainly now."

In Virginia Governor Thomas B. Stanley reacted by issuing a prepared statement two hours after the decision, which he said posed drastic change in the state's educational life. He did not seem to be alarmed, but he called for "cool heads, calm, steady and sound judgment." U.S. Senator Harry Flood Byrd, head of the political organization that gave Virginia its governors, promptly declared that the state faced "a crisis of the first magnitude." Stanley soon said that he was "convinced" the "overwhelming majority" of Virginians wanted to maintain segregated schools, and he proposed to use "every legal means at my command to continue segregated schools."

The goal of keeping the races separate in the schools without running afoul of the Supreme Court decision was shared by most of the governors. Even Governor Byrnes of South Carolina, with his background of experience as a justice on the Court, voiced "supreme confidence that we will find ways to lawfully maintain segregation." Governor Robert Kennon of Louisiana, a former state Appeals Court judge, declared, "It is not a violation of the Supreme Court ruling to continue a dual school system. The Supreme Court does not have jurisdiction over the state school systems." Kennon expressed the belief that "building equal facilities for both races largely will solve problems brought about by the Supreme Court decision," another viewpoint that he shared with Byrnes.

In Mississippi Governor White labeled the *Brown* decision "the most unfortunate thing that ever happened." Declaring that it was "impossible to mix the races together in the public schools of Mississippi," he promised that the state was "never going to have integration in its schools." Governor Marvin Griffin, who early in 1955 succeeded Herman Talmadge in Georgia, did not go as far as White. Immediately after assuming office, Griffin repeated his campaign pledge "to the mothers and fathers of Georgia" that so long as he held office "there will be no mixing of the races in the classrooms of our schools and colleges."

In the years that followed, the governors of the Southern states were to fall into the patterns cut by those who filled the states' top offices in the first year after the *Brown* decision. A few didn't quite fit the general pattern, even for their own states, but usually they represented variations on the main themes, not departures from them. All of them supported segregation, and most of them pledged that they would maintain it. Most of them attacked the Supreme Court, while calling for law and order and the keeping of the public peace. The majority urged that public schools be preserved, but some were willing to abandon public education rather than to permit white and Negro children to attend classes together. Almost without exception, the governors based their positions on the will of the people of their state.

Traditions and the Court

The Southern governors adopted a "wait and see" attitude during the year between the May 17, 1954, Supreme Court decision, and the May 31, 1955, decree to implement it. During this interim their reactions in most instances were restrained when related to their later behavior. Although the decree did not require immediate desegregation of the schools and was widely regarded as a victory for the South, its issuance reinvigorated the defense of Southern customs and traditions and the attack on the Supreme Court.

Luther Hodges of North Carolina was one of the first of the governors to react to the 1955 decree. Hodges, who had become governor late in 1954 upon the death of Umstead, said that "although first impressions of the Court's opinion may lead to the belief that the South achieved a measure of victory, a closer study of the Court's language reveals much greater possibilities than to date seem to have been realized." Urging that "some solution must be found to save our schools and our traditions," he advocated the continuation of "a dual system of schools in which the children of each race voluntarily attend separate schools." Hodges recognized the decision as "the law of the land" but expressed his conviction that it constituted "an unlawful usurpation of power" and gave notice of North Carolina's intention "to use every legal means at our disposal to preserve the segregated schools of this state."

While Hodges was determined in his defense of segregation and his attack on the Court, his language was moderate by comparison with that of some other governors. Governor Faubus of Arkansas likened the federal courts to the Nazi judiciary under Adolf Hitler and referred to "judicial dictatorship." When the Supreme Court ruled that laws he had sponsored were unconstitutional, Faubus said that the Court "usually rules on things without knowing what the hell they are all about." Governor Griffin, addressing the Georgia legislature at its first session after the 1955 decision, said that maintaining segregation was "the most vital question that has ever been before this legislative body since the state was created." He declared that the Supreme Court had "no authority to declare segregated public schools unconstitutional."

John M. Patterson, who followed Folsom as governor of Alabama, pledged that "if any school in Alabama is integrated, it will be over my dead body." He referred to the Supreme Court as a "super legislature" which in its school decisions "did not interpret but amended the Constitution."

George C. Wallace, governor of Alabama at the decade's end, was especially vitriolic in his attacks on the federal judges, whom he described at various times as "the sorriest in the world," "lousy and irresponsible," "a bunch of atheistic pro-Communist bums," and "bearded beatniks and faceless, spineless, power-hungry theorists and black-robed judicial anarchists."

As a candidate for governor, Wallace had said, "The best interest for the state is absolute and complete segregation. . . . We can maintain what we want to maintain in the South, and we can do it within the law. Nobody is smart enough to outsmart us." As governor, he assured the people of Alabama that he would "stand at the schoolhouse door, in person, if necessary" in order to resist a court order to desegregate schools.

Governor Ross Barnett of Mississippi went Wallace one better. As governor-elect, he pledged, "Ross Barnett will rot in a federal jail before he will let one nigra cross the sacred threshold of our white schools." Before taking office, he implored, "Let's keep the child from being brain-washed. Let's teach the child to love Christian principles and Southern traditions." In his inaugural address he said that "schools at all levels must be kept segregated at all costs." Shortly thereafter he expressed the opinion that "with integration will come intermarriage just as sure as God made little apples." He

7

also voiced the belief that "everywhere people have integrated long enough and extensively enough it has absolutely ruined every civilization."

Collins of Florida

Although a number of Southern governors recognized the legal force of the *Brown* decision, no other defended the Supreme Court as did LeRoy Collins, governor of Florida. Collins was elected in 1954 to fill the remaining two years in the unexpired term of Governor Dan McCarty, who had died soon after taking office in 1952. Charlie E. Johns, who was president of the state Senate at the time of McCarty's death, became acting governor, and was Collins's opponent for the office in 1954. Johns was an ardent segregationist. As a candidate, and after his election as governor, Collins also supported segregation. He issued a statement of principle, in which he said: "I favor segregation in our public schools. It is part of Florida custom and law. I will use all the lawful power of the governor's office to preserve this custom and law. Under our state constitution it is the governor's duty."

In January of 1957, following his election to a full four-year term, Collins sounded a different note in his inaugural address. "The Supreme Court decisions are the law of the land, and this nation's strength and Florida's strength are bottomed on the basic reverse premise that ours is a land of law," he said. Having sounded the note, he returned to it a number of times. Addressing a bar group in the spring of 1958, Collins, himself a lawyer, said, "At the head of the judicial system stands the Supreme Court of the United States, and its decisions must be accepted as to the meaning of the Constitution. . . . You can't have a baseball game without an umpire to interpret the rules, and you can't have constitutional government without the authority somewhere to interpret and apply the constitution." In his speech as outgoing chairman of the Southern Governors' Conference that fall he said: "One may feel very strongly that the 1954 decision is not well founded in the law. One may even feel that the Court exceeded its authority under the Constitution.

Even so, the Supreme Court as an institution is an essential part of the framework of our government, and its decisions cannot be disregarded without doing violence to our whole concept of government. If citizens may choose the decisions of the Supreme Court they like to live by and ones they do not like, law and order will soon disappear."

Soon after his 1957 inauguration, Collins also took a new tack on segregation. "If the South should wrap itself in a Confederate blanket and consume itself in racial furor," he said, "it would surely miss its greatest opportunity for channeling into a wonderful future the products of change now taking place." In a speech at a political dinner in Raleigh, North Carolina, early in 1958, he moved farther away from his former position favoring segregation when he observed, "The inevitable tide of human progress moves against racial discrimination. Universal brotherhood must be our goal." As his term of office neared its end, Collins said that the South must "look ahead" for answers to its problems instead of "always looking behind where the problems originated." He went on to say, "We have this problem with the race issue, and we've got to face up to it. We must accept the responsibility of meeting it and of working together to find the answers. We have got to learn to keep the routes of communication open between the Negro and white leadership."

Of all the Southern governors who served during the first decade after the *Brown* decision, Collins was the most active in seeking to find, as he put it, "solutions, not scapegoats." Soon after his election in 1956, he urged President Eisenhower to assemble a conference of all Southern governors, together with Southern educators, to discuss segregation. The President did not choose to act on the suggestion. As chairman of the Southern Governors' Conference at the time of the Little Rock crisis in 1957, Collins appointed a committee of five governors, including himself, to meet with the President and Governor Faubus in an effort to make possible the withdrawal of the federal troops dispatched to enforce court-ordered desegregation at Little Rock. The committee failed to achieve its purpose. In the spring of 1958, he proposed that Congress establish a civil rights commission in each of the states, with members appointed by the

President but recommended by the governors of the respective states. "Congress should take action setting up procedures to implement the Court's ruling in such a way as to protect the states against improvident action," he explained. Under the Collins plan, the state commissions would take over from the federal district courts original jurisdiction in school racial matters. The commissions would decide whether desegregation could be carried out or whether segregation should continue. When its actions were final, a commission's orders would be subject to review by the courts. Congress took no action on the Collins proposal, but the governor came back a year later with a request that Congress declare a six-month moratorium on federal district court decisions ordering desegregation. During that period, according to the plan, Congress would develop machinery to accomplish desegregation where feasible and to protect citizens "against improvident efforts to coerce" desegregation where it was not feasible. Again Congress failed to adopt the governor's proposal, but Collins attracted the attention of Senator Lyndon B. Johnson of Texas, the majority leader. Senator Johnson invited Collins to come to Washington for a discussion of his ideas. The Civil Rights Act of 1964 provided for the establishment of a Community Relations Service, and Johnson, then President of the United States, named Collins as its first director.

"Where Are the People in the Middle?"

LeRoy Collins gained a national reputation as a "moderate" on the school desegregation issue. But the people of his state deserted him as his term neared its end. In a radio-television address in the spring of 1960, Collins asked, "Where are the people in the middle? Why aren't they talking? Why aren't they working?" In the Democratic primary that year, Farris Bryant won the gubernatorial nomination. Bryant's position on segregation was that it was "preferable, natural and . . . inevitable." Collins opposed Bryant on the grounds that his nomination would lead to "reaction, retreat and regret." The election of Bryant generally was regarded as a repudiation of Collins.

Other governors whose words and actions caused them to be classified as "soft" or "moderate" on the desegregation issue were similarly repudiated. Both James Folsom in Alabama and J. P. Coleman in Mississippi failed in bids for re-election against candidates who were more vigorous in their support of segregation.

During his 1954-59 term as governor, Folsom had incurred the displeasure of the strong segregationists in Alabama. At the Southern Governors' Conference in 1954, he refused to sign a pledge to use every constitutional effort "to preserve the right of the states to administer their public school systems to the best interests of all the people." When the state legislature passed a pupil placement act in 1955, it became law without Folsom's signature. When in 1956 the legislature passed a resolution declaring the Supreme Court decision to be "null, void and of no effect" in Alabama, Folsom described it as "just a bunch of hogwash" and likened the action to "a hound dog baying at the moon." He pocket-vetoed several bills and resolutions in 1958, giving as his reason that "they wouldn't do any good and might stir up a lot of trouble." He urged "the leaders of both races to get together and settle their differences" because "eventually it will be done."

Under the Alabama Constitution, a governor could not succeed himself, but four years after he left office Folsom ran again. He campaigned in his characteristically humorous fashion. "You know down there in the black belt," he said in one of his favorite campaign stories, "they have a lot more Negroes than white folks, and there is a lot more of them light-skinned Negroes than black-skinned Negroes. Now my mama used to tell me that if the bed linen was dingy, you could hang it out in the sun and it would be bleached white, but those light-skinned Negroes were not bleached by the sun. If that ain't integration, I don't know what it is." He also told his audiences, "Them other fellows will tell you they can beat the federal government, but they know they can't and they will tell you in private they don't care about integration. They just care about votes." When the votes were counted, Folsom lost to George C. Wallace, fiery advocate of segregation and states' rights.

The experience of J. P. Coleman in Mississippi was similar to that of Folsom. As governor from 1956 to 1960, Coleman left no doubt about where he stood on segregation. Soon after taking office, he said that he regarded the Supreme Court school decision as "unconstitutional" and added that Mississippi would "resist enforcement by every legal and constitutional means available." At the same time he called the movement to nullify the Court's decision "legal poppycock" and "foolish." When chairman of the Southern Governors' Conference in 1958, he said that the decision was "the law." Coleman repeatedly implored the people of Mississippi "to keep cool heads and calm minds, and leave the solution of these problems to our duly chosen officials, which is the only way it can possibly be done." As the end of his term approached, he remarked, "Sometimes I think we are repeating step by step the same performance that destroyed us once before. Sometimes I think there is a curse on Mississippi that keeps us stumbling over the Negro problem and falling on our face."

In Mississippi as in Alabama, a governor cannot be elected to two consecutive terms. As the campaign to elect Coleman's successor gathered momentum, he warned that "a firebrand or a man who hasn't studied these problems could have this state in a mess in 24 hours." For himself, he said that he "had no intention of flipping matches into the gasoline barrel." To critics who accused him of being a "moderate" he replied that the problem of keeping schools open and yet avoiding integration calls for "clear heads and capable brains, not lungs and tongues." The attack on Coleman continued, and he made a radio-television address to the people of the state in June of 1959 in which he said, "I am aware that a little handful of my political adversaries have tried to destroy my place in the affections of my fellow Mississippians by claiming that I am a moderate. Apparently these people cannot tell a moderate from a successful segregationist." The voters elected Ross Barnett, whom Coleman opposed, to be their next governor. In his farewell address to the legislature, Coleman cited keeping the schools open and segregated as the greatest accomplishment of his administration. "If our children are deprived of schooling," he said, "if they are compelled by the mistakes of their elders to grow up in ignorance, we shall all be the easier victims for our well educated enemies."

After his nomination, Barnett exulted, "The day of the artful dodger in Mississippi is ended. The time of the apologist is gone." His reference to Coleman was obvious. Upon becoming eligible again, Coleman sought another term as governor. But in the Democratic primary of 1963 he lost to Paul B. Johnson, who as lieutenant governor during the Barnett administration had stood with Barnett in the attempt to block the admission of the first Negro to the University of Mississippi.

Almond of Virginia

While the voters rejected Folsom and Coleman and repudiated Collins's position, the governor who probably suffered the greatest agony of all those who served during the decade was J. Lindsay Almond, Jr., of Virginia. Almond was state attorney general under Stanley and, as the choice of the Byrd organization, took office as governor in January of 1958. It was his fate to preside over the collapse of Virginia's policy of massive resistance to school desegregation and to devise a new policy to replace it. In the process he lost favor with Senator Byrd and, consequently, his political future in Virginia.

As attorney general and in his first year as governor, Almond was a staunch and articulate advocate of massive resistance. In 1956 he criticized all appointments to the Supreme Court for the preceding twenty years as having been made "without regard to fitness or ability." He said, "The appointive power has been desecrated and degraded to the extent of political depravity for the purpose of paying political debts or for the support of minority pressure groups." In announcing his candidacy for governor, he pledged to "continue the fight with never diminishing faith that right will ultimately prevail."

Almond pursued this strong segregationist line in his inaugural address, saying, "Moderation may be indeed the noblest gift of heaven, but it is stark reality that confronts us here on earth. . . . I find no area of compromise that might be usefully explored. To compromise means to integrate. . . . I cannot conceive such a thing as a 'little integration' any more than I can conceive a small avalanche or a modest holocaust. . . . To sanction any plan which would legalize the mixing of races in our schools would violate the clear and unmistakable mandate of the people. . . . This I cannot do."

Under Virginia law Governor Almond that fall closed public schools in four communities to prevent their desegregation by court order. In doing so, he said, "I am willing to continue to fight till the last ditch and then dig another ditch. If we ever yield one inch, we are lost forever. There can be no compromise with principles. There can be no middle ground that will provide an avenue of escape." He told the state Congress of Parents and Teachers, "I will not permit white and colored children to be taught together in the public schools."

The governor suggested the strain he felt when he said late in 1958 that he was committed to do everything within his power "to prevent the amalgamation of the white and Negro races in Virginia, which would be the inevitable result of integrated schools." He added, "That's why I'm wrecking my life and my health to try to save public education."

On January 19, 1959, both the Virginia Supreme Court of Appeals and a three-judge federal court announced decisions that undermined the legal foundation of the state's policy of massive resistance. The following day, Governor Almond delivered a radio-television address to the people of Virginia in which he told them, "Be not dismayed. . . . We have just begun to fight." He assailed the "false prophets of a little or token integration" and "those who defend or close their eyes to the livid stench of sadism, sex, immorality, and juvenile pregnancy infesting the mixed schools of the District of Columbia and elsewhere." He pledged, "I will not yield to that which I know to be wrong and will destroy every rational semblance of public education for thousands of children in Virginia." He called on "the people of Virginia to stand firmly with me in this struggle."

A week later, addressing an emergency session of the state legislature, Almond recommended a policy of "passive resistance" or "containment." In an address which he read slowly and deliberately, the governor assured the legislators that "Virginia has not surrendered and does not surrender now." But he went on to say, "It is not enough for gentlemen to cry unto you and to me, 'Don't give up the ship; stop them; it must not happen; or it can be prevented.'" The governor referred to the segregationists who were demanding that Virginia not yield in its policy of massive resistance despite rulings of the courts. Directing his remarks to the segregationists, the governor admonished, "If any of them knows the way through the dark maze of judicial aberration and constitutional exploitation, I call upon them to shed the light for which Virginia stands in dire need in this, her dark and agonizing hour." To those who urged that the governor himself go to jail rather than condone desegregation, he replied, "I am willing to serve in durance vile with those who give the advice if it will accomplish the desired purpose." "But," he declared, "I know of nothing more futile than a penal sentence that contributes nothing but the ridiculous." The General Assembly passed a tuition-grant law and repealed the compulsory attendance law, as the governor recommended. It adjourned until a special study commission appointed by the governor could recommend other legislation to replace the defunct massive resistance laws.

Two months later the legislature reconvened to receive the report of the study commission, which recommended a policy of "freedom of choice" and "local option" in dealing with school desegregation. In an address to a joint session of the Senate and House, Governor Almond supported the commission's recommendations. At the same time, he defended his own shift in position. "The record permits me to state that I have fought as long and as hard to prevent this calamity as any man in Virginia's public service today," he said, "and yet, no man has been subjected to more insulting calumny." He added, "If we have failed to prevent integration in schools of Virginia, it is not because we have not tried. It is not because we have not evoked every resource known to the institution of the system in which we live. It is because we do not possess the power to override the supremacy of federal force." By a margin of one vote, the General Assembly approved the new laws that the study commission and the governor proposed.

Later Almond was to make frequent references to his shift in position during the week between the collapse of massive resistance and the convening of the special legislative session. As to his speech the day following the court decisions, he reflected, "I don't know why I made that damn speech. If I had listened to my wife, I wouldn't have. It's caused me a good deal of trouble and embarrassment. I saw the whole thing crumbling. I was tired and distraught. I agonized and gave vent to my feelings, which never should have been done. My underlying thought and motivation was to show the people that we had done everything we could do. I wanted them to know there wouldn't be any massive onrush of integration and that we would continue to try to contain it." Explaining the change in his thinking, he said that the only way to avoid desegregation was to abolish the public schools, and that "would confine a generation of children to the darkness of illiteracy, the pit of indolence and dependency and the dungeon of delinquency." Closing the public schools was "too big a price to pay" for maintaining segregation, he said, adding, "I had to take my position, and when I took it, the roof fell in on me so to speak."

The pillar that supported the political roof under which Almond had lived was the Byrd organization. Senator Byrd never forgot nor forgave Almond's abandonment of massive resistance. Almond related his attempts to discuss with Byrd the crisis that the court decisions on massive resistance had created. The governor had difficulty obtaining an appointment to see the senator in Washington. "As I recall," he said later, "we went to the senator's office but were then conducted to a secluded nook in the Capitol. We entered a labyrinth that was somewhat remindful of the catacombs of Rome. I had served in Congress myself, but I didn't know there was such a place in the precincts of the Capitol." Senator Byrd could not be budged from his conviction that massive resistance should continue. "I can't quote his exact words," Almond said, "but he made his feelings very clear that Virginia would have to hold the line. He expressed concern as to what his Southern colleagues in the Senate would think if Virginia gave up." President John F. Kennedy appointed Almond to the United States Court of Customs and Patent Appeals in April of 1962, but confirmation was delayed for months during which Senator Byrd, by his silence, was assumed to be opposed to the appointment.

Faubus of Arkansas

One governor who shifted his position while in office without damage to his political career was Orval Faubus of Arkansas. First elected in 1954, he was re-elected each two years throughout the decade. No other governor of the state had served more than three terms, and no other Southern governor remained in office during the full decade. From first to last, Faubus based his stand on "the will of the people."

Early in 1954, Faubus made a statement which he was to repeat with variations many times. "Integration is a local problem," he said, "and can best be solved on the local level according to the peculiar circumstances and conditions of each local school district." When he ran for governor the first time, he observed that the voters showed little interest in school desegregation; therefore, the Supreme Court decision was not a major issue in the campaign. He commented, however, that in his judgment "the people of the state are overwhelmingly opposed to any effort to bring about sudden and complete integration."

Two years later, when running for re-election, he declared that the segregation question was "the most important issue in the minds of the people of Arkansas." In an advertisement that appeared in all the daily newspapers of the state he predicted that "any attempt to force integration on an unwilling district will result in consequences which will be terrible for our people." He promised to give all the help he could "to any school district which wants to resist the abandonment of its segregated schools." He expressed his conviction that "the surest way to safeguard our public school system at the present time for all citizens, both white and Negro, is to preserve our segregated schools." He reminded the people that since he had been in office, "no school board has been forced to desegregate its schools against its will" and he assured them that no school board would be "forced to mix the races" while he was governor.

In his second inaugural address, in January of 1957, Faubus gave major attention to school desegregation. "The decision of 1954 placed psychology and sociology upon the judicial scales and overturned long established legal precedent and seeks to wipe out generations of human attitudes, traditions and customs based thereon," he said. "I do not know the ultimate answer. I doubt if anyone else does. However, I am convinced that the answer is not to be found in violence and disorder, nor in haughtiness, arrogance or the forcing of issues. And, above all, hate is not the answer. . . . It is folly to expect judicial dictation to compel social adjustments. These changes must be brought about in the hearts and minds of people. That is why I am opposed to forcible integration of our public schools. To me this is bad for the members of both races. These matters must be left to the will of the people in the various districts. The people must decide on the basis of what is best as a whole for each particular area."

In his comment about "the hearts and minds of people," the governor sounded much like President Dwight D. Eisenhower. Yet a few months later the governor and President were to be locked in dramatic conflict on the issue of the supremacy of federal over state sovereignty. As the time approached for court-ordered desegregation in Little Rock, Faubus accused the federal government of "cramming integration down our throats." With federal troops in Little Rock to enforce the court order, he said, "We are now occupied territory. There can be no question of the supremacy of the United States Army when used against a defenseless state." In a nationally televised address, he asked, "Must the will of the majority now yield under federal force to the will of the minority regardless of its consequences?" In his resistance to federal force, Faubus became the symbol of states' rights. On this score he said, "I never asked to become what I am now, but sometimes you become a child of fortune or circumstances."

Fortune favored Faubus's political ambitions. With the enthusiastic support of segregationists, he was elected in 1958 to a third term. He expressed his position then by saying, "I don't think the people are in a mood now to take integration." Yet in the spring of 1959 he indicated that he would not be opposed to "token integration" if that was necessary to resolve the deadlock at Little Rock, where the high schools were closed by the governor's order. This suggestion recalled Faubus's earlier statement that he never considered himself "either an integrationist or a segregationist" but that he was "opposed to forced integration." And in July of 1959 he returned to this point when he said, "I'm not arguing whether integration is right or wrong, but when the federal government sends troops with bayonets to force good, God-loving, church-going people to mix against their will, that is the beginning of tyranny."

The Little Rock schools reopened that fall, desegregated. The governor commented, "Whether the people like it or not, they're apparently reconciled to police state rule. . . ." In 1960 Faubus became the first man in history to be elected governor of Arkansas for a fourth term. He had continued his attacks on "judicial tyranny" and federal force and had upheld the right of the people to determine whether their schools should desegregate or remain segregated.

By 1962, when he was running for a fifth term, Faubus was saying, "I just regret that it all happened, but I wouldn't change anything I did. I just did what I had to do, what I felt the people of Arkansas elected me to do. . . . The people are as opposed to integration as they ever were, but they now have a feeling of hopelessness." The governor waged his campaign on the issue of industrial development of the state. Attacked by both the segregationists who formerly had supported him and by his long-standing opponents, he pictured himself as a man beset by "extremists on either side." Dr. Malcolm G. Taylor, a former president of the Little Rock Citizens' Council, lamented, "No longer will we thrill to the tirades of a toothless tiger. We must look elsewhere for leadership."

Faubus was unmoved by such criticism. Following his re-election, he interpreted the vote to mean that "the people do not wish to wander in the thickets of extremism to either the right or the left." He added that the voters had shown that they want "their feet planted firmly on the broad highway of progress" and "a good business climate in which to use their initiative and their money." Midway in his fifth term, he said that the people were "tired of this issue" of segregation. When he campaigned in 1964 for a sixth term, he had come full circle from his position during his first campaign ten years earlier. Again the people gave him their endorsement by re-electing him.

Signs of Change

While Orval Faubus showed his skill at correctly reading the political weathervane in Arkansas, the winds of change were blowing in other Southern states. Political leaders from Virginia to Mississippi adjusted their sails accordingly. As the decade neared its end, most of them continued to espouse segregation, but in words softer than their predecessors'.

In Virginia Albertis Harrison was the candidate of the Byrd organization to succeed Lindsay Almond. Harrison said in his inaugural address in January of 1962: ". . . if I were to venture even the slightest criticism of our beloved state, it would be that in times past we have not expanded sufficiently our intellectual, cultural and social horizons. . . . The changes brought by social forces and scientific developments of the past century have not brought in us a sufficiently timely response. . . . We may have erred in some areas by attempting to fit Twentieth Century problems to the Procrustean bed of Eighteenth Century solutions. . . . I myself am dedicated heart and soul to the concept of states' rights. I pledge that every ounce of my energy will be directed to preserving Virginia's powers as a sovereign state from continued attrition. Yet I would serve you poorly if I did not acknowledge candidly and realistically that in their application, historical principles of states' rights cannot always be trimmed to fit specific problems of our own day. The powers delegated to the central government by the constitution have to be exercised now in ways that were neither necessary nor proper then."

Two days later Governor Harrison appeared before the General Assembly to present the program of his administration. On that occasion he said, "My failure to mention the racial problem which has consumed so much of our time in years past is a deliberate omission. The progress that is so necessary to Virginia and the programs that I ask you to consider were designed for the welfare and happiness of all Virginians irrespective of their race, color or creed."

As governor, Harrison followed the course on school desegregation that Almond had set. The Byrd organization's support of Harrison in continuing the policies for which it had banished Almond was one of the political paradoxes of the time. Asked to comment on this situation, Almond said, "It is something of an enigma. My surmise is that Harrison went ahead and developed his chances for running for governor, and felt that he was on pretty solid political ground. Byrd must have made the same evaluation."

Like Almond in Virginia, Ernest Vandiver, who succeeded Marvin Griffin as governor of Georgia, led his state away from massive resistance to a local option plan. Vandiver ran as a confirmed segregationist, and as governor he pledged, "We are going to resist again, again and again. We will exhaust every legal means and remedy available to us." But, when the choice in 1961 was between some desegregation and no public education, he took the position that he would "not be a party to defiance of the law." In signing the "open schools" bills that he had recommended and the legislature had passed, he commented, "Thirty days ago I wouldn't have thought they'd have signed." One of the legislators gathered around his desk for the signing ceremony replied, "Sixty days ago I wouldn't have known they would have been recommended."

As president pro tem of the state Senate under Vandiver, Carl E. Sanders guided the open schools bills through a hostile Georgia Senate. As a candidate to succeed Vandiver, Sanders assured the voters that he would use forces "within the framework of the law" to maintain the segregated way of life in the state. As governor, Sanders said in his inaugural address in January of 1963: "This is a new Georgia. This is a new day. This is a new era. . . . We adhere to the values of respectability and responsibility, which constitute our tradition. We believe in law and order and in the principle that all laws apply equally to all citizens." A month later, he added: "While I am governor we are not going to resist federal court orders with violence, and we are not going to close any schools. We have seen some pretty sorry examples of that kind of folly in the South, and I want none of it in Georgia."

While Carl Sanders was taking office in Georgia, Donald S. Russell was breaking precedent at his inaugural as governor of South Carolina. More than a hundred Negroes attended the traditional barbecue on the mansion grounds—at the new governor's invitation.

In a message to the General Assembly, Governor Russell, who had been a law partner of former Governor Byrnes, reassured the legislators by saying, "We have not altered our convictions. We shall continue to seek to maintain these convictions by every lawful means, confident as we are in the ultimate rightness of our stand. But when we lose battles, we will abide by the lawful processes." Soon after Russell took office, South Carolina peacefully complied with orders of the federal courts to desegregate Clemson College. At a meeting of the National Governors' Conference in June of 1964, Russell spoke against the civil rights bill then before Congress, declaring that there already were too many laws affecting schools. He added, "Though many disagree with the United States Supreme Court decision, it has established the rights of all with respect to school admissions."

Even in Mississippi, the year 1963 was one of change. A new governor, who ran as an absolute segregationist, after assuming office began to steer the state toward acceptance of desegregation. Paul B. Johnson, lieutenant governor under Ross Barnett and son of a former governor, won an easy victory at the polls. Although he faced no effective opposition, he campaigned on a platform of states' rights and segregation. He pledged that he would "resist the integration of any school anywhere in Mississippi" and asserted that "we can and will maintain a system of segregated schools." Addressing a Citizens' Council conference, he said: "I promise here and now that when I am governor, I will stand firm. I will continue to uphold states' rights and racial integrity and to oppose federal encroachment in Mississippi. . . . Our enemies are highly organized and well financed. We must fight fire with fire, and under the dedicated leadership of men and women like yourselves, we can and will organize and unite the liberty-loving citizenship of conservative America into a strong and forceful unit dedicated to preserving the integrity of the white race."

In his inaugural address, Johnson made no mention of segregation, and he emphasized the need for national unity. "Hate, or prejudice, or ignorance will not lead Mississippi while I sit in the governor's chair," he said. He reminded the people of his state, "You and I are a part of this world, whether we like it or not; what happens in it, through no fault of ours, affects us. Too, we are Americans as well as Mississippians. As a practical matter, we are at this moment 'in the mainstream of national life.' National policies have direct bearing on our economy, on our political freedom, on our daily living, whether we like it or not." He pointed out that "the Mississippi economy is not divisible by political party or faction, or even race, color or creed." And he added, "As of this hour, Paul Johnson is working for everybody with every resource at his command." He concluded by asking God to bless "all Mississippians, both black and white, here and away from home." As his administration started, Johnson continued his efforts to change the national image of Mississippi along the lines that he suggested in his inaugural address.

In Louisiana the chief contenders for the Democratic nomination for governor in 1963 were John J. McKeithen and deLesseps Morrison. McKeithen was an attorney and a farmer, and Morrison was a former mayor of New Orleans and United States ambassador to the Organization of American States. Mrs. Blanche Long, widow of former Governor Earl Long, was McKeithen's campaign manager. One of her favorite tactics was to suggest that Morrison, if elected, would invite Negroes to the governor's mansion. McKeithen charged that Morrison was corralling the "Negro bloc vote" and referred to his "record as an integrationist." Morrison, who twice before had run unsuccessfully for governor, conducted what he called a "positive" campaign, stressing economic issues. On the race question, he described himself as a segregationist "within the rule of reason." McKeithen defeated Morrison in the runoff primary, and won over his Republican opponent in the general election.

Although McKeithen expressed stronger pro-segregation sentiments than Morrison, some Louisiana segregationist leaders criticized the governor-elect for the mildness of his position. In one of his campaign statements, McKeithen said: "I am not a hell-raising segregationist. I am frankly in favor of having all candidates make the same statement on segregation and dismiss the issue from the very beginning. . . . I will do everything legally possible to maintain our Southern way of life, but I will not close the schools to keep them from integrating." One of McKeithen's critics was William N. Rainach, a former state senator, first chairman of the Joint Legislative Committee on Segregation and a member of the State Sovereignty Commission. Rainach supported McKeithen's Republican opponent in the election. Soon after his election, McKeithen said that he was "prepared to make the sacrifice of standing in a schoolhouse door to resist integration attempts, should it be considered beneficial to the state by our finest constitutional lawyers." This statement evoked from Rainach the comment, "The longtime state sovereignty and segregation people welcome John McKeithen to our ranks. We take the position that a deathbed conversion is better than none at all—and we hope he sticks." After assuming office, McKeithen followed a moderate course on school desegregation.

While the governors of massive-resistance states—with the exception of Alabama—were taking a more relaxed attitude toward the race issue, in the Florida and North Carolina gubernatorial primaries in the spring of 1964, segregation and civil rights assumed renewed importance. In Florida Haydon Burns, mayor of Jacksonville, and Robert King High, mayor of Miami, went into a runoff for the Democratic nomination. Burns described High as the "candidate of the NAACP" and himself as the "candidate of the majority." High defended his "record for fairness and reason" and countered that Burns was stirring up "racial strife by reckless appeals which can only lead to violence in order to satisfy his own ambitions." Burns won the nomination.

In North Carolina that spring, there were three leading contenders for the Democratic nomination for governor. L. Richardson Preyer, who resigned a federal judgeship to run, had the support of outgoing Governor Terry Sanford; he took the Sanford position that the courts had settled the question of desegregation and that race was a closed issue in North Carolina politics. Dr. I. Beverly Lake, an attorney and former law professor whom Sanford had defeated four years earlier, ran again as a confirmed segregationist. He expressed the belief that the 1954 decision of the Supreme Court "is a violation of the rights of North Carolina under the constitution of our country" and that "our long-established school system is in the best interest of all our children." Dan K. Moore, also an attorney and a former state Superior Court judge, stood between Preyer and Lake. "I do not believe you can legislate equality," Moore said. "It must be earned. Toward that end, the Negro deserves and should be given equality of opportunity. This will not come through violence or by additional laws which take away private property rights in the name of civil rights." Preyer led in the first primary, but lost to Moore in the second primary when Lake switched his support—and his followers—to Moore.

The Power of Public Opinion

Soon after his candidate's defeat, Governor Sanford addressed to Southern moderates an appeal reminiscent of LeRoy Collins's plaintive questions four years earlier. "The South's great weakness today," he said, "is not the bigotry of its extremists. It is the inertia of its moderates. Moderates, by definition, are not activists. They don't raise their voices, don't make their feelings felt. And so extremists too often dominate politics and events. Southern moderates must ask whether they are any longer willing to let extremists present a caricature of the South to the world. If they are not, they must commit themselves to specific actions. . . . Politics will change the moment politicians know there is no longer anything to be gained from racism. The Southern moderate can indicate by his vote that he favors responsible change and disapproves of extremism. Leaders are far more likely to stand up and challenge extremists, if they believe the majority wants them challenged."

It is axiomatic that more than desire and willingness to serve are required to become governor of a state; it is necessary to obtain a majority of the votes. In the decade following the 1954 Supreme

Court decision, school desegregation was the predominant issue in Southern politics. In some states it appeared that the voters were not concerned about anything else, and in these states the candidates seemed to be judged by the relative strength of their stands for segregation.

Governor John Patterson of Alabama described the situation candidly when he said, "For some reason, the people in Washington can't seem to get it into their heads why public officials down here don't knuckle down to the *Brown* decision. If they did bow down to it, it would be their last term in office."

Other governors voiced variations on this theme. Governor Griffin of Georgia in the spring of 1956 commented, "Election results in several states and other straws in the wind indicate that the masses of the people in the South are not ready to abide by the action of the United States Supreme Court." In Louisiana Governor Long said that he was for segregation "one thousand per cent," but added, "I don't believe you should run for office on it" although "there are a lot of people who think that's the best way to get elected." After he had led Virginia from massive to passive resistance, Governor Almond said, "Always I was under the impact of the feelings and emotions of the people, and of my own emotions. . . . I can't say now that we should have done then what we eventually did, because it was not politically feasible. . . . Almost any political organization will sound the sentiments of the people and take advantage of it to stir them to act along the lines of least resistance."

Governors who did not "act along the lines of least resistance" made known their awareness of the power of public opinion. Governor Collins of Florida commented midway in his term that schools in his state would remain segregated "until there is some acceptance of integration in the hearts of the people." Mississippi's Governor Coleman began his term by declaring, "With all due respect to the mighty power of the United States government, it will never be able to force racial integration in Mississippi, nor in any other state where the people are unwilling to have it."

The will of the people was important to the governors of the states for reasons other than their desire to remain in office. Luther

Hodges said that his approach as governor of North Carolina was to recognize "the simple and fundamental fact that to have public schools we must have public support of those schools." Hodges added that in his judgment "the great majority of our citizens—both races included—prefer to keep our schools separate." Governor Kennon of Louisiana, speaking in similar vein, said, "If the public schools are made different from what the majority of taxpayers want, property owners might be reluctant to vote the necessary school funds."

Some of the governors claimed to have almost unanimous support for their positions. Governor Talmadge estimated that his opinion represented "the thinking of 98 per cent of the people of Georgia." Governor Stanley expressed the belief that his plan of massive resistance had the support of "95 per cent of the white people in Virginia."

While Southern governors expressed differing views about compliance with the *Brown* decision, whatever position they took, they usually represented it as being the will of the people of their respective states. Those who deviated too sharply from majority sentiment among the voters were unable to maintain their political leadership. Circumstances suggest that the governors in most instances were taking their lead from the people rather than leading them.

2.

The Legislators

Periodic outbursts of violence attracted the biggest headlines, but the greatest battles of school desegregation were fought between state legislators and federal judges—in the legislative halls and in the courtrooms, not in the streets.

Most legislators in the eleven states of the old Confederacy were determined to preserve segregation in the public schools, either absolutely or to the maximum possible degree. In these states the legislative debates almost never were between segregationists and integrationists. The opponents were segregationists of varying degrees of ardor who held different views on how best to maintain race separation.

In some of the states the legislators made a bow—albeit grudging —in the direction of the Supreme Court's authority and then promptly enacted laws designed to delay and restrict compliance with the Court's mandate. In other states the legislators were determined to defy the Supreme Court, to deny its authority and to prevent compliance with its decision.

In Florida, North Carolina, Tennessee and Texas, and at times in Arkansas, the legislators were more intent upon holding compliance to token proportions than they were upon defying the Court. In the Deep South states of Alabama, Georgia, Louisiana, Mississippi and South Carolina, the rallying cry was, "Never!" This was the hard core of resistance. Virginia, at first, shouted defiance with her Deep South sister states and indeed offered them philosophical leadership; but midway in the decade, Virginia joined the ranks of the token states.

In Arkansas the legislators were in tune with Governor Orval Faubus. Early in the decade Faubus discouraged some tentative legislative attempts to pass laws calculated to preserve segregation in the public schools. After 1957, in the prolonged Little Rock crisis, the legislators supported Faubus in his defiance. For a period of two years the governor was given most of the legislation he requested to bolster his position. Nearer the close of the decade, the Arkansas lawmakers, like the governor, returned to tokenism.

Virginia followed a somewhat different route. During the summer of 1956 political spokesmen in the Old Dominion enunciated the philosophy of massive resistance and, following the lead of U.S. Senator Harry Flood Byrd, assumed leadership of the defiant states. At that time Senator Byrd said, "Virginia stands as one of the foremost states. Let Virginia surrender to this illegal demand [the desegregation decisions of the Supreme Court] and you'll find the ranks of the Southern states broken."

Early in 1959 state and federal courts demolished the legal framework of massive resistance in Virginia; and, reluctantly, Virginia shifted to tokenism. The ranks were broken. Before the decade ended, Georgia, Alabama, Louisiana, and South Carolina were forced by court orders to abandon absolute resistance for tokenism.

When the legislative output peaked in 1956–60, several state legislatures found it necessary to establish screening committees to eliminate the duplications among the mass of bills in the hopper.

During the 1956 special session in Florida, Governor LeRoy Collins invoked a rarely used power to dissolve the General Assembly to avoid a deluge of segregation measures.

In 1960–61, when the Louisiana legislature met in one regular and five extraordinary sessions, the lawmakers passed ninety-two laws and resolutions designed to maintain segregation in the public schools. For more than a year the legislature passed laws. When, as was regularly the case, the federal courts promptly declared many of those laws unconstitutional, the legislators were ready with a new batch to replace the casualties.

Differences in Attitude

While the number of laws adopted in the respective states varied widely, most of the basic measures enacted in the defiant states also were passed in the token states. But the laws had different objectives. The spirit, the attitude, behind the laws was more significant than their letter in determining the uses to which they were put.

In the token states, governors, study commissions and some legislators sold the people on the proposition that a degree of compliance rather than massive resistance, in the long run, would buy the maximum of continued race separation in public education. Despite grumbling that "a little token desegregation is like a small bite of a rattlesnake," these states took positions of technical compliance with the Supreme Court decision. The laws their legislatures adopted were designed to assure that compliance would be no more than technical.

In the defiant states there was no thought of compliance, technical or otherwise. Here the attitude behind every law was an unswerving determination to maintain 100 percent racial separation in the public schools. The Supreme Court decision was branded "illegal." Laws that were considered primarily as "safety valves" in the token states were regarded in the defiant states as parts of a program of all-out resistance.

The defiant segregationist leaders declared that school desegregation would lead to racial intermarriage and interbreeding. They warned that "mongrelization" would mean the destruction of the white race. They insisted that the public schools must be kept racially segregated whatever the cost.

State Senator Sam Englehardt of Alabama capsuled the attitude of the hard-core states when he said, "As far as I am concerned, abolition of segregation will never be feasible in Alabama or the South. No brick will ever be removed from our segregation walls."

Because of these basic differences in the attitudes of legislators, similar laws enacted in moderate and defiant states might be almost identical in their wording but in the effects of their application bear little resemblance to one another.

Tailoring laws to the cut decreed by Southern policy makers required ingenuity and a high level of legal craftsmanship. In all of the Southern states money and appeals to white, regional patriotism were used to create teams of formidable legal talent. Governors and legislative committees recruited attorneys to help in devising crash programs to block or outflank the United States Supreme Court.

Working closely with the legislators, these teams of attorneys drafted laws intended to preserve the maximum degree of race separation in the public schools. The core of this legislative resistance is found in a series of basic laws: pupil placement acts, school closing laws, and laws providing for tuition grants and private school programs.

Pupil Placement Acts

All eleven state legislatures passed pupil placement acts. In ten of the states the power to assign students to schools was vested in local school boards. The purpose was to make it necessary to bring individual suits in each school district so that no single decision ordering desegregation could be effective against the whole state school system. In Virginia, the power to assign all children to schools was given to a single state board.

North Carolina and Alabama cut the patterns for the pupil

assignment acts adopted in the other Southern states. The North Carolina law established a few simple criteria by which assignments were to be made. The criteria in the Alabama law were both numerous and detailed. In litigation that went all the way to the Supreme Court, both laws were held to be not unconstitutional on their face, although the courts pointed out that the laws later might be held unconstitutional in their application.

The North Carolina law provides that school boards shall make student assignments for the orderly and efficient administration of the public schools and for the health, safety and general welfare of the pupils.

In the Alabama act, which was more widely copied, the criteria for assignment include (among many others) available room and teaching capacity, available transportation, adequacy of a student's scholastic aptitude and preparation, psychological qualifications of the pupil for the type of teaching and associations involved, effect of the admission of the pupil on the academic progress of others, possibility or threat of friction or disorder, possibility of breaches of the peace or ill will or economic retaliation within the community, home environment of the pupil, morals, conduct, health and personal conduct of the pupil.

The two types of laws both set up elaborate procedures for making assignments and transfers. Their effect was to require Negroes seeking to attend white schools to fill out application forms, take aptitude and achievement tests, submit to hearings and appeal adverse decisions through designated, and sometimes labyrinthine, channels. To save them from being declared unconstitutional on their face, they carefully omitted race as a basis for assignment.

These procedures were designed to discourage a Negro's attempting to go to a white school—or, if he did, to exhaust his patience and his purse in his pursuit of "available administrative remedies." They proved to be an effective deterrent to mass movement of Negro children into the white schools of the token states, and until late in the decade were an impregnable barrier in the defiant states. Through the first half of the decade, the federal courts ordinarily would not take jurisdiction of a school desegregation suit until the complainants had exhausted their administrative remedies provided by state statutes. Under the transfer provisions of the laws, it was difficult for a Negro child to gain admittance to a white school, but it was easy for a white child to escape from a desegregated school. The transfer plans were designed to have a calming influence on white parents by assuring them that no white child would be required to sit in a classroom with a Negro. In operation, the plans often produced resegregation of a desegregated school, since white children left a school when Negroes entered it.

In Arkansas, Florida, Tennessee and Texas, all of which adopted Alabama-type assignment laws, and in North Carolina, the purpose was to hold race mixing in the schools to a minimum. Some desegregation, however, was both anticipated and even quietly encouraged, because token desegregation was considered necessary to provide an aura of legality for the assignment acts themselves.

In the defiant states the pupil placement acts were passed by legislators who promised that no Negro would be assigned to any white school within the state at any time, anywhere. Assignment laws were one of many means to achieve that end.

Closing the Public Schools

Pupil placement provided a technique for restricting—or avoiding—admission of Negroes to white schools. In the event the placement acts failed in their purpose, as they ultimately did in state after state where they were relied on to prevent any desegregation, the extreme segregationists were prepared to close the public schools.

That closing schools was the keystone of massive resistance was recognized by State Senator L. Marion Gressette, who headed South Carolina's fight to preserve segregation. He said, "We cannot find anywhere in the U.S. Constitution where the right to operate a school has been delegated to the U.S. Government, nor can we find where it has been prohibited to the states; it therefore follows that this right was reserved for the states. This being true, the state cannot be forced to appropriate money for schools contrary to the public interest."

The voters of Alabama, Mississippi and South Carolina repealed constitutional requirements that the state provide public education. All of the defiant states except South Carolina gave either the governor or local school boards the power to close the public schools. All of the moderate states except Tennessee also adopted school-closing laws. These statutes generally declared that the power to close schools was to be exercised to prevent violence or breach of the peace, or to forestall the use of federal troops, or to serve the best interests of the students and the community, rather than to avoid desegregation.

Again, although their language was similar, the intent of the laws in the defiant states and in the token states was not the same. The legislators in the former intended that any white public school accepting Negro students, for whatever reason, would be closed. The threat implicit in these laws was directed to Negroes who might entertain the thought of going to a white school. Senator Englehardt of Alabama put it this way: "The National Association for the Agitation of Colored People forgets that there are more ways than one to kill a snake. . . . We will have segregation in the public schools . . . or there will be no public schools." In the token states the school-closing laws were intended to serve as lightning rods should desegregation brew a thunderstorm of public protest.

The power to close schools was used sparingly, even in the defiant states. Schools were closed in Little Rock, and in several places in Virginia, and briefly in Alabama. The federal courts blocked efforts to close schools in Louisiana.

Seven states passed laws to provide that funds be withheld from schools that desegregated. These laws became more of a hindrance than a help in time of need. In Georgia, when the state faced the choice of admitting Negro students to the university at Athens or withdrawing financial support, Governor Ernest Vandiver said the Georgia law had turned from "a source of hope to an albatross," and it was repealed. The attorney general of Texas first ruled that the law in his state did not apply when the schools were desegregated under court order and later expressed the opinion that it was unconstitutional.

Tuition Grants and Private Schools

All of the defiant states and two others (Arkansas and North Carolina) adopted laws providing for the payment of tuition grants and the establishment of private schools. The grants, roughly the per-pupil share of state and local expenditures for public schools, created an escape hatch for white students who objected to sharing classrooms with Negroes.

Neither Arkansas nor North Carolina paid any tuition grants, although Arkansas did make payments to the private Raney High School in Little Rock. In some of the defiant states, particularly Virginia and Louisiana, many pupils received grants.

In drafting their programs for tuition grants and private schools, several of the defiant states adopted modified versions of a doctrine known as "individual freedom of association." Leon Dure, a retired journalist living in Virginia, was its chief promoter. The heart of this concept, as explained by Dure, is that the state should "reserve to every child—of whatever color, whatever means—the individual choice of either attending the public school of his locality or obtaining an equivalent scholarship for use in any other public school system or qualified private school in the United States."

Dure appeared before a number of Southern legislatures to argue that the proper answer to the school problem was (a) to remove all restrictions on race in the public schools and (b) to pay tuition grants with which any student might defray the cost of attending any school of his choice, public or private, sectarian or nonsectarian.

The statutes adopted by legislatures in Virginia, South Carolina, Georgia and Louisiana reflected Dure's "freedom of choice" approach only in part. They did not remove all race restrictions in the public schools. They limited tuition grants to nonsectarian schools. In Georgia and South Carolina the grant programs were hedged with other limitations.

Germinated by actual or threatened desegregation and nourished by tuition grants of public funds, new private schools sprouted and old ones showed new growth. This was notably the case in Virginia and Louisiana.

Shackling the NAACP

If these basic laws were to be effective, it was necessary to protect them from successful attacks in the federal courts. Toward this end, most of the Southern states adopted a variety of laws to ban or curb activities of the National Association for the Advancement of Colored People.

As Representative Sam Nettles told the Alabama legislature in 1955, "Without such a proposal [to require a license fee from the NAACP] it would be very easy for the NAACP to slip into Wilcox County and teach the Negroes undesirable ideas."

With the exception of North Carolina, every Southern state enacted a variety of anti-NAACP laws. In North Carolina Representative William Womble and Senators Spencer Bell and Richard Long headed the opposition to anti-NAACP legislation endorsed by Governor Luther Hodges. In the course of that fight, Womble told the House in 1957, "I say to you that if you or I or any other citizen would want to organize or belong to a dues-paying group that either supports or opposes the separation of the races in the use of public facilities, we should be permitted to do so with freedom and dignity as we might on any other proposition of public concern without being singled out for treatment and burdens which this bill would impose."

The primary point of attack on the NAACP was barratry—the legal term for the persistent incitement and solicitation of litigation. Since NAACP lawyers were pressing the various school cases, it was inferred that this organization also was persuading reluctant Negroes to accept the risks entailed in a desegregation lawsuit. Laws were passed in an attempt to prevent that.

The barratry laws, according to Representative Charles G. Garrett of Greenville County, S.C., were designed "to protect our Negro citizens and colored public employes, most of whom are not members of the organization, from the intimidation and coercion of the NAACP, as well as to limit its activities against the best interests of our white citizens."

While the barratry laws were the basic tool used against the NAACP, other legislative shackles were put on the organization. There were racial lobbyist laws requiring NAACP officials to register with the state; laws making it a misdemeanor to employ a member of the NAACP and making membership in an organization advocating integration ground for dismissal from public employment; laws saying that all public employees must list the organizations to which they belonged and to which they made contributions; laws requiring the NAACP to file a list of its membership with the state; and laws defining the activities in which foreign corporations (those chartered in another state) could engage.

In several of the defiant states, investigation of the NAACP by legislative committees and state sovereignty commissions continued through the better part of the decade. Usually these investigations attempted to link the NAACP with the "Communist conspiracy" and to compel the organization to surrender its membership lists. The NAACP never was successfully tarred with the brush of Communism, and the organization declined to part with its membership lists. The Rev. Theodore Gibson, Florida NAACP leader, said in 1958, "We have nothing to hide and are willing to turn over all of our records to the committee, except the membership lists. We feel we cannot do this because of possible economic reprisals against members."

In every instance in which these anti-NAACP laws were carried to a court of last resort they were declared invalid. They, nonetheless, hampered NAACP activities. Alabama, for example, in 1956 obtained an injunction against all activities by the NAACP in that state. In 1964, after four trips to the United States Supreme Court, the case of *Alabama vs. NAACP* was still in litigation. Each round trip through the courts cost the NAACP something like $18,000. For a period of eight years, any NAACP activity in Alabama was almost certain to bring a contempt action by the state.

While the primary purpose of the anti-NAACP legislation was

to discourage school desegregation suits, it had another objective. It was to discourage Negro teachers—the best-educated, the most articulate and the most vulnerable segment of the Negro community —from actively participating in the desegregation struggle.

Chinks in the Wall

These four types of laws—pupil placement, school closing, tuition grants and anti-NAACP—were the bricks with which the wall of Southern resistance was built. In each state chinks in that wall were filled by other laws.

Each of the defiant states and several of the moderate ones approved resolutions of interposition (sometimes resolutions of interposition and nullification) in which they presumed to place the sovereignty of the state between its people and federal authority. Except for encouraging many Southerners to believe that there was a legal and time-honored justification for their defiance, the resurrection of the doctrine of interposition was an exercise in futility. It did provide an oratorical steam vent for the legislators who exhumed it—and for the federal judges who lowered it again into its grave.

All eleven of the Southern states amended or repealed their compulsory school attendance laws, so that no white child would be compelled to attend a school with Negro children. Six states modified their teacher-tenure laws so that teachers could be discharged by the simple expedient of failing to extend them new contracts. Six states authorized local school boards to segregate pupils by sex to avoid having white girls and Negro boys in the same classroom. Six states provided that public school property could be sold or leased in the event of desegregation.

Alabama urged the Supreme Court to "restore the rule of law." Georgia legislators adopted resolutions demanding the impeachment of six of the nine justices of the Supreme Court and calling on Congress to declare the Fourteenth and Fifteenth amendments invalid. Georgia and Alabama also proposed amendments to the United States Constitution to give the states sole power over schools and to deny any federal authority over schools.

The Arkansas legislature adopted laws permitting segregated classes within a desegregated school and authorizing school boards to hold their meetings in jail when one or more of the board members were incarcerated for failing to desegregate a school.

In some states it became a misdemeanor to teach a desegregated class, and any teacher who served in a desegregated school faced loss of certification. Louisiana law provided for the dismissal of any teacher, or even school bus driver, who advocated integration, and for the recall of any appointive officials by whose action a tax-supported facility would be desegregated. Mississippi made it illegal to attend a desegregated school.

A Louisiana law denying promotion or graduation to any student at a desegregated school caused Representative George D. Tessier of New Orleans to complain, "Under this bill a man could stay in first grade until he was fifty years old." Representative Eugene W. McGehee of Baton Rouge argued that the act would result in populating Louisiana with "segregated idiots."

During the height of the desegregation fight in New Orleans, the Louisiana legislature made it a crime to give or offer anything of value to parents in order to induce them to keep their children in a desegregated school.

Georgia forbade any person to enter school property closed by the governor. Georgia also deprived peace officers of their retirement and disability benefits if they failed to enforce the state's segregation laws.

In 1955 the Mississippi legislature required that the views of all speakers invited to appear on the campus of state-supported institutions of higher learning be screened. Speeches by advocates of desegregation were banned.

Salesmen for the South

Among the assignments given the legislative segregation committees was that of selling the Southern point of view outside the South.

In 1958 the Louisiana legislative committee headed by Senator

William Rainach purchased full-page advertisements in Northern newspapers. One such advertisement, which appeared in the New York *Herald Tribune* early in the year, said in part: ". . . It is significant that all of the communities in the South and, indeed, many of the communities in the North agreed that separation of the races in the fields of elementary and secondary education was essential." Rainach expressed delight at the results. He said, "From the response to the advertisement I'm convinced the South has a product for which there is a demand in the North—a racially separate social system. All we need to do is conduct a reasonable sales campaign."

The idea was widely shared. At one point the Georgia Education Commission had $376,000 to use in promoting the "Southern point of view." Under Governor Ross Barnett the state of Mississippi channeled money into the Association of Citizens' Councils for its information program. The Mississippi legislature played host to editors from the North so that they could travel about the state and determine for themselves that "the things they say about Dixie" weren't necessarily so.

Only a veto by Governor LeRoy Collins prevented the Florida legislature from appropriating $500,000 in 1959 to be used on a campaign to sell the segregationists' case in the North. As late as 1963, Florida's Governor Farris Bryant asked, but didn't get, funds to merchandise the South's way of life.

Representative Arthur Ravenel, Jr., of Charleston once proposed that the South Carolina General Assembly create a Commission of Information. When established, Ravenel said, the commission would raise $100 million and use this money as a revolving fund with which to purchase Northern newspapers, magazines, radio and television stations. The purpose, Representative Ravenel explained, was to get "the Southern point of view across to non-Southern audiences."

The Border States

By contrast to their counterparts in the former Confederate states, the legislators of the six border states accepted the *Brown* decision from the outset. They took no action to evade or nullify the Supreme Court's ruling. Their first and continuing reaction was to comply. Maryland, belatedly, ratified the Fourteenth Amendment.

In June, 1957, the Delaware General Assembly passed a law providing that no student could be transferred from one school district to another without the written consent of the majority of the two school boards involved. The law was intended to discourage transfers of Negroes to white schools. With this single exception the legislatures of Delaware, Maryland, West Virginia, Kentucky, Missouri and Oklahoma adopted no pro-segregation legislation.

Support from Congress

The state legislators were the shock troops in the South's fight to thwart the Supreme Court decision and to maintain segregation. They received strong moral and tactical support from most Southern representatives and senators in the United States Congress.

The outstanding example of moral support came in March, 1956, when 101 Southern members of Congress signed a "Declaration of Constitutional Principles" which came to be better known as the "Southern Manifesto." The declaration labeled the school desegregation decisions a "clear abuse of judicial power [which] climaxes a trend in the Federal judiciary undertaking to legislate in derogation of the authority of Congress and to encroach upon the reserved rights of the states and the people."

The manifesto rallied the forces of defiance in the South at a time when it appeared that more moderate leadership might prevail. Refusal to sign the manifesto was a factor in the defeat of two North Carolina congressmen (Charles B. Deane and Thurmond Chatham) while a third (Harold D. Cooley) won re-election only after a bitterly contested campaign.

Southern congressmen kept a sharp, investigative eye on conditions in Washington's desegregated school system. Their reports, often contested by educators and by Northern legislators, pictured what President Eisenhower expressed hope would become a "model" as a blackboard jungle in which all standards, academic and moral, had collapsed because of race mixing. Through most of the decade some Southern representatives and senators served as a sort of volunteer committee that welcomed and investigated all complaints concerning the schools in the nation's capital.

For a full decade after the *Brown* decision, Southern senators and representatives successfully blocked every effort to bring Congress and the executive branch of the federal government to the aid of the beleaguered United States courts in the school desegregation fight. The Civil Rights Acts of 1957 and 1960 left on the shoulders of Negro parents and such action groups as the NAACP the burden of bringing suits to desegregate schools.

President Kennedy sent civil rights messages to Congress on February 28 and on June 19, 1963. In the latter message the President said: "The Federal courts . . . have shown both competence and courage in directing the desegregation of schools on the local level. It is appropriate to keep this responsibility largely within the judicial arena. But it is unfair and unrealistic to expect that the burden of initiating such cases can be wholly borne by private litigants." The "omnibus civil rights act" that the President proposed contained several provisions pertaining to school desegregation. He asked that authority be given to the U.S. attorney general to initiate suits in the federal district courts, that technical and financial assistance be made available to school districts desegregating, and that the government be given discretion to withhold federal funds from "any program or activity in which racial discrimination occurs."

The Southerners in Congress acted with customary determination to impede action on the civil rights bill. The bill was stalled in committee at the time of President Kennedy's assassination on November 22. President Lyndon B. Johnson was the first Southerner to occupy the White House since Andrew Johnson a hundred years earlier had succeeded to the Presidency upon the assassination of President Abraham Lincoln. In an address to a joint session of Congress on November 27, President Johnson said: "No memorial oration or eulogy could more eloquently honor President Kennedy's memory than the earliest possible passage of the civil rights bill for which he fought so long. We have talked long enough in this country about equal rights. We have talked for 100 years or more. It is time now to write the next chapter—and to write it into the books of law."

The Texas background of the new President did not temper the reactions of his fellow Southerners in Congress. Senator Richard B. Russell of Georgia, leader of the Southern bloc in the Senate, characterized the proposed legislation as "not a civil rights bill" but "a special privilege bill." In the House, Representative William M. Colmer of Mississippi said: "Highly controversial legislation like civil rights should not be considered in an atmosphere charged with emotional hysteria. Moreover, the brutal assassination of President Kennedy, for whom we all mourn, has no bearing on the merits of these proposals. If they were right before his death, they are still right. If they were wrong, they still are wrong." He added that in his opinion "Congress should pass the remainder of the appropriations bills and go home." Congress adjourned without taking action on the civil rights bill.

President Johnson renewed his appeal for action on civil rights when Congress reconvened in January of 1964. In his State of the Union Address on January 8 he said that he wanted the session to be known as "the session that did more for civil rights than the last hundred sessions combined." The Southern leaders expressed fear that this time the bill might pass, and they began to prepare their constituents back home for that eventuality. Senator Russell conceded that "under the existing circumstances, the odds in favor of this shortsighted and disastrous legislation are very great." His colleague from Georgia, Senator Herman Talmadge, said: "Of course, we know that regardless of what the attitude of the people may be in any area of our country, when the full power and might of the federal government is brought to bear, the local people cannot withstand it. And that is the reason I think local people should get together and consider their relations with their fellow men and solve it on the local level rather than have oppressive, coercive legislation that would destroy really the freedom of all our people in the process."

Because the bill faced a certain filibuster in the Senate, action on it was pushed first in the House, where the rules do not permit unlimited debate. When the bill was reported from committee, Representative Edwin E. Willis of Louisiana called it "the most drastic and far-reaching proposal and grab for power ever to be reported out of a committee of the Congress in the history of our republic." The debate opened on January 31. The bill passed the House on February 10 by a vote of 290 to 130. Only 7 of the 95 representatives for the 11 Southern states voted for it; the 7 were from Florida, Tennessee and Texas. The House acted on some 140 proposed amendments. The only amendment to pass that affected school desegregation specified that the term " 'desegregation' shall not mean the assignment of students to public schools in order to overcome racial imbalance." Good humor and restraint characterized the House debate. Representatives who opposed the bill knew that the real fight on it would come in the Senate.

Senator Russell greeted the House action by serving notice that the Southern bloc intended "to fight this bill with all the vigor at our command." For seventy-five days the Southerners held forth with a stream of oratory, the longest filibuster in history. On June 10 the Senate, by a vote of 71–29 invoked cloture, the first time that debate ever had been limited on a civil rights bill. It was one of the few times that the vote of every member of the Senate had been recorded on a roll call. Only one Southerner, Senator Ralph W. Yarborough of Texas, voted for cloture. On June 19, exactly one year after President Kennedy had presented his last civil rights message to Congress, the Senate passed a bill drafted as a substitute for the House bill, although the major provisions of the House bill remained intact. The vote was 73 to 27, all members again voting. Senator Yarborough was the only Southerner voting for the bill. All of the border-state senators except Senator Robert C. Byrd of West Virginia favored the bill.

The battle shifted to the House, where the greatest obstacle in the path of the bill's final enactment was Representative Howard W. Smith of Virginia, chairman of the Rules Committee. To by-pass Representative Smith, who vowed to block the bill, the Rules Committee for the first time formally deprived its chairman of his control.

Before the bill came to a vote in the House on July 2, Representative Smith assailed it as a "monstrous instrument of oppression." The House debate lasted only one hour. It produced no surprises except for the announcement of one Southern congressman that he would change his previous negative vote. Representative Charles L. Weltner of Atlanta, Georgia, said that he was casting his lot with "those who seek reasoned and conciliatory adjustment to a new reality." He added, "I would urge that we at home now move on to the unfinished task of building a new South. We must not remain forever bound to another lost cause." When the votes were cast, the bill passed, 289 to 126. The same seven who voted for the first House bill, plus Representative Weltner, were the only Southern congressmen voting for the bill. President Johnson signed the bill into law a few hours after it was passed. It was the most sweeping civil rights legislation since the Reconstruction period.

The Southerners in Congress lost the battle of the Civil Rights Act of 1964, but some did not regard the war as ended and spoke of ultimate victory. Senator Russell said, "We reserve the right to advocate by legal means its repeal or modification. . . . It is now on the books, and it becomes our duty as good citizens to learn to live with it for as long as it is there." Time, such Southerners as Senator Russell hoped, would be on their side.

Time and the Tide

The Southern legislators, both in the state legislatures and in the United States Congress, always were fighting for time. In the spring of 1959 State Senator Larry Dumas of Alabama said, "If we can just postpone the situation and hold what we now have for ten or fifteen years, the tide will definitely turn and run in the opposite direction, in favor of our segregated schools."

Ten years after the *Brown* decision the tide had not turned. But in some of the Southern states it was moving so slowly as to seem not to be moving at all. And in none of them was it a flood tide.

Time was the legislators' principal weapon, and they made effective use of it. Their tactic of avoiding or delaying compliance through legislation, followed by litigation, was remarkably successful.

In the tenth school year after the Supreme Court had declared that compulsory segregation in the schools was unconstitutional, almost all of the children in the states of the old Confederacy still attended segregated schools. The Southern legislators could claim a great part of the credit for that. The Civil Rights Act of 1964, however, promised to accelerate the pace of desegregation in public schools and colleges. And the members of Congress who voted for the law could claim part of the credit for that.

3.
The Presidents

Three men occupied the office of President of the United States during the decade after the *Brown* decision: Dwight David Eisenhower, John Fitzgerald Kennedy and Lyndon Baines Johnson. The temper of the times and the circumstances while each held office differed. In addition, each brought to the Presidency his own peculiar background, personality and philosophy of government. The President shaped the approach of the executive branch of the federal government to the school desegregation issue.

When Eisenhower took office in 1953, the "separate but equal" doctrine of *Plessy v. Ferguson* was on shaky legs, but it still stood. With a military background, the former general was accustomed to working through channels, to delegating authority, to concerning himself with grand strategy while others took care of the details. Although he held the highest political office in the land, he did not consider himself to be a politician, and he appeared not to understand the workings of practical politics. Of particular pertinence to his handling of the school desegregation question was his reluctance to push the executive arm of the federal government into the affairs of the states.

By 1961, when Kennedy was inaugurated, the Supreme Court ruling that segregated education was "inherently unequal" was nearly seven years old. Almost all the Negro children in the eleven Southern states remained in segregated schools. Race relations had become, in the eyes of many observers, the gravest of all domestic problems. The "Negro revolt," fired by frustration, was fermenting. Kennedy's election generally was conceded to have been dependent on the Negro vote in the great urban centers. The new President was a Harvard-educated, wealthy Bostonian, who was steeped in the lore and art and practice of politics, and who was groomed for a career in public office. After having served six years in the U.S. House of Representatives, he was elected to the Senate in 1952, the same year that Eisenhower was elected President. A recognized master of practical politics, he also demonstrated his interest in ideas and ideals of government. He did not share Eisenhower's aversion to programs directed from Washington.

Having been elected Vice President on the ticket with Kennedy, Lyndon B. Johnson succeeded to the Presidency upon Kennedy's assassination on November 22, 1963. A soft-spoken, hard-dealing Texan who had spent most of his adult life in politics, Johnson's greatest fame had come while he was majority leader of the Senate, and he was best known for his boundless energy and skill in guiding bills through the legislative maze.

Until 1957, when he was instrumental in passage of the first civil rights act since Reconstruction, he was aligned with the Southern bloc in Congress. Upon becoming President, Johnson adopted the Kennedy program in toto, but he put his own stamp and style on his conduct of the office.

In a number of ways, the President could use the prestige and power of his office to exert influence or to cause action on school desegregation. His words affected the climate of public opinion. He had the obligation to uphold the orders of the federal courts. He could issue executive orders, as well as take action under the authority given to him by law. Through the Department of Justice he could participate in the judicial process in an effort to affect the course of desegregation. He could propose new legislation.

The President's Words

A President's words set the tone and tempo of his administration.

Eisenhower was cautious, restrained and conservative in his public statements on school desegregation. In his first State of the Union Message to Congress, in 1953, he had proposed "to use whatever authority exists in the office of the President to end segregation in the District of Columbia." And, following the 1954 decision, he expressed the hope that the District school system would become a "model" for other systems to follow. But he did not try to sell the model.

At no time while he was President did Eisenhower express any personal opinion about the correctness of the Supreme Court decision, and he made it clear that he thought it would be improper for him to do so.

In September, 1956, he told the press, "I think it makes no difference whether or not I endorse it [the decision in the *Brown* case]. The Constitution is as the Supreme Court interprets it, and I must conform to that and do my very best to see that it is carried out in this country."

Two years later, again speaking to reporters, the President added, "I have said here that I would never give an opinion about my convictions about the Supreme Court's decisions, because such a statement would have to indicate either approval or disapproval, and I was never going to do it about any of their decisions."

The press was persistent in questioning the President. At a press conference on January 21, 1959, William McGaffin of the Chicago *Daily News* commented, "Many persons feel you could exert a strong moral backing for desegregation if you said that you personally favored it." Then he asked, "If you favor it, sir, why have you not said so; if you are opposed to it, could you tell us why?"

Eisenhower answered: "Because, I'll tell you why. I do not

believe it is the function or indeed it is desirable for a President to express his approval or disapproval of any Supreme Court decision. His job is, for which he takes an oath, is to execute the laws. . . . I say I have got a particular function and I think it would make it more difficult to carry out that function if I indulged in that kind of, let's say, personal action with respect to court decisions." The President branded as "irresponsible" published reports that he privately disapproved the decision.

In October, 1963, almost three years after he had left office, Eisenhower for the first time gave his personal endorsement to the *Brown* decision. In an interview he said, "I believe the decision expressed the intentions of our Constitution and therefore is morally and legally correct."

While President Eisenhower never devoted a major address to the subject of civil rights, he touched on the issue a number of times and did this in a manner that revealed his thinking.

In his message to Congress of February 5, 1959, supporting his civil rights proposals, he said:

"Two principles basic to our system of government are that the rule of law is supreme, and that every individual regardless of his race, religion, or national origin is entitled to the equal protection of the laws. We must continue to seek every practicable means for reinforcing these principles and making them a reality for all.

"The United States has a vital stake in striving wisely to achieve the goal of full equality under law for all people. On several occasions I have stated that progress toward this goal depends not on laws alone but on building a better understanding."

With regard to implementation of the *Brown* decision, Eisenhower placed more emphasis on "understanding" than on "laws." He expressed the view that the process of desegregation must be gradual and that it required "forbearance and patience." We must, he said, ". . . educate ourselves, each of us, to reach the kind of understanding that does permit equality of opportunity among all citizens. . . ." Again he said, "The important thing . . . is that we make progress. This does not necessarily mean revolution. In my mind it means evolution."

In his opening statement at a press conference on October 1, 1958, the President said, "I continue to insist that the common sense of the individual and his feeling of civic responsibility must eventually come into play if we are to solve this problem." Earlier in that year Eisenhower commented, "I do not decry laws for they are necessary. But I say that laws themselves will never solve problems that have their roots in the human heart and in the human emotions."

Others occupying high positions in the Eisenhower administration reflected the President's thinking. Upon being named U.S. commissioner of education in 1956, Lawrence G. Derthick said: "I deplore extremes. They destroy reason and the spirit of brotherhood, the agents upon which we must depend to help solve the problems of integration with dignity to each person and to the nation." Vice President Richard M. Nixon said in 1959 that administration policy was not to seek "immediate total integration" but to take a firm position for progress that avoided extremes.

In February, 1960, in the last year of the Eisenhower administration and almost six years after the *Brown* decision, Attorney General William P. Rogers voiced the opinion that the pace of school desegregation had been "surprisingly good," considering the legal problems involved. At that time the public schools in five states were 100 percent segregated, and in all eleven states of the old Confederacy fewer than two-tenths of one percent of Negro schoolchildren were in classes with whites.

The attitude of the administration drew comment from Gordon M. Tiffany, who had been appointed by Eisenhower as first staff director of the United States Commission on Civil Rights. When he resigned on January 1, 1961, Tiffany said, "Civil rights have unquestionably been a White House orphan notwithstanding the sincere efforts of both the White House staff and the staff of the Commission to make it otherwise. As to the President and the White House staff," Tiffany continued, "emphasis should be placed on leadership and giving a public impression of conviction and continuing awareness of moral and legal obligations in this area."

As a United States Senator and as a candidate for the Presidency,

John F. Kennedy had been as outspoken as Eisenhower was reserved on school desegregation.

Addressing the New York Young Democratic Club on February 7, 1956, Kennedy urged that the Democratic party take a forthright stand backing the Supreme Court decision.

On October 17, 1957, he spoke in Jackson, Mississippi, to a meeting of Young Democrats. There he said, "I have accepted the Supreme Court decision as the law of the land." He added that he had "no hesitancy in taking the same stand here as I did in Boston on the question of integration."

In his television debate with Richard M. Nixon on October 9, 1960, Kennedy said: ". . . what will be done to provide equality of education in all sections of the United States? Those are the questions on which the President must establish a moral tone, a moral leadership, and I can assure you that if I am elected President we will do so."

A few days later, in a reference to the Eisenhower administration's handling of the school desegregation issue, Candidate Kennedy added, "There is more to the Presidency than just letting things drift and then calling out the troops. We lost valuable years by the failure of the President to assert leadership."

In the early part of his administration, President Kennedy seldom made a public statement about desegregation in education. A press conference on February 8, 1961, was one of the few such occasions. He was questioned about the situation in New Orleans. He replied, in part:

"I will, at such time as I think is most useful and most effective, I will attempt to use the moral authority or position of influence of the presidency in New Orleans and in other places. I want to make sure that whatever I do or say does have some beneficial effect. . . . It is my position that all students should be given the opportunity to attend schools regardless of their race. . . . I believe strongly that every American should have an opportunity to have maximum development of his talents under the most beneficial circumstances. . . ."

The President waited so long in selecting a time that he thought "most useful and most effective" that some groups interested in advancing civil rights chafed at the delay. They complained that Kennedy's presidential performance was not living up to his campaign promises.

On February 28, 1963, President Kennedy sent to Congress his first message devoted exclusively to civil rights. In the section on education he said: "Nearly nine years have elapsed since the Supreme Court ruled that state laws requiring or permitting segregated schools violate the Constitution. That decision represented both good law and good judgment—it was both legally and morally right...."

In April mass demonstrations began in Birmingham under the leadership of Dr. Martin Luther King, Jr. This gave new impetus to the movement not only to desegregate schools but to remove every form of racial discrimination.

President Kennedy responded on June 11 with an appeal to the conscience of the American people, asking their cooperation in meeting the growing crisis in American race relations. He warned of a "rising tide of discontent that threatens the public safety." He said: "The events in Birmingham and elsewhere have so increased the cries for equality that no city or state or legislative body can prudently ignore them. . . . Fires of frustration and discord are burning in every city, North and South. . . . Redress is sought in the streets, in demonstrations, parades and protests which create tensions and threaten violence and threaten lives. We face, therefore, a moral crisis as a country and as a people. It cannot be met by repressive police action. It cannot be quieted by token moves. . . . It is time to act in the Congress, in your state and local legislative body, and above all in our daily lives."

The President on June 19 sent a second civil rights message to Congress. Of education he said: ". . . The lack of equal educational opportunity deprives the individual of equal economic opportunity, restricts his contribution as a citizen and community leader, encourages him to drop out of school and imposes a heavy burden on the effort to eliminate discriminatory practices and prejudices from our national life."

The Kennedy attack on racial discrimination was not limited to the South. The President stressed that civil rights posed a national, not merely a regional, problem. Speaking to a college audience in San Diego in June, 1963, he said, "And we must recognize that segregation in education—and I mean the *de facto* segregation in the North as well as the proclaimed segregation of the South—brings with it serious handicaps to a large percentage of our nation's population. . . . Our goal must be an educational system in the spirit of the Declaration of Independence—a system in which all are created equal—a system in which every child, whether born a banker's son in a Long Island mansion or a Negro sharecropper's son in an Alabama cotton field, has the opportunity for an education that his abilities and character deserve."

As his appointment with tragedy neared, President Kennedy was using his position to "establish a moral leadership to provide equality of education in all sections of the United States."

In his early years as a United States representative and later as a senator from Texas, Lyndon B. Johnson consistently stood with the Southern bloc against civil rights legislation. In 1948, speaking in Austin, Texas, he described the civil rights proposals of President Harry S. Truman as "a farce and a sham" and "an effort to set up a police state in the guise of liberty." In 1949, in a Senate speech opposing a fair employment practices bill, he said, "We cannot legislate love."

Until 1957, Johnson never had voted for a civil rights bill. In that year and again in 1960, as Senate majority leader, he was instrumental in obtaining Senate passage of watered-down versions of bills that President Eisenhower proposed. The Civil Rights Acts of 1957 and 1960 generally were interpreted to represent victories for the Southern bloc, because the compromises that Johnson engineered removed the sections that were strongest, and thus the most objectionable to the Southerners.

In 1959 Johnson sponsored a bill to create a federal conciliation service to mediate racial disputes. Negro leaders rejected such a proposal out of hand. The bill caused NAACP leader Roy Wilkins to say, "Since no Negro in his right mind intends to submit his citizenship rights to a conciliation board instead of a court, why should the NAACP or anyone else pretend . . . that the Johnson bill might be acceptable?"

Senator Hubert Humphrey of Minnesota, attacking the same proposal, said it was "folly" to evade the issue by "substituting for responsible legal action presidential counsels of 'patience' and 'education' or even legislative gestures limited to 'conciliation' or to other forms of exhortation not backed by the equal protection of the law guaranteed by the Constitution."

With his nomination, and subsequent election, as Vice President in 1960, Johnson followed the position of the national Democratic party and of the Kennedy administration on school desegregation and broader civil rights questions.

Two speeches that Johnson made in the spring of 1963 showed the trend of his thinking. At a meeting of the Capitol Press Club he said: "As a prudent man—at least, I hope I am a prudent man—I know that frequently in life, I have had to settle for progress short of perfection. I have done so because—despite cynics—I believe half a loaf is better than none. But my acceptance has always been conditioned upon the premise that the half loaf is a step toward the full loaf—and that if I go on working, the day of the full loaf will come." At Gettysburg, Pennsylvania, he said, "Until justice is blind to color, until education is unaware of race, until opportunity is unconcerned with the color of men's skins, emancipation will be a proclamation but not a fact." In this speech, called the "second Gettysburg address," Johnson expressed dissatisfaction with the slow pace of the Negro's struggle against "injustice and inequality." "The Negro today asks justice," he said. "We do not answer him—we do not answer those who lie beneath this soil—when we reply to the Negro by asking, 'Patience.' "

To an even greater extent than was the case with Kennedy, Johnson assumed the Presidency at a time when the issue of school desegregation was inseparably linked to, or even submerged by, the larger question of civil rights for Negroes. Most of President Johnson's references to school desegregation, therefore, were parts of broad statements on civil rights.

Addressing a joint session of Congress on November 27, five days after taking office, Johnson endorsed Kennedy's civil rights proposals and urged enactment of the pending legislation embodying them "so that we can move forward to eliminate from this nation every trace of discrimination and oppression that is based on race or color." This message was disquieting to the Southern bloc. Civil rights leaders enthusiastically praised the President's words, but some of them were cautious. Roy Wilkins expressed "very great faith" in the President's attitude on civil rights, but he added that Negroes "naturally are skeptical of a man with a Southern background." James Forman, executive secretary of the Student Nonviolent Coordinating Committee, was blunter. "Where Mr. Kennedy because of his record and past actions in the civil rights field might have slipped by with words and promises," he said, "Mr. Johnson, being a Texan, will have to prove himself to Negroes and liberals by his actions."

In his State of the Union Message on January 8, 1964, Johnson again called on Congress to pass the civil rights bill. "As far as the writ of federal law will run," he said, "we must abolish not some but all racial discrimination." On July 2, Congress sent to the White House the Civil Rights Act of 1964. In signing it, President Johnson, in a televised statement to the nation, said: "Let us close the springs of racial poison. Let us pray for wise and understanding hearts. Let us lay aside irrelevant differences and make our nation whole." The Southerner in the White House had proved himself to Negroes and liberals by his actions, as well as his words.

Upholding the Courts

President Johnson's home state of Texas was the scene of the first attempt of a governor to prevent the execution of a court order to desegregate schools. When the fall term opened in 1956, Governor Allan Shivers dispatched two Texas Rangers to maintain peace and prevent violence in Mansfield, where Negroes were to be admitted to the high school under order of the Fifth Circuit Court of Appeals. The governor accomplished his purpose by maintaining segregated schools in Mansfield, despite the court order.

At a press conference on September 5, President Eisenhower indicated that he regarded the governor's action as a valid exercise of the state's police power. The President said, ". . . I want to emphasize . . . the locality's right to execute the police power in this country." He continued, "When the police power is executed habitually . . . by the federal government we are in a bad way. So, until states show their inability or their refusal to grapple with this question properly, which they haven't yet . . . we'd better be very careful about moving in and exercising police power."

The Mansfield incident created a momentary stir, but it soon was forgotten, although the governor of a state had blocked an order of the federal courts. Where Governor Shivers succeeded with two state policemen, Governor Orval Faubus, a year later, was to fail with the Arkansas National Guard.

Nine Negro children were to enter Central High School at Little Rock on the morning of September 3, 1957. Although Faubus was under unrelenting pressure from the segregationists to defy the desegregation orders of the federal courts, the governor did not commit himself. To most observers the signs indicated a quiet and orderly admission of the Negro students.

On the evening of September 2, Faubus announced in a television address that, "Units of the National Guard have been, or are now being mobilized with the mission to maintain or restore the peace and good order of this community."

On the morning of September 3 the nine Negro youngsters did not attempt to walk through the line of Guardsmen surrounding Central High School. When the Negroes appeared on the morning of September 4, they were turned back. The state of Arkansas stood in open defiance of the authority of the United States.

Throughout the summer of 1957, while the crisis in Little Rock moved toward its climax with such deceptive quiet, the Eisenhower administration had taken the position that the federal courts could and should handle developments as they arose. The administration had avoided further involvement.

By July Faubus was anxious to learn what the Eisenhower administration was prepared to do. The administration refused to commit itself. In August Arthur B. Caldwell, a former Arkansan who was an assistant to Assistant Attorney General Warren Olney III, called on Governor Faubus. "I had about an hour's conference with this man," Faubus said. "My main concern was to find out what, if anything, could be expected from the federal government in the way of assistance if disorder occurred. He reviewed the court procedures and ended up by saying virtually that there was nothing they could do except by court decrees."

On September 4, the day Guardsmen turned away the Negro children, Federal District Judge Ronald N. Davies asked Eisenhower's attorney general, Herbert Brownell, to order an FBI investigation of Faubus's claims that school desegregation in Little Rock was certain to lead to violence and mob action. The governor promptly sent a telegram to Eisenhower protesting any such investigation.

In his telegram the governor drew the issue as he saw it. "The question now is whether or not the head of a sovereign state can exercise his constitutional powers and discretion in maintaining peace and good order within his jurisdiction, being accountable to his own conscience and to his own people . . ." he said. "As the duly elected governor and representative of the people of Arkansas, I can no more surrender the rights [of a state] than you could surrender the rights of the duly elected chief executive of our nation."

To this the President replied on September 5, "When I became President, I took an oath to support and defend the Constitution of the United States. The only assurance I can give you is that the federal Constitution will be upheld by me by every legal means at my command."

On September 9 Judge Davies ordered the attorney general of the United States to appear in the Little Rock case as a friend of the court. He also ordered the attorney general to file a petition for an injunction against Governor Faubus and other state officials to prevent their interference with the Court's prior desegregation order.

The Department of Justice complied, and filed the petition the next day.

Judge Davies on September 20 granted a temporary injunction against the use of the National Guard for "restricting or preventing . . . the attendance of Negro students at Little Rock high schools." Judge Davies pointed out that "no acts of violence or threats of violence . . . had occurred."

Complying with the injunction, Governor Faubus withdrew the National Guard.

Three days later the nine Negro children entered Central High School. A mob gathered at the school. Violence grew in intensity during the day. The Negro youngsters were removed from the school for their own protection.

Angered by what he described as the "disgraceful occurrences" in Little Rock, President Eisenhower issued a statement in which he made two points:

"1. The federal law and orders of a United States District Court, implementing that law, cannot be flouted with impunity by any individual, or by any mob of extremists.

"2. I will use the full power of the United States, including whatever force may be necessary to prevent any obstruction of the law and to carry out the orders of the federal court."

The next day, on September 24, the President federalized the Arkansas National Guard and ordered troops of the 101st Airborne Division from Fort Campbell, Kentucky, to Little Rock. The Negro pupils re-entered the school on September 25 under federal protection and remained there for the rest of the year.

President Eisenhower had met the challenge to the authority of the federal courts.

President Kennedy twice faced defiance from state governors. His challengers were Governor Ross Barnett of Mississippi and Governor George C. Wallace of Alabama.

When James Meredith sought to enter the University of Mississippi at Oxford, both Governor Barnett and President Kennedy had the example of Little Rock to guide them. The President made strenuous efforts to settle the issue by persuasion, but nothing in the governor's public acts or words suggested compromise.

Barnett showed greater determination than Governor Faubus to uphold state sovereignty and to keep public education segregated. In September, 1962, when it became clear that Mississippi had lost its fight in the courts, Barnett issued a proclamation of interposition, denying the authority of the United States government in the field of education. He asked every state official "to go to jail, if necessary, to keep faith with the people" of Mississippi and called for the resignation of "any official who is not prepared to suffer imprisonment for this righteous cause." The governor ordered the jailing of any federal representative who attempted to arrest or fine any "state official in the performance of his official duties." The governor had the Board of Trustees appoint him "special registrar" of the university, and he personally blocked Meredith when the Negro student first attempted to register.

While all this was taking place, the President and Attorney General Robert F. Kennedy kept in touch with the governor and his staff, and the official attitude was reported to be one of optimism. In his private conversations with the Kennedys, Barnett had created the impression that, once he had made his opposition plain, he would step aside rather than engage the federal government in a test of strength. The Kennedys, publicly and privately, left no doubt that they would apply whatever force was necessary to uphold the authority of the United States courts, although they expressed the hope that no force would be required.

Until the moment rioting began on September 30, the Kennedys had assumed, they later indicated, that they had Barnett's pledge that Meredith would be brought quietly to the campus and enrolled and that the governor would maintain order rather than accept the responsibility for a second—and potentially more dangerous—Little Rock.

For whatever reason, Meredith's enrollment was anything but peaceful. In the riots two men were killed and many injured. Spokesmen for the Kennedy administration said that the governor "double-crossed" the President. Barnett laid the blame on "trigger-happy" U.S. marshals and a power-hungry national administration. As he had promised, Kennedy used all the force required to maintain federal authority. As many as twenty thousand troops were called to duty during the crisis.

Following the defiance at Oxford, Governor Barnett and Lieutenant Governor (later Governor) Paul B. Johnson were indicted for criminal contempt of the federal courts. Their case had not come to trial when the decade ended, but the Supreme Court had ruled that they were not entitled to a trial by jury, as they claimed. In arguing this point before the Supreme Court in October, 1963, Barnett's attorney, Charles Clark of Jackson, Mississippi, contended that the Court was not bound by previous decisions that defendants had no constitutional right to trial by jury in contempt cases. Clark argued that the Court need not be bound by precedent. "The Constitution," he said, "has meant different things at different times. . . . I don't think it is a dead document, and I know this court will constantly be asked to re-examine it." Barnett was a leading exponent of the theory that the *Brown* decision was illegal because it improperly departed from precedent.

After the bloodshed at Oxford, the defiance of Alabama Governor Wallace at Tuscaloosa was anticlimactic.

As a candidate, Wallace promised to "stand in the schoolhouse door" to bar any Negro who attempted to enter any white school in Alabama. He repeated the pledge many times after he took office.

The test of Wallace's defiance came in 1963 when the University of Alabama was ordered to admit two Negroes at the beginning of the summer term. On the appointed day the governor took his stand in the door of the registration hall on the Tuscaloosa campus. When the commanding general of the federalized Alabama National Guard asked him to step aside, Wallace did. The Negroes were enrolled. There was no violence or disorder. The governor had urged the people of Alabama to stay away from the campus, and none appeared.

President Kennedy, like President Eisenhower, used the full powers of the Presidency to uphold the authority of the federal courts. Their actions led to desegregation of education, but that was incidental to the central issue of the supremacy of the United States Constitution as interpreted by the Supreme Court.

President Johnson, in the months of the decade during which he served as chief executive, faced no crises of the proportions of Little Rock or Oxford.

Executive Action

Occasions were rare for such use of executive power as was made at Little Rock, Oxford and Tuscaloosa. But regularly proposals were forwarded that the President bring the authority of his office to bear against segregation in public education. President Eisenhower was cool to these suggestions.

Only once during his eight years in office did Eisenhower take executive action to desegregate schools. In January, 1954, four months before the Supreme Court decision in the *Brown* case, the President issued an executive order to end segregation in schools located on military bases.

Throughout the Eisenhower administration there was talk of cutting off the millions of dollars in federal financial aid that went annually to segregated public schools and colleges. The idea did not go beyond the discussion stage.

Except during the Little Rock crisis Eisenhower did not use his personal prestige in negotiations for compliance with desegregation decisions of the federal courts. Twice he conferred with Governor Faubus, but the President did not initiate the conferences. One was arranged by Representative Brooks Hays and the other by a committee of Southern governors.

President Eisenhower's concept of the executive role was expressed succinctly in 1956 by Neil McElroy, chairman of a White House Conference on Education. Asked why school segregation had not been on the agenda, McElroy replied, "It was properly out of our hands and under the wing of the Supreme Court."

The President told the press on November 5, 1958, that he was "not so certain" a White House conference would help to solve racial problems. "I believe that opinion does not have to be rallied always by some spectacular conference of that kind," he said. A few days later the National Council of Negro Women asked the President to confer with them on school desegregation problems. The President declined, giving as his reason that his schedule did not permit such a meeting. At another time Eisenhower said that he was skeptical of trying to "direct every single thing from Washington."

As a presidential candidate, Senator Kennedy charged that the Eisenhower administration had failed to assert leadership in dealing with school desegregation and other civil rights questions. Kennedy's election caused civil rights groups to anticipate a swift and decisive turn in national executive policy. The new President did not move as quickly or as firmly as had been expected.

In January, 1961, almost at the time Kennedy was sworn into office, the Southern Regional Council issued a forty-eight-page report outlining actions the executive departments might take "to strengthen civil rights and improve race relations." In March of 1962 the Council published a follow-up report in which it praised certain accomplishments but noted that "in some programs the administration has to date shown little concern for civil rights." The report cited a "lack of interest in moving beyond token school desegregation." A conclusion was: "In the South, the administration has had almost no goal except compliance with the federal law. It has not, in schools or in any other area, exerted its influence in behalf of integration beyond respect for law."

Near the end of the Eisenhower administration the Civil Rights Commission had issued a report on higher education. One of the Commission's recommendations was that federal grants be withheld from colleges and universities practicing racial discrimination. No action having been taken on the proposal, the Commission repeated it in January, 1961.

At a press conference on March 1, Kennedy was asked his opinion of such a fund cutoff. He replied that it was "a matter which is under consideration." He added, "It will be . . . a part of our general overall study of where the federal government might justfully place its power and influence to expand civil rights."

Federal funds went to colleges and universities under a number of programs. The National Defense Education Act of 1958 provided for grants to improve the quality of instruction in mathematics, foreign languages and student counseling. Research grants were made by a number of departments and agencies, including the Department of Defense, the Department of Agriculture, the Atomic Energy Commission and the National Science Foundation. The Federal Housing and Home Finance Agency made grants for dormitory construction. These were the grant programs the Kennedy administration studied.

The first fruits of the study became known on February 27, 1962. Secretary Abraham Ribicoff of the Department of Health, Education and Welfare appeared to testify at the opening day of hearings conducted by a subcommittee of the House Education and Labor Committee.

In response to questioning by members of the subcommittee, Secretary Ribicoff revealed that a policy of nondiscrimination had been adopted for the program of financial assistance under the National Defense Education Act. He told the congressmen, "We have made it a condition of contract with the institutions that there will not be segregation or discriminatory practices, and this has been in effect for a number of months. There has been no publicity on it."

Subsequently other grant programs in the area of higher education were brought under the same nondiscrimination policy. The National Science Foundation announced that effective in 1963 it would cease making grants to institutions that practiced racial discrimination. The Peace Corps took the same position. In the summer of 1963 all federal agencies were ordered to cease financing training programs in segregated public colleges and universities.

The same subcommittee that questioned Secretary Ribicoff about grants to higher education prodded the administration to review programs of grants to public education below the college level. Two 1951 laws provide for federal financial aid to school districts in so-called "impacted areas." These districts are saddled with an uncommon burden because military or other federal installations are located in them. Separate grants are made for construction and operation of schools attended by the children of federal personnel.

At his February 27 appearance before the committee, Secretary Ribicoff engaged in a verbal duel with some of the congressmen. Urged to withhold impacted-area funds from segregated school districts, or at least to test his legal authority to do so, Ribicoff told the congressmen: "You control the purse strings and you can determine how the money is spent. And this is a Congressional problem and not an administrative problem." He did agree to look into it, however.

On March 30 Ribicoff appeared again before the committee. He announced that, "Beginning in September, 1963, we will, exercising sound discretion, take appropriate steps as set forth in the law with respect to those children still attending segregated schools who by law are entitled to a suitable education." The key word was "suitable," which was interpreted to mean "desegregated."

According to the new policy, all children of personnel living on federal installations should have the opportunity to attend a desegregated school. School districts that maintained segregated schools faced the possibility of losing their impacted-area funds.

During 1961 approximately 65,000 school-age children lived on federal installations in the seventeen Southern and border states. Public schools serving these children received more than $12,250,000 in operating funds. Loss of this money would create a serious problem for many school districts.

Ribicoff resigned in 1962 from the Kennedy cabinet to run (successfully) for the U.S. Senate from his state of Connecticut. It fell to his successor, Anthony J. Celebrezze, to put the fund cutoff policy into effect. The practice was not to withhold funds. Instead, the possibility that they might be withheld was used as a bargaining point in negotiations to persuade local officials to desegregate their schools voluntarily.

Fifteen school districts in four states—Florida, Tennessee, Texas and Virginia—voluntarily desegregated rather than run the risk of losing federal money. No funds actually were withheld during the

1963–64 school year. Columbus, Mississippi, threatened with loss of impacted-area aid, closed the school serving military dependents and passed an order forbidding children from outside the city to attend city public schools. The federal government then backed off. When impacted-area funds were assured, the school was reopened —segregated.

In some instances the government decided to build on-base schools. This was done where the public schools were segregated and the number of children living on the base was great enough to justify providing a special school for them. Secretary Celebrezze announced plans to build schools to be operated by the federal government on eight military bases, located in South Carolina, Alabama, Georgia and Louisiana.

The Civil Rights Commission, in April of 1963, urged that the President go far beyond the withdrawal of federal aid from segregated schools. In a special interim report all six members of the Commission called on the President to "explore his legal authority" to withhold all federal funds—not just funds for education—from Mississippi until that state ended "its subversion of the Constitution." (In fiscal 1962 Mississippi paid $270 million in federal taxes and, in return, received $650 million in a wide variety of federal grants.)

Speaking to the American Society of Newspaper Editors a few days later, President Kennedy said, "I don't have the power to cut off the aid in a general way . . . and I would think it would probably be unwise to give the President of the United States that kind of power. . . ."

Kennedy, however, exerted pressure on segregated schools in ways besides a possible cutoff of federal funds.

In the summer of 1962 the President appointed a seven-member committee headed by Gerhard A. Gesell, a Washington attorney, to investigate racial discrimination in the armed forces. In July, 1963, the Gesell Committee reported that the most serious discrimination affecting the military occurred on off-base civilian facilities serving military personnel. Public schools, the committee noted, were a particular problem. The committee recommended that such schools be desegregated and added, "In accomplishing this, the full power of the base commander and of the service should be placed squarely on the side of the Negro parents as they attempt to overcome the administrative barriers which often accompany desegregation."

President Kennedy sent the Gesell report to Secretary of Defense Robert McNamara with an accompanying letter in which he observed, "Discriminatory practices are morally wrong, wherever they occur—they are especially inequitable and iniquitous when they inconvenience and embarrass those serving in the armed services and their families." McNamara instructed the commanders of military bases located in fifteen states to take the initiative in encouraging the desegregation of schools serving the children of military personnel. Such efforts as were made succeeded mainly in stirring the ire of Southerners, in and out of Congress.

Although the administration was attacked for doing too much and too little, the President persisted in efforts to encourage quiet, orderly school desegregation. By 1963 Kennedy was holding a series of conferences to discuss the question of school segregation. That same summer he wrote personal letters to the heads of school boards throughout the nation to ask for their support in solving the problem.

Each time a crisis developed the President intervened in an effort to head it off. In a single day he had as many as three telephone conversations with Governor Barnett about the developing crisis at Oxford. Months before the University of Alabama was opened to Negroes, the President attempted to guide defiant Alabama Governor Wallace off a collision course with the federal government.

Where schools were to be desegregated and trouble was feared, spokesmen for the administration conferred with local leaders to urge calm compliance with the law. In these meetings the emphasis was placed on avoiding violence. Token desegregation was acceptable and was praised when it occurred without incident.

The strategy of the Kennedy administration was to go slow on desegregation to avoid alienating the Southern bloc in Congress, whose support was needed to accomplish other important legislative objectives. But, as the civil rights groups applied more and more pressure for action, the President responded. In the months before his death, he gave more attention to civil rights than to any other domestic issue.

As Vice President under Kennedy, Lyndon Johnson headed the President's Committee on Equal Employment Opportunity. In this capacity he worked with Negro and business leaders to open more and better jobs to Negroes.

After he became President, Johnson asked all members of the Kennedy cabinet, and others in key positions, to remain at their posts. Without exception, they stayed, at least long enough to effect a smooth transition in the executive departments from one presidential administration to another.

As a consequence of Johnson's retaining Kennedy's official family, there was no change in policies or interruption in programs in progress when Kennedy was assassinated. The Johnson administration inaugurated no new programs prior to the end of the decade. The new President vigorously attacked old problems, however, and urged their solution as a memorial to Kennedy.

Participation in the Judicial Process

Of the executive departments the Department of Justice was the most actively and most continuously involved in the school desegregation issue. It was less active in the Eisenhower than in the Kennedy administration.

Under Eisenhower it was the general policy of the department to intervene in school desegregation suits only at the request of the courts. This occurred when the *Brown* case was being considered by the Supreme Court. In the arguments before the Court between the May 17, 1954, decision and that of May 31, 1955, the Justice Department appeared as a friend of the Court, at the Court's invitation.

After the United States District Court ordered the Justice Department to intervene in the Little Rock case, the Executive Office of the President issued a statement that expressed administration policy. It said: "Although the Federal Government has no responsibility to initiate action to desegregate public schools or to formulate any plans for desegregation, the courts have made it clear that the Department of Justice, at the invitation of the Court, must participate in litigation involving public school desegregation for the purpose of assisting the Court."

On two other occasions during the Eisenhower administration the Justice Department appeared in the role of friend of the court in school desegregation cases. On its own initiative the department in 1956 intervened on behalf of the local school board in the Hoxie, Arkansas, case. In New Orleans in November of 1960 intervention was at the invitation of the presiding judge.

There was discussion in 1959–60 of initiating desegregation suits against school boards that accepted federal impacted-area aid. The theory behind this proposed move was that where there are federal funds there is a federal interest. No such cases, however, were instituted.

The Department of Justice in the Kennedy administration recognized that it had no more authority to initiate school segregation suits than the department had had under Eisenhower. But it made greater use of the authority it did have and attempted to expand it.

Attorney General Kennedy on March 17, 1961, broke with previous Department of Justice policy in seeking to enter desegregation suits as a friend of the court. He asked U.S. District Judge J. Skelly Wright to permit the government to intervene in four Louisiana cases to "assist the Court in preventing potentially dangerous and critical situations from coming to a head."

In April the attorney general made an unprecedented move. The Justice Department filed a petition in the Prince Edward County, Virginia, case for permission to intervene as a co-plaintiff. Government intervention was declared necessary "in order to prevent the circumvention and nullification of the prior orders of this court and to safeguard the due administration of justice and the integrity of the judicial processes of the United States." Federal District Court Judge Oren R. Lewis denied the petition on the ground that to permit the government to enter the case would "delay and prejudice" it and would appear to be "contrary to the intent of Congress." He also held that the government did not have sufficient interest in the case to allow it to intervene as a matter of right.

After the appearance of Secretary Ribicoff before the Congressional committee in February, 1962, the Department of Justice again stuck its toe into untested legal waters. At the insistence of some members of the committee, Ribicoff agreed to explore "with officials of the Department of Justice the possibility of a lawsuit being brought on behalf of the United States to desegregate a school district receiving funds under the impacted area program." The first such suit was filed on September 17 against the school board of Prince George County, Virginia, seeking to end racial segregation in the public schools attended by the children of personnel at Fort Lee. In the 1961–62 school year, Prince George County received $224,328 in impacted-area aid; its total school budget was $1.3 million.

In a statement issued in conjunction with the filing of the suit, Attorney General Kennedy said:

"I think it should be made clear that this suit does not threaten an end to financial assistance to the Prince George County schools. The purpose, rather, of the suit is to seek an end to unconstitutional school segregation in an area where such segregation directly affects the armed forces.

"It makes no sense that we should ask military personnel to make sacrifices and serve away from home and at the same time see their children treated as inferiors by local requirements that they attend segregated schools. It is even more incongruous considering that these school systems are supported by public funds, contributed in part by the fathers of these children."

The filing of the Prince George County case marked the first time that the Department of Justice had initiated action to desegregate schools. Congress pointedly had denied the department authority to initiate such suits on behalf of individuals. The government based its action on the contract under which the county received impacted-area aid and also claimed that segregated schools impaired "the service and morale of its military and civilian personnel," and thus "unlawfully burdened the United States in the exercise of its war powers under the Constitution."

The main point at issue was whether the Justice Department had the authority to file the suit, whether it was a "proper party to the action." On June 23, 1963, U.S. District Judge John D. Butzner, Jr., ruled that the United States was a proper party to the suit because of its contract with the county. At the same time, he held that the Justice Department could not bring a desegregation suit on behalf of individual children, and he found no evidence that segregated schools "impinged upon the war powers of the United States." While the right of the government to bring the suit had been upheld, a year later the case had not been finally decided.

The government did not fare so well when similar suits were filed against school boards receiving impacted-area funds in Alabama, Florida, Louisiana, Mississippi and South Carolina. In every case that was decided, the judges ruled that the Justice Department lacked authority to institute civil rights cases except in the field of voting; that there was in fact no contract between local school districts and the federal government requiring that schools be desegregated; and that the government was not a proper party to the action.

Although the issue had not reached the Supreme Court for final decision, it seemed clear enough that if the government was to spur desegregation by filing suits, Congressional authorization was necessary. Presidents Eisenhower, Kennedy and Johnson proposed legislation to that end.

New Federal Legislation

President Eisenhower proposed civil rights legislation in 1956 and again in 1959. Although Congress did not give the President all that he asked, in 1957 and in 1960 the first Civil Rights Acts since Reconstruction were passed.

The 1957 Act established the United States Commission on Civil Rights and authorized the creation of a Civil Rights Division in the Department of Justice. Once established, both became increasingly active in the field of school desegregation.

Congress was unwilling to give the Department of Justice the authority to file suits on behalf of individuals in education and other civil rights cases, as the President had asked in 1956. In proposing additional civil rights legislation in 1959, Eisenhower omitted this earlier request. When efforts were made in Congress to insert this provision, the administration objected. Attorney General William P. Rogers, speaking for the administration, said that the change "might do more harm than good."

Four of the seven proposals made by Eisenhower in 1959 related to the schools. Two of them would have made it a federal crime to interfere with court-ordered school desegregation or to cross a state line in order to avoid prosecution for bombing a school. A third made provision for the education of children of military personnel stationed at places where the public schools were closed to avoid desegregation. A fourth would have provided technical and financial aid to school districts confronted with desegregation problems.

Modifications of the first three of these proposals were approved by Congress. The Civil Rights Act of 1960 did not provide for technical and financial assistance in desegregating schools.

As a candidate, President Kennedy pledged that he would seek to have the civil rights planks in the Democratic party platform of 1960 enacted into law. Among other things the platform said:

"We believe that every school district affected by the Supreme Court decision should submit a plan providing for at least first step compliance by 1963, the 100th anniversary of the Emancipation Proclamation.

"To facilitate compliance, technical and financial assistance should be given to school districts facing special problems of transition.

"For this and for the protection of all other Constitutional rights of Americans the Attorney General should be empowered and directed to file civil injunction suits in federal courts to prevent the denial of any civil rights on the ground of race, creed or color."

These proposals weren't original. President Eisenhower had included the last two in his programs. They were, however, considered to be the strongest platform statements on civil rights the Democratic party ever had adopted.

During the campaign Kennedy said that he had asked Senator Joseph Clark and Representative Emanuel Celler to draft civil rights bills "embodying our platform commitments for introduction at the beginning of the next session." When the bills were introduced, on May 7, 1961, Pierre Salinger, the President's press secretary, said that they were not administration bills. He said, "The President does not consider it necessary at this time to enact new civil rights legislation."

In the civil rights message that he sent to Congress on February 28, 1963, Kennedy urged broad civil rights legislation, but did not go as far as the Democratic platform of 1960. His proposals affecting education included technical and financial aid to desegregating school districts and elimination of the "separate but equal" clause from the Morrill Land Grant College Act. On June 19 he sent further civil rights proposals to Congress. Among other things he asked authorization for the Attorney General to initiate desegregation suits and sought power to withhold federal funds from "any program or activity in which racial discrimination occurs."

This legislative program was pending in Congress at the time of President Kennedy's death.

When Lyndon Johnson succeeded to the Presidency, the Southern bloc opposing the civil rights bill in Congress took little comfort from having a Southerner in the White House. "We would have beaten President Kennedy," Senator Russell said, "but now I won't predict. It will be three times harder."

The senator from Georgia continued, "Lyndon Johnson knows more about the uses of power than any man. Now he's President, with the greatest power in the world at his disposal. President Kennedy didn't have to pass a strong bill to prove anything on civil rights. President Johnson does."

As Senate majority leader, Johnson had promoted the compromises that led to the passage of the relatively weak civil rights acts of 1957 and 1960. As President, he proved that Senator Russell was an astute analyst. President Johnson did not compromise, and he used the power of his office to influence Congress to pass the Civil Rights Act of 1964. The law was even stronger in some respects than President Kennedy had proposed.

Slightly more than ten years had elapsed since the Supreme Court had declared that compulsory segregation of the races in public education violated the Constitution. The Supreme Court's decision now had the stamp of legislative approval in a law that went far beyond education. And the law gave to the executive branch of the federal government extensive new power to enforce its provisions for the protection of the civil rights of all Americans.

4.

The Schoolmen

The Supreme Court recognized in the *Brown* decision that local school authorities would have "the primary responsibility for elucidating, assessing and solving" the problems of desegregation. School boards and administrators were not always free to exercise this responsibility.

Where public opinion and political leaders accepted the Court's decision, school officials could proceed with plans for compliance. Where there was conflict, the schoolmen were trapped in the middle of it. Pulling from one side were state laws and local customs favoring segregated schools. Tugging from the other side were the federal courts and the advocates of change to a public educational system operated without racial distinctions.

The Decision to Desegregate in the Border Area

Compliance with the Supreme Court decision began in the border area, usually in the larger cities. Two of these cities—Washington, D.C., and Wilmington, Delaware—were defendants in the original cases before the Court. They moved promptly to desegregate.

For more than a year preceding the decision, the District of Columbia Board of Education and Superintendent Hobart M. Corning studied ways to desegregate a school system that had been segregated for ninety years by Congressional appropriation acts. A week after the decision the board issued a statement affirming its "intention to secure the right of every child within his own capacity, to the full, equal, impartial use of all school facilities and the right of all qualified teachers where needed within the school system." The board approved five principles to guide the superintendent in preparing a specific plan. Key points were the redrawing of school zone boundaries and the assignment of each pupil to the school serving the zone of his residence, with "no exceptions . . . for reasons of race."

Corning submitted a plan calling for a start toward desegregation in September of 1954, an intermediate step at the end of the first semester and completion of the process by the fall of 1955. He told the board that in his professional opinion full, immediate desegregation would be impossible.

Robert R. Faulkner, a member of the board, submitted a plan of his own under which the city would have three sets of schools. One would be exclusively white, another exclusively Negro and the third desegregated in student body and faculty. (This idea was to appear later in various places under the label "salt-and-pepper plan.") After the board tabled Faulkner's proposal, he voted with the majority to support the superintendent. Later, however, he referred to other board members as "modern John Browns."

The only member of the board who voted against Corning's plan was Mrs. Margaret Just Butcher, a Negro. She called his approach "gradual," a charge that the NAACP also made. Another group, the District Federation of Citizens Associations, criticized the board for acting too quickly and said that it would "go to court and compel these people to obey the Supreme Court and its rules." The organization sought an injunction to keep the board from "taking any further steps" until the Supreme Court issued its final decree, but Judge Henry A. Schweinhaut denied the request. When schools opened, the first phase of the plan worked so well that Superintendent Corning accelerated the second phase.

Wilmington took longer than Washington to put its plan into full effect and allowed pupils to transfer from one school to another rather freely. The first step, announced a few weeks after the *Brown* decision, was the desegregation of all the elementary grades in September, 1954.

Having made this announcement, Superintendent Ward I. Miller waited for public reaction. Almost none came, and Miller attributed this silence to a practice followed for several years before 1954 of bringing white and Negro students and teachers together. "As a result," he said, "a state of acceptance and readiness had been established by the time of the Court's decision." Soon after schools opened, Miller observed, "The success of our program is due largely to the fact that the people were well informed on the plans of the Wilmington Board of Education, and parents were given a chance to express their opinions to school officials and obtain transfers if they desired them for their children where space permitted." A liberal transfer policy was traditional in Wilmington and remained in effect after desegregation.

A year later Wilmington took a second step. The school board desegregated the seventh grade and gave all pupils in the tenth, eleventh and twelfth grades the privilege of transferring if courses they wanted to take were not available in the schools to which they otherwise would be assigned. In a third step the next year the whole system came under the plan.

Superintendent Miller emphasized the importance of "public understanding" in the accomplishment of desegregation "with so little friction and difficulty." "From the first," he said, "the public was taken into the confidence of the board. While individuals as such were not excluded from meetings and hearings, special effort was made to insure that several important organizations would send representatives qualified to speak for them and to discuss in a mature manner the issues involved."

Of the border cities that desegregated voluntarily, Baltimore acted first. As in Washington and Wilmington, the school board, under its president, Roszel C. Thomsen, and Superintendent John H. Fischer, anticipated the Supreme Court's decision and quietly prepared for it. Thomsen, an attorney, on the day of the 1954 decision took the oath as a United States district judge; while on the school board, he had coached its members on the law. Walter Sondheim, Jr., a department store executive, succeeded Thomsen.

The board conducted no program specifically designed to prepare the public, school personnel or pupils for desegregation. It assumed that the people of Baltimore would accept the Supreme Court decision. Superintendent Fischer expressed the view that the less said about desegregation the better, on the theory that it is best to let people do "what comes naturally." His reaction to the Court's decision was that it would not present "any special problems" and that he did not expect "any trouble at all so far as the children are concerned."

A few days after the decision, the school board asked City Solicitor Thomas A. Biddison for his opinion regarding the "duties and obligations of the Baltimore Department of Education." Before Biddison replied, Maryland Attorney General Edward D. E. Rollins advised the State Board of Education that, until the Court acted finally, state law requiring segregated schools would remain in effect and that it would be illegal for any local school system to "jump the gun" by desegregating. The Baltimore board met on June 3 and received the city solicitor's opinion that the local ordinance requiring segregation in education was "unconstitutional and invalid."

The board followed the advice of the city solicitor rather than the state attorney general. It adopted unanimously and without discussion a statement that "our school system should be conformed to a non-segregated basis to be in effect by the opening of schools in

September of this year" and asked the staff "to prepare material outlining the practical steps to be taken."

The plan that Superintendent Fischer presented to the board a week later called for continuation of previous assignment policies, except that "the race of the pupil shall not be a consideration." Under this policy every child had a free choice of attending any school in the system, unless the chosen school was restricted to avoid overcrowding. As to staff, the plan provided that "no person shall be denied any opportunity because of his race."

The "free choice" aspect of the Baltimore plan caused it to be described as "voluntary desegregation." The policy permitted any child to change schools for any reason, including race. Thus no child was required to attend a desegregated school against his will. Explaining this approach, Fischer said, ". . . our purpose was to open the door of all our schools to all children without discrimination, but not to push or pull anyone through a door. We have said that we believed it wrong to manipulate people to create a segregated situation. We believe it equally wrong to manipulate people to create an integrated situation." When the plan took effect in September of 1954, Board President Sondheim said that it operated "so smoothly there is no need for comment."

Immediately after the 1954 decision, the Missouri Board of Education asked State Attorney General John Dalton for his opinion of its effect. Dalton advised the board that the decision invalidated any law requiring school segregation. Until the Court issued its final decree, he added, school systems were under no compulsion to desegregate, although they might if they wished. St. Louis and Kansas City went ahead.

St. Louis followed the example of Washington more nearly than that of Baltimore. In June of 1954 the school board adopted a plan of desegregation to take effect in three stages over a period of one year. Conceding that it would be "possible" to desegregate the entire school system in September of 1954, the board expressed the opinion that to do so would be "educationally undesirable" for many children. The board also maintained that there would be "fewer mistakes and fewer misunderstandings if we proceed in orderly steps."

The first step, in the fall of 1954, was desegregation of the city's white and Negro teachers' colleges and special schools for handicapped children. Segregation ended in high schools on February 1, 1955, and in elementary schools when the new term began that fall. Under the plan, as in Washington, a student attended the school serving the district in which he lived.

Implementation of the plan was uneventful. Superintendent Philip J. Hickey said, "It was the quiet and undramatic culmination of years of education programming and democratic practice and the outcome of contributions to the building of good will by many diverse community agencies." In May, 1955, the Metropolitan Church Foundation of Greater St. Louis cited Hickey for "the thoughtful planning that went into successful integration of the high schools, the careful preparation of the people of the community for the step and the rapport established among community leaders and agencies of the city."

Kansas City also followed a three-phase, one-year plan, but with some variations from the St. Louis plan. Desegregation began in high school and junior college classes in the summer of 1954. Superintendent Mark W. Bills reported that the summer session "went off perfectly." With the start of the fall term, the junior college and vocational high school were desegregated. All schools in the system came under the plan in September of 1955.

In West Virginia both Governor William C. Marland and State School Superintendent W. W. Trent reacted to the Supreme Court decision by saying that the state would abide by it. Superintendent Trent sent a letter to all county superintendents suggesting that they "begin immediately to reorganize and readjust their schools to comply with the Supreme Court decision." In the fall of 1954 more than half of the state's biracial school districts desegregated.

By contrast to the pattern in Delaware, Maryland and Missouri, desegregation in West Virginia began in the counties that were predominantly rural and which had relatively few Negroes in their population. None of the six southern counties with the greatest numbers of Negroes desegregated the first year.

With two exceptions desegregation in 1954 began without incident. During the second week of the term white students at White Sulphur Springs in Greenbrier County demonstrated against going to school with Negroes. The County Board of Education held a session outside the meeting room. The board reversed its decision to desegregate. Negroes re-entered schools with whites the next year under court order. In Boone County similar demonstrations by white students and adults brought no change in school board policy.

In the fall of 1955, Kanawha County, which embraces the capital city of Charleston, desegregated the first, second and seventh grades. At the beginning of the next year, the entire system was desegregated. During the first year Superintendent L. K. Lovenstein received several anonymous telephone calls threatening violence, but none occurred. In the second year the superintendent called on P.T.A.'s, other citizens' groups and the press to cooperate. Dr. Herbert M. Beddow, president of the school board, said, "We couldn't have received better cooperation. Everybody agreed that integration must be made to succeed without violence."

The Board of Education of Raleigh County, with approximately the same number of Negro schoolchildren as Kanawha, also scheduled the beginning of desegregation for the fall of 1955. After a group of parents protested, three of the five members of the board held a meeting that President S. Austin Caperton had refused to schedule. The three rescinded the board's previous decision, whereupon Caperton and the fifth member resigned.

Within three years of the *Brown* decision all school districts in West Virginia in which both white and Negro schoolchildren lived had desegregated. Incidents of protest, some of them marked by violence, recurred occasionally in the state throughout the decade.

While Kentucky state officials reacted calmly and positively to the 1954 Court decision, public schools remained segregated during the 1954–55 term. The next fall some school districts desegregated, but the number of Negro children involved was small. One-third of

Kentucky's Negro population lived in the city of Louisville, where school authorities spent two years planning and preparing for desegregation.

On the day of the 1954 decision, the Louisville school board was in regular session. Informed of the Court's ruling, Board President William C. Embry said, "Our thinking and planning must start right now even if the decision allows us five years to carry out desegregation." Superintendent Omer Carmichael added that he expected to follow the law without undue delay and with no effort at subterfuge. In making plans for compliance, he said, consideration would be given to children, teachers and parents, in that order of priority.

Carmichael launched a "grass roots" program to "give us an idea of what our problems will be and how best to meet them." On the day of the 1955 decision, he said, "Now that the Court's final decision has been made we can go to work to develop a plan. . . . I believe another year of general background building, interpreting, and getting people to understand, is needed."

In November the superintendent presented to the board a twelve-point plan to take effect when schools opened the following September. The key points were that desegregation would be systemwide from the start, that school district lines would be redrawn without regard to race and that transfers would be granted "within the capacities of the schools." In explaining the plan, Carmichael said, "We decided on a simultaneous, systemwide change. There were several reasons for this. Experience elsewhere indicated that a partial or geographic change particularly might lead to mushrooming opposition. Desegregating a grade at a time or several grades at a time obviously would increase social confusion by having some children in a single family attend mixed schools while others remained in segregated schools. Administrative difficulties, too, obviously would be compounded by any partial program. And we decided that universality of participation by the entire school staff from the very beginning would greatly increase the chances of success."

When schools opened on September 10, 1956, the quiet implementation of the plan attracted wide attention. At his press conference the next day President Eisenhower commented, "I think Mr.

Carmichael must be a very wise man. I hope to meet him and I hope to get some advice from him as to exactly how he did it, because he pursued the policy that I believe will finally bring success in this." The President's compliment evoked from the superintendent the response, "The whole thing is no individual achievement. It represents teamwork within the school system and a school-community relationship capable of developing a climate of public opinion in which a program can succeed." Shortly afterward Carmichael did spend forty-five minutes in the White House telling the President about the Louisville approach to school desegregation.

As in Kentucky, no schools in Oklahoma desegregated during the 1954–55 term. State Superintendent Oliver Hodge said after the 1954 decision, "We'll follow the law, but it would be disastrous to do it right now. If we don't have to do anything about it until a year after September 1, it will be all right." The problem in Oklahoma was more financial than social. Two entirely different tax bases supported the separate Negro and white schools, and each biracial school district administered a dual budget. In a referendum in the spring of 1955, the voters approved an amendment to the state Constitution providing for a uniform school tax levy and merger of the separate school budgets. Soon after the vote, Governor Raymond Gary, the state attorney general, the State Board of Education and Superintendent Hodge issued a four-point policy statement declaring: (1) the state no longer would pay the bill for two school systems; (2) all state statutes conflicting with the U.S. Supreme Court order were void; (3) school aid would be calculated "consistent with the decisions of the Supreme Court"; (4) "transfers of children, both white and colored, to the schools of the choice of their parents will be recognized."

That fall desegregation began in Oklahoma City and Tulsa and in numerous other smaller school systems. There were almost as many variations in the plans of desegregation as there were school districts desegregating. The Oklahoma City school board drew new geographic zone lines and established new feeder relationships for its schools. The board continued the former policy of permitting a student to transfer if the school of his choice was not overcrowded and he could give a valid reason. Superintendent J. Chester Swanson said that neither white nor Negro children would be forced to attend certain schools for the sake of intermixture. He termed "rather unreasonable" the requests of Negro leaders who "would have us build fences and force people inside them." In Ardmore the school board policy was to let the problem solve itself. When questioned about the board's indefinite statement, Superintendent George D. Hann said, "We did that deliberately. If you couldn't understand what it means, then it was a pretty good statement, huh?"

In all the border states political and educational leaders immediately accepted the Supreme Court decision and moved to bring their schools into compliance with it. Desegregation began soon after the decision and spread quickly. Within three years more than 70 percent of all school districts in the area had desegregated. Generally the cities acted first, and the rural areas followed. The first steps toward desegregation were not always quiet or peaceful. Soon after desegregation began in Baltimore and Washington, objectors staged protest demonstrations, which subsided after a few days. Other incidents of protest took place in Delaware, Kentucky and West Virginia. In a few districts where resistance was strongest, schools remained segregated throughout the decade. But, after ten years, nine of every ten school districts had desegregated, and more than half the Negro children in the border area attended schools with white children.

The Decision to Desegregate in the Middle South

During the first three years after the 1954 decision, compliance was confined almost entirely to the border area. In the first year a few school districts in Arkansas and West Texas voluntarily desegregated. The second year saw voluntary compliance in Oak Ridge, Tennessee, then a federally owned and operated atomic city. Desegregation spread rapidly in West Texas, where few Negroes lived, and slowly in Arkansas and Tennessee. Until the fall of 1957, schools in other Southern states remained segregated.

Meanwhile the legislatures of all the Southern states had passed new laws designed to avoid or evade the Supreme Court decision or to soften its impact. Each state except Tennessee made it possible, or mandatory, to close schools rather than to desegregate them. Seven of the eleven states enacted laws that automatically cut off state funds from any school district that desegregated. No such obstacles stood in the way of desegregation in the border states.

With the opening of schools in the fall of 1957, Negroes entered schools with whites in Little Rock and Nashville under court order. Desegregation began voluntarily in North Carolina, where state law and policy discouraged, but did not prohibit, the assignment of white and Negro pupils to the same schools. These developments pointed the way toward the future of school desegregation in the South.

In the summer of 1954 Arkansas Education Commissioner Arch W. Ford said, "We will continue to have segregation unless and until the people at the local level are willing to accept integration. In my opinion, integration will come in some communities within a relatively short period of time. In others it will perhaps be many years. It is apparent that there can be no general statewide pattern of integration in our public schools." The commissioner was an accurate prophet. Two school districts in the state desegregated that fall, two more the next year and one the next—all voluntarily. In 1957, when Little Rock desegregated under court order, Fort Smith and Van Buren desegregated voluntarily. At the end of the decade 13 of the state's 228 biracial school districts had desegregated, and fewer than 400 of its 112,000 Negro schoolchildren attended formerly all-white schools.

One of the first districts to desegregate was Fayetteville, home of the University of Arkansas, which voluntarily had enrolled its first Negro students in 1948. Fayetteville admitted Negroes to its high school primarily for financial reasons. The number of Negro students was so small that the town had no separate Negro high school for them and had been sending them to Fort Smith and Hot Springs. The school board decided to save money by assigning the Negroes to the white high school. The board received about forty letters, all favorable except one, and it came from outside the state. Superintendent Wayne White said, "Not more than four patrons who have talked to me are bitter against the decision to integrate. Some others have said they did not like it but that it was inevitable. There has been no organized protest action and no written communication of protest."

Dollarway was the only other district in the state besides Little Rock that desegregated under court order. In 1960 the school board admitted one Negro child to a white school. "We have not given in," Board President Lee Parham said. "We have conceded a battle to win a war."

The Little Rock school board on its own initiative adopted a plan to desegregate the city's schools gradually, but the NAACP filed suit in an effort to cause immediate desegregation of the whole system. The federal courts upheld the board's plan and ordered it put into effect. The school board had taken its first action on May 20, 1954, three days after the *Brown* decision. In a formal statement the board then said, "It is our responsibility to comply with the Federal Constitutional Requirements and we intend to do so when the Supreme Court of the United States outlines the method to be followed." On May 24, 1955, a week before the Court issued its order, the board approved a plan of desegregation that Superintendent Virgil Blossom submitted. The plan provided for desegregation in three phases, starting in the high schools, then proceeding to the junior high schools and finally reaching the elementary schools. The board indicated that the first phase would start in the fall of 1957, although the plan did not include a timetable.

When the school board adopted its plan of desegregation, Dr. Dale Alford, an ophthalmologist, was its only member who was an outspoken segregationist. In the spring of 1957 two candidates who supported the plan won election to the board against segregationist opponents. After the federal courts approved the plan, few signs pointed to the confrontation between state and federal force that came with the opening of schools in September.

Early in 1958, with federal troops on duty outside Central High School, the school board asked United States District Judge Harry J. Lemley to suspend operation of the plan until January of 1961.

In their petition the board members said that they "were personally opposed to integration in the public schools" but believed they should obey the courts. "The principle of integration runs counter to the ingrained attitudes of many residents of the district," they added. "The transition involved in its gradual plan of integration has created deep-rooted and violent emotional disturbances. Any change in the attitudes of the residents of the district will come from educating them as to their obligations as American citizens and a concurrent extension of enforceable civil rights to the Negro minority, but such change will be slow in arriving." To describe their position they said, "The district, in its respect for the law of the land, is left standing alone, the victim of extraordinary opposition on the part of the state government and apathy on the part of the federal government." Judge Lemley granted the requested stay, but the Court of Appeals for the Eighth Circuit reversed his order and was upheld by the U.S. Supreme Court. Acting under state law, Governor Orval Faubus then closed the Little Rock high schools for the 1958–59 term to avoid their operation with white and Negro students enrolled in the same schools.

In November of 1958 Dr. Alford conducted an eight-day campaign for write-in votes for election to Congress. Running as a pro-Faubus segregationist, Alford defeated Representative Brooks Hays, who had held the seat for sixteen years. A week after Alford's election to Congress, the other five members of the school board resigned "in the light of recent events" and "the utter hopelessness, helplessness and frustration of our present position." Their last act, with Alford dissenting, was to vote to buy up, effective November 30, 1958, Superintendent Blossom's contract, which had until June 30, 1960, to run. Privately they said that they took this action because they feared the new board would not treat Blossom fairly. After he left Little Rock, Blossom gave his interpretation of what had happened there. "I believe the basic reasons for failure must be found in the vacillation of political leaders at state and federal levels," he said, "and in a deliberate plot by extreme segregationists all over the South to force a finish fight in Little Rock to delay or prevent a showdown on their own home grounds."

On December 6 the voters of Little Rock elected a new school board. Three of its six members—Ed I. McKinley, Jr., Traffic Judge Robert W. Laster and Ben D. Rowland—had the support of Governor Faubus and the Capital Citizens' Council. The other three—Everett Tucker, Jr., Ted Lamb and Russell H. Matson, Jr.—ran on a "businessmen's slate." In the campaign all described themselves as segregationists. At its first meeting the new board named Terrell E. Powell, principal of Hall High School, as superintendent. At the same meeting Assistant Superintendent Fred Graham resigned "to preserve my health, which has been impaired by the strain and tension of the past two years."

When the new board turned its attention to the desegregation problem, Judge Laster proposed that it maintain segregated schools, ignore the federal courts and "let the devil take the hindmost." When the board did not adopt this proposal, Laster presented a new one—automatically to cancel the contracts of teachers in a school that was desegregated so that it would be without a faculty. This plan failed to win adoption, too. Tucker, Lamb and Matson issued a statement in which they said that the choice was between desegregated schools and no schools; they favored keeping the schools open under a "controlled integration" plan, to be ready when the courts ordered the schools reopened. Governor Faubus proposed that Little Rock have two segregated and two desegregated high schools and that the desegregated schools be segregated by sex.

The school board was split three to three on all questions about desegregation. Then on May 5, 1959, the pro-Faubus members of the board—after the other three deliberately had left a meeting to deprive it of a quorum—voted to fire forty-four teachers. A group of business and civic leaders organized a committee, which they called Stop This Outrageous Purge (STOP), and circulated a petition to recall the three members of the board who had voted to fire the teachers. The Citizens' Council retaliated with a Committee to Retain Our Segregated Schools (CROSS) and petitioned for the recall of the other three. In the election the vote favored recall of the Faubus–Citizens' Council members and retention of the businessmen's slate. In June a three-judge federal court declared the Arkansas school-closing laws unconstitutional and ordered the school board to proceed with the original plan of desegregation. The Pulaski County Board of Education named three new members to the school board to replace those recalled. The schools reopened that fall, desegregated.

In the fall of 1962, Negroes were admitted to junior high schools with whites; in 1963 the plan was extended to the first and fourth grades; and in the fall of 1964 all Little Rock schools were to be desegregated. In the 1963–64 school year about 125 of more than 7,000 Negro students attended schools with whites.

Disagreement persisted on the school board, mainly between its chairman, Everett Tucker, and its secretary, Ted Lamb. The board, under Tucker's leadership, deliberately limited the number of Negroes admitted to white schools. Lamb advocated more admissions. In the spring of 1961 Lamb said, "The Tucker-dominated school board has insisted that by some devious means we could out-trick, out-maneuver and defy the federal government. Such a policy is as foolish as it is disastrous." Lamb said that school board policy was "leading Little Rock down the road to further strife and economic uncertainty." Superintendent Powell defended the pupil placement plan as the keystone to desegregation in Little Rock because it was acceptable, as a compromise, to the community. When the NAACP went back to court to seek acceleration of desegregation in Little Rock, Chairman Tucker said, "It is perhaps obvious by now that the extremists on both sides of the question will never be satisfied with the manner in which desegregation is accomplished."

In the fall of 1962, Wayne Upton, an attorney who served as chairman of the Little Rock school board in 1957 and 1958, reflected on the events of those turbulent years. Little Rock paid a rather high price for its resistance, he said, but "in view of what happened in other states . . . maybe it served a good purpose." He said that he had in mind other cities that later began desegregation peacefully.

Before schools opened in the fall of 1957, Nashville received more attention than Little Rock. The scheduled desegregation of schools in the Tennessee capital had stirred considerable local opposition and had attracted segregationists from outside the state. Trouble was expected in Nashville, not Little Rock.

The events that led to the admission of the first Negroes to schools with whites in Nashville started soon after the 1955 Supreme Court decision. The school board on June 9 referred the desegregation question to its Instruction Committee, of which Neil H. Wright was chairman. In a report on August 11 the committee suggested that "a portion of the problem should be handled first," that "the segment selected for handling should not be so large as to endanger the orderly administration of public schools in a system that has been wholly segregated for many years" and that "such segment should be sufficiently large to be a significant and worthwhile first step."

That fall twenty-one Negro children attempted to enroll in four white schools, but all were denied admission. Their parents filed suit in federal court, which held that the Board of Education was acting in good faith to comply with the Supreme Court decision and continued the case. In October of 1956 the board adopted a plan that called for geographic districting of schools without regard for race and gave pupils the privilege of transferring from schools in which their race was in the minority. Under the plan the first grades of all city schools were to be desegregated in September, 1957, but no further steps definitely were scheduled. U.S. District Judge William E. Miller approved the plan, as far as it went, but he directed the school board to submit before December 31, 1957, "a report setting forth a complete plan to abolish segregation in all the remaining grades of the city school system, including a time schedule therefor."

Early in 1957 the Tennessee legislature passed several laws that Governor Frank Clement recommended relative to school desegregation. One of these laws, known as the School Preference Act, authorized boards of education "to provide separate schools for white and Negro children whose parents, legal custodians or guardians voluntarily elect that such children attend school with members of their own race." Another was a pupil assignment act. The Nashville board went back to court to ascertain its authority under the school preference act, and Judge Miller ruled that the act was "on its face antagonistic to the principles declared by the Supreme Court in the two *Brown* cases and is, therefore, unconstitutional." The Nashville school board, as directed by the Court, in December filed a new plan of desegregation. Following the principle of the law that Judge Miller already had declared unconstitutional, the plan provided for the establishment of "three groups of schools," one for Negro students, one for white students and one for both Negro and white students. At the same time the board filed a motion for dismissal of the suit against it on the ground that the new state pupil assignment act afforded the plaintiffs an adequate remedy.

Judge Miller rejected the board's plan, finding that it "wholly fails to meet the test of constitutionality," and he ordered the board to "adopt a substantial plan and one which contemplates elimination of racial discrimination throughout the school system with all deliberate speed." He set April 7, 1958, as the deadline for submission of the plan. Judge Miller denied the motion to dismiss the suit, saying that he was "of the opinion that the administrative remedy under the act in question would not be an adequate remedy" because "to require the plaintiffs to go before a board committed in advance to a continuance of compulsory segregation would be to require them to perform a futile act." On the specified date the school board filed another plan, adding a timetable to its original plan. According to the schedule, an additional grade would be desegregated each year until the entire school system was covered. Judge Miller approved the plan, and both the Court of Appeals for the Sixth Circuit and the U.S. Supreme Court upheld his decision. Thus sanctioned, the Nashville grade-a-year plan was adopted by many other school districts in the South.

The superintendent of schools was the principal spokesman for the school board in Nashville. W. A. Bass was superintendent before desegregation began, and W. H. Oliver succeeded him upon his retirement during the first year of the plan's operation. The superintendents explained why the school board chose to begin desegregation in the first grade. Bass said that a basic reason was the difference in the "achievement level" of white and Negro pupils in the higher grades. Oliver gave as another reason that "there is a lot of difference in mixing five-year-olds and fifteen-year-olds." Bass conducted an intensive program to prepare the community for the change. In numerous speeches he confirmed the board's reluctance to desegregate. He said, "Your school board adopted this system with regret. They felt that the community is not yet ready for this step, but they were under compulsion to comply with the Supreme Court's decision. . . . You can get mad, cuss us out, call us names. But I'd like to ask you one question: What would you do if you were where we are?" After desegregation started, Oliver said, "There is no doubt that the great majority of the people in Nashville do not favor integration, but it is equally as obvious that they favor law and order."

Desegregation began in Nashville on September 9, 1957, in an atmosphere of vigorous protest. Shortly after midnight on September 10, the Hattie Cotton Elementary School, where one Negro girl had enrolled, was bombed. No one ever was charged with the bombing. When quiet returned, Oliver said, "At the most there were three hundred persons who were actively protesting. I think it safe to say that half of these people were from outside the city limits, in other words, people who were in no way affected by the school desegregation." Except for the incidents when schools opened in 1957, Nashville had no trouble. The plan proceeded as scheduled, and by the end of the decade it encompassed the first seven grades. About 775 Negroes then attended schools with whites; some 15,000 Negroes were enrolled in the city's school system. The Nashville grade-a-year plan contained the most gradual timetable that the federal courts approved, and for that reason it appealed to Southern school systems that preferred not to desegregate at all and to make the process as slow as possible once desegregation no longer could be avoided.

As it turned out, the pupil assignment plan developed in North Carolina proved to be more gradual in its effects than the Nashville plan. In principle, desegregation applied simultaneously to an entire school system that adopted a plan under the state pupil assignment law. In practice, very few Negroes successfully completed the administrative procedures established under the law as a prerequisite for admission to a school with whites.

The legislature passed the law in 1955. Although no schools in the state desegregated until 1957, some school boards made tentative moves toward desegregation before then. In July of 1955 Thomas J. Pearsall, chairman of the North Carolina Advisory Committee on Education, suggested that local school boards appoint their own advisory committees to study ways to deal with the Supreme Court decision. Some two dozen boards named such committees, which began their deliberations. In December W. W. Taylor, Jr., special counsel to the Pearsall Committee, wrote a letter to local school superintendents suggesting "that the activities of your local advisory committee be terminated . . . without publicity and by the simple expedient of having the person in authority refrain from calling the committee together." Some of the committees continued to meet, although the school boards of the state honored the request of Governor Luther Hodges and the Pearsall Committee that no action be taken during the 1955–56 school year.

The Wake County Board of Education adopted a statement of policy that beginning in September, 1956, "No child shall be assigned to any school in Wake County on the basis of color." The Winston-Salem school board also decided to desegregate at that time, then rescinded the decision; neither action was announced when it was taken. The Asheville Board of Education adopted a resolution of intent to "make an honest effort to comply with the Court's order." Governor Hodges was running for election on an appeal for "voluntary segregation." The people also were to vote that fall on the Pearsall Committee "safety valve" proposals for tuition grants and local option to close schools. These circumstances led state officials to discourage any desegregation in the fall of 1956.

Representatives of the school systems of Charlotte, Greensboro and Winston-Salem continued to hold unpublicized informal meetings at which they discussed mutual problems, including desegregation. The school boards of the three cities held simultaneous, official meetings on the night of July 23, 1957. They announced their decisions to assign Negroes to previously white schools and issued statements of policy. Each board acted under regulations drafted to conform with the state pupil assignment law, and together they assigned twelve Negro children to white schools.

Opponents of desegregation attended each of the meetings and expressed their views. In Charlotte, Kenneth Whitsett, a member of the Patriots of North Carolina, presented a petition which he said bore the signatures of sixteen thousand people who favored segregation. "Do you mean to say you can't get around this little bunch of niggers?" he asked. In Greensboro C. L. Shuping spoke for the Patriots. "If this board tonight permits integration of one single colored boy or girl to any branch of the school system of Greensboro, you shall be condemned, vilified, damned and cursed," he said. J. S. Kuykendall, also a Patriot, addressed the Winston-Salem board, basing his opposition to desegregation on the unequal taxes that whites and Negroes paid.

The start of desegregation was the occasion for incidents of protest in all three cities. The night before Yvonne Bailey was to enter Reynolds High School in Winston-Salem, someone painted in large letters on the school driveway the words "nigger go home." White students removed the paint before the Negro student arrived. In Charlotte white students harassed Dorothy Counts to the point that she withdrew from Harding High School. White students at Greensboro Senior High School threw eggs at Josephine Ophelia Boyd. Members of the Greensboro school board and Superintendent Ben L. Smith received a deluge of threatening letters. Smith had numerous anonymous telephone calls which he described as "vicious, profane and vulgar." At least one caller threatened his life. Police guarded his home after a brick was thrown through a large plate-glass window. When he retired in the spring of 1958 upon reaching sixty-five, Smith received the Greensboro Chamber of Commerce Distinguished Citizen Award.

These and other North Carolina school systems that desegregated later operated under similar plans. The rules and regulations that school boards adopted contained this language from the state pupil assignment law: "The board shall consider the best interests of the child, the orderly and effective instruction and the health, safety and general welfare of the pupils in the schools." In applying this broad policy, school boards used two basic concepts, which they labeled "normal attendance areas" and "feeder schools." The boards assumed that it was "normal" for the Negro children to attend schools with other Negro children and for white children to attend schools with other white children. They also assumed that a child "normally" attended the school nearest his home. Thus the school boards assigned Negro children to the Negro school nearest their homes and white children to the nearest white school. The result was two sets of attendance zones—one for white schools and one for Negro schools—and the zones frequently overlapped. Under the feeder system children graduating from specified elementary schools automatically were assigned to specified junior high schools, which in turn fed designated high schools. A pupil wishing to attend a school other than the one to which the board assigned him was given ten days in which to file an application for transfer. Should the school board decline to approve the transfer, the pupil had five days in which he could appeal for a hearing before the board. If, after the hearing, the board still failed to approve the requested transfer, the pupil could appeal to the state courts. School boards gave no reasons for their decisions on transfers. Under North Carolina law any child assigned against his will to a school in which his race was in the minority automatically had the privilege of transfer.

Ten years after the Supreme Court decision fewer than one-fourth of North Carolina's school districts had desegregated, and about one in two hundred Negro pupils attended a school with whites. Of the forty districts that had desegregated, all but two acted voluntarily. The state pupil assignment law and the administrative procedures established under it were factors in discouraging any massive movement of Negro pupils into white schools. The pupil placement idea, with local variations, became one of the principal means of controlling desegregation in the Southern states.

The North Carolina plan closely paralleled Virginia's first approach to the *Brown* decision. The Virginia Commission on Public Education, of which State Senator Garland Gray was chairman, in 1955 recommended a program that permitted local school systems to desegregate without requiring any child to attend a biracial school against his will. Basic elements in the Gray plan were pupil assignment by local school boards and public grants for private school tuition.

Immediately after the decision, it appeared that some Virginia schools would desegregate. State School Superintendent Dowell J. Howell said, "There will be no defiance of the Supreme Court decision as far as I am concerned. We are trying to teach school children the law of the land, and we will abide by it." In the summer of 1955 Paul Schweitzer, chairman of the Norfolk school board, said, "We intend, without mental reservation, to uphold and abide by the laws of the land." The Norfolk board began to consider plans of desegregation. In January of 1956 the Arlington County Board of Education adopted a plan of desegregation following the general lines of the Gray Commission proposals. The Arlington plan called for desegregation of elementary schools in the fall of 1956, junior high schools in 1957 and senior high schools in 1958; it specified that "any child in Arlington may attend a non-segregated school, if his parents so desire," but that "children whose parents object to their attendance at an integrated school will be assigned to a school that is not integrated."

The Gray plan never became law in Virginia. Instead the state embarked on a course of "massive resistance." At a special session in 1956 the legislature enacted a group of laws intended to maintain segregation in all schools of the state. The key laws denied funds to desegregated schools, gave the governor the authority to close schools to prevent their desegregation, and established a State Pupil Placement Board with jurisdiction over school assignments for all pupils in Virginia.

These laws effectively blocked any voluntary desegregation in Virginia. They did not stop the progress in the federal courts of desegregation cases brought against the school boards in Charlottesville, Norfolk and Warren County. In both Charlottesville and Norfolk the school boards adopted plans that required Negro pupils who applied for transfer to white schools to take special tests and to be interviewed; approval of transfer requests depended upon the outcome of the tests and interviews. With the approach of a new term in September of 1958, the school boards in the two cities prepared to comply with federal court orders to desegregate. A few days before schools were to open, the Warren County school board was ordered to desegregate its high schools. Governor J. Lindsay Almond, Jr., intervened and caused the closing of all schools that were to have been desegregated in the three systems. In January of 1959 both state and federal courts declared the "massive resistance" laws unconstitutional. The public schools in all three places reopened. While the schools were closed, the affected white children attended private schools. After the public schools reopened, the private schools continued to operate.

One school district in Virginia—Prince Edward County—was a defendant in the *School Segregation Cases* that the Supreme Court decided in 1954. The Prince Edward case was filed in 1951 and still was in the courts in 1964. The school board served notice in 1955 that it would close the county's schools rather than desegregate them, and white residents began to make plans for operating private schools for the education of their children. Upon the exhaustion of every appeal, the public schools did not open in the fall of 1959, and they remained closed for the rest of the decade.

With the collapse of massive resistance, Virginia adopted a "freedom of choice" program. It gave pupils the choice between attending the public school to which they were assigned or attending another school, public or private. Pupils who chose the latter received tuition grants from the state, supplemented by local grants. At the end of the decade Virginia had a higher ratio of desegregated school districts than any other Southern state.

Florida was the last of the Southern states outside the Deep South to lower segregation barriers in its public schools. State School Superintendent Thomas D. Bailey expressed the general attitude of other education and political leaders when he said early in 1956, "I believe some way can be found to maintain our segregated schools and to maintain the public school system." Top officials had met soon after the 1954 decision and agreed that state policy would be to do everything legally possible to delay desegregation. They relied primarily on laws that gave local school boards the responsibility for assigning pupils to schools and established criteria, tests and administrative procedures for the boards to follow. This program created so much paper work for the school systems that the local superintendents asked the state for an additional annual appropriation of $1,100,000 for extra personnel needed to assign each pupil individually.

Attention in Florida focused on Dade County, which includes the city of Miami, the largest school district in the state. Dade Superintendent W. R. Thomas said soon after the 1955 Supreme Court decision that desegregation would "move along as fast as the community will accept it." He added, "Our problem is to find what the community will accept." Within a few weeks a group of Negro parents filed a petition with the school board asking that segregation be abolished. The board's response was to adopt a formal statement of policy that it would continue to operate schools on a segregated basis "until further notice." The board's statement emphasized that the allocation of state funds to local schools was based on the "segregation principle" and that "it is essential, therefore, that no precipitate action be taken which would . . . endanger in any way the receipt of state funds, which pay about 35 per cent of the cost for the current operation of schools in Dade County." In the fall of 1956 the Negro parents filed suit in federal court in an attempt to force the board to desegregate the schools. Opponents of desegregation left the school board in no doubt about their views. David I. Hawthorne, president of the Dade County Property Owners, a group affiliated with the Citizens' Councils, appeared at a board meeting and said, "We have the names of people advocating integration, and these people are going to be taken care of at the proper time. They will be prosecuted for violating the laws of this state. Advocating racial integration is the same thing as breaking into the First National Bank."

In the fall of 1958 the Dade County school board made its first move toward desegregation. It ordered the staff to study the "practicability" of desegregation in an all-white school—Orchard Villa— in a neighborhood rapidly changing from white to Negro. In 1959 the legislature passed a number of laws to strengthen the state's defenses against impending desegregation. Early that year Governor LeRoy Collins called an off-the-record meeting of officials representing the five largest school systems in the state to determine whether any of them would be willing voluntarily to undertake "limited desegregation" for the purpose of protecting the pupil assignment law against attack in the courts. Questioned after the conference, the governor said, "There was no agreement as a group to do anything, and the matter is still up to the individual counties. But no school official was willing to proceed voluntarily with any token integration. The general feeling was that there would never be any integration until it is ordered by the courts." Dade County officials said, however, that they were going ahead with their Orchard Villa study.

In the spring of 1959 the Dade board announced that it would admit Negroes to Orchard Villa in September. This school was not involved in the court action against the board, and the start of desegregation there was considered voluntary. The board made it clear that white children would not be required to attend the school against their will. In the next few years desegregation spread in Dade County until, in June of 1963, the school board declared that the entire system was officially desegregated. In a statement endorsed by all members the board said, "This is an integrated school system and should be understood as such by all persons connected with it." The board announced that it would discontinue keeping records on a racial basis and no longer would classify schools as segregated or desegregated.

By the end of the decade one-fourth of the state's school districts with two-thirds of the population had initiated desegregation. Most school boards acted voluntarily, although all were under pressure of court action, as in Dade County. Most of them adopted grade-a-year plans, which when the decade ended were under attack as being too slow.

The Decision to Desegregate in the Deep South

The five Deep South states held out longest against desegregation. In these states no school board member or superintendent openly advocated compliance with the Supreme Court decision as a matter of principle. The question for them was whether to abandon public schools when desegregation became unavoidable. The Deep South schoolmen were squeezed tightly between state law on one side and the federal courts on the other.

No school board in the South felt this pinch more painfully than the one in New Orleans. U.S. District Judge J. Skelly Wright in February of 1956 ordered the board to desegregate the Orleans Parish schools "with all deliberate speed." The school board and Louisiana political leaders were committed to segregation. All members of the school board but one—Emile A. Wagner, Jr.—strongly favored keeping the schools open, even if desegregated. State political leaders showed determination to close the schools rather than to permit their desegregation.

At the time of the 1955 Supreme Court decision Dr. Clarence E. Scheps, comptroller of Tulane University, was chairman of the school board. In a statement on behalf of the board he said: "It must be remembered that our local schools are a part of the state system and as such are governed by the regulations of the State Board of Education and by the statutes and constitution as interpreted to us by the attorney general of Louisiana. Beyond this, however, we are aware that the legislature, the people of the state and the people of the community have declared themselves overwhelmingly in favor of the maintenance of a separate but equal school system for Negroes. The five members of the Orleans Parish school board are in unanimous agreement that the education of both races can proceed more effectively under a segregated system." The next spring the Louisiana School Boards Association joined in a statement that "the greater majority of our Negro people are not in favor of integration, and in order to protect them from a vicious radical minority it is essential that segregation be maintained."

Segregationist Wagner, a lawyer, succeeded Scheps as chairman of the school board. Wagner was the author of a state law that "froze" the racial separation of New Orleans schools by giving a four-man legislative committee authority over transfers of Negro children to white schools or white children to Negro schools. When in February of 1958 the U.S. Court of Appeals for the Fifth Circuit upheld Judge Wright's desegregation order, Wagner said, "The board is still dedicated to the maintenance of its policy of segregation." That fall Judge Wright issued a permanent injunction against segregation in New Orleans schools, and Wagner advocated closing the schools as a preferable alternative to complying. After further legal skirmishing, Judge Wright ordered the board to submit a plan of desegregation in the spring of 1960, and Wagner, no longer chairman of the board, said, "I would sooner have no public schools than the educational jungles and the moral swamps of Washington and New York."

Lloyd J. Rittiner, head of an engineering firm, then was chairman of the board. He expressed the view of all board members but Wagner when he said, "The federal government says we cannot operate segregated schools. The state says we cannot operate integrated schools and has the power to close the schools. We must submit a plan to Judge Wright by May 16. We don't have one. If we do submit one we cannot implement it because of the state law. Somewhere along the line the court is going to have to tell us what to do. I am a segregationist. I think it is to the best interest of the people of New Orleans of both races to have separate schools. If, however, I am faced with a choice of integrating or closing I am already on record as favoring integration to the extent that it is necessary to comply with law."

The school board declined to submit a plan to Judge Wright, so he ordered the desegregation of the first grades with the opening of schools in September. Maneuvering to maintain segregation continued, but in July Rittiner said, "There is absolutely nothing that the governor or the attorney general can do to maintain a segregated public school system in Louisiana. This may sound to some people like a defeatist attitude, but it is one thing to fight as far as humanly possible and still be able to recognize when you've reached the end of the road, and surrender, as difficult as the surrendering may be, and it is another thing to continue to fight without recognizing that you have reached the end of the road and be destroyed. I do not want the public school system to be destroyed."

In the weeks that followed, the school board, the governor, the legislature and the federal courts engaged in a flurry of moves and countermoves. Governor Jimmie H. Davis seized control of the schools, and the courts returned control to the board. Judge Wright extended the deadline for the start of desegregation to November 14. The school board prepared to follow the court order. The governor called the legislature into special session in an effort to block desegregation. State School Superintendent Shelby M. Jackson was a leader in the effort to maintain segregation. "I don't understand why we have to abide by the wishes of a small minority," he said, "when it is evident that a large majority of both races want the schools to remain as they are now." When Jackson attempted to declare a statewide school holiday to prevent the start of desegregation in New Orleans, he was cited for contempt of court.

The school staff took applications from Negro children who wished to transfer to white schools and administered psychological and ability tests to them. Superintendent James F. Redmond recommended that five of the applications be approved. Desegregated first grades would be segregated by sex, he said. In one of numerous actions Judge Wright issued a restraining order against 775 state and local officials, including the governor and all members of the legislature, to prevent their interference with desegregation. On November 14 four Negro girls entered two formerly white schools. A screaming throng, composed mostly of women, gathered around the schools for days. Very nearly all of the white students boycotted the schools.

The fight continued after the Negroes entered the white schools. The legislature remained in special session—one after another—passing laws to keep the schools segregated. As quickly as the legislature passed laws, the federal courts declared them unconstitutional. Desegregation in New Orleans advanced according to plan, and the number of Negro children in previously white schools gradually increased.

Just before desegregation began, the people of New Orleans voted to fill a place on the school board. Matthew R. Sutherland was re-elected on a platform of keeping the schools open, even if desegregated. After his victory, Sutherland said, "I believe that the majority which I received in this election is a complete vindication of the school board, which has been called a surrender board. It proves to me the people realize the board did all in its power to keep the schools open and segregated. We've heard a lot about mandates during this election, and I believe the mandate of the majority of the people in New Orleans to the governor and legislature is to keep our public schools open." Sutherland later was elected chairman of the board.

In the spring of 1962 Judge Wright ordered all elementary schools in New Orleans desegregated the following September. In his order he showed sympathy for the local school board. "The school board here occupies an unenviable position," he said. "Its members, elected to serve without pay, have sought conscientiously, albeit reluctantly, to comply with the law on order of this court. Their reward for this service has been economic reprisal and personal recrimination from many of their constituents who have allowed hate to overcome their better judgment. But the plight of the board cannot affect the rights of schoolchildren whose skin color is no choice of their own. . . ." Judge Frank B. Ellis, who succeeded Judge Wright, set aside the order to desegregate all the elementary schools and approved a grade-a-year plan.

No other school system desegregated in Louisiana until 1963. In the fall of that year East Baton Rouge, acting by court order, admitted twenty-eight Negro students to the twelfth grade under a plan that was to proceed downward a grade a year. The board was not unanimous in its action. One member, A. T. Furr, said, "The entire effort is purely political . . . a vote-getting gimmick. The Negro is being used as a pawn in a political power struggle."

Georgia in 1961 followed Louisiana into the ranks of Deep South states with forced desegregation. First the state was confronted with the choice between abandoning public education, as its laws required, or permitting some desegregation as the price of maintaining the schools. The choice was not easy.

Immediately after the first *Brown* decision, Georgia plotted a course aimed at substituting state-supported private schools for public schools, if necessary, to avoid desegregation. State law required the withdrawal of public funds from any school system that desegregated and provided for the payment of tuition grants for attendance at private schools.

State education leaders consistently opposed the private-school, tuition-grant approach. In 1954 the people of Georgia voted on a constitutional amendment to authorize the grants, and State School Superintendent M. D. Collins stumped the state to oppose it. He paraphrased Winston Churchill in saying that he was not elected state superintendent of schools to liquidate the public school system. He questioned whether private schools would guarantee segregation. The amendment passed, but opposition to it continued. In 1960, as the hour of decision neared, Dr. Claude Purcell, then state superintendent of schools said, ". . . I cannot do otherwise than take a stand for public education. . . . We cannot do without education in Georgia." Frank M. Hughes, executive secretary of the Georgia Education Association, used stronger language to voice his opinions. "I didn't think the private school plan would work when it was first introduced, and I still don't," he said. "When the plan fails, the GEA will move to support free, public tax-supported schools." Jim Cherry, DeKalb County superintendent, was another outspoken opponent of the private school plan. "Private schools for a hundred years had a free hand," he said, "and at no time were more than 15 per cent of the educable children attending schools."

Teachers in Georgia who deviated, or seemed to deviate, from the official state policy risked the loss of their jobs. The State Board of Education made it a rule to revoke the license of any teacher who was a member of the NAACP or "any allied organization, or any subversive organization" or who "supports, encourages, condones or agrees to teach a mixed class." The board also adopted a resolution prohibiting pupils, teachers, principals or any other persons connected with the public schools from participating in biracial meetings. The Georgia Teachers Association (white), at its 1955 meeting, noted that "in some quarters the loyalty of teachers of Georgia has been questioned with respect to our Southern traditions and customs in regard to segregation" and passed a resolution going on record in favor of segregation. The Georgia Teachers and Education Association (Negro) in 1956 approved a resolution calling for desegregation of state schools "with a spirit of fair play and good will" and labeled any attempt to "supplant" public schools with private schools "a serious menace to the educational process." In 1960 the white teachers group went on record favoring the continuation of public schools "where equal and separate school placement is violated."

By the time the courts required Atlanta to desegregate, official state policy had shifted to a position of permitting desegregation but holding it to a minimum through a pupil placement law and providing an escape from biracial schools through tuition grants to private, segregated schools. As early as 1955 the Atlanta school board had decided to study the question of desegregation but declared that there would be no "drastic, sudden or revolutionary changes." Miss Ira Jarrell, superintendent, pointed to the alternatives of maintaining segregation or closing the schools. "We are caught between state and federal laws," she said. When in 1959 U.S. District Judge Frank Hooper ordered the Atlanta school board to submit a plan for desegregation, he recognized this conflict and indicated that he would give the Georgia legislature time to change state law requiring that desegregated schools be closed. The legislature changed the law early in 1961 to avoid the necessity of closing the University of Georgia. The way was paved for desegregation in Atlanta.

Dr. John W. Letson then was superintendent of Atlanta schools, and A. C. Latimer was president of the Board of Education. They set the tone for Atlanta's approach to the change. "No modern city, no modern state, can continue to exist as a modern city or state without an education program to meet the needs of its people," Superintendent Letson said. "We must give more education, not less, not an emasculated program, not a limited program. We are going to do it. We are going to do it, for there is a way to do it without going through that devastating process that would brand our city for a long, long time." Latimer expressed the hope that "we can go through the period of transition—from an old order to a new . . . in an orderly, peaceful and dignified manner." Desegregation had strong opposition, but Mayor William Hartsfield and the business and civic leaders of the community organized to support the school board and administration.

The court approved a grade-a-year plan starting in the twelfth grade. Superintendent Letson later confessed that he at first had some "misgivings about starting with the 12th grade instead of the usual pattern of starting with the younger children" but that he changed his mind. The high school students "came to develop a sense of pride in taking and handling a difficult problem," he said, that "would not have been possible among first-grade students."

The first Negroes entered schools with whites in Atlanta in September of 1961, without incident. After schools opened Superintendent Letson said, "When the full story is told, it will be a thrilling account of an increasing groundswell for peaceful desegregation involving almost the total population of a community." Toward the end of the school year Letson said, "The board was determined to abide by authority but to do everything possible to prevent the schools from becoming a pawn between state and federal law." In his own evaluation of the first year Assistant Superintendent Rual W. Stephens said, "Atlanta, beyond question, has shown the rest of the state and nation that a school desegregation plan, well thought out, well prepared for, well executed, can work without the bloodshed or corrupted morals or deterioration of educational standards that the prophets of doom had called for."

When the decade ended, desegregation had started in three more of Georgia's 181 school districts in which both white and Negro students lived. Altogether in the 1963–64 school year fewer than 200 of the state's more than 337,000 Negro pupils were enrolled in schools with whites.

After desegregation began in Georgia in 1961, only Alabama, Mississippi and South Carolina remained on the list of states with completely segregated schools. The 1962–63 school year saw no change, but the next fall brought both Alabama and South Carolina into the desegregation column.

Alabama made a greater show of last-ditch resistance than did

South Carolina. In the highly volatile political atmosphere of Alabama, schoolmen for the most part kept a discreet silence. State Superintendent of Education Austin R. Meadows was the exception to the rule of silence, although he, too, was discreet. Immediately after the 1955 decision Meadows expressed the belief that "segregated schools in the state can be worked out on a voluntary basis," that "the overwhelming majority of Negroes realize that segregation is what the people in Alabama want" and that "the Negroes are friendly enough to co-operate with the majority who want segregation." Whether friendliness was the explanation or not, the Negroes of Alabama did not challenge the segregated system of education until late in the decade, except for a suit that the Rev. Fred Shuttlesworth filed in 1957 against the Birmingham Board of Education. In that case the Alabama Pupil Placement Act was held to be constitutional "on its face."

In 1957 the legislature passed a law to provide for the closing of public schools and the payment of tuition grants for private schools. Superintendent Meadows attacked the plan. "We can't solve the school dilemma in any respect, financially or racially, by running away from it," he said. "To abolish the public school system in favor of private schools would be like tearing down a house to put out a fire in the cellar. . . . The danger of private school plans is that they could destroy our system of education, including the legitimate private schools." After the law passed, Meadows said that he would cooperate, but he contended that "if you set up private segregated schools, somebody will set up integrated private schools, and you will have more integration with private schools."

In the spring and summer of 1963 federal courts ordered a beginning of desegregation in Birmingham, Huntsville, Mobile and Macon County (Tuskegee). In September state troopers acting under orders from Governor George C. Wallace blocked Negro students who reported to white schools in Birmingham, Mobile and Tuskegee. Desegregation began in Huntsville unimpeded. All five federal district judges in Alabama joined in restraining the governor from any further interference. White students boycotted the desegregated schools everywhere but at Huntsville. The boycotts collapsed after a few days except in Tuskegee, where all white students withdrew to attend a private school.

South Carolina, along with Virginia, was one of the Southern states in which a school district was a defendant in the original *School Segregation Cases*. The Clarendon County school board was under a court order throughout the decade to desegregate "with all deliberate speed," but its schools remained segregated. Until 1960 Negro parents in the county made no effort to force the issue, and a suit filed then was not pursued. The statements of school officials describe the situation. J. D. Carson was chairman of the school board when the 1955 Supreme Court decision came down. "We will keep the races separate. If we have to close the schools, we'll close. If we close one school, we will close them all. . . . If any Negro applies for admission to the white school when the next term starts, we will just close down the school." J. W. Phillips, principal of the consolidated white school, added, "I think the minute there is a choice between integration and closing down, we will close down. There will be nothing else to do. The Negroes have us outnumbered eight to one. I certainly would not want to be responsible for maintaining order and good feeling under integration." County School Superintendent L. B. McCord said, "If we desegregate, neither race will receive any benefit. Both races will be hurt. Here is the situation. The Negro children have not had the educational advantages in the past that the whites have had. They haven't even taken advantage of the opportunities that they have had." Later McCord said, "Frankly, I'm sick of outsiders who tell us how to run our schools. . . . A small group of loud-mouth agitators keeps telling us how we ought to do this and how we ought to do that. We've been living here practically all our lives and we understand the situation. How could they understand it when they are hundreds of miles away?"

South Carolina followed a policy of resistance in common with the other Deep South states. When the ultimate choice between no schools and desegregated schools had to be made, the state went the way of the other states. It permitted desegregation and adopted a program of tuition grants for private schools.

In September of 1963 Charleston became the first school district in the state to admit Negroes to a school with whites. It was the only district to desegregate during the decade.

With the crack in the segregation wall in South Carolina, Mississippi stood alone among the states in maintaining absolute segregation of the races in its public schools. Using all the devices employed by the other states to prevent desegregation, Mississippi also placed unusual emphasis on equalizing Negro schools. The theory was that Negroes would be more nearly satisfied to remain in their own schools if the schools were equal to those for whites. It was estimated that it would take $120,000,000 to do the job. State School Superintendent J. M. Tubb reported in 1962 that "the expenditure per pupil in average daily attendance for whites was $81.86 and for Negroes it was $21.77." The report dealt with local supplements to state school funds.

Superintendent Tubb incurred the wrath of state political leaders in 1961 by a speech he made before the Mississippi Education Association. He said that if segregated schools were challenged, "the solution must be found through the efforts of dedicated leaders who put the welfare of the children and the future of our state and nation above all else. In the day of last resort, our people must know that to abolish the public schools would be to close the door of hope for many ambitious youth in this state." Some school people also criticized Tubb for this statement. Superintendent G. L. Tutor of Magee said, "I think every red-blooded Mississippian would not go to the extent of saying public schools at any cost. We cannot forsake our precious heritage, our customs, our social obligations to our children, our obligations to the colored race and to our God."

In a letter to Negro parents, O. S. Jordan, Negro principal of a school in Carthage, discouraged their seeking desegregation. "Do you know that if a suit is filed here, it calls for the automatic closing of all schools?" he wrote. "Do you have enough money to pay for a private school? How many jobs can you give to members of your race? Are you educationally prepared to obtain employment in some other area? Are you willing to allow your anger to override your better judgment? Do you believe in the Christian concept of life?"

The Negroes who wanted desegregated schools were undeterred. In Carthage, Biloxi and Jackson they filed suits in 1963. U.S. District Judge Sidney C. Mize dismissed the suits, saying that "none of the plaintiffs have exhausted any of the administrative remedies provided for" in the Mississippi pupil assignment law "or in any way attempted to use" them. The Fifth Circuit Court of Appeals reversed Judge Mize and ordered him to give the cases "prompt consideration" on their merits. Judge Mize ordered the three school boards to submit plans to desegregate at least one grade each year beginning with the 1964–65 term.

Post-Desegregation Problems

Desegregation, once begun, brought new problems for students, teachers and administrators. For students the problems were mainly academic and social. For teachers, maintaining discipline sometimes was difficult. Negro teachers in some areas faced loss of their jobs. The problems of the students and the teachers in turn were problems for the administrators.

The principal academic problem was the "achievement gap" between white and Negro pupils of the same age and grade level. In general, the gap widened as the children advanced into the higher grades. Various reasons were given—and debated—for the disparity in scholastic performance: the inferiority of segregated Negro schools, the culturally deprived environment in which most Negroes lived, an increasing awareness of what it means to be a Negro in a white-dominated society, the inherent inferiority that some ascribed to the Negro race. Whatever the reason, the gap was a common phenomenon. Tests given in many communities showed that white students in general ranked higher than Negro students in general, although some Negroes ranked very high and some whites very low.

School administrators and teachers had the problem of planning an instruction program in a desegregated school that would meet the needs of all students, white and Negro. The District of Columbia school system developed a "four-track" plan for its high schools. Students were assigned to one of four learning programs—

honors, regular, general and basic—according to their scores on tests. Assistant Superintendent Carl F. Hansen, who was the chief architect of the plan and who later became superintendent, said that the plan's purpose was to provide students with instruction suited to their needs and was "not associated with desegregation." Other school systems used variations of the track plan. One of them was Baltimore, where Superintendent John Fischer agreed with Hansen that problems stemming from differences in achievement "were not created by desegregation." Fischer said, "We have long known that, regardless of race, the social and cultural pattern of a child's family affect his learning and interest in school." In St. Louis Dr. Samuel Shepard, Jr., who directed the "Banneker group" of twenty-three elementary schools in a depressed, predominantly Negro area, developed a program to stimulate and motivate children toward higher achievement. Within a period of four years the level of achievment by students in these schools rose as much as two years. The St. Louis Newspaper Guild selected Shepard for its Page One Award. The citation read, "The results can be evaluated statistically on the basis of highly improved reading ability, and corresponding gains in the number of eighth graders prepared for top track high school work. The changed spirit in the once depressed schools may prove to be even more important than the measurable accomplishments."

In Montgomery County, Maryland, a group of white parents organized a voluntary tutoring service for Negro pupils. The project began when four Negro schools were closed and their pupils reassigned to nearby white schools. Mrs. Clara Eugster, who served as executive secretary of the program, described it at a hearing conducted by the U.S. Commission on Civil Rights. "With few exceptions," she said, "the educational achievement of these [Negro] children lagged from one to five grades behind their white classmates." White volunteers—including lawyers, scientists, businessmen and social workers—spent an afternoon or an evening a week tutoring the Negro pupils, usually in the children's homes. Mrs. Eugster reported that the school work and attitudes of the children improved.

Extracurricular activities also presented problems that sometimes were more sensitive than academic ones. Should Negro students admitted to white schools be permitted to join clubs, play in the band, attend school dances? Should Negroes be members of school athletic teams? School boards and administrators had to find answers to these and related questions.

District of Columbia schools dropped dances during the early stages of desegregation. In Baltimore dances continued, with a tacit understanding that no stags would attend and that couples would be of the same race. In St. Louis each principal decided the policy for his school. In Virginia most desegregated schools discontinued social activities. In July of 1962 the Albemarle County, Virginia, school board forbade "all school activities which bring about social contacts." A year later the county trustees fired the entire school board because its members refused to reconsider their ruling.

Interracial athletics were the subject of lively controversy in some places. Delaware offers an example. White schools in Sussex County canceled their football games with schools in New Castle and Kent counties that had Negroes on their teams. The Dover high school played against Negroes in its home games, but not away from home. In Greenwood the school board announced a policy of banning any sort of interracial activity; within a month the board reversed its field under pressure from the students.

Desegregation of a school sometimes aggravated problems of discipline. St. Louis Superintendent Philip Hickey said he was "at a loss to know how to cope with the problem of mushrooming little everyday skirmishes between kids into racial incidents simply because they occur between white and colored kids." A Washington principal who was a former Marine told the superintendent that he felt "more like a warden than an educator." Representative James C. Davis of Georgia, who was chairman of a Congressional committee that investigated desegregation of the Washington schools, said that "as an experiment in human relations" it was "a nightmare." Superintendent Hansen called it "a miracle of social adjustment."

When schools desegregated, Negro teachers often lost their jobs. Almost four hundred Negro teachers were displaced in Oklahoma. In Missouri, Texas and West Virginia desegregation caused significant unemployment among Negro teachers. The situation began to change, however, toward the end of the decade. The urban centers of the border states adopted policies of employing and promoting teachers by nonracial criteria. Gradually the number of Negro teachers and administrators increased. In the eleven Southern states there was very little desegregation of teaching staffs. Court decisions in several cases, however, applied the principle of the *Brown* decision to school personnel.

Regardless of its effect on employment of Negro teachers, desegregation emphasized one of the products of segregated education. In general, Negro teachers were not as well prepared as white teachers, although many of the Negro teachers held more advanced degrees than white teachers. Superintendent Omer Carmichael of Louisville said, "The average Negro teacher is not as good as the average white teacher." W. D. Galbreath said that the Memphis school boards, of which he was president, used two sets of standards in hiring teachers, one for whites and one for Negroes. "If we applied equal standards," he explained, "83 per cent of our Negro teachers would be eliminated." Superintendent Fischer of Baltimore observed, "On the whole the colored teachers do not make as good scores on the professional examinations as the white teachers and a number of them come from colleges that could not honestly be called the equal of the colleges from which most of our white teachers are drawn. Many of these teachers have made heroic efforts to improve their competence and some of them have become very good indeed. But the average competence of our Negro teachers is probably not as high as the average of all our white teachers. We are living with the consequences of our past mistakes in segregating and depressing a large section of our population."

Resegregation

Population movements affected the course of desegregation. In some instances a single school was involved, in others an entire school system. Miami's Orchard Villa school converted within two years from all-white to all-Negro. The school was located in a neighborhood that rapidly shifted from white to Negro, and the racial composition of the school's student body changed correspondingly. This resegregation—the return of segregation to a school that had been desegregated—occurred on a large scale in such border-area cities as Washington, Baltimore and St. Louis.

At the time of the 1954 Supreme Court decision, 61 percent of the pupils enrolled in the District of Columbia schools were Negroes; ten years later Negroes comprised almost 86 percent of the enrollment. Numerous schools went through the segregated-desegregated-resegregated cycle. In 1964 the District had about two dozen all-Negro schools, four all-white schools and many predominantly Negro schools. Superintendent Hansen said of this situation, "We have no embarrassment about the enrollment ratio. It is symptomatic of an urban problem that needs adjusting beyond the scope of the school system—in such fields as housing and public service."

The pattern was similar in Baltimore. When desegregation began, less than one-third of the students in the public schools were Negro; ten years later well over half were Negro. Dr. Houston R. Jackson, a Negro assistant superintendent of schools, said in 1961 that Baltimore had "more Negro children today in essentially segregated situations than we had when segregation was compulsory." The trend continued. In the year before desegregation started, Baltimore had about 52,000 Negroes in segregated schools. At the end of the decade about 80,000 Negroes were in all-Negro schools or schools with less than 5 percent white enrollment.

Deputy Superintendent William A. Kottmeyer of St. Louis said in 1961 that there was more segregation in the public schools of his city then than in 1955, when the system completed official desegregation. The reason, he said, was the tendency of white residents to leave an area when Negroes moved into it. He added that, once Negroes became a sizable proportion of the students in a school, the proportion of whites declined rapidly. In the spring of 1964, Kottmeyer, then superintendent, reported to the Board of Education that the school system was adding 3,000 Negro children annually and losing 1,100 white children. Between 1953 and 1963 the proportion of white students declined from 65 percent to 43 percent.

Private Schools

Of the eleven Southern states all but three—Florida, Tennessee and Texas—adopted plans under which state and local funds could be used to make grants toward tuition at private, nonsectarian schools. The amount of the grants usually was determined by the per-pupil contribution of the state and local governments to the cost of operating the public schools.

Public school officials, as a rule, opposed these plans. They expressed concern about the quality of instruction that children would receive in the private schools. They also voiced fear that the expenditure of public funds for private school tuition would divert money from the public schools.

A private school spawned by desegregation opened in Kentucky in 1957. White parents who objected to sending their children to biracial schools in Sturgis organized Union County Independent Schools, Inc., and started a school at Grove Center. Wright Waller, Jr., chairman of the private school group and president of the Union County Citizens' Council, commented that "this is what the unconstitutional usurpation by the federal government of local police power and local school board management of the local schools is driving us to." Kentucky, in common with the other border states, made no contribution to the support of private schools. After one year of operation the Grove Center Academy closed, and Waller explained, "We found you can't pay taxes and be independent at the same time."

In the fall of 1958 Governor Faubus of Arkansas closed high schools in Little Rock and Governor Almond of Virginia closed high schools in Charlottesville, Norfolk and Warren County to avoid desegregation. In each place private schools for white children opened with state financial support. When the public schools reopened in Little Rock, the private school closed. In Virginia the private schools continued to operate, and others sprang up as desegregation spread to additional communities in the state. North Carolina, the only other state outside the Deep South to enact a private-school, tuition-grant law, made no payments under its plan during the entire decade.

In the Deep South desegregation started in Louisiana, which had a strong private school tradition. After desegregation began in New Orleans in 1960, enrollment rose in established private schools. In 1963–64 grants to more than ten thousand students in fifty-eight private schools totalled $3,500,000. Despite the grants, some private schools organized as a direct result of desegregation had financial difficulties. The largest of the new private schools, Junior University of New Orleans, closed in the spring of 1964. In Georgia the tuition grants program inaugurated in 1961 aroused so much opposition that the legislature amended the law in 1963 to require that local school boards and the county government certify a need for the program and pay part of its cost. In the 1962–63 school year more than twelve hundred students received grants; during the next year only nineteen grants were paid. The beginning of desegregation in Alabama, South Carolina and Mississippi at the end of the decade stimulated the organization of private schools in those states.

Although Louisiana had the most extensive and expensive private school program, the movement in Virginia attracted the most attention. With the threat of closed schools hanging over the state in the summer of 1958, Virginia Superintendent Davis Y. Paschall said in an address to district superintendents, "If there ever was a time for a courageous stand in defense of the public school system, a keystone to the future of representative government in this country, this is the time. Sensible people cannot permit the public school system to be destroyed without recognizing the corollary of destruction of that representative government." That fall the Tidewater Education Association, which organized a private school in Norfolk, asked for help from teachers in the public schools closed by order of the governor. All the teachers refused, on the grounds that they would not be a part of the "massive resistance" program. Instead they set up "tutoring groups" for children not attending any school, and about four thousand enrolled. The teachers stopped this program because, they said, it lulled parents into feeling that the makeshift classes were a solution to the school crisis. The public schools reopened in Norfolk, Charlottesville and Warren County in February, 1959, after both state and federal courts declared Virginia's school-closing law unconstitutional. The private schools remained open, and their students continued to receive tuition grants.

In the spring of 1959 the Virginia Education Association's Educational Policies Commission, headed by Superintendent H. I. Willett of Richmond, warned that hastily organized private schools would result in inferior education. In a report endorsed by the VEA Board of Directors, the commission said, "The citizens of this commonwealth must recognize that the Virginia public school system has been built with painstaking care at great cost and that it has produced impressive results. Non-public schools of high quality also have benefited from a long period of effective development. New non-public schools can only be organized with great difficulty if they have due regard for quality education."

Soon after the commission made its report, the Board of Supervisors of Prince Edward County voted not to appropriate funds for public schools for the fiscal year starting July 1. Almost immediately after the decision, white residents of the county began to make plans and to raise money for private schools. With the exhaustion of the last appeal in the courts, the public schools of the county closed. The white children went to the private schools that opened in the fall of 1959. Negro parents rejected offers to provide segregated private schools for their children. During the 1963–64 academic year almost sixteen hundred Negro children and a half-dozen white children attended schools operated by the Prince Edward Free Schools Association with contributions from foundations and individuals.

Developments in two other Virginia counties provided variations on the Prince Edward experience. Surry County desegregated its public schools under court order in 1963. All the white children withdrew from the public school system and enrolled in the new private school for whites. Only Negroes remained in the "desegregated" public schools. Powhatan County schools also desegregated in the fall of 1963, and a private school for white students was formed. In Powhatan, however, a group of white parents joined in an organization that they called Citizens for Public Education, with the purpose of encouraging as many white students as possible to remain in the public schools. The white students split almost evenly between the public and the private schools, the latter attracting a slight majority.

Under Virginia law any child who did not wish to attend the public school serving his neighborhood was eligible for grants toward the cost of attending any other nonsectarian school, public or private, segregated or desegregated, anywhere in the United States. During the 1963–64 school year more than twelve thousand pupils received almost $3,000,000 in tuition grants, approximately half from state funds and half from local funds. The students who received grants were a small fraction of the one million children in the public schools, but the number of grants increased steadily and at an accelerating rate each year.

The establishment and the subsequent success or failure of private schools showed a close correlation to the degree of resistance to desegregation. Where resistance was weak, desegregation had little effect on existing private schools and produced no new ones. Where resistance was strong, desegregation caused enrollments in existing private schools to increase and prompted formation of new ones. Where resistance wavered, new private schools had tough sledding.

Outside the South

The Supreme Court ruling that "separate educational facilities are inherently unequal" clearly invalidated laws requiring racial segregation in the public schools. But did the principle of the *Brown* decision apply to racial segregation in the schools whatever the reason for it?

After 1960 this question repeatedly arose in the United States district courts. Judge Irving R. Kaufman held in January of 1961 that the school board of New Rochelle, New York, deliberately had drawn zone lines to create and maintain a predominantly Negro school. Judge Kaufman said in his decision: ". . . I see no basis to draw a distinction, legal or moral, between segregation established by the formality of a dual system of education, as in *Brown*, and that created by gerrymandering of school district lines and transferring of white children. . . . Having created a segregated school, the Constitution imposed upon the Board the duty to end segregation. . . ." Two years later, in deciding a case from Gary, Indiana, Judge George N. Beamer said: "The problem in Gary is not one of segregated schools but rather one of segregated housing. . . . The fact that certain schools are completely or predominantly Negro does not mean that the defendant maintains a segregated school system. . . . Racial balance in our public schools is not constitutionally mandated." The Supreme Court declined to review either the New Rochelle or the Gary decision.

Judge John F. Dooling in 1962 refused to dismiss a suit against the school board of Hempstead, New York. His reason was widely cited. He said, "Segregated education is inadequate and when that inadequacy is attributable to state action it is a deprivation of constitutional right." Judge Joseph C. Zavatt referred to Dooling's ruling in January of 1964, when he ordered the school board of Manhasset, New York, to submit a plan to end segregation in the elementary grades the next fall. In his opinion Judge Zavatt said, "The court does not hold that . . . racial imbalance and segregation are synonymous or that racial imbalance, not tantamount to segregation, is violative of the Constitution. It does hold that, by maintaining and perpetuating a segregated school system, the defendant Board has transgressed the prohibitions of the Equal Protection Clause of the Fourteenth Amendment."

In the absence of any decision by the Supreme Court, the legal question remained in doubt. For school boards and administrators the practical problems of racial imbalance in the schools would not wait for resolution by court decision. In most of the major cities of the country, and in many of the smaller ones, both Negro and white groups protested the action and inaction of school authorities. By petitions, boycotts, picketing and other forms of demonstration they attempted to influence official decisions. On the whole, these protests outside the South exceeded those in the South in frequency, magnitude and intensity.

There was no precise definition of "racial imbalance." Judge

Kaufman said in the New Rochelle case that racial imbalance existed in a school with 94 percent Negroes. The U.S. Commission on Civil Rights defined as "segregated" a school with 90 percent or more Negroes. James E. Allen, Jr., commissioner of education for the state of New York, said that ". . . a racially imbalanced school is defined as one having 50 per cent or more Negro pupils enrolled." Allen directed all local superintendents and school boards to report to him what they were doing toward elimination of racial imbalance.

Educators held conflicting views on the problem and what to do about it. Two statements by the same man—one who changed his mind—were representative of the chief opposing arguments. Dr. John H. Fischer, superintendent in Baltimore when desegregation started there, expressed one opinion in 1962 at a conference called by the Civil Rights Commission. Then dean of Columbia University Teachers College, Fischer spoke strongly against "social engineering" to achieve racial balance. He said, "In the administration of schools . . . the manipulation of pupils on purely racial grounds is irrelevant and improper. . . . The most offensive aspect of the engineered approach is the assumption that any group can be improved if members of another race are introduced into it. . . . We cannot have it both ways. We cannot say that race *per se* makes no difference and then argue that important decisions should be based on this inconsequential factor." Two years later, as president of Teachers College, Fischer wrote, "When any school becomes improperly exclusive in fact or in spirit, when it is viewed as being reserved for certain groups or as protecting special interests, or when its effect is to create or continue a ghetto-like situation, it cannot serve the purpose of democratic education. . . . The new problems of race relations in the public schools . . . must be answered, and in virtually every case the answers must come from the local school boards."

The California Board of Education in 1962 adopted a policy of avoiding "insofar as practicable, the establishment of attendance areas which in practical effect discriminate upon an ethnic basis against pupils or their families or which in practical effect tend to establish or maintain segregation on an ethnic basis." Max Rafferty, California superintendent of public instruction, said in a speech about a year later: "There is no question some schools are completely segregated. This is bad for the children, education and the schools, but it is not all the fault of the schools. I hate racial prejudice, but an artificial ratio of Negroes to whites is not the answer. This would be bad for education. We are going to help lick the problem of integration but we cannot sacrifice the principle of good education to solve a problem that originated outside of the schools. Neighborhood segregation is the real problem. We don't want to use the schools to kid people there is an easy way to solve this national problem." The California legislature in 1963 authorized the appointment of a special commission to assist local school districts "in problems involving the ethnic distribution of pupils in school attendance."

The Illinois legislature also acted to correct racial imbalance in the state's public schools. A law passed in 1963 requires school boards to avoid segregation in "erecting, purchasing or otherwise acquiring buildings" and to review attendance areas and to revise them "in a manner which will take into consideration the prevention of segregation."

The governor and Commission of Education of New Jersey joined in an effort to eliminate segregation in the schools. Governor Richard J. Hughes said: "While *de facto* segregation may be no one's fault, its attempted correction must be everyone's business, if the American and New Jersey pledge of equality of educational opportunity is to be fulfilled." Education Commissioner Frederick M. Raubinger issued a series of quasi-judicial orders in which he reflected the governor's philosophy. In a case involving the city of Orange, Raubinger said, ". . . the Commissioner is of the opinion that in the minds of Negro pupils and parents a stigma is attached to attending a school whose enrollment is completely or almost exclusively Negro, and that this sense of stigma and resulting feeling of inferiority have an undesirable effect on attitudes related to successful learning." He added that such racial imbalance, although *de facto* in nature, "constitutes a denial of equal opportunity under New Jersey law which the school district is required to correct."

In a memorandum to local school officials in New York State,

Commissioner Allen said: "The position of the Department . . . is that the racial imbalance existing in a school in which the enrollment is wholly or predominantly Negro interferes with the achievement of equality of educational opportunity and must, therefore, be eliminated from the schools of New York state. It is recognized that in some communities residential patterns and other factors may present serious obstacles to the attainment of racially balanced schools. This does not, however, relieve the school authorities of their responsibility for doing everything within their power, consistent with the principles of sound education, to achieve an equitable balance."

At the center of the controversy about racial imbalance was the concept of the neighborhood school. Most educators endorsed the traditional practice of assigning a pupil to the school nearest his home, particularly in the elementary grades. In the South, where students were assigned by both race and residence, the opponents of segregation often demanded assignment by residence alone as a means of achieving biracial schools. Outside the South assignments by residence produced many schools that were altogether or predominantly nonwhite. For this reason the advocates of racial balance attacked the idea of the neighborhood school, and school officials sought alternatives to it.

Pupils in nonwhite schools were given the privilege of transferring to other schools attended by whites. Attendance-zone lines were redrawn. New schools were located with racial balance in mind. Predominantly white and predominantly nonwhite schools were paired, and students were swapped between them. Pupils were transported by bus to schools outside their neighborhoods. Children were permitted to attend the schools of their choice, under a plan of open enrollment. The attendance areas of two or more schools were combined, and all pupils in certain grades were assigned to the same school. Whatever the approach, the purpose was to achieve better racial balance in the schools.

The problems of racial imbalance were not confined to the North and West. School authorities in the major cities of the border area also had to deal with them. In the summer of 1963 representa-

tives of school systems in all three areas held a conference in Baltimore for "a free exchange of ideas so as to clarify the role of the public schools in mitigating the effects of *de facto* segregation." The
meeting was closed to the press and public, but a report published
later said that "the participating superintendents and state commissioners gained a sense of urgency in working toward the solution of
problems of *de facto* segregation."

Dr. Robert J. Havighurst of the University of Chicago made a
study of the steps being taken to meet these problems. He observed
that the school officials were in the position of "a man swimming
upstream at the rate of two miles an hour while the current is carrying him back at the rate of five miles an hour."

5.
The Colleges

"A state institution is very close to the people of the state," Chancellor J. D. Williams of the University of Mississippi told the Commonwealth Club of San Francisco early in 1963. "In many ways this is good, for the ideal state university is delicately responsive to the varying needs of those whom it serves. At the same time this closeness makes for effective political and social pressures which are hard to withstand."

When Williams spoke, federal troops occupied his campus at Oxford. The pressures that accompanied the court-ordered admission of James Meredith to Ole Miss were the most severe to strike any desegregating college; but storms of controversy buffeted many Southern institutions, catching administrators, students and faculties in their cross-currents.

The Legal Background

When the attack on segregated higher education began, the controversy was confined largely to the courtrooms. In a series of decisions between 1938 and 1950, the United States Supreme Court applied the *Plessy v. Ferguson* "separate but equal" principle to graduate and professional schools. In none of these cases was segregation itself the basic issue; in question was the equality of education offered in separate institutions for Negroes.

The first of the college cases did not reach the Supreme Court. In 1935 Donald Murray, a Negro, filed a suit to gain admission to the University of Maryland Law School. Maryland, like other Southern and border states, followed the practice of granting out-of-state scholarships to Negro students who sought training that was not available in the state's institutions for Negroes. The Maryland Court of Appeals held that the state must afford equal educational opportunities in its own institutions, and the University of Maryland Law School admitted Murray.

The Supreme Court of the United States in 1938 followed this same principle in the *Gaines* case. Lloyd Gaines, a Missouri Negro, sought admission to the University of Missouri Law School. The Supreme Court decreed that "the state was bound to furnish [to Negroes] within its borders facilities for . . . education substantially equal to those which the state has afforded for persons of the white race."

In 1948 the Court handed down a decision in the case of Ada Lois Sipuel, an applicant for admission to the University of Oklahoma Law School. The Court said that a state not only must provide equal facilities to both races within its own borders, but that they must be made available to one applicant as soon as to another.

In 1950, the Court held that G. W. McLaurin, a Negro student in the University of Oklahoma Graduate School of Education, "must receive the same treatment at the hands of the state as students of other races." On the same day the Court ruled in the *Sweatt* case. Heman Sweatt applied in 1946 for admission to the University of

Texas Law School. The state courts granted Texas six months in which to set up a law school for Negroes equal to that for whites at the University at Austin. Sweatt refused to enroll in the Negro school, and his legal fight to gain admittance to the University Law School culminated successfully in the Supreme Court's decision in his case.

Chief Justice Fred Vinson wrote the Court's opinion, in which he said: ". . . the University of Texas Law School possesses to a far greater degree those qualities which are incapable of objective measurement but which make for greatness in a law school. Such qualities, to name but a few, include reputation of the faculty, experience of the administration, position and influence of the alumni, standing in the community, tradition and prestige."

From the *Sweatt* decision the Supreme Court did not have far to go to conclude in the *Brown* case that ". . . in the field of public education the doctrine of 'separate but equal' has no place." On the Monday following the public school decision, the Court directed the Supreme Court of Florida to reconsider "in the light of" *Brown* the case of Virgil Hawkins, who sought to enter the state university's law school. In the fall of 1955, a three-judge federal court ordered the University of North Carolina to admit Leroy Frasier and others as freshmen, a decision that the U.S. Supreme Court upheld the next spring. Thus the principle of the *School Segregation Cases* soon was extended to higher education, both graduate and undergraduate, with one important difference: the Court declared the right of qualified Negroes to attend public colleges and universities to be immediate, whereas it gave local school boards time to make the transition to desegregation in elementary and secondary schools.

The Negro plaintiffs in the cases that broke college segregation barriers did not themselves always enjoy the fruits of their victory. Lloyd Gaines, in whose favor the Supreme Court ruled in 1938, never made an appearance at the University of Missouri. Heman Sweatt failed in his courses at the University of Texas Law School. Virgil Hawkins fought in the courts for nine years to establish the right of Negroes to enter the University of Florida, only to be declared ineligible under new and higher admission standards. Leroy Frasier left the University of North Carolina at the end of his sophomore year because his grades fell below the average required to enter the junior class. Autherine Lucy, the first Negro student at the University of Alabama, was expelled after three days. Although these trailblazers fell by the wayside, they helped to prepare the way for growing numbers of other Negroes who enrolled in previously all-white colleges.

Resistance to Desegregation

Despite the rulings of the federal courts, Southern white colleges hardly welcomed Negro students. The Deep South states, especially, erected obstacles to keep them out. Some colleges revised their admission requirements, and some took advantage of procedural technicalities to rule applicants ineligible. State legislatures passed laws to help maintain college segregation. Various forms of persuasion and pressure supplemented the regulations and laws.

Mississippi exerted the greatest effort, and could claim the greatest success, in excluding Negroes from its white colleges. Medgar Evers, state field secretary for the NAACP, applied in 1955 for admission to the law school at Ole Miss. The Board of Trustees of State Institutions of Higher Learning rejected his application and adopted a new policy requiring that all future applications be approved by at least five alumni in the county of the applicant's residence. Evers dropped his efforts to enter Ole Miss but continued his work for the NAACP. In 1963 a sniper's bullet fired from ambush killed him outside his home in Jackson.

Clennon King, a professor at Alcorn A. & M. College for Negroes, was the next to try. In 1958 he applied for admission to the university to work on his doctorate. He inserted a full-page advertisement in a Gulfport newspaper soliciting letters of endorsement from alumni, but none responded. On June 5 King attempted to register, but the highway patrol removed him from the campus and jailed him under a charge of disturbing the peace. The next day, following a lunacy hearing from which his lawyer was ejected, King was committed to the state mental hospital. After a twelve-day observation period the hospital director released King; the staff in a unanimous report said that it "could find no evidence of mental disorder." That same day King left Mississippi by plane for his father's home in Georgia. In a statement to the press he said that he had "no plans whatsoever" for any further attempt to enter the university.

While King knocked at the door of Ole Miss, Clyde Kennard quietly sought to enter Mississippi Southern (later the University of Southern Mississippi) at Hattiesburg. Kennard had studied political science at the University of Chicago from 1952 to 1955, then had returned to Mississippi to help his mother run a chicken farm. Deciding to continue his education, in 1956 he applied for admission to Mississippi Southern, a fifteen-minute drive from his home.

Kennard did not push his application, mainly as the result of talks he had with President W. D. McCain; but neither did he withdraw it. In 1958 Governor J. P. Coleman invited Kennard and President McCain to his office in Jackson, where Kennard declined the governor's offer to pay his expenses to any college in the United States. By the fall of 1959 Kennard made it known that he would wait no longer and that he would attempt to register at Mississippi Southern.

The night before registration day, McCain telephoned Kennard, asking him to come to the president's office for an interview before reporting to the registrar. When Kennard appeared, Zack Van Landingham, chief investigator for the State Sovereignty Commission, was with McCain. Upon returning to his parked car after the interview, Kennard was arrested by two county constables, who charged him with speeding. At the police station he also was charged with the possession of five half-pints of liquor, which one of the constables said he found under the front seat of Kennard's car. He was fined $600. Meanwhile President McCain issued a statement that Kennard "was denied admission because of deficiencies and irregularities in his application papers."

The end of Kennard's troubles was yet to come. A few weeks later he was accused of being an accessory in the burglary of $25 worth of chicken feed from the Forrest County Co-operative Warehouse. The illiterate, nineteen-year-old warehouse helper who testified that he stole the chicken feed for Kennard went unpunished and even kept his job. Kennard was sentenced to seven years in the state penitentiary at Parchman. Because of his persistent complaints about "stomach trouble," he was sent to the state hospital in Jackson, where an operation revealed that he had cancer. After another year at Parchman, during which his case attracted national attention, Kennard was released in January, 1963, by Governor Ross Barnett, who suspended his sentence. Kennard went to Chicago, where a few months later he died.

The experiences of Evers, King and Kennard did not deter James Howard Meredith from his desire to enter the University of Mississippi. A Mississippi native, he served for nine years in the Air Force. During that time he maintained his legal residence in Attala County, where he owned three farms. In the fall of 1960, soon after his discharge, he enrolled in Jackson State College for Negroes as a sophomore, having been given credit for college courses he took while in the Air Force. He registered to vote in Hinds County, where Jackson State is located. His residence, his voting registration, his educational background and his Air Force record became important questions in his effort to enroll at Ole Miss.

In January, 1961, he applied for admission to the university "because it is the best institution in the state, and I think I should like to graduate from the state's best institution." In May the registrar notified Meredith that his application had been rejected because Jackson State was not accredited by the Southern Association of Colleges and Schools (soon after that it was) and because he did not submit the required letters of recommendation from five university alumni. A few days later Meredith filed suit in the United States district court over which Judge Sidney C. Mize presided.

The case bounced up and down through the federal courts for more than a year. Attorneys for the state of Mississippi maintained that Meredith's rejection had nothing to do with his race. To the reasons given by the university registrar, they added others: that Meredith had violated legal residence requirements when he registered to vote in Hinds County; that his medical history in the Air Force showed a "compulsive neurosis" based on "his nervous reaction when the racial question was discussed"; that he was a "trouble-maker" interested only in desegregating the university, not in obtaining an education.

Judge Mize consistently ruled with the state, holding that Meredith was not refused admission because of his race and that the university was "not a segregated institution." The judges of the Court of Appeals for the Fifth Circuit—divided two to one—just as consistently overruled Judge Mize. The Court of Appeals majority held the alumni-recommendation requirement unconstitutional, and in so doing said that "Meredith should be able to get an education without having to follow winding trails through sharp thickets in constant tension."

Meanwhile the state legislature was meeting in what became the longest session in its history. When it adjourned on June 2, it had passed new laws to strengthen the state's hand in repelling Meredith's assault on the gates of Ole Miss. On June 6 Meredith was arrested on the charge that he had "falsely registered" to vote in Hinds County; the Appeals Court almost immediately enjoined the county attorney from prosecuting Meredith.

On June 25, 1962, Meredith's twenty-ninth birthday, the Court of Appeals majority ruled that he had been denied admission to the university "solely because he was a Negro" and ordered Judge Mize to restrain university officials from denying his enrollment. The Court said, "We see a well-defined pattern of delays and frustrations, part of a Fabian policy of worrying the enemy into defeat while time worked for the defeaters." The judges called the false voter registration charge against Meredith "frivolous." As to Meredith's military medical history, they said that the "record shows just about the type of Negro who might be expected to try to crack the racial barrier at the university: a man with a mission and with a nervous stomach." The end of the "winding trails" was in sight, but the legal fight to keep Meredith out of Ole Miss continued unabated until his admission on September 30. Even then, United States marshals and troops were needed to assure his admittance and to protect him while he was a student. In its June 25 decision, the Court of Appeals said, "The hard fact to get around is that no person known to have been a Negro has ever attended the university." After Meredith's admission,

Harry S. Murphy, Jr., a Negro of New York City, revealed (and university records confirmed) that he had attended Ole Miss in 1945–46 as a Navy V-12 student.

Other states also acted to keep their colleges segregated. The Board of Regents of the University System of Georgia adopted new entrance requirements, including a personal interview with every applicant for admission and the signatures of two sponsoring alumni and his home-county clerk. The Georgia legislature set age limits for college admission at twenty-one for undergraduates and twenty-five for graduate students. Georgia law also required the withholding of public funds from any desegregated school or college. The legislature repealed both of these laws when they proved hindrances to white colleges.

The South Carolina legislature in 1956 included in a general appropriations bill a provision that any college ordered by a court to desegregate should be closed. The bill specified that if any other college was closed to avoid desegregation, the South Carolina College for Negroes "shall likewise be closed." The 1960 appropriations bill did not contain these provisions and they did not appear subsequently.

All of the Deep South states had admitted Negroes to their white colleges by 1963. The number of Negro students involved was small, except in Louisiana, where in 1963–64 about 850 Negroes attended formerly white colleges. Desegregation began in the graduate schools at Louisiana State University in 1950, under court order but without incident. Resistance stiffened after the *Brown* decision, and in 1956 the legislature passed a pair of laws intended to resegregate the state's colleges. One law required a registrant to obtain certificates of "good character" from his high school principal and district superintendent. The other made it a firing offense to sign such a certificate for a Negro attempting to enroll at a white college. Federal courts declared both laws unconstitutional.

Resistance to college desegregation in the six remaining states of the old Confederacy was less determined than in the Deep South. Usually it was limited to a court fight against the first effort to breach the segregation wall. In all of the border states, college desegregation began before 1954 and proceeded rapidly. By 1964 every public college in the border area had a biracial student body.

Minority-Race Students on the Campus

Admission to a predominantly white college did not launch a Negro into the mainstream of student life. Dr. Guy B. Johnson, University of North Carolina sociologist, in 1955 made a survey of desegregated Southern colleges. He found that "in the strictly social aspects of student life . . . the amount of interracial contact is close to zero." The experiences of many Negro students in white colleges throughout the decade confirmed this finding.

After he had been at the University of Mississippi for several months, James Meredith described himself as possibly "the most segregated Negro in the world." He added, "Just having a Negro in residence does not mean that the university has been integrated. So many unusual and unique things have been a part of my stay here that I seriously doubt that I am in a true sense a student of the university. Through it all the most intolerable thing has been the campaign of ostracizing me. The ostracizers not only don't associate with me, but assume the right to see that no one else associates with me."

White students at the University of Georgia gave Hamilton Holmes and Charlayne Hunter, the first Negroes admitted, a cool reception. Holmes described the atmosphere on the campus as one of "uncordiality." His mother said, "It's lonely for him down in Athens. You'd think some students there would make overtures to a boy in a situation like that. It's hard for me to believe that nobody would bother, unless the boy was objectionable. I guess I'll never understand." Miss Hunter reported, "Many students have gone out of their way to be cordial to us, but there still is considerable reserve from the majority." After her graduation Miss Hunter married a white fellow student.

Harvey Gantt, the first Negro to enter a white college in South Carolina since Reconstruction, said that at Clemson College "the apparent attitude has been one of indifference." Henri Monteith reported a similar attitude at the University of South Carolina. "The university has been formally integrated, but that's all," she said, adding that "a lack of communication exists" and that "too many students are indifferent." Both Gantt and Miss Monteith said that students and faculty members had treated them fairly. At the University of North Carolina, Student Government President Don Fowler said, "The presence of these Negroes causes so little interest that most of us are unaware they are here unless we happen to have a class with them. Nobody resents them; or if they do, they certainly don't show it. I think most of us look on this thing—integration— as something that has become a fact of life, and that the only thing to do is to find intelligent, constructive ways of making it work." Florida strenuously resisted desegregation of its colleges, but the first Negro admitted to the university, George Starke, Jr., said at the end of his first semester, "Everybody has treated me as just another student." Other Negro students who followed Starke reported similar experiences.

Whether Negro students should be housed in dormitories, permitted to participate in extracurricular activities, included in campus social affairs and allowed to represent the college in athetic contests were troublesome questions on many campuses. Dormitories and athletics attracted the most attention. Long after the University of Texas had accepted Negro students, Thornton Hardie, chairman of the Board of Regents, announced that athletics and certain dormitories would remain segregated "until the people of Texas are ready for a change." The regents would know when that was, he explained, because "we come from all over the state and we think the members of the board are pretty well advised of the sentiment of the legislature and the people." In Texas, and in most other states, restrictions on Negroes tended to disappear as their presence receded from the area of public controversy.

Participation of Negroes in intercollegiate athletics was a persistently sensitive point. Louisiana was the only state to have a law banning interracial sports (the law was declared unconstitutional), but official policy in other states firmly opposed athletic competition involving both whites and Negroes. When the policy kept Southern teams from taking part in intersectional playoffs and national championship games, it was abandoned—even in Mississippi. It was late in the decade before predominantly white Southern colleges began to include Negroes on their own teams. The Southwestern Conference led the way, and by 1964 all its members except Rice University had announced policies of desegregation. The University of Kentucky in 1963 became the first member of the Southeastern Conference to do so. The University of Maryland, also in 1963, gave notice that in the future it would recruit Negro athletes, setting the precedent in the Atlantic Coast Conference.

Academically, the Negro students at the predominantly white colleges were on their mettle. Guy Johnson in his 1955 study reported that Negro students were not coming up to the white students in their performance. Esther M. Langston, a Phi Beta Kappa graduate of Fisk University, failed as a medical student at the University of Florida, but she regarded her failure as "emotional not intellectual." All of the first three Negro undergraduates admitted to the University of North Carolina had to drop out because of poor grades. Some Negroes established high scholastic records. Julius LeVonne Chambers led his class in the Law School at North Carolina and was named editor-in-chief of the *Law Review*. Hamilton Holmes was a Phi Beta Kappa student at the University of Georgia. Charles Fletcher Christian ranked first in a class of eighty-eight at the Medical College of Virginia. At the University of Texas the grades of Negro students averaged the same as those of white students.

Negro students at formerly white colleges in the border states generally were accepted on the same footing as other students. There occasionally was a tendency to give them favored treatment. "Immediately after Negro students were first admitted," Dr. Philip Davidson, president of the University of Louisville, reported, "a lot of white students leaned over backwards to have a Negro student on every committee, and things of that sort."

At two colleges in West Virginia, white students who attended formerly all-Negro institutions were said to be targets of discrimination. After West Virginia State had changed from all-Negro to 70 percent white, President William Wallace addressed an open letter to the student body in which he said that the students seemed to be seeking to preserve "all honors and all positions of importance for Negro students . . . regardless of ability or merit." Further, he said, "There are indications that students, right here on this campus, are as prejudiced as the meanest demagogue in the South. . . ." Felix L. Paul, a member of the faculty of Bluefield State College, in resigning accused the college of discrimination against its white students, who comprised two-fifths of the enrollment. In a letter to President L. R. Allen, Paul said that no white students worked in college offices, lived in dormitories, or were members of the football and basketball teams. "When dances, plays and other festivities are held, Bluefield State looks like an all-Negro institution," he wrote.

The Negro Colleges

The *Brown* decision raised serious questions for the Negro colleges. Would there be any further need, or justification, for them? Could they compete with the desegregated formerly white colleges?

Prominent Negro educators, who strongly favored the principle of desegregation, defended the place of the Negro college in the system of higher education. Dr. R. O'Hara Lanier, president of Texas Southern University, said in a 1954 report to the State Commission on Higher Education, "Because of human behavior and social backgrounds and patterns, long existent, the large majority of [Negro] students will come to us because they prefer to do so. Such students will very likely prefer to continue to study with homogeneous groups and will feel strongly that more sympathetic attention will be given to them . . . in our institutions than in some other school." Dr. E. B. Evans, president of Prairie View A. & M., Texas' other Negro college, joined President Lanier in urging expansion of the Negro colleges rather than their absorption into the state's white institutions. President Rufus B. Atwood of Kentucky State College, which was threatened with closure, contended that Kentucky's need was "not for fewer colleges but more." President Jerome Holland of Delaware State College urged that his institution be kept open because many of the students there would not make the grade at the University of Delaware; he cited three reasons—financial, psychological and academic. In an address at Fisk University, Dr. Mordecai W. Johnson, president emeritus of Howard University, said in 1961 that the need for Negro institutions "is greater than ever before, and it will be 25 years at least until Fisk, and institutions like Fisk, will be able to take the accent off the word 'Negro.' " Dr. Benjamin Mays, president of Morehouse College, said that desegregation was a "two-way street" and that the Supreme Court decision meant that Negro as well as white institutions should open their doors to all students. "Negro colleges have been 'segregated' institutions but they never have been 'segregating' institutions," Dr. Mays wrote. "The Negro colleges have had to restrict their enrollment to Negroes by custom and law and not by any desire or design to exclude white students."

Custom remained effective after segregation laws were declared unconstitutional. Together with other factors, varying local customs accounted for substantial differences in the experiences of the Negro colleges. Some closed; some lost their identities through mergers; some prospered.

The Negro colleges in the border states were under the greatest pressures to close. Usually they had relatively high per-student operating costs and low enrollments. Their courses of study duplicated those offered in the white colleges. Public opinion generally was amenable to desegregation.

Some Negro colleges in the border states did close. When the University of Louisville desegregated in 1950, the Louisville Municipal College for Negroes closed. Storer College at Harpers Ferry, West Virginia, closed in 1954 when the state, following the Supreme Court decision, withdrew its annual subsidy. In both the District of Columbia and the city of St. Louis separate Negro and white teachers colleges merged in 1954. Montgomery County, Maryland, and Kansas City, Missouri, merged their Negro and white junior colleges.

In the eleven Southern states the prospect of desegregation strengthened the position of the Negro colleges. When Dr. Luther H. Foster, president of Tuskegee Institute, appeared before the Alabama legislature to make his appropriation request, John H. Pinson, a former state senator, supported him. Pinson told the House Ways and Means Committee, "If you don't want integration at the university, then you better continue this appropriation." Otherwise, he said, the Tuskegee students "would just hop on a bus or train and go over to Auburn and Tuscaloosa and enroll." Theo Congelosi, president of the Louisiana State University Board of Supervisors, expressed essentially the same idea when he said, "The very year Southern University [Negro] put in a graduate school, colored enrollment at LSU dropped from 260 to 99. My personal view . . . is that it is evident that colored folks would rather go to school among and with their own people if the facilities are provided."

Not only did political leaders in some of the Southern states want to keep the Negroes in Negro colleges; they also frowned upon the admission of whites to Negro colleges, even private colleges. In 1956 André Toth, a Hungarian refugee, enrolled at Allen University, a church-supported institution in Columbia, S.C. Governor George Bell Timmerman, Jr., retaliated with charges that three members of the Allen faculty were Communists. The charge led to a legislative investigation and a ruling from the State Board of Education that Allen graduates would not be certified to teach in the state. Toth finished his year but did not return; the three faculty members were dismissed; the college was restored to approved standing. In another incident Tougaloo Southern Christian College for Negroes at Tougaloo, Mississippi, was criticized when it admitted two white women students. Tougaloo students and faculty members participated in antisegregation demonstrations, causing Lieutenant Governor Carroll Gartin to call it "a haven for political agitators and possibly some Communists" and to propose a legislative investigation of the institution. A bill introduced in the legislature to repeal the college's charter (issued in 1871) died in committee. Another bill to deprive the college of its state accreditation passed.

The Student Protest Movement

In the first five years following the *Brown* decision, college students demonstrated sporadically against racial segregation and discrimination. The demonstrations caused the expulsion of some students and the firing of some faculty members and one college president.

The all-white Board of Trustees of South Carolina College for

Negroes termed a student demonstration "an insurrection," ordered sixteen students expelled and did not renew the contracts of three faculty members. After students of Florida State (white) and Florida A. & M. (Negro) universities staged a bus boycott in Tallahassee, the board of control of the state university system ruled that students "who stir up trouble" should be dismissed. When students at Alcorn A. & M. College in Mississippi boycotted their classes, the Board of Trustees dismissed President J. P. Otis and the president of the Student Council. These and other incidents were local and unrelated, but they were forerunners of an organized, regionwide student protest movement.

On February 1, 1960, about seventy-five students from A. & T. College in Greensboro, North Carolina, sat at the lunch counter in Woolworth's variety store and asked to be served. Within a week white and Negro students were conducting "sit-in" demonstrations in several North Carolina college towns. The demonstrations spread quickly through the South and from lunch counters to other private businesses catering to the general public. Government-operated facilities also were targets, as were churches. In April student leaders from the eleven Southern states and the District of Columbia met at Shaw University, a private Negro institution, in Raleigh, North Carolina. From this meeting emerged the Student Nonviolent Coordinating Committee, with John Lewis of Fisk University at Nashville, Tennessee, as its chairman.

Nashville, as a training center and testing ground for the techniques of nonviolent protest, offered something of a cross-section of the student movement. Under President Stephen J. Wright, private, predominantly Negro Fisk gave the movement intellectual and practical leadership. Tennessee A. & I. University for Negroes was under the control of the State Board of Education. Education Commissioner Joe Morgan, with the support of Governor Buford Ellington, instructed heads of all institutions under the board's jurisdiction to dismiss any students arrested and convicted "on charges involving personal misconduct." President Walter S. Davis expelled thirteen A. & I. students arrested during "freedom ride" demonstrations in the summer of 1961. U.S. District Judge William E. Miller ruled that the students were entitled to a hearing before the university's discipline committee, and they all were readmitted.

In March of 1960 the Executive Committee of the Board of Trust of private, predominantly white Vanderbilt University at Nashville officially requested James Lawson, a Negro student, to withdraw from the Divinity School. The reason given was his "strong commitment to a planned campaign of civil disobedience." Lawson refused to withdraw, and Chancellor Harvie Branscomb expelled him. The university took no action against students who demonstrated within the law. Three months after Lawson's expulsion, the Divinity School faculty recommended that he be admitted to summer school. When Chancellor Branscomb disapproved this recommendation, Dean J. Robert Nelson and ten members of the Divinity School faculty submitted their resignations. Chancellor Branscomb accepted Dean Nelson's resignation, but invited the other faculty members to withdraw theirs, which they did, on the basis of a proposal that would have allowed Lawson to receive his degree from Vanderbilt. One result of the Lawson episode was the formulation by a faculty committee that Chancellor Branscomb appointed of a new policy on principles and procedures to be followed in disciplinary cases involving "conscience or academic freedom." This policy was invoked by Chancellor Alexander Heard, Branscomb's successor, in the fall of 1963, when Vanderbilt students picketed a segregated off-campus grill. The university took no disciplinary action against those participating.

Reactions to student demonstrations ranged from their acceptance and open encouragement in the border states to their absolute prohibition in the Deep South. When white and Negro students at Washington University refused to leave a St. Louis restaurant and were arrested, Chancellor Eathan A. H. Shepley commented, "It's a free country and a free campus." The president, executive vice president and assistant to the president of the University of Louisville signed a petition circulated by students to ask off-campus restaurants to "give equal service to all students."

In 1962 the Alabama State Board of Education, at the insistence of Governor John Patterson, vacated the presidencies of the state's two Negro colleges. Both President H. Council Trenholm of Alabama State College and President Joseph W. Drake of Alabama A. & M. had been in their jobs for thirty-five years. The board gave Trenholm an unrequested year's leave of absence and dismissed Drake. The official reason given in both instances was "poor health." At the time of the student demonstrations in 1960, the governor had revealed the shape of things to come. He suggested then that President Trenholm should be replaced with "someone . . . who is loyal to the state of Alabama." Patterson said that the demonstrations at A. & M. made it essential to get a president "who will require discipline, make the students behave themselves." The board ordered the firing of any faculty member who encouraged student protests.

The Louisiana State Board of Education directed the automatic expulsion of any student arrested or jailed and banned student participation in any "demonstrations that are not sanctioned by the institution." Mass student demonstrations in 1962 caused President Felton G. Clark to close Southern University, near Baton Rouge. When Southern, the largest Negro college in the nation, reopened, the demonstration leaders were denied admission.

Chancellor Gordon W. Blackwell of the Woman's College of the University of North Carolina took a middle ground. In a talk to the students he advised them "to refrain from any public demonstration" and to remember that "on and off the campus you represent this institution." Governor Luther Hodges liked Blackwell's talk so well that he circulated it to heads of all the state's colleges.

Restraints on Freedom of Expression

Faculty members and students, mostly in the Deep South, sometimes found that freedom of speech did not extend to the expression of unorthodox views about school segregation. The tradition of academic freedom was not strong enough to protect some teachers' jobs. Students encountered suppression, reprimand or expulsion. Placing shackles on freedom involved risks for a college, too, in the form of censure or loss of accreditation.

The University of South Carolina was the scene of an incident early in the decade. Dean Chester C. Travelstead of the School of Education in April of 1955 wrote a letter to Governor George Bell Timmerman, Jr., criticizing a pro-segregation speech by the governor. University President Donald S. Russell advised the dean that "such letters make politicians mad" but in July reappointed him for the next year. In August Travelstead said in a speech, "It is my firm conviction that enforced segregation of the races in our public schools can no longer be justified on any basis and should, therefore, be abolished as soon as practicable." Two weeks later President Russell dismissed Dean Travelstead "in the best interest of the university."

Dr. Joseph Margolis did not return to the South Carolina faculty in the fall of 1958. Earlier that year he had written an article for the *Bulletin* of the American Association of University Professors. He said, "Taken singly, the Southern segregationist can find answers for the inexplicable plight of the Negro only in unreasonable mouthings about racial inferiority and contradictory testimony of the ingratitude, disease, stupidity, childishness, arrogance, viciousness, irresponsibility, contentedness, well-being and cunning of the Negro."

Officials of Furman University, a Baptist institution at Greenville, in May, 1955, seized an issue of the *Echo*, student literary magazine, prior to its distribution. It contained an article by Joan Lipscomb, who described the Supreme Court decision as "a fact which all the emotionalism of Southern politicians cannot alter with all their oratorical eloquence." Co-editors Lipscomb and Huby Cooper resigned.

The Louisiana Chapter of the American Civil Liberties Union in 1958 circulated a petition on college campuses in the state urging the legislature to defeat bills designed to preserve school segregation. The petition, the idea of Dr. Waldo McNeir of Louisiana State University, did not accomplish its intended result. The legislature passed the bills and also appointed a committee to investigate "subversive activities" at tax-supported colleges. H. W. Ibser circulated the petition at Northwestern State College and was dismissed from the faculty for "insubordination." The LSU Alumni Council defended "the good name of LSU and its reputation for independent expression of its faculty members." At private Tulane University the Senate (composed of the president, deans and directors) took a stand opposing "legislative investigations when employed to intimidate petitioners" and said that they "implied denial of the right to free speech and petition." The Tulane Chapter of the AAUP took a similar stand.

The investigation did not deter Dr. McNeir. He persisted in pressing his views on legislators. In letters to leading segregationists among them he said that "segregation is wrong" and called the state's pro-segregation laws "a disgrace and a national scandal." The legislature passed a resolution condemning McNeir and authorizing a full-scale investigation of LSU by its Un-American Activities Committee. Representative Wellborn Jack called the professor "a dangerous man" who has "got to go." University authorities resisted demands that McNeir be fired, but in January, 1961, he resigned, giving "outside threats and inside pressures" as the reasons. Two days later 117 LSU faculty members signed a petition conceding the right of the legislature to investigate the university, but saying that when "its actions curtail freedom of expression or create an atmosphere of fear, it does a great disservice to the university and to the state which it serves."

In 1956 Autherine Lucy, the first Negro student at the University of Alabama, accused university officials of conspiring against her, and they expelled her because of what she said. The university officially announced that six professors gave the Lucy incident as their reason for resigning; unofficial reports placed the number as high as "21 or more."

Philosophy Professor Iredell Jenkins wrote in an article that the only course for the future was "to make real the paper promise of equal opportunity." He expressed concern "with the moral dilemma that now confronts all those professors who share my convictions." They were looking, he said, for a middle course between the alternatives of "resigning or cultivating one's garden." He concluded that, "What such men desperately want is to participate in the formation of present policy and in the determination of impending events." Robert Shelton, national grand wizard of the Knights of the Ku Klux Klan, later said that the Klan would "keep an eye" on Jenkins and other Alabama faculty members, students and student organizations adjudged "too liberal." He added that student Klansmen were infiltrating campus organizations to collect information.

It was 1963 before the Tuscaloosa institution admitted another Negro. James Hood, who enrolled then, soon followed Miss Lucy's example. In an off-campus speech, which state investigators tape-recorded, he criticized Governor George Wallace and accused university officials of trying to "trick" him into a situation that would require his expulsion. Before authorities decided whether to expel him, he withdrew "in order to avoid a complete mental and physical breakdown," his attorney said.

At Alabama Polytechnic Institute (later Auburn University) Professor Bud R. Hutchison in 1957 wrote a letter to the student newspaper, the *Plainsman*. He expressed sympathy toward the efforts of the New York City Board of Education to "come to grips with the difficult problems of effectively integrating their education system." President Ralph Draughon dismissed Hutchison and explained that his opinions were "contrary to the views" of the institution. The Board of Trustees adopted a new policy toward academic freedom, stating that in the future the board would "take such action as it shall deem necessary to protect the institution and its employes from the storms of controversy. . . ." The AAUP formally censured the university for "infringement of academic freedom" in the Hutchison case.

The *Plainsman* in 1961 published an editorial saying that racial desegregation "is inevitable, and those who think it is not are either miserably stupid or living in self-delusion." A cross was burned in front of the editor's fraternity house, and he was burned in effigy on the drill field. The Board of Student Publications censured the paper for "overstatement and lack of judgment." The Board of Trustees adopted a resolution requiring student publications to "advise the dean of student affairs on editorial or news items of public affairs having a bearing on the good name of Auburn University before they are published."

The State Board of Education in the summer of 1960 ordered President Trenholm of Alabama State College to fire Dr. Lawrence D. Reddick, head of the history department, "before sundown today." Governor John Patterson had branded Reddick, biographer of the Rev. Martin Luther King, Jr., an agitator and Communist sympathizer. One member of the board objected to firing Reddick without a hearing. Reddick appealed for a review of his dismissal, saying that it "violated every principle of decency, fair play and justice" but the board took no action on the request. The AAUP, the Civil Liberties Union, the NAACP and other groups protested the firing. Governor Patterson said that if these groups opposed him, he must be right. The AAUP, in a report published in its *Bulletin,* charged that the governor had acted "in haste and in complete disregard of the requirements of the academic due process." In the wake of the Reddick incident, three Alabama State professors with doctoral degrees resigned.

Academic freedom was a lively issue at the University of Mississippi during most of the decade. The incidents fell into two general periods—before and after the admission of James Meredith in the fall of 1962.

One of the first, and most-publicized, early incidents involved the Rev. Alvin Kershaw, an Episcopal rector of Oxford, Ohio. After Kershaw had accepted an invitation to speak during Religious Emphasis Week, university officials discovered that he was a member of the NAACP, to which he had donated his winnings on a television show. The university withdrew the invitation, and the Board of Trustees adopted a rule that in the future all speakers must be screened and approved. Five other ministers scheduled to speak on the same program with Kershaw returned their invitations. The Student Senate protested withdrawal of the invitation as being "in direct opposition to the constitutional standards of freedom of speech and freedom of thought." Two faculty members resigned.

In 1957 Chancellor J. D. Williams took note of rumors of an exodus of professors who complained of restraints on academic freedom. He said that in the previous two years the forty-one resignations from a full-time staff of two hundred "may be a little more than normal, but not alarmingly so." To the rumors the chancellor replied, "The administration is trying to protect academic freedom. We attempt to maintain a climate on the campus that is non-political, strictly objective. . . . The university operates in a context of social conflicts which may not exist elsewhere, but it cannot divorce itself from these issues. . . ." He expressed the opinion that better salaries elsewhere caused most of the resignations. One of the professors who left in 1957 was Dr. Charles Bigger, who said, "In spite of what the administration says there is a lack of academic freedom at Ole Miss. . . . The state's super-sensitive militancy toward the race question poses a very real threat to the scholastic reputation of the university."

Some alumni felt that there was too much freedom of expression on the campus. In 1958 a group of them filed charges with the Board of Trustees that "the chancellor and a large number of others in key positions at the university" were "teaching and conspiring to accomplish apostasy, subversion and the violation of Mississippi law and tradition." The board "unanimously and unreservedly" expressed confidence in the chancellor and his administration.

In the spring of 1962 Dr. William P. Murphy of the Law School resigned under pressure. Segregationists had attacked Murphy since 1954, when soon after the Supreme Court decision he said that "the adoption of legal subterfuges in the long run will be of no avail." The Murphy resignation was the last of the pre-Meredith incidents. That fall the first known Negro entered Ole Miss in the company of U.S. marshals, and the campus was for one night a battleground.

At the time of the rioting Sidna Brower, editor of the *Mississippian,* the campus newspaper, called editorially for "law and order." The Student Senate reprimanded her for "failing to uphold and represent the rights of her fellow students." The faculty adopted a resolution saying that "by holding to the American ideal of a responsible free press, Miss Brower has significantly contributed to the preservation of the university's integrity."

On February 1 Chancellor Williams advised members of the faculty, staff and student body that "public statements and press, radio and television interviews which appear likely to create disorder or impair the effectiveness of the educational program at the University of Mississippi must be regarded as unacceptable behavior on the part of all those associated with the university." He added that "disagreement is understandable, but methods of expressing disagreement are unacceptable when they are contrary to legal orders."

Soon a method of expression perhaps not covered by the regulation stirred new controversy. Art Professor G. Ray Kerciu included in an exhibit of his work five impressions of the rioting. A law student, who filed charges in magistrate's court, accused the artist of obscenity and desecration of the Confederate flag, which was used as a backdrop for the five paintings. Dr. Charles Noyes, university provost, ordered the offending paintings removed from the exhibit. The local chapter of the AAUP called on the administration to "support Professor Kerciu . . . and to defend him openly and officially through the services of the university attorney." The resolution continued, "If this is not done, it is the belief of this body that the individual members of this faculty can only conclude that they will be abandoned to the whims of any pressure group which may be offended by the conscientious and legitimate exercise of their academic obligations." The charges were dropped before Kerciu was brought to trial.

In his San Francisco speech Chancellor Williams said, "When I consider the price that has been paid for this determined attempt to integrate the University of Mississippi and the equally determined attempt made by powerful forces to resist such integration—the cost in money, in reputation, in good will, in human suffering—I am appalled. . . . Some able men will leave us, shaking the dust off their feet as they turn away; but others will stay to see the struggle through." At the end of the year, the chancellor announced that sixteen members of the faculty had resigned. The Associated Press reported the number at thirty-five, and another report put it at fifty. Dean Robert J. Farley of the Law School was one of those who stayed. "The white muslim branch of the Citizens' Councils had attempted in recent years to have me ousted," he said. "However, I withstood their attempts and remained." Dean Farley retired that fall upon reaching the age of sixty-five, not having been extended the customary invitation to those in "strategic places" to remain until seventy.

Two Ole Miss professors attracted wide attention by speeches they made in November of 1963. Dr. James W. Silver, in his presidential address to the Southern Historical Association, spoke on "The Closed Society" in Mississippi. He said: "Perhaps the greatest tragedy of the closed society is the refusal of its citizens to believe that there is any view other than the orthodox. In recent years there has been a hardening attitude among college students, who do not want to hear the other side. In such a twilight of nondiscussion, minds not only do not grow tough, they do not grow at all. Intelligent men with ideas are isolated from the rest of the community. . . . One reason the Ole Miss faculty failed to protest an ugly situation just before the insurrection was that, through one means or another, freedom of speech had long been curtailed." In a speech at the University of Illinois Professor Russell H. Barrett said: "Faculty members and students at Ole Miss who supported James Meredith in his successful integration bids were subjected to various forms of harassment. . . . The treatment varied with the moral depravity of the abuser, and it included telephone calls, letters, property damage, anonymous publication of libelous material and even some annoying of children. Those who supported Meredith were appointed as 'honorary niggers' by the white Citizens' Council, and the appointees considered it to be an honor."

Legislators criticized both professors, and some called for Silver's discharge. Senator Corbett Patridge said of Silver, "I am outraged that the taxpayers have to pay the salary of a man like this. I can't see why the legislature will tolerate such an idiot to teach in this state." Silver, a member of the faculty for twenty-eight years, received a leave of absence to teach at Notre Dame University during the 1964–65 academic year.

The events surrounding Meredith's efforts to gain admittance to Ole Miss caused the Southern Association of Colleges and Schools to threaten all eight Mississippi colleges and universities with loss of accreditation. At a meeting in Dallas in November, 1962, the association issued a stern warning against "any encroachment by pressure groups, investigating committees or other agencies upon the freedom of faculties and administrations or the students to learn or teach." The threat, removed a year later, was regarded by some as an explanation for the outspokenness of some faculty members.

The Deep South had no monopoly on incidents involving academic freedom. They occurred in other states—notably Arkansas, Florida and Texas. But the episodes in the Deep South were the ones that attracted the most attention.

The Private Colleges

The court decisions on educational segregation applied only to public institutions, but many private colleges voluntarily desegregated—for both ethical and practical reasons. Some said that to exclude students because of their race was morally wrong. A racially exclusive admissions policy also made an institution ineligible to receive grants from the federal government and major foundations.

Boards of trustees were not always free to abandon a policy of segregation. State laws and conditions imposed by benefactors sometimes bound them to admit only one race. Some institutions asked the courts to remove these restrictions.

Tulane University at New Orleans in the spring of 1961 made known its desire to admit Negro students "if it were legally permissible." Paul Tulane and Sophie Newcomb had specified that their grants to the institution were to be used for the education of "young white persons." The university invited a friendly suit to test the validity of this restriction. U.S. District Judge J. Skelly Wright issued a summary judgment ordering admission of the Negro plaintiffs in the case. He said that ". . . Tulane University cannot discriminate in admissions on the basis of race. . . . The bitter fruit of the board's segregation policy of the past should not be visited on the young men and women of the future, of all races, who seek admission to the university." Judge Wright did not stop there, which was as far as the university wanted to go. Tulane had argued that, because of its private status, it was free to discriminate in admissions as it chose. Judge Wright questioned "whether any school or college can ever be so 'private' as to escape the reach of the 14th Amendment." Further, he commented that the suit was "designed to rescue the university from the unfavorable position in which it now finds itself, particularly with regard to large foundations created to dispense funds to institutions of higher learning." Tulane appealed, and Judge Frank B. Ellis, Wright's successor, set aside the summary judgment. After hearing the case on its merits, Judge Ellis ruled that Tulane was a private institution and could not be compelled to desegregate under the Fourteenth Amendment; but he upheld the university's right to admit Negroes.

While the Tulane case was in the courts, Emory University at Atlanta issued a public statement that it wanted to desegregate. Standing in the way were the Georgia Constitution and state laws extending tax exemption to private educational institutions only if they operated on a racially segregated basis. Emory said that its financial resources already were strained and that it could not afford to run the risk of losing state tax exemption. In a test case the Georgia Supreme Court unanimously ruled that Emory could enroll Negroes without losing its tax exemption.

Rice University at Houston was in a situation similar to that of Tulane. William Marsh Rice in 1891 left his estate for the establishment of a university "for the instruction and improvement of white inhabitants." His will also specified that such instruction would be free. In 1963 the Rice trustees filed suit in state district court to construe the will to permit the admission of Negroes and the charging of tuition. At the trial President Kenneth S. Pitzer testified that continued segregation would be "the beginning of the end of Rice as an important institution" and "would indicate Rice was trapped in the customs of a half-century ago." He added that no professor of outstanding ability would want to be with an institution on the decline and that the loss of good faculty soon would cause the loss of research grants. When asked specifically whether in his opinion Rice could obtain a Ford Foundation grant if it maintained its racial restriction, Pitzer replied, "I am convinced that it cannot." District Judge William M. Holland ruled that Rice could admit Negroes and charge tuition.

Most of the private colleges in the region were church-related, and for them the morality of the desegregation issue was of special significance. The Methodist Board of Education, meeting in 1955, adopted a resolution saying, "Since church-related colleges and universities profess to stand for Christian principles, there is an obligation here which should be more compelling than the legal compulsion which has been placed on the public schools." Dr. Herman Long of Fisk University in 1960 conducted a survey for a commission of the National Council of Churches. He reported that "public institutions appear to be responding to legal and political forces more effectively than private institutions are responding to the moral and religious influences central to their church-relatedness." Dr. Long found that about twice as many public as private, church-related colleges admitted both white and Negro students. The gap was closing by the end of the decade, but the percentage of desegregated institutions remained higher for public than for private, church-related colleges. Segregation was most prevalent among the private, secular colleges.

In a speech in 1956, Alexander Heard, political scientist then on the faculty of the University of North Carolina, said, ". . . The problem [of school desegregation] has been taken over by the politicians, and the politicians have tended to exploit it for purposes not always connected with a concern for wise social and educational policy. The problem belongs with the politicians all right, but not with them alone. The debate could be carried on better, and solutions could be found quicker, in other forums. . . . It is clear that the universities have joined but little in the discussion."

Seven years later, as the decade neared its end, Chancellor Williams of the University of Mississippi commented that "political and social pressures" on a state institution were "hard to withstand." More often than not, the colleges and universities of the South yielded to the pressures that were exerted on them, both for and against desegregation of education. They joined but little in the discussion of public policy, leaving it to the political leaders and the people to make the basic decisions.

6.

The Police: Order, Disorder
and Violence

"The modern officer in dealing with racial tensions is much like 'the man on the tight rope.' One false step may lead to disaster. The law enforcement officer's critical position cannot be overemphasized."

Chief Jesse E. Curry and Captain Glen D. King of the Dallas, Texas, police department expressed this judgment in their book *Race Tensions and the Police*. Numerous incidents accompanying the desegregation of schools showed how critical the law-enforcement officer's position could be.

The First Protests

When schools opened in September, 1954, some of them were desegregated. At first all was quiet. But soon rumblings of discontent were heard in Milford, Delaware, a town of five thousand population in a farming area sixty-five miles south of Wilmington. The school board had decided to desegregate the Milford High School but had made no announcement until the night before the term was to begin. The news was broken at a meeting of the Rotary Club.

Eleven Negro children were admitted to the formerly white school. For ten days the community was calm, on the surface. Then, without warning, about fifteen hundred people converged on the American Legion home, where they conducted a mass meeting to protest the board's action. Other meetings followed, and they attracted Bryant W. Bowles of Washington, D.C., founder and president of the National Association for the Advancement of White People. With Bowles on the scene, the protest rallies grew in size and intensity, climaxing on Sunday afternoon, September 26, when some four thousand people gathered to hear him speak.

Fearing violence, the school board had closed the schools on Monday, September 20, and they remained closed for the rest of the week. On orders of the Delaware State Board of Education, the schools were reopened on September 27, with the Negroes in attendance at Milford High School. The local board resigned under the pressure, and a new board promptly ousted the Negroes. Later the State Supreme Court ruled that the Negroes had been enrolled illegally.

The police played a small part in the Milford incident. On the day of the first spontaneous mass meeting, extra state troopers and special police were called to duty to handle traffic. When schools reopened after the one-week cooling-off period, fifteen state troopers and ten Milford policemen were on hand. But the crowds of protesters were not unruly, and the removal of the Negro children from the white school restored calm.

Bowles was charged with counseling parents not to send their children to school and with conspiring with parents to keep their children at home. Tried before Common Pleas Judge Arley B. Magee, he was convicted and sentenced to pay a fine of $300 or spend six months in jail on each of the two charges. On appeal, a jury found him not guilty. Bowles expressed his attitude toward the police when he said, "I'm from the South, and in the South, police have guns to protect the white from the colored and the colored from the white."

From Milford the spotlight turned to Baltimore, where immediately after the 1954 Supreme Court decision, the Board of Education had announced that the city's school system would be desegregated in the fall. Schools opened without incident, and there was no trouble until September 30. Then, inspired by the successful protest movement in Milford, groups of Baltimore parents who favored segregated schools began to take action. They picketed some schools, and students in large numbers boycotted those schools. Bryant Bowles hastened to Baltimore.

The political, educational and civic leadership of the city closed ranks to stop the disorder. They joined in appeals to the demonstrators, and, when their words were ignored, the leaders demanded and supported sterner measures to be taken by the police.

The police commissioner of Baltimore is named by the governor of Maryland, a procedure designed to keep law enforcement above local politics. The Baltimore police commissioner was Colonel Beverly Ober, a veteran National Guardsman.

The demonstrations began on a Thursday. On that day and the next the police broke them up and ordered students taking part to "go home or go to school." On Monday it was apparent that the appeals for an end to the disorders were not being heeded. Colonel Ober warned the demonstrators that "it is the duty of this department to stop all picketing or assembly in the neighborhood of our various public schools. Such picketing will cease or the police will take appropriate action." The commissioner cited Maryland laws against inducing children to absent themselves from schools and against creating a disturbance outside a school while classes are in session.

That same night Bryant Bowles addressed a meeting—held just outside the city limits. "I can't tell you to picket, and I'm not telling you not to," he said. "I understand the commissioner of police is predicting he's going to arrest everyone. I don't know him—or his color—but I do know he'll have to build a bigger jail."

Bowles was wrong. On Tuesday most of the students returned to their classes. Adults made a few half-hearted attempts at picketing, but the police quickly dispersed them. Superintendent John H. Fischer warned that truancy penalties would be applied against students. The holdouts came back to school on Wednesday, and there was no more picketing. Within a week after the demonstrations began, order was fully restored.

During the Baltimore demonstrations, rumors circulated that the District of Columbia schools would be next. They were. On Monday, October 4, about 2,500 of Washington's 104,000 public school students remained away from their classes and staged street demonstrations. One student said, "If Delaware and Baltimore can do it, so can we. We don't want them in our schools."

Bryant Bowles traveled the forty miles from Baltimore to preach his gospel at home. On Tuesday night he held a street-corner meeting with a group of students. He made other efforts to inject himself into leadership of the protests, but he didn't cut much of a figure.

The District police had been prepared for trouble when schools had opened in September. A uniformed officer had been stationed near each school, and these assignments continued for the first few weeks. Deputy Police Chief Howard V. Covell in a directive to the force said, "It is reasonable to expect some friction." When none developed, the policemen were withdrawn.

With the start of demonstrations on October 4, Chief Robert V. Murray, under the plan adopted but not used for the opening of the school term, quickly dispatched foot and mobile units to the trouble spots. Samuel Spencer, president of the District Board of Commissioners, and School Superintendent Hobart M. Corning made appeals for law and order.

The Washington episode paralleled closely the one in Baltimore. Appeals for order did little good. But threats of stern action sent the students back to school. Chief Murray announced that a section of the District code dealing with unlawful assembly would be enforced. Superintendent Corning warned that all pupils who were not in their classes by Friday morning would be penalized. On

Friday attendance returned to normal, and the demonstrations had ended.

A common denominator in all three of these incidents of organized protest in the first year of school desegregation was the participation of Bryant W. Bowles. He moved to the small town of Houston, Delaware, and took an active part in local politics for a while. Then he went to California. Later he was tried and convicted on a murder charge in Texas and was sentenced to life imprisonment.

The Beginning of Violence

The first really violent protest against desegregation erupted at the University of Alabama in Tuscaloosa on February 3, 1956, when Miss Autherine Lucy, a Negro, attended her first classes. Three days later she was spirited off the campus in a state highway patrol car. President O. C. Carmichael told a faculty meeting that she had been in danger of "being murdered on the campus."

Industrial workers in Tuscaloosa and persons from other states and other places in Alabama outnumbered university students in the rioting that began on the campus and spread into the town. Ku Klux Klan and Citizen's Council literature was distributed.

Some faculty members said that "ineffectiveness of police" was a cause of the rioting. At the faculty meeting which President Carmichael addressed, Professor Fred Ogden asked "why police protection had not been more adequate."

Campus police had taken stations at entrances and in the corridors of the buildings in which Miss Lucy attended classes. During the riotous demonstrations, town police rerouted traffic but made no arrests. Tuscaloosa Police Chief W. C. Thompkins and University Police Chief A. O. Rayfield announced that they did not plan to make any arrests. The state highway patrol limited its participation to removing Miss Lucy from the campus.

At the height of the demonstrations on February 6, university officials asked Governor James E. Folsom to send the National Guard to Tuscaloosa. He declined the request but said that the "state stands ready at all times to meet any situation properly." He added, "It is normal for all races not to be overly fond of each other. . . . We are not excited." After Miss Lucy had left the campus, never to return as a student, and after the general excitement had ebbed, the governor took a strong stand against mob action, saying, "I will use every power at my command to prevent mob rule from running any branch of the state government."

While Governor Folsom did not feel it proper to use the Alabama National Guard at Tuscaloosa, the governors of Tennessee and Kentucky called out the Guard to quell large-scale disorders in their states in the fall of 1956. Governor Frank Clement sent the Tennessee state police and Guard to Clinton and Governor A. B. Chandler dispatched the Kentucky police and Guard to Clay and Sturgis.

Clinton is a town of about four thousand nestled in the Cumberland Mountains about fifteen miles northwest of Knoxville. The school board had announced its plan to desegregate its schools when the fall term began on August 27. The white people of the community weren't happy about it, but they seemed to be resigned to the board's decision.

On Saturday before the schools were to open on Monday, Frederick John Kasper of Washington, D.C., executive secretary of the Seaboard White Citizens Council, came to town and started a campaign to arouse opposition to letting the Negroes attend the white schools. His efforts were so successful that he was arrested and jailed on charges of vagrancy and inciting to riot, but he was released for lack of evidence. Two days later Kasper was jailed again on order of U.S. District Judge Robert L. Taylor; the charge this time was contempt of court for having violated an injunction against hindering or impeding desegregation of the Clinton high school.

By then, however, news of the protest movement blossoming at Clinton was attracting national attention, and segregationists from distant points congregated there. Asa "Ace" Carter, president of the North Alabama Citizens' Council and organizer for the Ku Klux Klan, came from Birmingham. Jack Kershaw, secretary of the Tennessee Federation for Constitutional Government, came from Nashville and said that he was there to help maintain peace, "because that is the only way we can achieve our ends." Other organizations represented were the Pro-Southerners, the Tennessee Society to Maintain Segregation, and the States' Rights Council of Tennessee.

By Wednesday the mob was out of hand, and Anderson County Sheriff Joe K. Owen telephoned Captain George Burdette of the State Highway Patrol office in Knoxville to ask for help. "Has anyone been hurt?" the sheriff was asked. He replied, "Well, no blood has been spilled, but we're afraid there may be." To which the answer was, "Sorry, we can't help you unless actual violence has been committed."

The six-man Clinton police department was unable to maintain order, and a young lawyer, Leo Grant, Jr., organized an auxiliary volunteer police force. "Maybe we didn't do the right thing," he said later, "but the police were sitting around wringing their hands and not doing anything, and the time comes when somebody has to get up and do something."

On Saturday the Board of Aldermen declared that a state of emergency existed in Clinton. Mayor W. D. Lewallen and Sheriff Glad Woodward flew in a chartered plane to Nashville to deliver to Governor Clement a written request for state help. That night 39 highway patrol cars, occupied by 110 state patrolmen equipped with riot guns and submachine guns, sped into the little town. The next day brought more than 600 battle-ready National Guardsmen, accompanied by M-41 tanks and armored personnel carriers. Ten days later, order restored, the last of the Guardsmen left Clinton.

In sending the highway patrolmen and National Guardsmen to Clinton, Governor Clement said, "I am not doing this to promote integration or segregation. I am doing this to promote law and order and to preserve the peace." Later in a statewide radio address he said that he could not "sit back as governor and allow a lawless element to take over a town and county in Tennessee."

When school desegregation sparked trouble in Sturgis and Clay, small mining and farming towns near Kentucky's western border,

Governor Chandler acted promptly on his own initiative to end it. He sent National Guardsmen in tanks to both towns. The Guardsmen escorted the Negro children to the schools and maintained order, although protests continued and white students boycotted the schools.

In explaining why he had called out the Guard, Governor Chandler said, "Mobs led by bad-tempered men were taking over. You can't let mobs enforce the law. The rights of people were at stake. Streets were closed. Lives were in danger. The tanks were taken along for the proper psychological effect. Some men won't let a soldier with a gun push them. No man is going to argue with a tank."

State Attorney General Jo M. Ferguson was more effective than the guns and tanks in restoring the tranquillity of the disturbed white people of Sturgis and Clay. On September 24 he ruled that the Negro students had been "illegally enrolled," and they were ousted from white schools.

While tanks were rolling in Tennessee and Kentucky, Governor Allan Shivers found a few Texas Rangers sufficient to restore order in Mansfield and Texarkana. But there was a fundamental difference in objectives. Governors Clement and Chandler had used the National Guard to support school boards that had desegregated schools. Governor Shivers used the Rangers to restore segregation in schools that were under court orders to desegregate.

Mansfield is a town of about fifteen hundred population just outside Fort Worth. Its residents were strongly segregationist, and during the summer of 1956, before desegregation of the high school was to start, had expressed their disapproval in a number of ways. Crosses were burned, Negro effigies were hung, anti-Negro signs were strung across the main street, and a Citzens' Council was formed. On the day school opened, a crowd of some five hundred gathered around the school and turned the Negroes away.

Governor Shivers sent two Rangers to Mansfield with orders to arrest anyone "whose actions are such as to represent a threat to the peace." At the same time he advised the school board to "transfer out of the district any scholastics, white or colored, whose attendance or attempts to attend Mansfield High School would be reasonably calculated to incite violence." The Negroes were transferred, and the Mansfield schools remained segregated throughout the decade.

The governor sent four Rangers—also in 1956—to Texarkana, where Texarkana Junior College was under court order to admit two Negroes. A mob barred the Negroes, who turned to the Rangers for help. Sergeant Jay Banks told them, "Our orders are to maintain order and to keep down violence. We are to take no part in the integration dispute and we are not going to escort anyone in or out of the college." In 1963 the college admitted its first Negro student.

From Little Rock to New Orleans

The next fall, when desegregation was to begin under court order in Little Rock, Governor Orval Faubus took his cue from Governor Shivers. He used his powers as governor to prevent desegregation and the violence he said it would cause, but he failed to prevent either desegregation or violence.

The Eighth Circuit Court of Appeals in May of 1957 had approved a plan for desegregation in Little Rock. Although there was some dissatisfaction, the community seemed prepared to accept the inevitable. The governor said in August, "Everyone knows that state laws can't supersede federal laws." Mayor Woodrow W. Mann and Police Chief Marvin H. Potts expected no trouble.

Then Governor Marvin Griffin of Georgia addressed a rally of the Capital Citizens' Council. He made a rousing speech and asked, "If Georgia doesn't have integration, why does Arkansas have it?" After that Chief Potts said, "I don't know what's going to happen."

What happened was that Governor Faubus, without prior notice, called out the National Guard "to maintain or restore the peace and good order of this community," which he said would be impossible "if forcible integration is carried out tomorrow in the schools of this community."

Mayor Mann in a statement said: "The Governor has called

out the National Guard to put down trouble when none existed. He did so without a request from those of us who are directly responsible for preservation of peace and order. The only effect of his action is to create tensions where none existed." He added that "the Governor's excuse for calling out the Guard is simply a hoax."

While the Guard carried out the governor's orders to keep the Negroes from entering Central High School, peace did prevail. On Friday, September 20, the governor withdrew the Guard when he was ordered by the federal district court to stop obstructing the admission of the Negro students to the school. During the next three days large-scale mob violence developed. The Little Rock police, some 150 strong and under the direction of Assistant Chief Eugene Smith, erected barricades around the school. On Monday the police brought the Negro students into the school, but, as a safety measure, removed them around noon. Outside the barricades the size of the mob was growing, and its fury raged unchecked. On Tuesday President Eisenhower federalized the Arkansas National Guard and sent paratroopers of the 101st Airborne Division, commanded by Major General Edwin A. Walker, to Little Rock. Order was restored, and the Negro children returned to the school the next day.

The dramatic events in Little Rock deflected attention from other places where school desegregation was to begin in the fall of 1957. One of them was Nashville, Tennessee, where responsible public officials had reason to be apprehensive.

After lengthy litigation and extensive general public debate, Negro children were to be admitted to first grades with white children when schools opened on September 9. Most of the upholders of segregation who had been in Clinton were active in Nashville, including John Kasper and Asa Carter and the Ku Klux Klan and the Tennessee Federation for Constitutional Government. Many individuals and organizations called for peaceful public acceptance of desegregation.

Registration for all first-grade pupils was held on August 27 at fifteen formerly white schools that Negroes were eligible to attend. Police Chief Douglas E. Hosse stationed ninety-two officers, including twenty detectives, at the schools. They were ready for any disturbance, but there was none. Superintendent W. A. Bass expressed his delight and pride in the people of Nashville.

On Sunday, September 8, Chief Hosse announced that the police would arrest anyone appearing at the desegregated schools who was disorderly or who attempted to intimidate children or parents. The next day 115 policemen were on duty at seven formerly white schools that Negroes attended for the first time. Barricades were placed a block from each school. Persons who could not explain their presence at the schools were turned away. As demonstrators appeared, police dispersed them and arrested their leaders.

John Kasper appeared at several schools during the day and that night he spoke at a rally held downtown. Shortly after midnight the Hattie Cotton School, one of those desegregated, was bombed and damaged extensively. Kasper and others were arrested, although no one ever was charged with the bombing.

Mayor Ben West and the police department moved quickly to meet the challenge to law and order. Chief Hosse addressed a police detachment and told them, "This has gone beyond a matter of integration. These people have ignored the laws and they have shown no regard for you or any citizen." There was no further serious disorder accompanying the desegregation of schools in Nashville.

The police in Little Rock again took the center of the stage in the fall of 1959. Governor Faubus, acting under state law, had closed the high schools for the 1958–59 academic year to avoid desegregation. The schools reopened—desegregated—in September, 1959, without the protection of federal troops. Eugene Smith had become chief of police, and the entire force had been trained in the techniques of professional police work.

During the spring and summer of 1959 Smith and his men planned for the reopening of the schools, scheduled for August 12. On the night of August 11 Governor Faubus appeared on television. He said that there was "nothing to be gained tomorrow by disorder and violence." The governor then complained that integration was being forced on Little Rock. Attacking Chief Smith, he said, "The city police force is in charge of one who will make every effort tomorrow to apply the force necessary to forcibly integrate the public schools. He and his associates will call it law and order. That's the same term used by the Hungarian puppet and his Russian masters." The governor added, "The general consensus around here is that Gene Smith has been bought and paid for to see that integration is effected."

On the morning of August 12 a crowd of segregationists gathered at the steps of the state capitol. The governor spoke to them briefly and then, marching behind the United States, Arkansas and Confederate flags, they started toward Central High School. They never completed the trip. Along the way they encountered a police roadblock. Smith told the protesters to disperse. When they refused, the police, assisted by fire hoses, waded in and fragmented the mob. There was no further trouble in Little Rock.

Smith's actions made him the subject of abuse from the governor, the Citizens' Council and from anonymous letter writers. One person wrote Smith, "I just now seen your picture in the paper. You think you look so darn pretty in your uniform. Well, I hate you worse than niggers. I'd like to come up and kill you."

The Little Rock police and Chief Smith were praised as well as criticized. "Chief Smith has been slandered by the rabble-rousers," J. Gaston Williamson, chairman of the Committee for the Peaceful Operation of Our Free Public Schools, said. "The vast majority of the citizens of Little Rock are deeply grateful to Chief Smith and his men." Before the school year ended—in March—Chief Smith shot and killed his wife and himself. He left no note to explain why.

Police chiefs in other Southern cities that had not experienced the start of school desegregation took note of what happened in Little Rock in 1959. Chief Herbert Jenkins of Atlanta wrote Chief Smith, "You are not only making history, but you are establishing a precedent and a procedure that most of us will benefit by because sooner or later many of us will have a similar problem."

Chief Jenkins's turn came two years later, and he was to show that he had learned the lessons of Little Rock. The first large city to have the opportunity to benefit from Chief Smith's example, however, was New Orleans. There Police Superintendent Joseph Giarusso had his problems.

Almost no one in authority supported desegregation in New Orleans. But the Orleans Parish School Board had exhausted every legal recourse to avoid it, and on November 14, 1960, four Negro girls entered the first grade in two New Orleans schools. Some of the noisiest demonstrations of the decade followed. The white children boycotted the two schools, and mobs composed mostly of mothers and teen-age truants gathered daily to shout taunts and epithets at the Negro girls, the U.S. marshals accompanying them and the few white parents who returned their children to the schools.

Superintendent Giarusso kept scores of policemen, selected from his twelve-hundred-man force, on twenty-four-hour alert for six days. They kept the crowds pushed well back from the schools. At one point seventy-two officers ringed one of the schools to prevent a band of teenagers from entering it. Policemen mounted on horses and motorcycles kept the mobs back; fire hoses also were used.

One mother grabbed Superintendent Giarusso and tearfully pleaded, "Chief, help us, not the United States government." He replied, "We'll help you if you do it in an orderly manner, but we are not going to let you take over the city."

Within two weeks most of the mothers had gone home, and New Orleans was quiet again.

Athens, Oxford and Tuscaloosa

After New Orleans most of the demonstrations and violence during the remainder of the decade took place at Southern universities—at the University of Georgia in 1961, the University of Mississippi in 1962 and the University of Alabama in 1963.

In February, 1960, Governor Ernest Vandiver of Georgia pledged, "We are going to resist again and again and again. . . . We will exhaust every legal means and remedy available to us." In

January, 1961, two Negro students were admitted to the University of Georgia at Athens, the choice having been made to keep the university open and desegregated rather than to close it.

Hamilton Holmes and Miss Charlayne Hunter, the Negro students, had registered on Monday, January 9, and their appearance on the campus had caused no disorders. There was a rock-throwing demonstration on Tuesday night. Tension mounted during the day on Wednesday. That night Georgia Tech beat Georgia in a basketball game at Athens. The game ended about 9:45, and a wild riot began. It centered around Myers Hall, the dormitory to which Miss Hunter had been assigned.

Sensing possible trouble, Mayor Ralph Snow and Police Chief E. E. Hardy had alerted the entire forty-one-man police force. By 10 P.M. it was clear that the local police could not handle the situation. The mayor called the Athens post of the state highway patrol to ask for help. He was told that no patrolmen could be sent until the request was cleared with a superior officer. Repeated requests to the patrol office brought no response, although it was reported that thirty troopers were standing by. At 11 P.M. the mayor ordered the fire department to assist the police, and hoses were turned on the rioters, but their spirits were undampened.

At 11:30 Mayor Snow drove to the highway patrol post, where he called Colonel William P. Trotter, director of the Department of Public Safety, in Atlanta. Colonel Trotter said that no action could be taken without consulting the governor. Governor Vandiver ordered the troopers to go to the scene of the disturbance, but when they arrived, at 12:20, the riot had ended. The mayor returned to the campus, where the local police, using tear gas and fire hoses, had dispersed the mob.

During the rioting Miss Hunter was removed from the campus for her personal safety. Holmes was living off the campus. He was picked up, and both students were taken to Atlanta. U.S. District Judge William A. Bootle on Friday ordered that the students be readmitted by 8 A.M. on Monday, and he obtained assurances from state officials that the state would keep order at the university. The

Negro students returned to their classes on Monday, and there were no further disorders.

The University of Mississippi at Oxford was the scene of the next, and most severe, violence that desegregation of education produced during the decade. Two men were killed in a night of rioting after James Meredith was admitted to Ole Miss on September 30, 1962.

Governor Ross Barnett did everything within his power to prevent Meredith's enrollment. In the process Mississippi and other parts of the South became inflamed. For days before September 30 an army of state highway patrolmen and sheriffs from all parts of Mississippi surrounded the university to keep Meredith out. They wore steel helmets, carried clubs but no guns, and had been issued gas masks. Highway patrolmen formed a human wall around Governor Barnett's office in Jackson to prevent the serving of court papers on him. Thousands of men lined the highways leading into Oxford, seat of the university, silently watching.

On Sunday afternoon, under an agreement between Governor Barnett and federal authorities, Meredith was brought to the campus in a state police car. A contingent of more than three hundred U.S. marshals had preceded him. As the word spread that the Negro was at Ole Miss, segregationists converged on Oxford. Among those who came to observe and to encourage the protesters was Major General Edwin A. Walker, who had commanded the federal troops at Little Rock. That night President Kennedy in a television address called upon the students at the university to "return to their normal activities." By that time rioting had begun, and it grew in size and intensity.

The Lyceum Building, where federal officials made their headquarters on the campus, was the target of the rioters. United States marshals, equipped with tear-gas guns and grenades, formed a protective ring around the building. As the shouting rioters attacked, throwing rocks and bottles and other missiles, the 250 state highway patrolmen on the scene attempted to push them back. One of the marshals fired a tear-gas grenade at close range, and it was reported to have hit one of the patrolmen in the back. The patrolmen withdrew, but thirty minutes later returned. The rioting continued, and the patrolmen withdrew again, leaving the marshals on their own. It was then 10:30 P.M.

At 2 A.M. on October 1 the first units of the federalized Mississippi National Guard were ordered into action. At 4:15 the first federal troops, specialists in riot control, marched onto the campus. Four hours later Brigadier General Charles Billingslea, in charge of the military operations, said, "I now declare this area secure."

The behavior of both the state patrolmen and the federal marshals was hotly debated. Federal officials said that Governor Barnett had assured them that the state would maintain order when Meredith was brought to the campus, but that the patrolmen withdrew at a time when the rioting could have been brought under control with their assistance. U.S. Attorney General Robert F. Kennedy accused the governor of having ordered the withdrawal. Barnett "emphatically and positively" denied the accusation. He countered by calling the marshals "inexperienced, nervous and trigger-happy," and he charged them with "instability and unwarranted brutality." Barnett said that the firing of the first tear gas "point blank into the backs of the state officers" was "the direct cause of the violence on the campus."

Mayor Robert W. Elliott of Oxford said that he asked the highway patrol for help when the rioting spread from the campus to the town and was told, "We have orders not to interfere." He said that "patrolmen actually saw cars demolished and saw mobs on the streets and did nothing about it." The mayor had deputized the town's thirty firemen to augment the seven-man police force, but he said that together they were "no match for the rioters." Mayor Elliott asked the FBI to call for federal troops. The Army restored order in the town as it had on the campus.

The next, and last, display of force on a college campus during the decade was at Tuscaloosa. The University of Alabama had been under court order to admit Negroes since 1956, when Autherine Lucy had been enrolled briefly. From then until 1963, the student body at the university was all-white.

George C. Wallace was inaugurated as governor of Alabama in January of 1963. During the campaign for election he repeatedly pledged that he would defy any court order to desegregate education in the state "even to the point of standing at the schoolhouse door in person."

The new governor did not have to wait long to honor his pledge. On May 21 U.S. District Judge H. Hobart Grooms ordered the admission of two Negroes to the university at Tuscaloosa on June 11 and another to the university center at Huntsville on June 13. By contrast to 1956, wide public support was voiced for peaceful compliance with the court order.

Although he maintained his stance of defiance, the governor continued to give assurance that he would maintain law and order. He asked the people of Alabama to stay away from the campus and let him handle the situation. As a precaution he ordered a 500-man unit of the Alabama National Guard to Tuscaloosa along with 150 highway patrolmen and other state police. President Kennedy put 2,000 federal troops on alert.

On the appointed day Governor Wallace took his stand in front of Foster Auditorium, where the Negroes were to register. The two students, Miss Vivian Malone and James Hood, soon arrived with officials of the U.S. Justice Department. The governor read a five-page statement, which concluded, "I denounce and forbid this illegal act." The students and the federal officials retired. Less than an hour later President Kennedy federalized the Alabama National Guard. A contingent of Guardsmen escorted the Negro students to Foster Auditorium. Brigadier General Henry C. Graham of Birmingham was in command. The general asked the governor "to step aside." Wallace returned to the state capital in Montgomery. There was no disorder then or later at Tuscaloosa. The governor decided not to repeat his gesture in Huntsville, and the university center there admitted its first Negro student two days later without incident.

The decade's final outburst of violence took place when the first public schools in Alabama were desegregated. After standing in the door at Tuscaloosa, Governor Wallace had pledged his resistance to desegregation of the high schools of his state. "At the moment there is no court order telling us to admit Negroes to our high schools," he said. "Whenever the time comes, I will take appropriate action in keeping with the dignity of our state. I can assure you it will be a forceful stand, whatever I do."

The time was not long in coming. In August federal courts ordered that desegregation must begin in September in Birmingham, Huntsville, Tuskegee and Mobile. The governor kept his word by taking a forceful stand. Schools were scheduled to open on September 2. Governor Wallace dispatched state troopers to all the schools, despite the expressed disapproval of local authorities. Confusion was general; schools were opened and closed again during the week, but no Negroes were admitted to the white schools. On September 9, all the schools opened, but under an executive order from the governor, state troopers turned away the Negroes everywhere except in Huntsville. No explanation for the omission of Huntsville was made.

On Tuesday all five of the federal district judges in Alabama joined in issuing an injunction restraining the governor from further interference with school desegregation. Wallace responded by replacing the state troopers with National Guardsmen. President Kennedy promptly federalized the Guard, and he issued a statement accusing the governor of being "desperately anxious to have the federal government intervene in a situation in which we have no desire to intervene." Wallace retired from the fray, saying, "I can't fight bayonets with my bare hands."

The Prevention of Disorder

From 1954 on, police executives met regularly at the local, state, regional and national level to discuss law enforcement and race tensions. These conferences and seminars were sponsored by agencies such as the Ford Foundation, the National Conference of Christians and Jews and the International Association of Chiefs of Police. In these sessions the underlying theme was the need for police work which upheld the law, protected lives and property and which did not use law enforcement as a means for promoting either segregation or integration.

One of the obstacles to impartial law enforcement was the personal attitude toward Negroes of white officers who shared the predominant segregationist sentiment of other white Southerners. Judge J. Spencer Bell of the Fourth Circuit Court of Appeals observed, "Woe unto a Southern Negro who fails to address a policeman as 'sir.' "

Before 1954 segregation not only was imbedded deeply in Southern culture; it had the support of law. White segregationist policemen could enforce the law without violating their personal beliefs. Although the Supreme Court changed the law, white policemen continued to regard Negroes as they had in the past. Chief Curry and Captain King of Dallas wrote in their book, "It would be absurd to presume that the mere act of donning a uniform and a badge would remove ideas, opinions and prejudices instilled from childhood." They added, "When law enforcement is concerned, the officer must sublimate his personal opinions to his official duties." An objective of police training courses was to establish the principle that law enforcement should be color blind.

Some police agencies were trained in dealing with race friction long before 1954. In Louisville the police force began hiring Negroes in 1923. In 1949 the department brought in Dr. Joseph Lohman, then sheriff of Cook County, Illinois, and later dean of criminology at the University of California, to train officers in police work with minority groups. The Louisville police department incorporated part of Lohman's book, *Police Work with Minority Groups,* in its training manual.

The first Negroes were admitted to schools with whites in Louisville in the summer session of 1956 without any difficulty. Planning for general desegregation of the Louisville schools was under the direction of School Superintendent Omer Carmichael. He had the full backing of political and community leaders. Police Chief Carl Heustis, working closely with the superintendent, was kept informed of all plans and developments.

Late in the summer there had been sporadic picketing by members of the Citizens' Council. Plans for picketing when the schools opened were called off when Millard D. Grubbs, chairman of the Kentucky Citizens' Councils, Inc., was unable to obtain assurances that pickets would not be arrested. Instead, Chief Heustis gave notice that the police intended to use whatever means necessary to see that the rights of all people were protected. Although the Louisville desegregation was voluntary, the chief said that the mandate of the Supreme Court would be enforced. When schools opened there were no disorders. A few pickets showed up at City Hall and at the Board of Education office, but within an hour they had disappeared.

Louisville had less reason to fear disorder when school desegregation began than did cities in the Southern states, where sentiment for segregation was stronger. That these fears were well-founded was realized in Little Rock, Nashville and New Orleans. Even in these cities, the police had shown that mob violence could be controlled and suppressed.

Other large cities in the South took note and began to make their plans to prevent disorder. When their schools were desegregated in 1961, Atlanta, Dallas and Memphis profited from the experience of others.

Atlanta had been ordered to begin desegregation in its schools in 1960. On January 4 of that year, in his annual message to the Board of Aldermen, Mayor William B. Hartsfield had said: "I regard the vigilance and support of our citizens to the cause of continued public education as the most important thing which confronts us during the fateful year of 1960. . . . I know the people of Atlanta, who are proud of their city, its marvelous growth and good reputation, will rise to this challenge. There are those who will, as usual, shout hatred and confusion, but the great majority will live up to the traditions of our town."

The mayor did know his town. Both the proponents of segregation and the defenders of public education marshaled their forces. Mayor Hartsfield ordered "the entire city government" to place itself "squarely behind the preservation of public education." This, of course, included the police department, headed by Chief Herbert T.

Jenkins. The courts gave Atlanta a year of grace so that the legislature would have an oportunity to change the laws designed to preserve school segregation, as was done in 1961 when the University of Georgia admitted its first Negroes rather than close.

Meanwhile Chief Jenkins had gone ahead with his plans. He had studied carefully police experience in Little Rock—both in 1957 and 1959. When race trouble erupted in New Orleans, Montgomery and Jacksonville, he sent observers there from his department.

Police officers in Atlanta were required to read *With Justice for All,* published by the Anti-Defamation League of B'nai B'rith and the International Association of Chiefs of Police; George McMillan's booklet, *Racial Violence and Law Enforcement;* the 1961 report of the U.S. Commission on Civil Rights; and Dr. Robert A. Matthews's book, *How to Recognize and Handle Abnormal People.*

The police identified potential trouble-makers and put them under surveillance. The chief made it clear that when the time came to desegregate the schools, order would be maintained and the law would be enforced. With respect to law enforcement his credo was, "if a man acts like a gentleman, or a woman acts like a lady, I believe in treating him or her like a gentleman or a lady, regardless of race, color or creed. If they act like hoodlums, I believe in treating them like hoodlums, regardless of race, color or creed."

The public schools in Atlanta desegregated without trouble. At one school the police arrested four white residents. At another school a member of the American Nazi party from Alexandria, Virginia, was arrested. Asked later to explain Atlanta's experience, Chief Jenkins said, "There was never any hesitation, nor the slightest sign of weakness on the part of anyone. . . ."

Dallas police officials, like Atlanta's, had made a close study of what happened in Little Rock. Mayor P. L. Thornton and City Manager Elgin Crull sent Police Chief Carl Hansson on a secret mission to Little Rock in 1957. The chief and M. W. Stevenson, head of the criminal investigation division, were instructed to learn what they could about police problems in handling "the situation." When it became known several months later that he had been to Little Rock, Chief Hansson said he thought Dallas could profit from Little Rock's experience. One thing he learned, he said, was the need for "close cooperation" between police, school and government officials. Dallas provided that cooperation to a high degree.

Immediately upon his return from Little Rock, Chief Hansson began to make plans for a police training program aimed at "any outbreak of mob violence" arising from the eventual desegregation of Dallas public schools. A ninety-page *Training Manual on Community Tensions* was prepared. Before the training program was begun Hansson retired, but his successor, Jesse E. Curry, carried out the plan. In the spring of 1960, when it was thought that Dallas schools might desegregate that fall, all policemen were required to attend an eight-hour course with the manual as a textbook. Inspector J. Herbert Sawyer told the men, "Regardless of your private views regarding minority groups, you, as officers of the law, must not compromise the performance of your public duty." The course of study covered crowd behavior, mobs and police tactics, mobilization of community resources and quelling riots.

During the summer of 1961—with public school desegregation in Dallas scheduled for September—the more than one thousand members of the department were given refresher courses. In this same period potential trouble-makers—both groups and individuals —were identified and kept under surveillance, as had been done in Atlanta. Chief Curry repeatedly made it clear to the public that the police were prepared to "get tough" in the event of trouble.

There was no trouble when school desegregation began in Dallas.

Memphis also was under court order to begin desegregation in its schools in the fall of 1961, but unlike Atlanta and Dallas waited until several weeks after the term opened to admit the first Negro children to white schools. The desegregation was "executed like a well-rehearsed military operation," according to reporters who covered it.

As in Dallas, the top leaders of the community had worked together to assure peaceful change. Jack Petree, attorney for the school board, was in charge of carrying out the plan. "This is going to be a thoroughly policed operation," he said. "It's vitally important that no incident occur, intentionally or otherwise. Police will be all over everywhere."

Police Commissioner Claude Armour assigned 160 policemen equipped with clubs to patrol the schools that were being desegregated. He made it clear that no disorders would be tolerated. The chief told his men to arrest "anyone who gets out of line—I don't care who it is." He continued, "Anyone who can't carry out this assignment can hand in his badge." On desegregation day an elaborate communications system was in effect so that school, police and other city officials would remain in constant touch with one another. At the end of the day a police official commented, "There was no apparent resistance to integration." As a precaution against possible violence, police guards were stationed at each of the schools at night for some time. Nothing happened.

Even where resistance to desegregation was strongest, accommodation to change could be peaceful. South Carolina provided the showcase in 1963, first at Clemson College and then at Charleston.

Harvey B. Gantt enrolled at Clemson on January 28. State officials had pursued every legal recourse to keep him out, but they were determined that upon his admission nothing would happen to reflect discredit on South Carolina. Governor Donald S. Russell said that the state was "perfectly capable of maintaining order," adding, "We are not going to have any violence." Other state leaders appealed for peace and order. Taking no chances, a tight security network was thrown up around the college the day Gantt was to register. Many law enforcement officers were stationed on the campus, operating under a carefully preconceived plan. Roadblocks were set up on all highways leading into the town of sixteen hundred population. Identification cards were issued to each of the four thousand students at the college. Gantt was admitted without incident.

When eleven Negro children entered four high schools in Charleston in September, they attracted almost no attention. Mayor

J. Palmer Gaillard was prepared for trouble, if it came. Police units were poised to reach any of the schools within minutes. The only police in evidence the day classes began were those guarding street crossings. There was no need for the others.

In the decade following the *Brown* decision, thousands of schools in the affected region were desegregated. In the vast majority of instances, segregation ended peacefully. In the absence of any public disturbance, the local police were not called upon to perform extraordinary duties. Where there was organized effort to prevent desegregation or to restore segregation, the action or inaction of the police was a significant factor in shaping events.

In most instances of disorder, persons from outside the community where it occurred struck the spark to pentup feelings. Those who were strongly committed to segregation seemed to be especially susceptible to outside influences.

The small towns had more than their share of trouble. When their police forces were incapable of coping with it, their appeals for outside help were not always met promptly and adequately. In the larger cities, the police showed that they could handle most situations, if ordered, or permitted, to do so.

Unlike others in key roles, the policemen were not free to set their own courses of action. Law-enforcement officers—town constables, city policemen, state highway patrolmen, United States marshals, federal troops—all took orders. Political office holders—mayors, governors, the President of the United States—issued the orders. The peaks of violence were reached when there was conflict between political leaders, as at Little Rock and Oxford.

After the decade ended, Atlanta's Chief Jenkins commented that, in meeting the challenge created by social changes, the police had been handicapped by "misguided leadership of some of our public officials." The support of the elected officials to whom the police were responsible was essential to effective law enforcement. Even where resistance to school desegregation was strongest, public passions seldom erupted into disorder and violence if the political leaders were determined to maintain order.

7.

The Lawyers

"I consider my nomination a public mandate to carry on an all-out fight to maintain segregation," MacDonald Gallion said in 1958 upon becoming the Democratic candidate for attorney general of Alabama. After his election he went before the state legislature to ask for extra money "to take the attack to the enemy."

The enemy was the National Association for the Advancement of Colored People. By winning the *School Segregation Cases* before the United States Supreme Court in 1954, NAACP lawyers set in motion a cycle of legislation and litigation that was to occupy many attorneys in the Southern states for years to come.

Lawyers were at the center of much of the school desegregation activity that followed the *Brown* decision. Others—the governors, the legislators, the schoolmen—often took the spotlight, but not far offstage were the lawyers who wrote the script and did the prompting.

As did Gallion, attorneys general of all the states of the old Confederacy gave high priority to keeping the schools segregated. The attorneys general acted as legal advisers to the governors and legislators of their states, and sometimes to the educators. They drafted laws to preserve segregation or to delay desegregation as long as possible. They defended the states and their political subdivisions in the courts when suits were filed to desegregate schools and colleges or to challenge the constitutionality of the laws that the legislatures had passed.

The attorneys general did not stand alone in waging the battle. They had the help of leading lawyers in their states. Attorneys, usually considered experts on constitutional law, served on official bodies charged with plotting legal strategy. Some of these groups were legislative committees, and their lawyer-members were legislators. In other instances the governors made the appointments, including lawyers both from their state's legislature and from private practice.

Local school boards had their own attorneys, who advised on how to desegregate—whether voluntarily or under the stimulus of court action—or how to resist desegregation. They represented the boards in court.

The initiative lay with "the enemy"—the lawyers for the NAACP. They chose those targets that promised the greatest chance of success, either in achieving desegregation or in establishing or clarifying legal principles.

The ultimate outcome of a court action against segregation rooted in law was easily predictable. The federal courts would not permit the continuation of such segregation. But to bring about desegregation through court action was not always easy or quick. The attorneys for the resisting school boards were masters of the legal techniques for delaying disposition of a case. Years could elapse between the filing of a suit and its final adjudication.

Trial of these cases required lawyers and money. The NAACP had the advantage of the *Brown* decision, but the Southern states had more lawyers and more money than the NAACP.

Standing somewhat aloof from the legislative and courtroom battles and yet deeply engaged in the segregation war was the attorney general of the United States. Under federal law he lacked the authority to file desegregation suits. On matters of school desegregation, however, the attorney general often was the spokesman for the administration in office in the great legal and public debate that preceded and followed the *Brown* decision.

The School Segregation Cases

The courts do not institute the cases that come before them. Someone with a grievance seeks to have it rectified through the courts. Attorneys present the arguments upon which judges reach decisions.

The arguments in the chain of cases that led to the *Brown* decision started in the mid 1930's. The issue was whether the quality of education in separate colleges for Negroes met the requirements of the "separate but equal" principle that the Supreme Court established in 1896. Under court rulings in the college cases, Negroes gained admission to white colleges because the Negro colleges were judged to be inferior.

In the public school cases attorneys for the Negro plaintiffs followed the direction signs of the college cases and took a step beyond them. They made a frontal assault on the constitutional validity of the "separate but equal" doctrine. They contended that segregation and equality were incompatible and that segregation based on law violated the constitutional mandate for "equal protection of the laws."

Public officials for the segregation states were alert to the significance of the public school cases coming through the courts. They marshaled their legal forces to fight the threat. The attorneys upholding the segregated school systems emphasized the "separate but equal" precedent that had stood for more than half a century. They also stressed the Tenth Amendment's reservation to the states of all powers not delegated by the Constitution to the United States, pointing out that the Constitution contains no mention of public education. They predicted violence and bloodshed if Negroes and whites attended the same schools.

Lawyers for the NAACP mapped the grand strategy for the assault in the courts on segregation. The campaign began in 1934 with the employment of Charles H. Houston, vice-dean of the Howard University Law School, as its part-time director. Beginning July 1, 1935, Houston made it his full-time job, and his was the legal mind that conceived the approach to the Supreme Court decision of 1954. When Houston resigned in 1938 to enter private practice, Thurgood Marshall became special counsel for the NAACP. Marshall had graduated from the Howard Law School in 1933 and for five years engaged in private practice. In 1939, to obtain tax exemption, the NAACP Legal Defense and Educational Fund was established as a separate organization, with Marshall as its counsel-director. In this capacity he was the principal attorney for the plaintiffs in the *School Segregation Cases.*

Heading the roster of attorneys for the defense was John W. Davis of New York, who had been retained to represent Clarendon County, South Carolina. During his long career at the bar, Davis argued cases before the Supreme Court 140 times, more than any other lawyer in history.

The arguments before the Supreme Court began on December 9, 1952, and continued for three days. Instead of handing down a decision during that term of court, the justices issued an order restoring the cases to the docket and assigning them for reargument in the next term. The Court posed five questions on the Fourteenth Amendment, the powers of the Court and of Congress, and procedures to follow if segregation was declared unconstitutional. These arguments were heard in December, 1953.

On May 17, 1954, the Court announced its decision that "separate educational facilities are inherently unequal" and "a denial of the equal protection of the laws." Still the Court did not issue a decree to put its decision into effect. Instead it again restored the cases to the docket and asked for further arguments on procedures for implementation. This round of arguments was conducted April 11–14, 1955.

The United States and six states filed briefs and made oral arguments as friends of the Court. The NAACP attorneys contended that the Court should order desegregation by a fixed date, preferably by

September, 1955, but in no event later than September, 1956. The lawyers for the Southern states asked the Court to provide adequate time for compliance with its decision and to allow the federal district courts to supervise its implementation, taking account of differences in local conditions. The solicitor general of the United States took a middle course, agreeing that the cases should be remanded to the district courts but with a deadline for compliance.

The Supreme Court handed down its decision on May 31, 1955. It recognized that implementation of the constitutional principles it set forth on May 17, 1954, "may require solution of varied local school problems" and said it was up to school authorities to solve these problems. It required of the defendants in the cases before it "a prompt and reasonable start" toward achieving "a system of determining admission to the public schools on a non-racial basis." The cases were "remanded to the district courts to take such proceedings and enter such orders and decrees consistent with this opinion as are necessary and proper to admit to public schools on a racially nondiscriminatory basis with all deliberate speed the parties to these cases."

The State Attorneys General

The Supreme Court decisions in the *School Segregation Cases* opened new vistas to the attorneys general of the eleven Southern states—new opportunities for political advancement, new work, new trouble. In the border states the decisions made little difference in the personal fortunes and functions of the attorneys general.

Eugene Cook of Georgia perhaps expressed the views of most of the Southern attorneys general when he said after the 1954 decision, "The people of Georgia don't want to comply. . . . We mean to reverse it, and we mean to reverse it peacefully." A few months later in his address as retiring president of the National Association of Attorneys General, Cook advocated that Congress pass a bill to strip the Supreme Court of jurisdiction over state education systems as "the only effective answer, nationally."

During the decade following the first decision, about thirty men served as attorneys general for the eleven Southern states. Cook was one of two who held office for the entire ten years. The other was Richard W. Ervin of Florida. Four of the attorneys general became governors. In Virginia both J. Lindsay Almond, Jr., and Albertis S. Harrison were elected governor after serving as attorney general. The others were J. P. Coleman of Mississippi and John Patterson of Alabama.

Coleman was attorney general in 1954. After the first *Brown* decision he asked every member of the State Bar Association (white) to accept appointment as a special assistant to him in defending school desegregation suits. He said that more than twelve hundred lawyers, "all but two or three of the practicing active members," replied affirmatively. These special assistants were authorized "to represent, in co-operation with the attorney general, any school district or any public school official in any suit or other legal proceedings which may hereafter be instituted for the purpose of impairing or destroying separate schools for white and Negro races in Mississippi."

Getting ready for court action was of greater concern to Coleman than was the passage of new laws. In one regular and two special sessions in 1954 and 1955 the state legislature had enacted ten laws to deal with the Supreme Court decision of 1954. Just before the 1955 decision Coleman said, "Mississippi has enough laws now to preserve segregation, regardless of the decision handed down by the Supreme Court." After the decision Coleman, then a candidate for governor, said, "We are prepared to resist everywhere. We have laws to keep integration out indefinitely. We will gerrymander districts . . . assign pupils where we want them or abolish public schools as a final step. If a local board is sued for refusing to integrate schools, the school district could be abolished one day and re-established the next under a new set of trustees." He added, in a statement that expressed one of the basic objectives of his counterparts in other Southern states, "We could keep the Court busy for years in that way."

Despite all these preparations, or perhaps because of them, Coleman said that he was "wholly unworried as to any possibility of desegregation in Mississippi." As it turned out, when his term as governor expired in 1959, there had been no occasion to call on the twelve hundred private attorneys to defend school desegregation cases. The first such suit in Mississippi was filed in 1961, when James Meredith sought to gain admittance to Ole Miss. The first public school cases were filed in 1963.

Joe T. Patterson succeeded Coleman as attorney general and continued in the office for the remainder of the decade. As late as 1964 he was saying, "We still think Mississippi has the right to conduct its own affairs, and we won't give up on a single case involving state's rights until it makes a complete round of the courts and we are left with no alternative but to comply."

Lindsay Almond of Virginia was the only other attorney general in office in 1954 who later was governor of his state. Like Coleman he promised "a fight to the finish," but unlike Coleman he called for more laws to help him in the fight. While Mississippi was free from litigation until late in the decade, Virginia was a favorite target of the NAACP lawyers. In June of 1956 Almond, in urging that the legislature be called into special session, said, "I have fought to the end of the legal rope, and as counsel for the state it is my judgment that we must have state legislation on this subject in order to meet the attacks of the National Association for the Advancement of Colored People. . . . I have fought with my back to the wall in an effort to save the public school system of Virginia from destruction. In this fight I have exhausted every available legal defense."

When Almond spoke, Virginia had taken only two legislative measures in response to the *Brown* decisions—a constitutional amendment permitting the payment of tuition grants and a resolution of interposition. The legislature convened on August 27 in a special session at which it passed two dozen laws designed to preserve segregation. One of the laws authorized the state to provide legal defense for school boards and their members in desegregation suits; another directed the attorney general to assist local school boards in such cases. Attorney General Almond got state laws to help him in his fight, but they did not stop the onslaught. The NAACP met the challenge of these and later laws by filing more suits in Virginia than in any other state.

The most successful of the attorneys general in fighting the NAACP was John Patterson of Alabama. He launched an "all-out fight" in which he obtained an injunction that effectively barred the NAACP from operations in his state from 1956 through the remainder of the decade. The case of *NAACP v. Alabama* went to the U.S. Supreme Court four times. In its last decision, on June 1, 1964, the Court told the Alabama Supreme Court to enter a prompt decree vacating the order that barred the NAACP from registering as a corporation in the state.

Attacking the NAACP was a common practice of the Southern attorneys general. Although they could not claim the results that Patterson obtained in Alabama, Eugene Cook of Georgia and Bruce Bennett of Arkansas relentlessly lambasted the NAACP. Cook wrote a book entitled *The Ugly Truth about the NAACP*. He stumped the South making speeches castigating the Supreme Court and the NAACP. In one of these speeches, in Miami, he said, "Two-thirds of the officers of the NAACP have subversive or communist backgrounds. . . . We in Georgia are dedicated to the proposition that we are not going to let the NAACP dictate to us how we are going to run our schools or how we are going to raise our little children." Bennett sponsored a bevy of anti-NAACP laws, which the Supreme Court in 1961 held unconstitutional; the laws did not prevent NAACP activity in Arkansas.

Attacks on the Supreme Court were common, too. John Ben Shepperd, Texas attorney general, voiced a popular refrain when, in addressing the Arkansas State Bar Association in 1955, he said, "In its ruling the Court rode boot and spur right across 105 years of legal precedent and 150 years of social tradition repeatedly upheld under the federal Constitution. School segregation has been upheld by federal courts in 77 cases, at least 13 of which were before the United States Supreme Court. When the Court junked the line of cases, it was demoralizing to the legal profession whose every legal concept must be based on precedent."

In a 1956 speech attacking both the NAACP and the Supreme Court, Attorney General T. C. Callison of South Carolina touched on several oft-repeated themes. "The ultimate goal of the NAACP and their allied minority," he said, "is to completely integrate the races. . . . Members of the NAACP, certain politicians and other minority groups should know and should have it forcibly called to their attention that they are engaged in and carrying out the real program which was mapped out by the communists 25 or 30 years ago. . . . In every case which has gone to the U.S. Supreme Court where minority groups have been arraigned against the vast majority of the people, the decisions have been favorable to the minority. The great masses of the people have no civil rights which the Court feels they should protect."

Not all of the Southern attorneys general attacked the Supreme Court. Tom Gentry, who was attorney general of Arkansas in 1954 and whom Bennett succeeded, said, "Desegregation has been declared the law of the land, and we are going to abide by it." Malcolm Seawell of North Carolina in 1958 made a series of speeches that stirred strong and mixed reactions. Seawell said that defiance of the law "will never result in anything but irreparable damage to the state and its people." Then he added, "However distasteful may be the job assigned to me by law, I intend to take my stand on the side of law—and neither through public utterance nor in any other manner will seek to advise a people to take any other stand than that which I know under law is the only stand we may take. If this is politically inexpedient, dangerous or fatal, I'll just have to be content with what the future holds for me." In 1960 Seawell ran for governor and was defeated. Among his opponents was Dr. I. Beverly Lake, who as assistant attorney general had argued before the Supreme Court in 1955 and who championed segregation and states' rights; he lost, too. Bennett of Arkansas was another attorney general who ran unsuccessfully for governor—in 1960 against Orval Faubus.

The governor and the attorney general of a state almost always worked in harmony in their approach to school desegregation. The one glaring exception was in Alabama when George C. Wallace was governor and Richmond Flowers was attorney general. The conflict between them had been apparent during their pre-election campaigns, but it was boldly underscored when they were inaugurated on January 14, 1963. It was in his inaugural address that Governor Wallace had pledged "segregation now, segregation tomorrow, segregation forever." In his inaugural statement Flowers said that blanket defiance of federal court decisions could "only bring disgrace to our state, military law upon our people and political demagoguery to the leaders responsible." While promising "to do battle for our Southern tradition," he said that "the people of this state must discern and distinguish between a fighting chance and a chance to fight."

The first educational desegregation crisis in Wallace's administration came when Negroes were ordered admitted to the state university in June, 1963. Wallace called the order "unwarranted interference" by the federal courts "with the internal affairs of this state." He said, "I embody the sovereignty of this state and I will be present to bar the entrance of any Negro who attempts to enroll at the University of Alabama. This is legal resistance and legal defiance." Flowers took a different view, saying that "as attorney general, I do not question, challenge or pass judgment on the validity and wisdom" of the University Board of Trustees in deciding to admit Negroes to the university under court order. Then he added, "As dark as these days are, defiance that would provoke violence would only make days darker and upon those who resort to these measures must lie the blame if federal troops are used in the state of Alabama." A few months later, in a speech in Birmingham, Flowers called Wallace's "schoolhouse door" stand at the university "the greatest production since 'Cleopatra.'" He said that the governor's tactics had been to "stand up, stick up and back up." The attorney general continued to take verbal potshots at the governor when the occasion permitted.

By the end of the decade even Deep South attorneys general expressed their reconciliation to defeat in the courts. After the 1955 Supreme Court decision Eugene Cook of Georgia had pledged to fight it "so long as there is any legal recourse." In the spring of 1963 he said, "All the legal arguments . . . have been resolved." In Louisiana Attorney General Jack P. F. Gremillion said in 1962, "We will continue to be unsuccessful in the federal courts, in my opinion. I don't intend to give up my fight for segregation. But if we are going to continue to offer resistance, we must start looking at this from a new viewpoint." He suggested that "local committees from each of the races could co-operate in discussions to determine possible areas for getting along together." He expressed the belief that "such steps would go a long way toward eliminating the interference from outside agitators, including the federal government, and would keep them out of our affairs."

Occasionally the attorneys general made rulings of their own that had far-reaching effects. Among the more significant was one by Will Wilson of Texas. In the fall of 1960 he ruled that school systems desegregating to comply with court orders would not lose state funds. A 1957 Texas law required approval of desegregation in a local referendum as a condition of continued state aid. On January 1, 1963, his last day in office after an unsuccessful race for governor, Wilson stated his opinion that the referendum law was unconstitutional. Another ruling of some importance was that of Attorney General Gremillion of Louisiana that teachers in the state's public schools would not automatically lose their jobs if they belonged to the National Education Association. A 1956 state law provided for the dismissal of any teacher who advocated integration, and the NEA had adopted a resolution favoring desegregation, thus raising a question about the job status of Louisiana teachers who were members. While teachers were permitted to maintain their NEA membership, Gremillion held that "if a member of a group which advocates integration personally joins in any advocacy, then he would be subject to removal."

Attorneys for the Defense

The beleaguered attorneys general received much help from other white lawyers in their states. Some were legislators who served as chairmen or members of committees to assist in the drafting of bills. Some were official attorneys for school boards or for cities or counties. Others were in private practice. They joined forces to combat the common enemy—the NAACP—in the legislative halls and in the courtrooms.

One of the lawyers who was chairman of a legislative committee served throughout the decade. He was State Senator L. Marion Gressette of Calhoun County, South Carolina. The legislature relied heavily on his judgment about the best ways to preserve segregation. Senator Gressette expressed confidence that his state would abandon public education rather than admit Negroes to white schools. Soon after the 1955 decision he said: "We cannot find anywhere in the U.S. Constitution where the right to operate a school has been delegated to the United States government, nor can we find where it has been prohibited to the states. It therefore follows that this right was reserved for the states. This being true, the state cannot be forced to appropriate money for schools contrary to the public interest." In the summer of 1959, speaking before a meeting of leaders of the Citizens' Councils of South Carolina, which he endorsed, he said, "The people of South Carolina intend to operate their schools in accordance with their own wishes so long as they are allowed to do so. When this right is denied to them, they will close the public schools and seek some other method for the education of their children." In 1963, faced with the choice between closing its schools and desegregating them, South Carolina abandoned Senator Gressette's advice and took the latter course.

In Alabama State Senator Albert Boutwell, a Birmingham lawyer, headed the legislative study committee during the crucial early years of the decade. Later he was elected lieutenant governor, and then mayor of Birmingham.

State Senator Mosby G. Perrow, Jr., a Lynchburg attorney, headed one of the two committees that formulated Virginia's laws to deal with the Supreme Court decision. In 1964, after serving for twenty years as a state senator, Perrow was defeated in his bid for re-election; but he was elected chairman of the State Board of Education.

Florida had a nonlegislative committee composed entirely of lawyers. Governor LeRoy Collins in the spring of 1956 appointed an official eight-man commission to seek legal sanctions for the maintenance of segregated schools. The members were selected by the governor and Attorney General Richard W. Ervin on recommendations of state officials and legislative leaders. The chairman was L. L. Fabisinski of Pensacola, a retired circuit court judge. One of the members was Cody Fowler of Tampa, a past president of the American Bar Association. Collins later named Fowler chairman of a state committee on race relations.

Thomas J. Pearsall of Rocky Mount, a lawyer and former speaker of the State House of Representatives, headed North Carolina's committee. William T. Joyner of Raleigh, an attorney, was vice-chairman. In 1956, soon after the committee's recommendations had become law, Joyner, in a speech before the State Bar Association, said, "I think that some mixing is inevitable and must occur. . . . One of the nightmares which besets me on a restless night is that I am in a federal court attempting to defend a school board in its rejection of a transfer requested by a Negro student, when a showing is made that nowhere in all the state of North Carolina has a single Negro ever been admitted to any one of the more than 2,000 schools attended by white students. I ask that you as attorneys or prospective attorneys of school districts picture yourselves in such a situation in the fall of 1957 or in the fall of 1958. Would not your legal position be greatly strengthened, would it not be almost unassailable, if you could point to one or more instances in your county where a Negro has been admitted to a white school, or to instances in other counties where that has occurred?" The next year school boards in Charlotte, Greensboro and Winston-Salem voluntarily admitted the first Negroes to school with whites. Joyner and attorneys for school boards in North Carolina could sleep easier.

Throughout the South lawyers gave advice and counsel to school boards. Frequently their advice was to desegregate without waiting for a court order. If school board policy was to resist desegregation until it was forced by court order, the lawyers used their skill in taking advantage of the law's delays. When the time came to desegregate, the lawyers helped to devise plans that they hoped would meet with the approval of both the federal courts and local school patrons.

The advantage of voluntary desegregation was that it avoided court-imposed plans as well as the expense and turmoil of a court contest. But where white public opinion was adamantly opposed to desegregation, the day of reckoning could be postponed for years by skilled lawyers. Attorneys for the school boards of Clarendon County, South Carolina, and Prince Edward County, Virginia, showed what could be done. Both of these school systems were parties to the *Brown* cases and were affected directly and immediately by the Supreme Court decision. But, when the decade ended, neither had admitted a single Negro child to a school with white children. Robert McC. Figg, Jr., of Charleston and S. E. Rogers of Summerton were attorneys for Clarendon County.

The Clarendon case was relatively inactive during most of the decade, but the Prince Edward case was in the courts almost constantly, and the Virginia county was represented by a number of attorneys. Until his death in 1964 Collins Denny, Jr., of Richmond was chief counsel for the board. He was a staunch segregationist and outspoken critic of the Supreme Court. "Had I not been led into this fight because of my strong aversion to the Supreme Court's usurpation of legislative power, I, in all probability, would have gotten into it because of my racial views," he said.

Among the more colorful of the attorneys was Leander Perez of Plaquemines Parish, political boss in southeast Louisiana. He wrote most of the laws for the Joint Legislative Committee on Segregation while Senator William M. Rainach, not a lawyer, was its chairman. Perez's fiery tongue always was ready to sear the Supreme Court and its desegregation decisions. "The Court itself cannot expect the Southern states to comply with its unlawful communistic decree," he said. "The Court has plainly usurped powers it does not have under the Constitution. . . . The decision, based on direct repudiation of the Constitution . . . was nothing more or less than a fellow-traveler blank check to the pro-communist decrees for forced racial integration, regimentation and the ultimate amalgamation of the American people, to our certain destruction and, in the end, the surrender to the worldwide communist conspiracy."

In Georgia a number of private attorneys joined the fight to preserve segregation. Among them were Hugh Grant and Roy V. Harris of Augusta, Charles J. Bloch of Macon, Carter Pittman of Dalton and Newell Edenfield of Atlanta. These attorneys, and others, advised and represented the state and local governments. They also spread the word through their speeches and writing. Grant was a leader in the States' Rights Council of Georgia; with Perez he said that success of the NAACP in desegregating Southern schools would result in "amalgamation, mongrelization and the passing from the American scene of the Negro race." Harris was the publisher of the Augusta *Courier,* a principal organ for the dissemination of the segregationist view, and became president of the Citizens' Councils of America. Edenfield was president of the State Bar Association in 1960, when the University of Georgia and Atlanta public school cases were working toward their climax. He proposed that Georgia repeal all of its segregation laws. "I found," he said, "that while a school board may not win a suit if the state has no [segregation] laws, it is absolutely and utterly impossible to win if it does have such laws." Bloch and Pittman, in the Chatham County (Savannah) case, persuaded Federal District Judge Frank M. Scarlett that desegregation was harmful to white children for the same reasons that the Supreme Court held segregation harmful to Negro children. The Fifth Circuit Court of Appeals reversed Scarlett's decision and rebuked the judge.

Alabama went to great effort to develop the theme that the Negro is inherently inferior to the white and that it is injurious to a white child to attend the same school with Negroes. Ralph Smith, a Montgomery attorney who was designated by Governor John Patterson to represent him in all racial litigation, gave this explanation of the Alabama approach: "It was my feeling, and one shared by Governor Patterson, that we should explore every avenue in our efforts to preserve racial segregation. I think that many people in the South sincerely believe that the mental capacity of the Negro is inferior to that of a white, yet these same people think that science has proved to the contrary. Actually, scientific data supports the contention that the white race, intellectually, is superior to the Negro, and that is the point we seek to make with this study." The study to which Smith referred was done by Dr. Wesley C. George, an anatomist of the University of North Carolina.

In other Southern states the pattern was similar. The white

lawyers were united behind the political leaders in the defense of segregation. Rarely did a white lawyer in the South speak a good word for the Supreme Court. One who did was Irving Carlyle of Winston-Salem, North Carolina. He opposed the Pearsall plan in his state and in a speech in 1957 said, "The vituperation being hurled against the Court in this state and elsewhere does no harm to the Court or its members—it only undermines the respect of the people for the Court and for the law. Therefore, it only hurts the people." At the midwinter meeting in 1964 of the American Bar Association, the Lawyers' Committee for Civil Rights under Law reported that Negroes in many Southern communities could not obtain counsel "because a white lawyer involved in civil rights litigation representing Negroes faces loss of clients, impairment of social status, public criticism, and often threats of physical harm to himself and his family."

Attorneys for the Plaintiffs

Negro parents who had to get a court order to enroll their children in a desegregated school turned for counsel to the NAACP and to the NAACP Legal Defense and Educational Fund, Inc. The staff of lawyers in the New York office and a group of cooperating Negro attorneys in the Southern states were kept busy with school desegregation and other civil rights suits.

Thurgood Marshall headed the Legal Defense Fund from its origin in 1939 until 1961, when President Kennedy named him a judge of the Second Circuit Court of Appeals. Born in Baltimore in 1908, Marshall graduated *cum laude* in 1929 from Lincoln University at Oxford, Pennsylvania. He was first in his law class at Howard. In the term before Marshall's appointment to the bench, only the federal government had more cases before the Supreme Court than the NAACP. During his career as an NAACP attorney, Marshall appeared before the Supreme Court thirty-two times; he won all but three of his cases.

When Marshall went to work for the NAACP in 1938, he and Charles Houston comprised the legal staff, and their total budget was less than $10,000 a year; Marshall's salary was $2,600. By 1958 the budget had grown to $300,000 and Marshall's salary to $15,000. In his report for that year he said, "Now we're in for some real hard legal maneuvering in court, countermotions and back and forth. They're going to try to delay. We're going to try to push ahead. It's going to be more litigation now than ever before. We're going into a lot of fast play around second base. . . . I think that in many areas of the South they will find the price of delay is too costly. This litigation is very costly, and it costs them much more than it does us. Their lawyers get paid terrific fees. I mean, say $25,000 retainer and $500 a day." The NAACP estimated that it cost from $10,000 to $50,000 to take a single case to the Supreme Court.

Marshall's successor as director-counsel of the Legal Defense Fund was Jack Greenberg, a young white attorney. Greenberg had joined the fund staff shortly after his graduation in 1948 from Columbia University Law School as a Harlan Fiske Stone Scholar. As chief assistant counsel for the fund he had worked on the *School Segregation Cases* and was the only white lawyer to appear before the Supreme Court on behalf of the plaintiffs. When he became general counsel, the nine attorneys on the fund staff were responsible for more than four hundred pending civil rights cases involving more than two thousand persons.

Mrs. Constance Baker Motley stepped into Greenberg's old job. She had been a member of the staff since 1946 and was the principal trial attorney in many of the major public school and college desegregation cases. Among them was the James Meredith case in 1962. Soon after Meredith had been admitted to the University of Mississippi, Mrs. Motley commented, "Not a single public official of any description in Mississippi called for respect for law, let alone support of integration orders of federal courts. . . . Leading members of the bar supported the Governor of Mississippi. . . . Not even college degrees command the respect of the gentry of Ole Miss, for not once was I addressed in the courtroom by other than 'Constance' and the newspapers referred to me consistently as 'that Motley woman.' " In 1964 Mrs. Motley became the first Negro woman to be elected to the New York State Senate.

Several of the leading Negro attorneys in the school cases achieved prominence and recognition outside the NAACP. Three of them served, successively, as dean of the Howard Law School— James M. Nabrit, Jr., Spottswood Robinson III and Clarence C. Ferguson, Jr. Nabrit became president of Howard in 1960. President Kennedy appointed Robinson to the United States Commission on Civil Rights and later named him a United States district judge for the District of Columbia. Ferguson served as general counsel to the Civil Rights Commission.

The staff lawyers of the Legal Defense Fund worked closely with "cooperating attorneys." Thurgood Marshall in 1959 put the number of these lawyers at 50; in 1964 Jack Greenberg said there were 120. The cooperating attorneys sometimes were necessary to meet the requirements of federal judges who insisted that plaintiffs be represented by local counsel. U.S. District Judge C. C. Wyche of South Carolina expressed this view in remarks addressed to Matthew J. Perry of Columbia, one of the attorneys for Harvey Gantt in his successful effort to enter Clemson College. "I know you and you are trustworthy," Judge Wyche said to Perry. "But I don't know about any foreign lawyers. The examiners should be lawyers within the jurisdiction of this court." The foreign lawyers to whom the judge referred were Greenberg, Mrs. Motley and Derrick Bell, Jr., a trio who appeared together in many Southern courtrooms.

To increase the number of attorneys in civil rights practice, Greenberg in 1963 inaugurated an internship program. Under it young lawyers were to serve six months to a year on the New York staff before going to a community in the South. The first intern, Julius LeVonne Chambers, graduated from the University of North Carolina Law School, where he had been editor of the *Law Review*.

In May of 1964 the Legal Defense Fund held a special convocation in New York to observe its own twenty-fifth anniversary and the tenth anniversary of the *Brown* decision. On that occasion Greenberg announced that the budget for the fund would be $1,500,000 a year in 1964 and 1965 and $2,000,000 in 1966. The full-time staff of attorneys in New York was being increased to twenty, he said. Mrs. Motley served notice that new suits would be filed to speed up desegregation that already had started, to eliminate dual attendance zones and to require the assignment of teachers on a nonracial basis. At the time of the convocation the fund had seventy-six public school cases pending in thirteen states.

The U.S. Attorneys General

Until passage of the Civil Rights Act of 1964, the attorney general of the United States lacked clear statutory authority to initiate school desegregation suits. The Department of Justice did intervene occasionally as a friend of the court. The attorney general proposed and drafted civil rights legislation. And next to the President he was the administration's principal spokesman on civil rights. Each of the three men who served as attorney general during the decade— Herbert Brownell, Jr.. William P. Rogers, Jr., and Robert F. Kennedy—supported the Supreme Court decision in the *Brown* cases and defended the justices against their critics.

As attorney general under Eisenhower in 1954 Brownell filed a brief on the questions the Supreme Court posed for reargument. "Racial segregation in public schools is unconstitutional," he said, "and will have to be terminated as quickly as possible, regardless of how much it may be favored by some people in the community. There can be no 'local option' on that question." The brief also said, "The responsibility for achieving compliance with the Supreme Court's decision in these cases does not rest on the Judiciary alone. Every officer and agency of the Government, Federal, State and local, is likewise charged with the duty of enforcing the Constitution and the rights guaranteed under it. And ultimately it is the obligation of every citizen to respect and abide by the law, once it is authoritatively declared."

In the spring of 1956 Brownell addressed the National Association of State Attorneys General, meeting in Phoenix, Arizona. He called for solid support of the Supreme Court and said that "attacks upon any branch of the government sooner or later breed disrespect for every other branch." At this meeting Brownell made a survey for President Eisenhower among Southern delegates on the prospect for implementation of the school decision. He reported to the President that large sections of the South would not accept racially mixed schools under any circumstances for the foreseeable future.

A year later, speaking at Columbia University Law School, Brownell returned to the subject of his remarks to the state attorneys general. "Any attempt to wantonly discredit the Supreme Court is a disservice to freedom itself," he said. "Criticism should be fair, responsible and informed if it is to be respected. It should not be an invitation to defy the rulings of the Court." To the contention that the Constitution does not mention education, Brownell replied, "This cannot be denied. For that matter the Constitution does not refer to agriculture. Does that mean that the Congress may not provide price supports for cotton, soybeans or wheat? Obviously not." As to the Court's overruling previous decisions, he said, "The Court adjusts, qualifies, extends, and overrules federal precedents and in doing so, tends to stabilize and reconcile the counteracting social, economic, and other forces that erupt in each new era."

Brownell was the chief adviser to President Eisenhower in the Little Rock episode of 1957. After federal troops had been used to enforce the Court order to desegregate Central High School, Brownell told the Connecticut State Bar Association that obedience to Supreme Court decisions "is the sturdy foundation upon which our country's stability, success and freedom have long rested." Upon Brownell's resignation to return to private law practice, Deputy Attorney General William P. Rogers, Jr., succeeded him.

Rogers was cautious in his initial approach to school desegregation and other civil rights questions. He called for a "cooling off period" and said that the Justice Department had "a duty to exercise caution in what we say and not to aggravate the situation." But in the summer of 1958 he took a different tack. His speech to the American Bar Association was regarded as the strongest statement on school segregation made to that date by any spokesman for the Eisenhower administration. He began by saying that the Supreme Court decision in the *Brown* cases was "the law of the land for today, tomorrow and I am convinced for the future—for all regions and for all people." Granting that the Court had allowed time for compliance, he added, "The crux of the matter then is one of intention. The problems are difficult at best, but they become hazardous if the underlying intent of those who are opposed to the decision of the Court—particularly those in official positions who are opposed to the decision—is one of defiance. Time to work out constructive measures in an honest effort to comply is one thing; time used as a cloak to achieve complete defiance of the law of the land is quite another."

In a later speech, the text of which President Eisenhower is known to have approved, Rogers expanded on this theme. "Individuals may not determine for themselves when they will obey the decrees of the courts and when they will ignore them," he said. The proper way to overcome a constitutional decision, he added, is "by the orderly process of constitutional amendment," not by "defiance or lawlessness." Noting that both federal and state officials take an oath to support the Constitution, he continued, "The duty embraced by the oath of office requires support of the Constitution not as each individual officer, Federal or State, believes it should or might be interpreted, but as it is interpreted by our courts."

With the inauguration of President Kennedy in 1961, his brother, Robert F. Kennedy, became attorney general. The policy of the new administration at first was to speak softly on the school segregation issue. In a "progress report" to the President on civil right activities during his first year in office, the attorney general said his belief had been strengthened that "Americans are law-abiding people who wish to live by the law, do not want to circumvent court decisions, and are opposed to actions which will result in violence." He said that the Justice Department had "worked informally" throughout the summer with state and local officials "to help bring about peaceful school desegregation." He emphasized that the basic policy of his department was "to seek effective guarantees and action from local officials and civic leaders voluntarily and without court action" and added that this was done "quietly and without publicity."

The next year brought the crisis at the University of Mississippi. In September, shortly before the rioting began in Oxford, Attorney

General Kennedy, speaking by telephone, told the members of the American Bar Association meeting in San Francisco, "One of my great disappointments in our present efforts to deal with the situation in Mississippi, as lawyers, has been the absence of any expression of support from the many distinguished lawyers of the state. Whether they agree or not, they still have their obligations as lawyers."

Kennedy returned to this theme, and broadened it, in a speech to the Missouri Bar Association a year later. "To a far greater extent than most Americans realize," he said, "the crisis in civil rights reflects a crisis in the legal profession—in the whole judicial system on which our concept of justice depends." Speaking of lawyers and public officials who "obstruct the enforcement of laws and court orders," he added: "With regard to the *Brown* decision, I think we can all agree that the probability of its permanence is so overwhelming as to counsel the abandonment of anyone's hope for the contrary. The decision was, after all, a unanimous one. Since 1954 there have been six vacancies in the Supreme Court, which means that by now a total of 15 Justices have endorsed it. . . . To suggest, at this point in history, that there is any real likelihood of the *Brown* decision's being reversed is irresponsible to the point of absurdity. No lawyer would advise a private client to contest the validity of a decision as solidly established and as often reiterated as this one; he would not want to victimize his client by raising frivolous questions. Yet a client is being victimized every time this frivolous question is raised today— and the client is the American public itself."

The "crisis in the legal profession"to which Attorney General Kennedy referred brought further comment from Burke Marshall, assistant attorney general in charge of the Civil Rights Division of the Justice Department. Speaking of the events at the University of Mississippi, he said that lawyers, particularly those in the South, "could have done great service through their influence and potential effect on public opinion simply by speaking out in favor of obedience to the law." Deputy Attorney General Nicholas deB. Katzenbach condemned the "deafening silence" of the nation's lawyers, North and South, in the wake of the Supreme Court's school desegregation decision, and expressed the opinion that by their silence the lawyers had contributed to the violence at Ole Miss.

The Bar Associations

When Attorney General Rogers made his speech to the American Bar Association in 1958, he received a standing ovation. Charles S. Rhyne of Washington, the president, praised Rogers for his "courage and leadership" and said to him, "We of the bar, who have provided leadership in this country since time immemorial, will accept your challenge to provide leadership on this tremendously important matter." While Rhyne and other ABA presidents expressed their personal views, supporting and opposing the Supreme Court decision, the association avoided the issue. Chief Justice Earl Warren resigned from the ABA in 1958. It was widely speculated that he did so to protest the organization's failure publicly to advocate obedience to the law. Warren neither confirmed nor denied the reports.

Writing in the Atlanta *Constitution* in October, 1962, Ralph McGill said, "Where the bar associations of the South were silent, individual attorneys, described glowingly as 'constitutional authorities,' were publicly and slanderously denouncing the federal judiciary and assuring a troubled and indecisive public that the United States Supreme Court's school decision was not legal, did not have the force of law and was communistically inspired. That this stoked the fires of violence is unquestioned."

Although no Southern white bar associations supported the Supreme Court school decision, some criticized it. The Mississippi Bar Association by unanimous vote in 1955 endorsed a speech by Hugh G. Wall in which he said, "It is a strange coincidence, indeed, that following the public doctrine of the communists, we find the Supreme Court of the United States outlawing segregation." The Alabama Bar Association in 1957 adopted a resolution denouncing the Court; only one of 450 members present voted against it. That same year the State Bar of Texas adopted three resolutions critical of the Supreme Court. One of them, offered by U.S. District Judge

T. Whitfield Davidson, urged that appointments to the Court be restricted to attorneys of at least ten years experience as judges or practicing lawyers.

Occasionally groups of lawyers, official and unofficial, defended the Court. In 1956 a group of one hundred lawyers, including a number from the South, issued a statement deploring the attacks on the Court "precipitated by the school segregation decision." The statement said that "these attacks have been so reckless in their abuse, so heedless of the value of judicial review and so dangerous in fomenting disrespect for our highest law that they deserve to be repudiated by the legal profession and by every thoughtful citizen."

After the rioting at Ole Miss in 1962, a group of fifty-seven professors and deans of law schools, including four in the South, sent a message of support to President Kennedy. They said, "The real issue . . . is whether the rule of law which our profession and our country are striving to promote among all nations, may be flouted and dishonored at home. It is time for the leaders of the bar in every part of the country, and of every political persuasion, to make it plain that the only alternatives are anarchy or law."

The following summer 129 deans and professors at 25 Southern law schools issued a statement on "Law and Race Relations." Regarding the doctrine of interposition they said, "It is a backward doctrine that is as out of date as feudalism." Pointing to the Constitution, they commented, "Observe that the Constitution and the federal laws are made the 'supreme Law of the Land.' . . . Nearly 150 years ago it was held, through Chief Justice Marshall, that the Supreme Court of the United States, not a State Supreme Court, is the final interpreter of national law. . . . The official who would deny controlling effect to our national law violates his oath of office as well as our fundamental law."

In September, 1963, a group of fifty-three Birmingham lawyers issued a statement saying "whether we agree or disagree with the result in any case, the court's decision is the law and must be obeyed." That same month the executive committee of President Kennedy's Lawyers' Committee on Civil Rights Under Law said of Governor George C. Wallace, "In his latest efforts to interfere with the integration of public schools in Alabama, Governor Wallace has again sought to substitute the rule of force for the rule of law. As lawyers we feel compelled to speak out against his actions."

The *Brown* decision, Justice Robert Jackson said in 1954, opened the way for "a generation of litigation." Ten years later, after passage of the Civil Rights Act of 1964, Assistant Attorney General Burke Marshall said the new law created "a legal situation which hopefully makes the nation's racial problems soluble in the courts over the next two generations." The prospect was that lawyers would continue to be occupied with school desegregation and a broad range of civil rights questions.

8.
The Judges

Southerners who favored segregated schools reacted to the 1955 *Brown* decision like Br'er Rabbit being tossed into the briar patch. The Supreme Court gave to the federal district judges, "because of their proximity to local conditions," the initial responsibility for implementing its 1954 ruling against compulsory segregation in the public schools.

Tom J. Tubb, an attorney of West Point, Mississippi, hailed the second decision as "a very definite victory for the South." "We couldn't ask for anything better than to have our local, native Mississippi federal district judges consider suits in good faith and act accordingly in the 'as soon as feasible' element," he exulted. "Our local judges know the local situation and it may be 100 years before it's feasible." Throughout the South others expressed a similar point of view.

Judge John R. Brown of the Court of Appeals for the Fifth Circuit suggested the unjudicial influences on judicial decisions when he observed that, ". . . lifetime tenure insulates judges from anxiety over worldly cares . . . but it does not protect them from the unconscious urge for the approbation of their fellow man, and fellow man most often means those of like interests and backgrounds, business and professional experiences and predilections and even prejudice."

Attitudes of Southern Judges

The expressed attitudes of Southern federal judges toward the *Brown* decision ranged from strong disapproval to equally strong approval. Some judges voiced neither approval nor disapproval, but obviously were reluctant to order desegregation. Many of the men on the bench followed the guidelines given them by the Supreme Court without revealing their personal feelings.

Among the outspoken judges, those who disagreed with the Supreme Court were most numerous. Immediately after the 1955 decision Judge George Bell Timmerman of South Carolina said that "the Court rested its opinion in the *Brown* case almost exclusively upon sociological and psychological factors." Judges William H. Atwell and T. Whitfield Davidson presided over the trial court in the Dallas, Texas, case. Both were in their eighties, and they held similar views. "My personal feeling about segregation is that it is neither immoral nor unconstitutional," Judge Atwell said. Judge Davidson remarked from the bench, "The Supreme Court has placed your state, your country and your schools . . . over a barrel. . . . The white man has a right to maintain his racial integrity, and it can't be done so easily in integrated schools." In ordering desegregation of the East Baton Rouge, Louisiana, schools, Judge E. Gordon West said, "I personally regard the 1954 holding of the United States Supreme Court in the now-famous *Brown* case as one of the truly regrettable decisions of all times. Its substitution of so-called 'sociological principles' for sound legal reasoning was almost unbelievable. As far as I can determine, its only real accomplishment to date has been to bring discontent and chaos to many previously peaceful communities, without bringing any real attendant benefits to anyone."

Judge Sidney C. Mize heard the first college and public school desegregation cases in Mississippi. In the James Meredith case he found "as a fact" that the University of Mississippi was "not a racially segregated institution." To this finding the Fifth Circuit Court of Appeals retorted, "This about-face in policy, news of which may startle some people in Mississippi, could have been accomplished only by telepathic communication among the University's administrators. . . ." Before Meredith's admission, an unprecedented situation developed on the Fifth Circuit Court. Circuit Judge Ben F. Cameron three times issued decrees staying action on Appeals Court orders that the University of Mississippi be desegregated. His Fifth Circuit Court associates severely reprimanded Judge Cameron, setting aside his stay orders as "unauthorized, erroneous and improvident." Undaunted, Judge Cameron charged that his colleagues used "unorthodox procedures" in handling segregation cases "in order to accomplish a desired result." He accused Chief Judge Elbert P. Tuttle of "gerrymandering" panels of judges to hear Mississippi cases. All of the other eight Fifth Circuit judges joined in a formal reply to Judge Cameron. "The court believes that in no given case has there been a conscious assignment for the purpose of accomplishing a desired result," they said. His rebuff in the Meredith case did not deter Judge Mize from dismissing the first public suits in Mississippi on the grounds that none of the Negro plaintiffs had been denied any rights. Under the mandate of the Appeals Court, he ordered desegregation to begin in the fall of 1964, but in doing so he said, "In the opinion of this Court, the facts in this case point up a most serious situation, and, indeed, 'cry out' for a reappraisal and complete reconsideration of the findings and conclusions of the United States Supreme Court in the *Brown* decision. . . ."

A few of the Southern district judges were emphatic in their approval of the *Brown* decision. One was Judge J. Skelly Wright of New Orleans, who expressed his views about the Supreme Court at a testimonial dinner in his honor following his appointment in 1962 to the Court of Appeals for the District of Columbia. "In the present great struggle between the East and the West for the minds of men, 90 per cent of the people of the world are colored," he said. "If we're going to make any progress with that 90 per cent we had better practice what we preach. . . . The Supreme Court is more than a law court—it is a policy court, or, if you will, a political court. It is an instrument of government, and while most judges have the habit, through long years of precedent, of looking backward, the Supreme Court must look forward through a knowledge of life, of people, of sociology, of psychology. The Supreme Court is the final interpreter of the Constitution, a living document. It should not be interpreted with reference to the time in which it was written but rather in reference to the present, or, better still, the future."

In handing down decisions that they knew were unpopular, judges sometimes defended their positions. When Judge H. Hobart Grooms ordered the admission of Autherine Lucy to the University of Alabama in 1956, he remarked in court, "There are some people who believe this court should carve out a province, man the battlements and defy the U.S. Supreme Court. This court does not have that prerogative." Judge Frank A. Hooper, in ordering desegregation of Atlanta schools, said, "For this court to declare as law that which is not law would not only be a futile gesture, but a great disservice to our people. It would add to the confusion already existing in the public mind, and it would build up hopes destined to be destroyed on appeal, and it would delay the efforts now being made by our people to find the best solution possible for a critical and urgent problem."

Many of the Southern judges were appointees of President John F. Kennedy. At a news conference a few months before his assassination, he was asked to comment on charges that he had named "segregationist judges." The President replied: "I think that some of the judges may not have ruled as I would have ruled in their cases. In those cases, there is always a possibility for an appeal. On the whole, I believe—and this is not true just of this administration but of the previous administration—I think the men that have been appointed to judgeships in the South, sharing, perhaps, as they do, the general outlook of the South, have done a remarkable job in fulfilling their oath of office."

Public Opinion and the Law

"Judges must speak for the will of the people," Judge John E. Miller of Arkansas said in addressing the Sebastian County Bar Association at Fort Smith. "Our greatest problem is the inclination of some of the appellate courts of the land to arrogate unto themselves the power to declare for us certain standards contrary to the mores and conditions which have existed for centuries in this country."

The Supreme Court, in returning the school cases to the lower courts, declared that "it should go without saying that the vitality of these constitutional principles cannot be allowed to yield simply because of disagreement with them." Many of the federal judges in the Southern states were caught in the conflict between local public opinion and the *Brown* decision.

Public opinion was a major issue in the Hoxie, Arkansas, case, filed in the fall of 1955 before Judge Thomas C. Trimble. The Hoxie school board asked the court to enjoin the activities of persons who sought to prevent desegregation. Judge Trimble enjoined the defendants from "interfering with the free operation of schools . . . by acts of trespass, boycott or picketing . . ." or "in any other manner." Upholding Judge Trimble, the Court of Appeals for the Eighth Circuit said that the school board had a right "to be free from direct interference in the performance" of its duty.

Soon after Judge Trimble's order, Judge Joe Estes dismissed a suit seeking desegregation of the Mansfield, Texas, schools on the grounds that it was "impractical and likely to bring about emotional reactions." The Court of Appeals for the Fifth Circuit reversed Judge Estes's ruling and held that the plaintiffs were entitled to a declaration of their right to attend public school without regard to their race and "uninfluenced by private and public opinion as to the desirability of desegregation in the community." The Supreme Court upheld the Court of Appeals.

In the early stages of the New Orleans case, a three-judge court came to grips with the role of public opinion. Writing for the court, Judge J. Skelly Wright said, "The problem of changing a people's mores, particularly those with an emotional overlay, is not to be taken lightly. It is a problem which will require the utmost patience, understanding, generosity and forbearance from all of us, of whatever race. But the magnitude of the problem may not nullify the principle. And that principle is that we are, all of us, freeborn Americans, with a right to make our way, unfettered by sanctions imposed by man because of the work of God." More than three years later, after the violence in Little Rock, New Orleans still had not begun to desegregate its schools. In ordering the school board to prepare a plan of desegregation Judge Wright said, "The choice as to whether New Orleans will become another Little Rock is not the school board's alone. Our news media, our public and private leaders, our churchmen and the public generally will share the responsibility of that decision. It is only with their help, their intelligent and active support, that the board will be able, without civic excitement, to comply with its duty under the law."

In Little Rock the question put to the courts was not mere "interference" or "disagreement," but violence to prevent compliance with a court order. Governor Faubus said that his purpose in using the Arkansas National Guard to block the admission of Negroes to Central High School was to avoid violence. To this the Eighth Circuit Court of Appeals rejoined, "A rule which would permit an official whose duty it is to enforce the law to disregard the very law which it was his duty to enforce, in order to pacify a mob or suppress an insurrection, would deprive all citizens of any security in the enjoyment of their life, liberty or property. . . . Use of troops or police for such purposes would breed violence. It would constitute an assurance to those who resort to violence to obtain their ends that if they gathered in sufficient numbers to constitute a menace to life, forces of law would not only not oppose them but would actually assist them in accomplishing their objective."

A few weeks after this ruling by the Appeals Court, District Judge J. Harry Lemley granted the request of the Little Rock school board for a two and one-half year moratorium in its desegregation plan. In his opinion Judge Lemley commented that "on account of the popular opposition to integration, the year was marked by repeated incidents of more or less serious violence directed against the Negro students and their property. . . . The personal and immediate interest of the Negro students affected must yield temporarily to the larger interest of both races. . . . The granting of the board's petition does not, in our estimation, constitute a yielding to unlawful force or violence, but is simply an exercise of our equitable discretion and good judgment so as to allow a breathing spell in Little Rock, while at the same time preserving educational standards at Central High School. . . . It is one thing to say that the school board must make a start in the direction of integration without regard to public feelings on the subject . . .; but it is quite another thing to say that when a school board has had experiences with its plan which the Little Rock board has had, and when, after observing the results of that plan in operation, it comes into federal court seeking not to abandon or to lay it aside indefinitely, but merely a moratorium, the court must close its eyes and ears to the practical solution with which such board is confronted. Such a judicial attitude would be most unrealistic. . . ."

The Appeals Court quickly reversed Judge Lemley. Circuit Judge Marion C. Matthes of St. Louis, speaking for the Court, wrote: ". . . A person may not be denied enforcement of rights to which he is entitled under the constitution of the United States because of action taken or threatened in defiance of such rights. . . . An affirmance of 'temporary delay' in Little Rock would amount to an open invitation to elements in other districts to overtly act out public opposition through violent and unlawful means. . . . We say the time has not yet come in these United States when an order of a federal court must be whittled away, watered down, or shamefully withdrawn in the face of violent and unlawful acts of individual citizens in opposition thereto."

The U.S. Supreme Court upheld the Court of Appeals. In its first major opinion on school desegregation since the *Brown* decision, the Supreme Court said: "The constitutional rights of respondents are not to be sacrificed or yielded to the violence and disorder which have followed upon the action of the governor and legislature. . . . Thus law and order are not there to be preserved by depriving the Negro children of their constitutional rights. . . . In short, the constitutional rights of children not to be discriminated against in school admission on grounds of race or color declared by this court in the *Brown* case can neither be nullified openly or directly by state legislators or state executives or judicial officers, nor nullified indirectly by them through evasive schemes for segregation whether attempted 'ingeniously or ingenuously.' . . ."

Some states recognized the role of public opinion in laws providing for a vote of the people as a prelude to desegregation. A 1957 Texas law denied state funds to any school district that desegregated without first obtaining approval in a referendum. Four days after the law became effective the Court of Appeals for the Fifth Circuit, in ruling that Dallas must desegregate its schools "with all deliberate speed" said that the new statute "cannot operate to relieve the members of this Court of their sworn duty to support the Constitution of the United States, the same duty which rests upon the members of the several state legislatures and all executive and judicial officers of the several states." Four years later the Appeals Court again ruled that Dallas must desegregate, this time setting September, 1961, as the date for starting. The Court said that "the holding of an election . . . should not be made a condition of a plan of desegregation. It goes without saying that recognition and enforcement of constitutional rights cannot be made contingent upon the results of any election." A Louisiana law provided for local option to close schools by popular vote. A three-judge federal court, in striking down the law, said, ". . . the requirement of a popular referendum on the question of closure adds nothing to the challenged statute. One of the purposes of the Constitution of the United States was to protect minorities from the occasional tyranny of majorities. No plebiscite can legalize unjust discrimination. . . ."

The Meaning of Brown

When in 1954 the Supreme Court established the legal principle that "in the field of education the doctrine of 'separate but equal' has no place," it did not spell out what would be required to comply with its decision. In the second *Brown* decision, a year later, the Court assigned to the lower federal courts the job of giving precise meaning to the broad generality of the first.

The early lower court decisions dealt as much with what *Brown* did not require as with what it did. The opinion written in 1955 by Fourth Circuit Court Judge John J. Parker in the Clarendon County, South Carolina, case, after it was remanded to the lower court, was frequently cited in subsequent decisions. Judge Parker said: "... it is important that we point out exactly what the Supreme Court has decided and what it has not decided in this case. It has not decided that the federal courts are to take over or regulate the public schools of the states. It has not decided that the states must mix persons of different races in the schools or must require them to attend schools or must deprive them of the right of choosing the schools they attend. What it has decided, and all that it has decided, is that a state may not deny to any person on account of race the right to attend any school that it maintains. This, under the decision of the Supreme Court, the state may not do directly or indirectly; but if the schools which it maintains are open to children of all races, no violation of the Constitution is involved even though the children of different races voluntarily attend different schools, as they attend different churches. Nothing in the Constitution or in the decision of the Supreme Court takes away from the people freedom to choose the schools they attend. The Constitution, in other words, does not require integration. It merely forbids discrimination. It does not forbid such segregation as occurs as the result of voluntary action. It merely forbids the use of governmental power to enforce segregation. The Fourteenth Amendment is a limitation upon the exercise of power by the state or state agencies, not a limitation upon the freedom of individuals."

Judge Albert V. Bryan observed in the Arlington County, Virginia, case that "the ruling of the Supreme Court . . may well not necessitate such extensive changes in the school system as some anticipate." Judge Johnson J. Hayes, in a North Carolina case, commented that "federal judges are ill-prepared to sit in every school squabble" and added that the Supreme Court "did not require a federal judge to become a substitute for local school boards." In his opinion in the Dade County, Florida, case, Judge Emett C. Choate said, "It is not for the courts to make the policy of the school boards, but to consider the adequacy of any plan the defendant may propose to meet these problems and to effectuate a transition to a racially nondiscriminatory school system."

"A Prompt and Reasonable Start"

In its 1955 decision the Supreme Court directed the lower courts to "require that the defendants make a prompt and reasonable start toward full compliance with our May 17, 1954, ruling." The decision referred specifically to the defendants in the five cases before the Supreme Court, but the principle was intended to apply to other cases. What happened in the five cases suggests the flexibility with which the decision was implemented. Three of the defendant school boards complied immediately. The other two did not, and their school systems remained segregated past the end of the decade.

Most school districts in the border states complied promptly, and usually voluntarily, with the desegregation decision. In the Southern states few school districts acted "promptly" to desegregate, even after they were taken to court. Delay was the first line of defense in the fight against desegregation. Many Southern school boards and their attorneys, and even some federal judges, took full advantage of the law's delays.

The Prince Edward County case offers an extreme example of delay despite intensely active court action. The case was filed in 1951 and still was in the courts in 1964. After the Supreme Court decision of 1955, a three-judge court ordered desegregation of the schools "with all deliberate speed" but authorized delay for making arrangements. In early 1957 District Judge Sterling Hutcheson declined to set a deadline for the start of desegregation. In his opinion he said, "I believe the problems to be capable of solution but they will require patience, time and a sympathetic understanding. . . . It would be unwise to attempt to force a change of the system until the entire situation can be considered and adjustments gradually brought about. . . ."

The Court of Appeals for the Fourth Circuit then ordered

Judge Hutcheson to fix a starting date "without further delay." Judge Hutcheson set "the beginning of the school year of 1965" and repeated his view that "over-hasty action necessitating a backward step is less conducive to proper law enforcement than action taken after carefully considered delay." The appellate court in May of 1959 directed Judge Hutcheson to order qualified Negro students admitted to the white high school in September. Rather than comply with this order, the county closed its public schools. The litigation continued. When the case was before the Fourth Circuit Court in the summer of 1963, Judge J. Spencer Bell expressed the view that "the defendants closed the schools solely in order to frustrate the orders of the federal courts that the schools be desegregated. . . . It is tragic that since 1959 the [Negro] children of Prince Edward County have gone without formal education. Here is a truly shocking example of the law's delays."

District and appeals court judges also clashed sharply about delay of desegregation in the Dallas, Texas, case. The case was filed in 1955, and District Judge Atwell dismissed it. The Court of Appeals ordered the district court "to afford the parties a full hearing on the issues." Again Judge Atwell dismissed the suit "in order that the school board may have ample time, as it appears to be doing, to work out this problem." In his opinion Judge Atwell said: "We have civil rights for all people under the national Constitution, and I might suggest that if there are civil rights, there also are civil wrongs. It seems to me, in view of the facts, that the white schools are hardly sufficient to hold the present number of white students; that it would be unthinkably and unbearably wrong to require the white students to get out so that the colored students could come in. That would be the result of integration here."

The litigation continued to seesaw between the district and appeals courts. Judge Davidson, who took over the case from Judge Atwell, in the summer of 1959 again refused to "name any date or issue any order" and held that the school board had "made a prompt and reasonable start toward good faith compliance at the earliest practicable date with the May 17, 1954, ruling of the Supreme Court." The patience of the Court of Appeals wore thin. At a hearing in the spring of 1960, Chief Judge Richard T. Rives of the Court of Appeals told an attorney for the school board, "Words without deeds are not enough. We've been engaging in legal literature for five years without action. Do you think that a mere study over a period of five years is a prompt and reasonable start as ordered by the Supreme Court?" The Court of Appeals directed Judge Davidson to order that desegregation of Dallas schools start in September, 1961, and he complied with this mandate.

In the Mansfield, Texas, case, Judge Estes found in 1955 that the "rural school board composed primarily of farmers" was "struggling with breaking the tradition of generations; opening their meetings with prayer for solution; studying articles in magazines and papers; holding numerous meetings; passing resolutions and appointing a committee to work on a plan for integration...." He held that "This school board has shown that it is making a good faith effort toward integration and should have a reasonable length of time to solve its problems and end segregation...." At the end of the decade the Mansfield schools still were segregated.

In its 1955 decision the Supreme Court recognized that "school authorities have the primary responsibility for elucidating, assessing and solving" the problems of implementing desegregation. The Chattanooga, Tennessee, school board in 1955 adopted a program of "elucidation" to prepare the community for desegregation. When, in 1960, Negroes filed a suit for desegregation, the school board asked Judge Leslie R. Darr to enter a decree approving its "plan for elucidation, thereby giving the necessary time in which to educate, reconcile and bring about acceptance of a plan of desegregation for the schools." Judge Darr responded, "This is simply a request for postponement of the trial." Observing that "getting people ready is not a plan," he ordered the school board to present a plan of desegregation. In arguing his case before the Court of Appeals for the Fifth Circuit, Raymond B. Witt, Jr., attorney for the school board, said that the board had held more than three hundred meetings in its "elucidation program." He said that delay in desegregation had resulted from the need "to change the attitude of the community" and that "our main responsibility is to design a plan to continue support for public education as well as support for the Supreme Court decision." Agreeing with Judge Darr that "elucidation" by itself was not compliance with the *Brown* decision, the Court of Appeals returned the case to the district court to work out a plan of desegregation. The plan took effect in 1962.

In the spring of 1963 the Supreme Court handed down a unanimous decision in a public parks case from Memphis, Tennessee. Justice Arthur J. Goldberg wrote the opinion, in which he commented on delay in complying with the *Brown* decision. He wrote: ". . . It is now more than nine years since this Court held in the first *Brown* decision . . . that racial segregation in state public schools violates the Equal Protection Clause of the Fourteenth Amendment. . . . *Brown* never contemplated that the concept of 'deliberate speed' would countenance indefinite delay in elimination of racial barriers in schools. . . . It must be recognized that even the delay countenanced by *Brown* was a necessary, albeit significant, adaptation of the usual principle that any deprivation of constitutional rights calls for prompt rectification. The rights here asserted are, like all such rights, *present* rights; they are not merely hopes to some *future* enjoyment of some formalistic constitutional promise. The basic guarantees of our Constitution are warrants for the here and now and, unless there is an overwhelmingly compelling reason, they are to be promptly fulfilled. . . ."

With a few exceptions, the question of delay in making "a prompt and reasonable start" toward desegregation was settled with the Supreme Court's pronouncement in the Memphis parks case. Time for delay had run out for school boards taken to court. But school boards choosing to delay until forced to act still could wait, insofar as court implementation of the *Brown* decision was concerned. No school board was compelled to desegregate its schools until it was placed under specific court order. The Civil Rights Act of 1964 promised to change that situation. The act provided for withholding federal funds from segregated schools, and the executive branch of the government gave evidence of its intent to enforce the law.

"With All Deliberate Speed"

In the second *Brown* decision the Supreme Court said, "Once
. . . a start has been made, the courts may find that additional time
is necessary to carry out the ruling in an effective manner. The burden rests upon the defendants to establish that such time is necessary in the public interest and is consistent with good faith compliance at the earliest practicable date." The Court remanded the
cases "to the District Courts to take such proceedings and enter such
orders and decrees consistent with this opinion as are necessary and
proper to admit to public schools on a racially nondiscriminatory
basis with all deliberate speed. . . ."

The pace of desegregation was a key question in most of the
cases filed in the district courts. The answer depended upon the
district judge's interpretation of the requirements of *Brown* in the
light of local circumstances. In some instances judges approved
"stairstep" plans that extended the process over periods as long as
twelve years. In other cases the judges required immediate, complete
desegregation of entire school systems. Toward the end of the decade, judges tended to order acceleration of plans they earlier had
approved.

In the Little Rock case the district court in the spring of 1957
approved a plan of desegregation to take effect in three steps over
a period of six years. On appeal the Negro plaintiffs sought total,
immediate desegregation. The Court of Appeals for the Eighth Circuit upheld the three-phase plan. Writing the opinion for the Court,
Judge Charles J. Vogel said, "A reasonable amount of time to effect
complete integration in the schools of Little Rock, Arkansas, may be
unreasonable in St. Louis, Missouri, or Washington, D.C. The
schools of Little Rock have been on a completely segregated basis
since their creation in 1870. That fact, plus local problems . . . may
make the situation at Little Rock, Arkansas, a problem that is extremely different from that in many other places."

At approximately the same time that the Eighth Circuit Court was handing down its decision in the Little Rock case, District Judge William E. Miller approved the plan of the Nashville, Tennessee, school board for desegregation of the first grade in the fall of 1957. "It is the considered opinion of the school authorities, after mature deliberation," Judge Miller said in his opinion, "that a change from a system of segregated schools should be upon a gradual or step-by-step basis. They have concluded that an abrupt change in all of the city schools would be inconsistent with the public interest and with the efficient functioning of the school system itself. They believe that the soundest approach to the problem is to begin with desegregation in the first grade and to make plans for the future based upon the experience thus gained. . . . The Nashville plan . . . merely postpones complete desegregation to provide time for the solution of varied administrative problems without impairment or denial of adequate educational opportunities to both races during the period of transition. . . ." A year later Judge Miller approved extension of the Nashville plan to the remaining grades in the school system at the rate of one additional grade each year. In his opinion at that time, Judge Miller said, "Admittedly the problem is not susceptible of an easy solution. The Supreme Court of the United States has made it clear that adjustments must be made in accordance with the exigencies of each case and that the concept of 'all deliberate speed' is a flexible one. For this reason decisions applying the desegregation doctrine in other cities or areas where different conditions obtain are of little value. Local conditions call for the application of local remedy." The Court of Appeals for the Sixth Circuit upheld Judge Miller's decision, and the Supreme Court declined to review it.

In response to court orders, the Delaware State Board of Education in 1959 submitted a plan that called for grade-a-year desegregation over twelve years, following the precedent of Nashville. In his opinion approving the plan, District Judge Caleb R. Layton said, "Any thought of a total and immediate integration of the Delaware School System is out of the question." The Third Circuit Court reversed Judge Layton, and in the opinion Chief Judge John Biggs, Jr., wrote: ". . . the circumstances of . . . Nashville . . . are not analogous to those at bar. The number of Negro children involved in the Nashville schools was substantially larger than the number with which we are concerned. . . . Moreover, the City of Nashville lies in the deep South, a part of our Nation where emotional reactions concerning school integration are more intense than in our own State of Delaware. . . . In short, integration in the State of Delaware, which already has integrated many of its schools, particularly in the Wilmington metropolitan area, should not be viewed, gauged or judged by the more restrictive standards reasonably applicable to communities which have not advanced as far upon the road toward full integration as has Delaware. To apply such standards to the Delaware school system is not permissible in the light of the Supreme Court's mandate. . . ." The Court of Appeals ordered the State Board of Education to submit to a district court a plan "for the integration at all grades for the public school system of Delaware . . . of all Negro children who desire integration. . . ." After the Supreme Court had denied an application for a stay of the appellate court's order, the Board of Education complied, and the statewide plan took effect in the fall of 1961.

Nowhere except in Delaware did the courts order statewide desegregation, either immediate or gradual. A three-judge court in 1964 threatened to take such action in the Macon County, Alabama, case. "However," the judges said, "in this case, *at this particular time,* this Court will not order desegregation in all the public schools of the State of Alabama . . . This Court, under the evidence in this case, could and possibly should now order the State of Alabama Board of Education to cease the illegal and unconstitutional practice of distributing public funds for the purpose of operating segregated schools. . . . Needless to say, it is only a question of time until such illegal and unconstitutional support of segregated school systems must cease. These State officials and the local school officials are now put on notice that within a reasonable time this Court will expect and require such support to cease. These school officials should now proceed to formulate and place into effect plans designed to make the distribution of public funds to the various schools throughout the State of Alabama only to those schools and school systems that have proceeded with 'deliberate speed' in the desegregation of their school systems as required by *Brown*. ...." Jack Greenberg, general counsel of the NAACP Legal Defense Fund, called this decision "the most sweeping decree in the history of the Legal Defense Fund's integration campaign." And Richmond Flowers, attorney general of Alabama, described it as "the most far-reaching since the 1954 decision." Flowers said, "Our backs are really to the wall now. If we appeal it, it may be made the law of the land by the Supreme Court. We're afraid to appeal. I don't think our school officials realize how important this ruling is."

While no courts in the Southern states ordered statewide desegregation, as time passed district judges showed a growing inclination to order immediate desegregation of entire local school systems. In the fall of 1961, Judge William E. Miller ordered the school systems of the city of Lebanon and Wilson County, Tennessee, to reassign all students by January 2, 1962, and to notify them of "nonracial rezoning and reassignment." Soon after this ruling, Judge Bailey Brown rejected a grade-a-year plan submitted to him by the Obion County, Tennessee, school board and ordered the board to submit a plan for the abolition of segregated schools in all grades by the fall of 1962. From the bench Judge Brown said, "I don't think the idea should get around that every school district can simply wait until they are sued and then come in with the most conservative plan that has ever been approved and expect to have it approved. ... It is clear that this school board doesn't need much time." When a case from the nearby city of Jackson was in his court in 1963, Judge Brown said to Superintendent C. J. Huckaba, "The Court would not really be forcing something on you if it ordered complete desegregation tomorrow since you have known about this since 1954." This threat caused Huckaba to exclaim, "Oh, Judge, I hope you don't do that!" Judge Brown gave Jackson four years to complete its desegregation program. In the summer of 1963 District Judge Edwin M. Stanley ordered the school board of Durham, North Carolina, to submit to him "not later than May 1, 1964, ... a plan for the total and complete desegregation of the Durham City School System for the 1964–65 school year, and for subsequent years. ...."

In the Memphis parks case, the Supreme Court suggested its dissatisfaction with the slow pace of desegregation. "Given the extended time which has elapsed, it is far from clear that the mandate of the second *Brown* decision requiring that desegregation proceed with 'all deliberate speed' would today be fully satisfied by types of plans or programs for desegregation of public educational facilities which eight years ago might have been deemed sufficient," the opinion said. Still the Court did not specify how fast "all deliberate speed" should be. Early in 1964, the Supreme Court heard arguments in the Atlanta, Georgia, case, in which acceleration of the grade-a-year plan was a principal issue. During the proceedings, Chief Justice Warren commented, "It's quite evident that we're confused." The confusion arose from changes that had been made in the Atlanta plan, and the Supreme Court sent the case back to the district court for "a proper evidentiary hearing" on the new developments. Atlanta Superintendent John W. Letson voiced his relief when he said, "There was some feeling that the Court might use the Atlanta case to redefine 'deliberate speed.'" On the same day that the Supreme Court returned the Atlanta case to the district court, it handed down a decision in the Prince Edward County, Virginia, case. Acceleration was not the issue in the case, but Justice Hugo Black, who wrote the opinion, made some pointed comment on the subject. "There has been entirely too much deliberation and not enough speed in enforcing the constitutional rights which we held in *Brown* . . . had been denied Prince Edward County Negro children," he wrote. "The time for mere 'deliberate speed' has run out. . . ."

In the absence of any specific definition by the Supreme Court, the judges in the lower federal courts began to fashion their own constructions of "deliberate speed." In New Orleans, when the school board failed to produce a plan of desegregation, Judge Skelly Wright ordered a grade-a-year plan to take effect in the fall of 1960. In the spring of 1962 Judge Wright ordered that all of the elementary grades be desegregated the following fall. "Generations of Negroes," he said, "have already been denied their rights under the separate but equal doctrine of *Plessy v. Ferguson* . . . and, at the present pace in New Orleans, generations of Negroes yet unborn will suffer a similar fate with respect to their rights under *Brown* unless desegregation and equal protection are secured for them by this court." District Judge Frank B. Ellis, upon succeeding Judge Wright, granted a stay on Judge Wright's order and later approved continuation of desegregation on the original grade-a-year plan. Negroes continued to press for acceleration, but Judge Ellis commented at a hearing in the fall of 1964 that they had not taken advantage of their opportunities under the plan in effect.

In Knoxville, Tennessee, schools were desegregated in the fall of 1960 under a grade-a-year plan approved by District Judge Robert L. Taylor. The Sixth Circuit Court of Appeals in the spring of 1962 ruled that "more grades than contemplated by the board's plans should now be desegregated." The school board complied by desegregating the first six grades by the fall of 1963 and all remaining grades in 1964.

In the fall of 1963 desegregation began in the schools of Birmingham and Mobile, Alabama, under grade-a-year plans approved by federal district judges. The following summer the Court of Appeals for the Fifth Circuit ordered an acceleration so that all twelve grades in the school systems would be desegregated in six years. Writing the Court's opinion, Judge Walter P. Gewin said, "Plans providing for the integration of only one grade a year are now rare; and the possibility of judicial approval of such a grade-a-year plan has become increasingly remote due to the passage of time since the *Brown* decisions."

The Fourth Circuit Court, in the Lynchburg case, held on July 8, 1963, that grade-a-year plans "cannot now be sustained." In the Charleston, South Carolina, case decided a few weeks later, District Judge J. Robert Martin ordered that desegregation start in the fall of 1963 and that it be extended to cover all Negro students in the school system the following year. District Judges Robert W. Hemphill and Charles E. Simons, Jr., in the Sumter County and Orangeburg County, South Carolina, cases, in 1964 followed Judge Martin's precedent, ordering a start that fall and completion of the process the next year.

Some of the district judges still weren't convinced. Three days before the Supreme Court decision in the Memphis parks case and a full year after the Court of Appeals decision in the Knoxville case, District Judge Marion S. Boyd approved a grade-a-year plan for Memphis. In delivering his opinion from the bench, Judge Boyd said, "Too much haste is not . . . conducive to the sound solution of the problem." The primary purpose of the Negroes, he added, "apparently is speed and more speed without proper consideration for costs or consequences." After the Memphis parks decision, Judge Boyd approved an amendment of the school plan, under which desegregation would be accelerated and completed in seven years. In his opinion on the amended plan, Judge Boyd said, "Desegregation of the Memphis school system demands elaborate and time-consuming preparation with parents, teachers, principals and students. Chaos would result if white and Negro children were assigned to desegregated schools without this planning, work and cooperation. The education process would be seriously and adversely affected by a plan of desegregation which is more rapid than that proposed by the Board of Education." On appeal the Sixth Circuit Court ordered further acceleration so that all grades would be desegregated by the fall of 1966. The attorney for the school board welcomed the decision, saying that it "relieves the board of the responsibilities to consider that matter further" and that "the time and effort which have gone into the consideration of this subject can be devoted to other areas that will lead to a better school system."

In the summer of 1964 Judges Ben Connally and Whitfield Davidson declined to order acceleration of grade-a-year plans in Houston and Dallas. Judge Connally said that the Negro plaintiff in the Houston case "in effect is asking that the program for orderly transition from a segregated to an integrated school system be junked and that all of the schools be subject to immediate integration." Judge Davidson told the Negroes in Dallas, "You already have all your legal rights." He continued, "If a key doesn't open a lock the first time you try, you work with the key in the lock, and after awhile it usually opens. If you get impatient, however, and take a wrench and turn the key in the lock, you will break either the lock or the key." When Judge Mize approved a grade-a-year plan for three Mississippi school systems, effective in the fall of 1964, attorneys for the Negro plaintiffs reminded him that this pace did not meet the "minimum standards" that the Fifth Circuit Court had set in the Alabama cases. Judge Mize was unmoved; he said that he considered the plan the "best procedure for amicable and orderly desegregation of the schools." At approximately the same time however, District Judge Claude Clayton ruled that the Clarksdale, Mississippi, schools should complete desegregation in six years.

Most Southern school boards took full advantage of the delays inherent in legal procedures, first to postpone a start toward compliance with *Brown* and then to advance at the slowest possible pace. In some instances, the federal judges prodded the school boards to go faster. Often, however, the reluctant boards had the full approval and cooperation of the judges.

Plans of Desegregation

While a "stairstep" arrangement was a key feature of many plans of desegregation, some plans were built around other ideas. One that had tough sledding in the courts appeared in several places under different labels. The basic idea was that parents should be allowed to determine whether their children were to attend all-white, all-Negro or desegregated schools.

The Tennessee legislature passed a school preference law in 1957, which Judge William E. Miller promptly declared to be "antagonistic to the principles declared by the Supreme Court" and "unconstitutional on its face." He said, in the Nashville case: ". . . the act would directly authorize the school board of the City of Nashville to take a census and then to set up separate white schools and separate schools for colored children, whose parents so elected. After those schools were so set up, they would not only be separate schools, but they would be separated because of race and for no other reason. In addition, the separation, once made, would be compulsory." The idea of giving pupils a choice between segregated and desegregated schools was implicit in the plan to abolish compulsory segregation in "selected schools" that the Chattanooga Board of Education submitted in 1960 to Judge Leslie Darr. In rejecting the plan, Judge Darr said, "My idea is that the desegregation, if started gradually, should start in the whole system and not just part of the system." The Sixth Circuit Court upheld Judge Darr's ruling.

When in 1960 the Dallas school board submitted a grade-a-year plan to Judge Davidson, he expressed the opinion that "the plan . . . will manifestly lead to an amalgamation of the races." He recommended instead "that the school authorities set aside schools within the city limits in which all those of either race who desire integration may be enrolled. . . . Since the children would be there together by their parents' consent there is at least one reason why good will would prevail in these schools that might not prevail in schools where children are brought together by force and without the approval of their parents." Judge Davidson's proposal became known as the "salt-and-pepper plan." The school board complied with Judge Davidson's order, but when the plan went to the Fifth Circuit Court for review, Judge Richard T. Rives said, "That plan evidences a total misconception of the nature of the constitutional rights asserted by the plaintiffs. Negro children have no constitutional right to the attendance of white children with them in the public schools. Their constitutional right to 'the equal protection of the laws' is the right to stand equal before the laws of the State; that is, to be treated simply as individuals without regard to race or color." Following the mandate of the Court of Appeals, Judge Davidson approved a grade-a-year plan for Dallas to take effect in the fall of 1961, but in so doing he took a parting shot at the circuit judges. "Should a judge act when his conscience says no and where every sense of right and fair play says no, or should he under such conditions hold himself disqualified?" he wrote in his formal opinion. "To abolish a long established social status or educational system by force is un-American. Such may be amicably done only by consent of the parties affected. The Court's decree may take effect through the office of the United States Marshal or with the soldier's bayonet, it is force just the same. . . . History will mark this as an epoch in the lives of the American people and particularly so as a rift in the judicial powers of our nation. Though we sign the decree as required by the mandate of our higher court, so deeply do we feel the effects upon the future we must let the record show that at least one judge would dissent."

Plans providing a personal "freedom of choice" by pupils of the schools they wished to attend were approved by both district and appeals courts. The intent of these plans, however, was opposite to that of the Tennessee School Preference Act and Judge Davidson's "salt-and-pepper" plan. Their purpose was to remove barriers to the admission of Negro children to predominantly white schools.

The "freedom of choice" concept began to appear in court decisions late in the decade. In 1962 Judge John Paul held in the Charlottesville, Virginia, case that "attendance at the high schools in Charlottesville is to be based solely on the student's decision as to which school he prefers to attend." Judge Edwin M. Stanley entered "freedom of choice" orders in a number of cases arising from North Carolina communities. The leading cases were from Caswell County and the city of Durham. Judge Stanley ordered that children should have "complete freedom to transfer to a school which is attended solely or largely by pupils of another race." The Fourth Circuit Court upheld the decisions in both the Charlottesville and North Carolina cases. In the Obion County, Tennessee, case Judge Brown approved a freedom-of-choice plan, although attorneys for the Negro plaintiffs opposed it on the ground that it "would allow segregation." In the Wilson County, Tennessee, case Judge Miller ruled that "children . . . have the absolute right to attend . . . any school of their choice. . . ."

Pupil Placement Laws

The Southern states found pupil placement laws to be an effective way to limit the number of Negro children admitted to schools with white children. These laws had a number of common characteristics. They vested in school boards or other bodies the authority to assign pupils to schools. They established administrative remedies for those who claimed that their assignments were illegal. They enumerated criteria by which assignments and transfers might be made. The basic concepts of the laws and the application of their specific provisions were involved in numerous cases.

One of the first cases arose from McDowell County, North Carolina, where prior to the *Brown* decision Negroes filed suit for equal school facilities, not desegregation. Judge Wilson Warlick dismissed the suit in the summer of 1955 on the ground that the relief asked was inappropriate in the light of *Brown*. Meanwhile the state legislature passed a pupil assignment act, and the plaintiffs in the case sought admission to white schools. On appeal, the Fourth Circuit Court returned the case to the lower court with instructions to "give consideration not merely to the decision of the Supreme Court but also to the subsequent legislation of the State of North Carolina providing an administrative remedy for persons who feel aggrieved with respect to their enrollment in the public schools of the state." The circuit judges added that, "it is well settled that the courts of the United States will not grant injunctive relief until administrative remedies have been exhausted. . . ."

When the case returned to the appellate court in the fall of 1956, the Court upheld the constitutionality of the pupil placement act. Judge John J. Parker wrote the opinion, saying "It is argued that the pupil placement act is unconstitutional; but we cannot hold that the statute is unconstitutional upon its face and the question as to whether it has been unconstitutional upon its face and the question as to whether it has been unconstitutionally applied is not before us, as the administrative remedy which it provides has not been invoked. . . . It is clear, however, that the appeals to the courts which the statute provides are judicial, not administrative remedies and that, after administrative remedies for the school boards have been exhausted, judicial remedies for denial of constitutional rights may be pursued at once in the federal courts without pursuing state court remedies. . . ." The Supreme Court declined to review this decision.

For the next six years the doctrine of the McDowell County case was applied in many other North Carolina cases. In 1962, however, the Court of Appeals held in the Durham case that the pupil placement law was being administered in an unconstitutional manner. Judge Simon Sobeloff wrote for the Court. "The inescapable conclusion from the evidence," he said, "is that the assignment of pupils to the Durham public schools is based, in whole or in part, upon the race of those assigned. It is an unconstitutional administration of the North Carolina Pupil Enrollment Act to assign pupils to schools according to racial factors."

The federal courts dealt with the question of administrative remedies in Virginia before the state passed a pupil placement law. Negroes were denied admission to white schools in Arlington and Charlottesville because they had not exhausted the administrative remedies available to them. In July of 1956 District Judges Albert Bryan and John Paul ruled for the Negroes, and the school boards appealed. Judge Parker, writing the opinion of the Fourth Circuit Court in these cases, said, ". . . in view of the announced policy of the respective school boards any . . . application to a school other than a segregated school maintained for colored people would have been futile; and equity does not require the doing of a vain thing as a condition of relief." The Supreme Court declined to review this decision.

In September of 1956 the Virginia legislature passed a pupil placement law, giving to a State Pupil Placement Board full authority to assign pupils to specific schools. The following January District Judge Walter E. Hoffman, in the Norfolk and Newport News cases, ruled that the law was "unconstitutional on its face and must be disregarded." He said that "the Pupil Placement Board would indeed be derelict in its duty if it ever permitted admission of a Negro child in a school heretofore reserved for white children, and vice versa." He added, "The pattern is plain—the Legislature has adopted procedures to defeat the *Brown* decision." Referring to the Fourth Circuit Court decision in the McDowell County case, he commented, "Obviously, the remedies afforded by North Carolina do not lead to a complete 'blind alley' such as Virginia has prescribed." The Fourth Circuit Court and the Supreme Court upheld Judge Hoffman's decision.

The legislature amended the law in 1958, but the board still assigned no children to biracial schools. The Norfolk case again came before Judge Hoffman, and in the fall of 1959 he said in his opinion that "the findings of fact and conclusions of law emphatically demonstrate the unconstitutional application of a law which is constitutional on its face. . . . The Board candidly admits that the race of the child is the controlling factor wherever a child of one race seeks admission to a school solely or predominantly attended by children of the opposite race. . . . Thus, the melody of massive resistance lingers on. . . ." Judge Hoffman warned the Placement Board that he would take action against its members if they failed to assign Negro children to white schools in Norfolk. He instructed Norfolk school authorities to disregard the Placement Board until it "changes its attitude." On advice of counsel, the board complied with the Court's order, and after that assigned Negroes to schools with whites in a growing number of Virginia school systems.

The Louisiana legislature in 1954 passed a pupil assignment law. In February of 1956, in the New Orleans case, District Judge J. Skelly Wright declared the law "invalid on its face." He said that it "was part of the legislative plan, enacted subsequent to the Supreme Court's decision in *Brown* . . . to avoid the effect of that decision in order to retain segregation in the public schools of the state" and that it detailed "means by which segregation is to be achieved." He added, "To remit each of these minor children and the thousands of others similarly situated to thousands of administrative hearings . . . to seek the relief to which the Supreme Court of the United States has said they are entitled, would be a vain and useless gesture, unworthy of a court of equity. It would be a travesty in which this court will not participate." The Supreme Court declined to review this decision. The Louisiana legislature in 1958 passed a new pupil assignment law, and in 1960 amended it to conform to the Alabama law, which the Supreme Court had upheld. In 1962 Judge Wright and the Court of Appeals for the Fifth Circuit ruled that the new law could not be used so long as New Orleans operated a dual school system. "However valid a school placement act may be on its face, it may not be selectively applied," Judge

Wright held. "Moreover, where a school system is segregated there is no constitutional basis whatever for using a pupil placement law. A pupil placement law may only be validly applied in an integrated school system, and then only where no consideration is based on race. To assign children to a segregated school system and then require them to pass muster under a pupil placement law is discrimination in its rawest form."

The Alabama pupil placement law, passed in 1955, served as the most popular model for other states. A three-judge court in 1958, in the Birmingham case, held the law to be constitutional "upon its face." In writing the opinion for the Court, Circuit Judge Rives said, "The School Placement Act furnishes the legal machinery for the orderly administration of the public schools in a constitutional manner by the admission of qualified pupils upon a basis of individual merit without regard to their race or color. We must presume that it will be so administered. If not, in some future proceeding it is possible that it may be declared unconstitutional in its application. The responsibility rests primarily upon the local school boards, but ultimately upon all the people of the state." The Supreme Court denied review of this decision. In the summer of 1964, in the Macon County case, another three-judge court considered the constitutionality of the Alabama placement act. "The record in this case indicates that the State Board of Education regards the Alabama School Placement Law as a law to be used merely when a school board is faced with demands for desegregation," the Court said in its opinion. "Such a use of the Alabama Placement Law, since such is clearly unconstitutional, will be enjoined by this Court. . . . This Court is not willing at this time, however, to declare the Alabama Placement Law unconstitutional. Future use of this law by the school authorities in the State of Alabama may, if it is applied in a constitutional manner, serve a good purpose, not only for the Alabama public school system but for Alabama citizens of both races."

Court decisions in numerous cases established the right of school authorities to make pupil assignments, provided race was not a factor. The constitutionality of the state pupil assignment laws depended upon their application. The laws could not be the basis for compliance with *Brown* where schools were segregated, nor was it necessary in such situations to follow the administrative remedies that the laws stipulated.

In cases from Florida and Tennessee, court decisions established another point. State placement laws could not be used by local school boards as plans of desegregation. In the Dade County, Florida case, the Fifth Circuit Court in 1959 reversed a district court decision that the state law "met the requirements of a plan of desegregation of the schools." Judge Rives said in the opinion that the law did "no more than furnish the legal machinery under which compliance may be started and effectuated . . ." and that there was nothing in the law "clearly inconsistent with a continuing policy of compulsory racial segregation." He added, "Obviously, unless some legally non-segregated schools are provided, there can be no constitutional assignment of a pupil to a particular school."

Two district judges in Tennessee in 1961 came to opposite conclusions on the use of the state placement law as a plan of segregation. Judge Marion S. Boyd held that "the Tennesee Pupil Assignment Law furnishes a fully adequate and efficient plan of operating the Memphis City School System on a racially non-discriminatory basis." Judge William E. Miller, in the Wilson County case, held, "The Court cannot approve the Tennessee Pupil Placement Law as a plan for accomplishing desegregation of the schools. This law, as shown on its face, is not a plan for desegregation, nor is desegregation a part of its subject matter or purpose. . . . The Pupil Placement Law at best provides a most cumbersome and time-consuming procedure to accomplish transfers of students. . . ." The decision of Judge Boyd in the Memphis case was appealed, and the Sixth Circuit Court reversed him. "The Pupil Assignment Law might serve some purpose in the administration of a school system," Circuit Judge Lester L. Cecil wrote, "but it will not serve as a plan to convert a biracial school system into a non-racial one." The Supreme Court upheld the Court of Appeals.

The pupil placement laws provided criteria and tests by which assignments and transfers might be made. In the early court cases, the use of these standards was approved. The Fifth Circuit Court in the Dallas case said in 1957, "Pupils may, of course, be separated according to their degree of advancement or retardation, their ability to learn, on account of their health, or for any other legitimate reason, but each child is entitled to be treated as an individual without regard to his race or color." Judge Hoffman held in the Norfolk case in 1959 that there was nothing "arbitrary, capricious or illegal" in the school board's use of criteria in making assignments and that "the standards, criteria and procedures are not unconstitutional on their face"; he warned, however, that they "must be equally applied to all applicants." In the Alexandria case, the Fourth Circuit Court a year later upheld the use of tests and criteria, but said, "If the criteria should be applied only to Negroes seeking transfer or enrollment in particular schools and not to white children, then the use of the criteria could not be sustained." In the fall of 1961 Judge Paul said in the Charlottesville case, "The soundest basis for all future questions is that Negroes and whites must be treated exactly alike in determining their rights." This rule, formulated most clearly in the Virginia cases, was applied generally by judges in other states.

An important factor in determining the assignment of pupils was the place of their residence. A school board might draw attendance-zone lines so that certain schools would be predominantly, or even exclusively, of one race; this was known as gerrymandering. Or the board might establish a dual system of overlapping white and Negro zones, assigning white students to the white school nearest their homes and Negro students to the nearest Negro schools. The courts ruled against both practices. In the Dade County, Florida, case, Judge Emett C. Choate said in 1957, "The issue is whether this gerrymandering, or whatever you call it, denies the rights of students. The rule of thumb, I think, is that pupils go to the nearest school." The Fifth Circuit Court held in the Escambia County, Florida, case that "there cannot be full compliance with the Supreme Court's requirements to desegregate until all dual school districts based on race are eliminated." The Fourth Circuit Court said in the Alexandria, Virginia, case, "Obviously, the maintenance of a dual system of attendance zones based on race offends the constitutional rights of the plaintiffs and others similarly situated and cannot be tolerated."

For a period of years, one type of transfer in which race was a factor had the approval of the courts. It was known as the "minority race transfer," under which pupils assigned to schools in which their race was in the minority had the privilege of changing to a school in which their race predominated. Judge Miller approved the minority race transfer provision of the Nashville plan. He held that "provisions which merely confer upon white and Negro students a non-discriminatory right to transfer would not appear to violate the Constitution." The Sixth Circuit Court upheld Judge Miller's decision, saying, "If the child is free to attend an integrated school, and his parents voluntarily choose a school where only one race attends, he is not being deprived of his constitutional rights." The Supreme Court, by a six to-three vote, declined to review the decision.

When Dallas included the Nashville transfer provision in its plan, the Fifth Circuit Court in 1961 ruled that it "should be stricken" because it recognized "race as an absolute ground for transfer of students, and its application might tend to perpetuate racial discrimination." The Fourth Circuit Court took the same position in the Charlottesville case, holding, "It is of no significance that all children, regardless of race, are first assigned to the schools in their residential zone and all are permitted to transfer if the assignment requires the child to attend the school where his race is in the minority, if the purpose and effect of the assignment is to retard integration and retain segregation of the races. That this purpose and this effect are inherent in the plan can hardly be denied."

Many school systems adopted minority race transfer provisions with the approval of federal judges. Among them were Davidson County and Knoxville, Tennessee, and the Supreme Court agreed to hear arguments in cases in which the transfer plans of these two school boards were attacked. In June of 1963 the Court handed down its decision. Justice Tom Clark said in the opinion: "It is readily apparent that the transfer system proposed lends itself to perpetuation of segregation. Indeed the provisions can only work toward that end. . . . Here the right of transfer, which operates

solely on the basis of a racial classification, is a one-way ticket leading to but one destination, *i.e.,* the majority race of the transferee
and continued segregation. . . . The recognition of race as an absolute criterion for granting transfers which operate only in the direction of schools in which the transferee's race is in the majority is
no less unconstitutional than its use for original admission or subsequent assignment to public schools."

State Sovereignty

Throughout the decade, as the start of desegregation spread
from one state to another, claims were made that under the Tenth
Amendment to the Constitution education was the exclusive province of the states and that under the Eleventh Amendment a state
could not be sued without its consent. Some federal judges upheld
these claims of state sovereignty and state's rights. But ultimately
they all fell under rulings of the federal courts.

The question of the immunity of a state to suit arose early—in
1956 in the New Orleans case. Judge Wright ruled that "a suit
against officers or agents of a state acting illegally is not a suit against
the state." The state immunity issue reached the Fourth Circuit
Court in the Charlottesville and Arlington County, Virginia, cases
about the same time that Judge Wright gave his decision in the
New Orleans case. Writing the opinion for the Court, Judge Parker
said, "We see nothing in these decrees of which the defendants can
complain. The decrees do not attempt to direct the school officials
as to how they shall perform their duties or exercise the discretion
vested in them by law, but simply forbid them to discriminate
against the plaintiffs, or other Negro children similarly situated, on
the ground of race or color, in violation of their rights under the
Constitution of the United States as declared by the Supreme Court.
A suit for such relief is not a suit against a state within the meaning
of the 11th Amendment to the Constitution but is a suit for the
protection of individual rights under the Constitution by enjoining
state officers and agencies from taking action beyond the scope of
their legal powers." The Supreme Court declined to review this
decision.

In 1964 Federal District Judge E. Gordon West declined to rule on a case because the Louisiana State Board of Education was named as the defendant. "A sovereign state simply cannot be made a defendant in a suit in a federal court," Judge West said, "either by suing it directly, or by suing it indirectly through one of its agencies, without its express consent, without running afoul of the provisions of the Eleventh Amendment to the United States Constitution. . . ." The Fifth Circuit Court quickly, and with evident impatience, overruled Judge West. Speaking for the Court, Judge Rives said, "Five times this Court has held that there is no immunity for a state agency from a suit to enjoin it from enforcing an unconstitutional statute which requires segregation of the races. . . . We see no reason why this Court (or the district court) should depart from our previous holdings."

When the New Orleans case came to the Fifth Circuit Court, the Tenth Amendment issue was injected into it. The state contended that the maintenance of segregated schools was "in the exercise of the state police power to promote and protect public health, morals, better education and the peace and good order in the State, and not because of race." Judge Tuttle wrote the Court's opinion. "Appellant nowhere in his brief undertakes to explain the process of reasoning by which it seeks to have this Court conclude that racial segregation in the schools is any less segregation 'because of race' merely because the stated basis of adhering to the policy is in the exercise of the State's police power," he wrote. "The use of the term police power works no magic in itself. Undeniably the States retain an extremely broad police power. This power, however, as everyone knows, is itself limited by the protective shield of the Federal Constitution." The Supreme Court declined to review the lower court decisions.

Some state judges persisted in the opinion that the *Brown* decision was an invasion of states' rights. The Florida Supreme Court, in the University of Florida case, said, "It is a 'consummation devoutly to be wished' that the concept of 'state's rights' will not come to be of interest only to writers and students of history. Such a concept is vital to the preservation of human liberties now." The Virginia Supreme Court of Appeals, in declaring that the massive resistance laws violated the State Constitution, deplored "the lack of judicial restraint evinced by the Supreme Court in trespassing on the sovereign rights of this Commonwealth reserved to it in the Constitution of the United States."

The most extreme expression of states' rights was the doctrine of interposition—the placing of the power of the state between its people and the federal government. The federal courts demolished the doctrine in the Little Rock case in 1958 and in the New Orleans case in 1960. In the Little Rock decision of 1958 the Supreme Court, in a unanimous opinion, said: ". . . we should answer the premise of the actions of the Governor and Legislature that they are not bound by our holding in the *Brown* case. It is necessary only to recall some basic constitutional propositions which are settled doctrine. Article VI of the Constitution makes the Constitution the 'supreme Law of the Land.' In 1803, Chief Justice Marshall, speaking for a unanimous Court, referring to the Constitution as 'the fundamental and paramount law of the nation,' declared in the notable case of *Marbury v. Madison* . . . that 'It is emphatically the province and duty of the judicial department to say what the law is.' This decision declared the basic principle that the federal judiciary is supreme in the exposition of the law of the Constitution, and that principle has ever since been respected by this Court and the Country as a permanent and indispensable feature of our constitutional system. It follows that the interpretation of the Fourteenth Amendment enunciated by this Court in the *Brown* case is the supreme law of the land, and Article VI of the Constitution makes it of binding effect on the States 'any Thing in the Constitution or Laws of any State to the Contrary notwithstanding.' Every state legislator and executive and judicial officer is solemnly committed by oath . . . 'to support this Constitution.' No state legislator or executive or judicial officer can war against the Constitution without violating his undertaking to support it. . . ."

In the New Orleans case a three-judge federal court in 1958 discussed at length the efforts of Louisiana to resort to "interposition" as a means of avoiding compliance with *Brown*. "The conclusion is clear that interposition is not a *constitutional* doctrine," the Court said. "If taken seriously, it is legal defiance of constitutional authority." The Supreme Court, within less than two weeks, upheld the lower court and added: "The main basis for challenging this ruling is that the State of Louisiana 'has interposed itself in the field of public education over which it has exclusive control.' This objection is without substance. . . ."

Tuition Grants and Private Schools

As a part of their programs to prevent desegregation or to avoid its effects, most of the Southern states adopted laws under which grants could be made to students for the payment of tuition at some school other than the public school to which they normally would be assigned. In most instances the intent of these laws was to make it possible for students to attend segregated, private, nonsectarian schools rather than desegregated public schools. In Virginia the grants were available to pay tuition at any nonsectarian private school or any public school outside the student's district, whether the school to be attended was segregated or desegregated.

Virginia was the principal legal testing ground for tuition grants, but before the Virgina cases had progressed far enough to yield key decisions the question came before the courts in the Little Rock and St. Helena Parish cases. In its 1958 opinion in the Little Rock case the Supreme Court said, "State support of segregated schools through any arrangement, management, funds or property cannot be squared with the Fourteenth Amendment's command that no State shall deny to any person within its jurisdiction the equal protection of the laws." At a special session in 1958 the Arkansas legislature had passed laws permitting the governor to close schools and providing that state aid withheld from closed schools might be paid to schools attended by pupils transferring from the closed schools. When Governor Faubus closed the high schools at Little Rock, the school board contemplated leasing the buildings for operation as private schools. The Eighth Circuit Court of Appeals prohibited this arrangement and later declared the laws involved "invalid and completely ineffectual" and "clearly unconstitutional."

In the summer of 1961 a three-judge court ruled, in the St.

Helena Parish case, that the Louisiana law providing for private schools and tuition grants was unconstitutional. The Court said that the "subsurface purpose" of the act was "to provide a means by which public schools under desegregation orders may be changed to 'private' schools operated in the same way, in the same buildings, with the same furnishings, with the same money, and under the same supervision as the public schools." The judges called the law "a transparent artifice designed to deny the plaintiffs their constitutional rights to attend desegregated public schools." The decision continued, ". . . The state might not be doing business at the same old stand; but the state would be participating as the senior, and not silent, partner in the same sort of business. The continuance of segregation at the state's public-private schools, therefore, is a violation of the equal protection clause." The Supreme Court upheld the three-judge court.

The payment of tuition grants was one of the issues before the courts in the later stages of the Prince Edward County, Virginia, case. In the fall of 1961 District Judge Oren R. Lewis ruled that tuition grants could not be paid to private schools so long as public schools in the county were closed. Almost exactly ten years after the *Brown* decision, the Supreme Court handed down a decision in the Prince Edward case. The Court observed: ". . . the record in the present case could not be clearer that Prince Edward's public schools were closed and private schools operated in their place with state and county assistance, for one reason, and one reason only: to ensure, through measures taken by the county and the State, that white and colored children in Prince Edward County would not, under any circumstances, go to the same school." The Court specifically upheld Judge Lewis when it said, "The injunction against paying tuition grants and giving tax credits while public schools remain closed is appropriate and necessary since those grants and tax credits have been essential parts of the county's program, successful thus far, to deprive petitioners of the same advantages of a public school education, enjoyed by children in every other part of Virginia." But that was as far as the Supreme Court went. The Court did not declare unconstitutional the use of public funds to pay grants for private school tuition.

Closed Schools

The laws providing for public support of private schools, through tuition grants or other means, usually were parts of a legislative program that, as a last resort, permitted the closing of a public school to avoid desegregation. Wherever schools were closed or threatened with closure, these laws came under the scrutiny of the federal courts.

When Governor Faubus closed the high schools in Little Rock, the Arkansas Supreme Court ruled that his action was a valid exercise of state police power. A three-judge federal court held, however, that the state law under which the governor acted was "clearly unconstitutional under the due process and equal protection clauses of the Fourteenth Amendment, and conferred no authority upon the Governor to close the public high schools in Little Rock." The Supreme Court upheld this ruling.

As the Atlanta case proceeded through his court, District Judge Frank A. Hooper showed acute awareness of the Georgia laws providing for withholding state funds from desegregated schools and authorizing the governor to close them. Governor Ernest Vandiver in the summer of 1959 warned that, if the Court ordered desegregation in the Atlanta schools, he would have no recourse but to close them, and he expressed the hope that "the federal courts will not force the closing of a single school in Georgia." Judge Hooper in a decision on June 16 said, "This court fully recognizes the difficult position in which defendants herein are placed. If they integrate the schools, all state money under existing laws will be cut off and it may be that such funds are necessary for the operation. The continued operation, however, with discrimination as in the past, will not be permitted." Judge Hooper delayed his desegregation order to give the Georgia legislature time to repeal the laws. In remarks at a hearing in December of 1959, he said: "The decision of closing the schools is on the people of Georgia, and not on this court. . . . It's my purpose to carry out the command of the Supreme Court and the Fifth Circuit Court of Appeals to eliminate segregation. But as far as I personally have any part in that, it is my purpose

. . . to give, if I can, the people of Georgia an opportunity to say whether or not they would have a gradual integration . . . or whether their answer would be in the negative and they would say on the other hand we would rather close every school in Georgia than to have one Negro to enter a school with the whites." The legislature repealed the laws, and desegregation began in Atlanta in 1961.

The question of closing schools figured prominently in the St. Helena Parish case in 1961. At issue then was the constitutionality of the "local option school-closing" law that the Louisiana legislature passed earlier that year. After hearing arguments, the three-judge court in April asked for the filing of further briefs. "We have an open mind on the constitutionality of the statute," the opinion said. "We point out, however, that national policy and state policy require us to scrutinize carefully any statute leading to the closing of public schools. When there is now such a manifest correlation between education and national survival, it is a sad and ill-timed hour to shut the doors to public schools."

In its decision, handed down on August 30, the Court said: ". . . the act is assailable because its application in one parish, while the state provides public schools elsewhere, would unfairly discriminate against the residents of that parish, irrespective of race. . . . Thus, it is clear enough that . . . a state cannot close the public schools in one area while, at the same time, it maintains schools elsewhere with public funds. . . . There can be no doubt about the character of education in Louisiana as a state, and not a local, function. . . . When a parish wants to lock its school doors, the state must turn the key. If the rules were otherwise, the great guarantee of the equal protection clause would be meaningless. . . . The consequence is that the local option device cannot save Act 2. . . . No plebiscite can legalize an unjust discrimination. . . ." The Supreme Court upheld the decision, which avoided the broad question of whether a state could, under the Fourteenth Amendment, totally abandon its system of public education.

The question remained unanswered, even in the extensive litigation of the Virginia cases. The Prince Edward County case had the longest history of all those from Virginia, and the prospect of closing the schools was apparent almost from the start. At a hearing before a three-judge court in 1955 Judge Armistead M. Dobie of the Fourth Circuit Court asked, ". . . if all through the South they would abolish the public schools, that would be a perfect compliance with the Supreme Court's decree, wouldn't it?" He was questioning Spottswood Robinson, an attorney for the Negro plaintiffs. When in the fall of 1957 the Fourth Circuit Court ordered Prince Edward County to make "a prompt and reasonable start" toward desegregation of its public schools, it said in its opinion, "The fact that the schools might be closed if the order were enforced is no reason for not enforcing it. A person may not be denied enforcement of rights to which he is entitled under the Constitution of the United States because of action taken or threatened in defiance of such rights." Having exhausted every legal recourse to keep the schools open and segregated, Prince Edward County closed its public schools in the summer of 1959, and they remained closed until the fall of 1964. Meanwhile the courts were occupied with questions about the obligations of the county and the state of Virginia to operate public schools.

On January 19, 1959, a three-judge federal court and the Virginia Supreme Court of Appeals both handed down decisions on Virginia's massive-resistance laws, under which the governor had ordered schools closed in several communities. One of the places was Norfolk, where six schools were closed while the remainder were open. In the Norfolk case, the federal court held: "While the State of Virginia, directly or indirectly, maintains and operates a school system with the use of public funds, or participates by arrangement or otherwise in the management of such a school system, no one public school system or grade in Virginia may be closed to avoid the effect of the law of the land as interpreted by the Supreme Court, while the state permits other public schools or grades to remain open at the expense of the taxpayers. . . . We do not suggest that, aside from the Constitution of Virginia, the state must maintain a public school system. That is a matter for state determination." The decision of the State Supreme Court of Appeals was on an action brought by Attorney General Albertis Harrison, later governor, to test the validity of the massive-resistance laws under the State Constitution. The Court held that the constitution "requires the State to *'maintain* an efficient system of public free schools *throughout the state'* [Court's emphasis]. That means that the State must support such public free schools in the State as are necessary to an efficient system, including those in which the pupils of both races are compelled to be enrolled and taught together, however unfortunate that may be." These decisions caused the collapse of Virginia's massive-resistance laws, but they only partially settled the school-closing question. They declared the state's obligation to provide support for a system of public schools, and they prohibited the closing of any part of a local school system so long as other parts were open.

In the fall of 1961 the attorney for the Negro plaintiffs in the Prince Edward County case petitioned the State Supreme Court of Appeals for a writ of mandamus to compel the county Board of Supervisors to levy taxes and make appropriations for public schools. The following spring the court denied the writ, and said in its opinion: "We find in neither . . . the Constitution nor in the statutes implementing it, any support for the petitioners' contention that the Board of Supervisors is under the mandatory duty to levy local taxes and appropriate moneys for the support of public free schools in the county. . . . It is not our function here to say whether the action of the Board of Supervisors of Prince Edward County in refusing to make these appropriations is proper, wise, or desirable. . . ."

Following the State Supreme Court decision that Virginia law did not require the county to operate public schools, Federal District Judge Oren R. Lewis reached the conclusion that closing the schools violated rights created by the equal protection clause of the United States Constitution. In his opinion Judge Lewis said, "This Court holds that the public schools may not be closed to avoid the effect of the law of the land as interpreted by the Supreme Court while the Commonwealth of Virginia permits other public schools to remain open at the expense of the taxpayers. . . . The School Board of Prince Edward County is herewith directed to complete plans for the admission of pupils in the elementary and high schools of the county without regard to race or color and to receive and consider applications to this end at the earliest practical date." The case went again to the Fourth Circuit Court, and Judge Clement F. Haynsworth wrote the opinion. "Transmuted, this old case, in its new flesh and pregnant with questions, comes before us again," he began. The appellate court, holding that Judge Lewis should not have acted until the Virginia Supreme Court had resolved "issues resting upon interpretations of state law," vacated the district court judgment.

When late in 1963 the case again was brought to the State Supreme Court, the question was whether the state had a constitutional obligation to operate the schools if a county refused to operate them. The Court answered: "Because of the refusal of the County Board of Supervisors of Prince Edward County to appropriate funds, the public free schools in the county are closed. We find nothing in the provisions of the Constitution that makes it the duty of the General Assembly in that case to take over these schools and operate them. . . . The Constitution and laws of Virginia have given to its localities an option to operate or not to operate public schools." The Court also held that neither the county's failure to operate public schools nor the operation of private schools violated the federal Constitution.

On May 25, 1964, the U.S. Supreme Court upheld Judge Lewis's 1962 decision and sent the case back to the district court "with directions to enter a decree which will guarantee that these petitioners will get the kind of education that is given in the State's public schools." Justice Black, in writing the Supreme Court opinion, said, ". . . We agree with the District Court that closing the Prince Edward schools and meanwhile contributing to the support of the private segregated white schools that took their place denied petitioners the equal protection of the laws. . . . The District Court may if necessary to prevent further racial discrimination, require the Supervisors to exercise the power that is theirs to levy taxes to raise funds adequate to reopen, operate, and maintain without racial discrimination a public school system in Prince Edward County like that operated in other counties in Virginia." Judge Lewis promptly issued an order such as the Supreme Court directed, and the county supervisors levied the necessary taxes to reopen the schools in the fall.

Closing the public schools was the segregationist South's ultimate weapon in the defense against the *Brown* decision. In no case, however, did closing the schools succeed in preventing desegregation, except temporarily.

School Personnel

The *Brown* decision applied directly and specifically to the "segregation of children in public schools on the basis of race." After several years the federal courts were asked to decide whether the principle of *Brown* also embraced teachers and other school personnel. Desegregation of personnel was sought in cases filed in 1960 in Tennessee and Florida, and thereafter it became standard procedure to include the personnel issue in school suits.

At first the judges declined to consider the question, on the ground that any right of Negro teachers to be free from discrimination would be personal to them and could be asserted only by them. Early in 1960 District Judge Leslie Darr ruled in the Chattanooga case that no rights of pupils were affected by teacher assignments. Upon Judge Darr's retirement, Judge Frank Wilson restored the personnel question to the Chattanooga case, and the Sixth Circuit Court affirmed his decision. "We read the attack upon the assignment of teachers by race not as seeking to protect rights of such teachers, but as a claim that continued assigning of teaching personnel on a racial basis impairs the students' rights to an education free from any consideration of race," the Court said in its opinion of July, 1963, emphasizing that it was "not passing upon the legal question presented." In the Davidson County case, Judge William E. Miller in 1961 reserved judgment on the issue, saying, "The difficulties and problems which will be encountered in making the transition from a segregated to a non-segregated system would be enhanced and complicated if the Court should at this time require the assignment of teachers and supporting personnel in the schools of the system on a basis different from that which has heretofore been followed."

The Florida cases initially took the same direction as those in Tennessee. Then, in 1962, Judge Bryan Simpson handed down decisions in cases from Duval and Volusia counties, in which he used identical language on the personnel issue. "There may be no determinations based upon race or color, in whole or part, with respect to the operation of the public school system, or any of its components," he said. "The *Brown* case is misread and misapplied when it is construed simply to confer upon Negro pupils the right to be considered for admission to a 'white' school." Judge Simpson enjoined the school systems from "assigning teachers, principals, and other supervising or supporting personnel to schools on the basis of the race and color of the persons to be assigned and/or the race and color of the pupils attending the schools to which the personnel are assigned." The Duval County school board appealed. The Fifth Circuit Court affirmed Judge Simpson's decision, and the Supreme Court denied review, but none of the courts set a deadline for the start of personnel desegregation.

The Atlanta case was the only one argued before the Supreme Court in which the application of *Brown* to personnel was an issue. The Fifth Circuit Court had agreed that District Judge Hooper "did not err in postponing the consideration of the teacher assignment question." In arguing the Atlanta case before the Supreme Court on March 31, 1964, Mrs. Constance Baker Motley of the NAACP Legal Defense Fund said, "When a school has an all-Negro staff or an all-white staff, that labels the school as an all-Negro school or an all-white school just as effectively as a sign on the door saying 'Negro' and 'white.'" Since the Supreme Court returned the case to the district court for further hearing of the evidence, its ruling was postponed.

Several district judges did not wait for Supreme Court determination of the issue to order desegregation of personnel. Judge Mac Swinford in April of 1963 ordered "assignment of faculty members . . . without regard to race . . . as of the fall term 1963" in Bowling Green, Kentucky. That summer Judge H. Church Ford approved desegregation plans for Frankfort, Richmond and Jessamine County, Kentucky, all to take effect in the fall. The plans contained provisions that "no teacher or other personnel of the public schools . . . shall be employed, assigned, denied employment or denied assignment on the basis of race or color." Judge Luther Bohanon ordered Oklahoma City "to establish a policy of integrating supervisory and teaching staffs, in good faith, and with deliberate speed . . . beginning in September 1963." In his opinion Judge Bohanon said, "Inasmuch as the Superintendent of Schools has established the proof necessary that Negro teachers are equal in quality to the white teachers, it seems only reasonable and fair that in all schools, mixed or otherwise, the School Board would and should make a good faith effort to integrate the faculty, in order that both white and Negro students would feel that their color was represented upon an equal level and that their people were sharing the responsibility of high-level teaching. . . . To me, to send Negro children . . . to a white principal and all-white teachers would be a deterrent to the Negro students not having before them Negro teachers who are as well qualified as whites to set an example to them of integration."

The applicability of the *Brown* decision to school personnel as well as to pupils was not firmly established a decade after the decision was handed down. Judges showed reluctance to deal with the question. A few who did, near the decade's end, concluded that school systems must employ and assign personnel without regard to race.

The Reverse of Brown

Chief Justice Warren in the first *Brown* decision wrote of Negro children in segregated schools, "To separate them from others of similar age and qualifications solely because of their race generates a feeling of inferiority as to their status in the community that may affect their hearts and minds in a way unlikely ever to be undone. . . . Whatever may have been the extent of psychological knowledge at the time of *Plessy v. Ferguson,* this finding is amply supported by modern authority." A footnote to the opinion cited a number of these authorities.

During the latter half of the decade, white parents sought to intervene in desegregation suits filed by Negro plaintiffs. Their attorneys took Justice Warren's words and turned them around. They argued that desegregation would be harmful to white children because of their association with Negroes, whom they claimed to be inferior to whites in various ways; and they assembled their own supporting authorities.

Judge Wright denied a motion by whites to intervene in the St. Helena Parish case in 1960, and Judge Simpson denied a similar motion in the Duval County case the next year.

When the Atlanta school board announced that it would admit a few Negroes to formerly all-white schools in the fall of 1961, a white student, Sandra Melkild, asked transfer from a desegregated school to an all-white school. The board denied the request, and her parents appealed to the State Board of Education. They claimed that their daughter wished "to maintain freedom of association" and "that the existing decision compelling her to attend an integrated school would result in intolerable psychological damage to her person." The state board ruled in the girl's favor. The Atlanta board then applied to Federal Judge Hooper for clarification of his previous orders. In pleadings filed before the court, attorneys for the state said, "There has never been a stable free society which has been either Negro or Mulatto and the only explanation therefore is genetics—not environment. . . . Integrated education imposed and maintained by official act has a detrimental and deleterious effect on the education, morals and mental development of the whites who are forced to associate with Negroes." Judge Hooper upheld the city school board's position and enjoined the state board from interfering with the court-approved desegregation plan in Atlanta.

Judge Frank M. Scarlett in 1963 permitted white intervention in the Savannah–Chatham County, Georgia, desegregation case, terming the approach "novel." Over objections of attorneys for the Negro plaintiffs, he expressed his determination to permit a thorough airing of the psychological evidence the attorneys for the whites said they were prepared to introduce. Psychological, sociological, anthropological, educational and medical testimony was presented. Attorney General Eugene Cook, of Georgia, put it briefly when he said, "Enforced integration inflicts far greater injury upon personality development and education processes than any ills heretofore thought to flow from enforced separation."

In a lengthy opinion Judge Scarlett reviewed the testimony of the witnesses for the white intervenors. Among his twenty "findings" were these: "Substantially all the difference between these two groups of children is inherent in the individuals and must be dealt with by the defendants as an unchangeable factor in programming the schools for the best educational results. . . . Failure to attain the existing white standards would create serious psychological problems of frustration on the part of the Negro child, which would require compensation by attention-creating antisocial behavior. . . . Total group integration as requested by the plaintiffs would seriously injure both white and Negro students in the Savannah–Chatham County schools and adversely affect the educational standards and accomplishments of the public school system. . . . Selective integration would cause substantial and irremovable psychological injury both to the individual transferee and to other Negro children. . . . Each study presented to the Court, confirmed by the opinions of the witnesses, showed that the damaging assumptions of inferiority increase whenever the child is brought into forced association with white children." Judge Scarlett concluded, "The classification of children in the Savannah–Chatham County schools by division on the basis of coherent groups having distinguishable educability capabilities is . . . a reasonable classification." He dismissed the Negroes' complaint.

The Fifth Circuit Court quickly overruled Judge Scarlett. In a sharply worded opinion, Chief Judge Elbert Tuttle said for the unanimous Court: "The trial judge permitted an intervention by parties whose sole purpose for intervening was to adduce proof as a factual basis for an effort to ask the Supreme Court to reverse its decision in *Brown v. Topeka Board of Education.* The Court then permitted evidence in support of this approach by the intervenors, and denied the appellants' motion for preliminary injunction solely on the basis of such evidence. . . . The district court for the Southern District of Georgia is bound by the decision of the United States Supreme Court, as we are. Unless and until that Court overrules its decision in *Brown v. Topeka,* no trial court may, upon finding the existence of a segregated school system, refrain from acting as required by the Supreme Court merely because such district court may conclude that the Supreme Court erred either as to its facts or as to the law." The Appeals Court said that "it was a clear abuse of its discretion for the trial court to deny appellants' motion for a preliminary injunction" and directed Judge Scarlett to require desegregation of the schools, starting in September of 1963.

Essentially the same group of witnesses for the white intervenors in the Savannah case testified in the Charleston, South Carolina, case. Judge J. Robert Martin admitted their testimony on the inherent inferiority of Negroes "to develop the record" in the event of appeal. "But," he added, "that is not the issue." Judge Martin ordered desegregation of Charleston schools, and the Fourth Circuit Court upheld his decision.

Both the Savannah and Charleston cases were appealed to the Supreme Court. The justices showed no inclination to reverse *Brown*. They declined to review the decisions of the Circuit Courts.

A Decade of Definition

During the ten years after the first *Brown* decision, the federal courts repeatedly reaffirmed and strengthened the principle that "in the field of public education the doctrine of 'separate but equal' has no place." Scores of decisions brought the broad language of *Brown* into sharper focus and gave it more precise definition.

The judges recognized the force of local customs and traditions, but they made it clear that disagreement with the rule of the *Brown* case, no matter how violent, was not a valid reason for failure to comply with the orders of federal courts to desegregate. Through most of the decade, they permitted delay in the start of compliance and gradual extension of desegregation once it began, depending upon varying local circumstances. By 1964, however, the judges were demanding less deliberation and more speed.

Of the laws and devices adopted to avoid or minimize desegregation, many were declared unconstitutional, the ultimate test being the effect of their application. The judges showed increasing intolerance of any move to perpetuate segregation. They insisted that school systems treat all children alike, insofar as their race was concerned. The net effect of all the court decisions was to narrow the area of maneuverability for those states and school systems that resisted desegregation.

Some of the judges made no secret of their belief that the "separate but equal" doctrine that the Supreme Court established in 1896 still was the correct interpretation of the Constitution, and their decisions on school desegregation reflected their personal convictions. But they were in the minority. At the height of the New Orleans school crisis in 1960, Congressman Otto Passman addressed a special session of the Louisiana legislature. "My friends," he lamented, "it is not pleasant to contemplate, but it appears to be true that at least some federal judges take their orders directly from the United States Supreme Court." By the tenth anniversary of the *Brown* decision, even the most recalcitrant of the judges was taking orders from the Supreme Court.

9.
The Editors

"My situation is this: How can I lead when I look behind me and no one is following?"

J. Q. Mahaffey, editor of the Texarkana *Gazette,* expressed a dilemma that he faced in common with many other Southern newspaper editors. In the fall of 1956, when he made this comment, his community had been the scene of an incident that attracted wide attention. Two Negroes sought admission to the local junior college, but protesting whites gathered, and the Negroes were kept out. Mahaffey wrote:

"When a newspaper in this part of the country supports compliance with the Supreme Court ruling, it finds that it has little or no public support from the white people and its stand merely serves to aggravate the situation.

"We have begged our people to be calm about the matter and

247

have editorialized at length against any type of violence or intimidation. This was not a very strong stand. I was not proud of it but I felt that any other position would have the effect of creating a situation which could have led to violence.

"In all of my newspaper experience I have never had a more difficult situation to deal with. I have been assailed by my conscience of what is right on the one hand and by my common sense of wanting to do the best thing for the public on the other. . . ."

An examination of press performance in the seventeen-state region during the first decade of school desegregation suggests that, like Mahaffey, most editors were looking over their shoulders to see who was following them. This offers an explanation of the close correlation between the editorial positions taken by newspapers and prevailing public opinion in their places of publication.

The newspaper editors of the Southern and border states recognized that the Supreme Court's decision placed an unusual responsibility on them. From their typewriters flowed a torrent of editorial opinion. From their desks went orders to their news staffs to give the delicate school desegregation story special handling.

As a subject for both editorial comment and news reporting, school desegregation received handling as varied as local public reaction. Through the influence of the editorials and news they print, newspapers generally are regarded as being "molders of public opinion." But on the school-race issue, the public seemed to be molding newspaper opinion as much as the newspapers were molding public opinion.

The general pattern is clear. In the border area, where the Supreme Court decision was widely accepted, the major newspapers supported the ruling and urged compliance. Around the outer fringe of the eleven Southern states, public reaction was to recognize the authority of the Court but to hold compliance to a minimum; this was the position taken by most newspapers in these states. In the Deep South the controlling whites denounced the decision and resolutely resisted compliance; the majority of newspapers were in tune with this point of view.

For Full Compliance

In the border states and the District of Columbia, major newspapers gave strong editorial endorsement to the desegregation decision and called for compliance with it. And, as a rule, their communities did comply, without delay and without serious public protest.

The District of Columbia schools desegregated immediately after the 1954 decision, with the encouragement of the Washington *Post*. The District school system became a constant target for the criticism of segregationists, but the *Post* said at the end of the second year: "Desegregation has been accomplished here with surprising ease, understanding and good sense, and it has been accomplished without disrupting the school system. . . . As a community we can be proud of the accomplishment to date."

St. Louis, Missouri, also desegregated its schools in 1954. The *Post-Dispatch* approved enthusiastically, and by the end of the first year was advocating desegregation of faculties. "Certainly the color line must not be removed from one end of the classroom only to be redrawn in front of the teacher's desk," it editorialized.

When Louisville desegregated its schools peacefully in 1956, the *Courier-Journal* was given credit for having played a major role in creating a climate of public opinion favorable to the change. The school board plan for desegregation evoked from the paper this comment: "The entire program seems to us to be in the spirit of full and sensible compliance with the ruling of the Supreme Court. And one of its soundest aspects, it seems to us, is the acceptance of full desegregation at the beginning of the 1956 school year—from kindergarten through the 12th grade—rather than the grade-a-year approach hesitatingly endorsed by some less forthright planners elsewhere."

West Virginia desegregated its schools to an extent and with a dispatch unequaled in any other entire state. Harry G. Hoffman, editor of the Charleston *Gazette,* outlined the editorial policy of his paper: "We are for equality and freedom of the individual, regardless of race or creed, to go to the school of his choice . . . to lead his own life with no restrictions except respect for the law and his fellow man." Superintendent C. D. Tamplin of the Boone County schools acknowledged that "the work of the Charleston *Gazette* was of tremendous help in preparing our people for the integration process."

The Negro Press

The Negro newspapers were very nearly unanimous in insisting upon compliance with the school desegregation decision and upon removal of every vestige of racial discrimination from American life. The Baltimore *Afro-American,* the Norfolk *Journal and Guide,* the Birmingham *World,* the Atlanta *World* and other Negro papers published in the region were as vigorous in their editorial positions as were the Chicago *Defender* and the Pittsburgh *Courier.*

One Negro paper, the *Arkansas State Press,* perished in the fury of Little Rock. Established by L. C. and Daisy Bates in 1941, the *State Press* by 1957 had built a circulation of some twenty thousand in Arkansas alone. Then the segregationists turned the screws. State and local advertising completely vanished, and 90 percent of the paper's national advertising was canceled. Circulation dropped to less than five thousand. The last edition, published on October 30, 1959, carried an editorial explanation that the *State Press* was "a survivor of terror but a victim of boycott."

A few Negro editors urged the continuation of segregation. They argued that the help of the white man was necessary to Negro progress and that the greatest gain was to be made within the framework of a segregated society. The writings of these Negro editors were reprinted and widely distributed by white segregationists.

In the Middle

Harder to find than a Negro segregationist editor in the eleven Southern states was a white integrationist editor. Many recognized the authority of the Supreme Court and counseled calm and cautious acceptance of the school desegregation decision. But, to remove any doubt or suspicion on the point, they emphasized that they were not "integrationists."

These editors voiced the opinions of newspapers in the layer of states surrounding the Deep South. This tier of states lay between the border area and the Deep South both geographically and in point of view. Majority white public opinion there favored segregated schools but was amenable to desegregation, provided it could be held to "token" proportions. The editor with his ear to the ground— or looking over his shoulder—could determine that by taking this position he would not run the risk of losing his followers.

North Carolina offers an example of a state that took a stance between substantial compliance and massive resistance. Scores of editorials appeared in the state's major daily newspapers in the decade after the May 17, 1954, Supreme Court decision. The decision itself, the passing of the state pupil assignment act and the first desegregation of public schools in the state were among the key developments that prompted editorial comment. All of the newspapers expressed opinions of marked similarity.

Commenting on the May 17 decision, the Winston-Salem *Journal* said: "The long-awaited Supreme Court order in the public school segregation cases is about as lenient as it possibly could be. . . . The court has given North Carolina and the other segregation states the time they sought to work out compliance with its decision in the light of local conditions. With the emphasis thus placed upon local solutions, it is incumbent upon each affected state and community to begin to make its plans for the future. . . . The opportunity to find the right solution is best if we begin to seek it now. If we wait until we are forced, part of that opportunity will be lost."

The heart of the North Carolina approach to the Court decision was the state pupil assignment law, of which the Charlotte *Observer* said: "The genius of the pupil assignment law . . . is that it will enable local school boards to control desegregation by keeping it a limited, selective process instead of a sudden mass overturning of community relationships. But it will do that only if it is fairly and honestly administered. That means that here and there in North Carolina, properly qualified Negro students must be enrolled in the white schools as individuals or in small groups."

The first test of the assignment law came in the summer of 1957. The school boards of Charlotte, Greensboro and Winston-Salem approved the applications of a few Negro pupils for transfer to white schools that September. Typical of editorial reaction in all three cities was that of the Charlotte *News:* "The Charlotte City School Board has acted to preserve the schools. It has acted to prevent massive, court-decreed integration. It has acted to retain local control of the schools. It has acted in honesty and good faith. Citizens who seek the same goals will respect the board's painful but honest decision."

And so it was as each new wave in the school crisis crested. The major daily newspapers of the state spoke almost as with a single editorial voice. They called for orderly, but limited, desegregation. They deplored violence, whether in North Carolina or elsewhere. To them, closing schools was unthinkable as an alternative to desegregation. Other editors in the middle tier of states took similar stands.

Advocates of Resistance

In the Deep South also the major newspapers and their white readers were in general agreement. They were for segregation. They denounced the Supreme Court justices and their decision. Their resistance to compliance was relentless. Sometimes they found themselves backed into a corner, but they did not surrender. They merely retreated to another prepared position.

Loudest of the segregationist editorial voices was that of the late Fred Sullens of Jackson, Mississippi. A native of Missouri, Sullens went to Jackson as a young man. He acquired fame not only for his fire-breathing editorials, but also for physical combat with public officials who stirred his ire.

To Sullens there was no middle ground on the school segregation issue. In an editorial on the front page of his *Daily News* he proclaimed "You Are For Us Or Against Us." "This is a fight for white supremacy," he wrote. ". . . the school integration order eventually means miscegenation, mixed marriages and widespread mongrelization, followed by complete social equality in all its uglier forms. . . . In the awakening being sought there will be no room for neutrals or non-combatants. . . . If you are a member of the Caucasian race, a white man or woman, then you must stand up and be counted."

The *Daily News* greeted the 1954 Supreme Court decision with a front-page, black-bordered editorial entitled "Blood on the White Marble Steps" in which it fixed on the Court the blame for any violence that might follow. In other editorials Sullens called the justices "those nine muddy-minded political jurists" and "fellow-conspirators" and their decision "infamous." He urged U.S. senators from the South "to institute impeachment proceedings against all members of the court and to prosecute those proceedings with all possible vigor."

Sullens emitted a steady barrage of such comment in his editorials and columns until his death in 1957 at the age of eighty. Jimmy Ward picked up the cudgels; in his column "Covering the Crossroads" he loosed a daily diatribe against integrationists and heaped praise on segregationists.

No less voluble or determined than Sullens and Ward in his defense of segregation, but much more genteel in his language, was Thomas R. Waring, editor of the *News and Courier* in aristocratic Charleston, South Carolina. For sheer volume and variety of his editorial fusillades against the Supreme Court, Waring was without peer. Day after day he defended the advantages of segregation and attacked the evils of race mixing.

Of the May 17 decision Waring wrote that "the Supreme Court has cut deep into the sinews of the Republic." When the Clarendon County, South Carolina, school board expressed its determination to close its schools rather than desegregate them as the Court ordered, he said: "The court has ruled. Now the people will act, according to their own fashion." The public schools of the county remained open, and segregated, throughout the decade.

When Negroes entered Central High School in Little Rock, Waring commented: ". . . The Supreme Court has twisted the Constitution to mean things it never said. If this perverted 'law of the land' continues, people will find other ways to maintain a way of life. South Carolinians, we believe, will reluctantly close their public schools before they mix the races. Means then will have to be found to educate white children unable to afford private schooling."

Ultimately Charleston's moment of decision came, and it kept its public schools open at the price of some desegregation. In September, 1963, the first Negroes entered schools with whites in the city where, as the local saying goes, the Ashley and the Cooper rivers join to form the Atlantic Ocean. In the spirit of Charleston, Waring accepted the unpleasant reality with these words: ". . . Much as Charlestonians resent the federal courts usurping the function of the city's school board, we don't believe they would have approved violent resistance and demonstrations. . . . Most things in life come quietly, as integration came to Charleston's public schools. A cancer often eats away while one feels fit and well. . . . While integration began peacefully in Charleston, it will proceed at a high cost in genuine education."

The segregation barrier having been broken in the public schools, Waring continued to support the establishment of private schools. "The 'can do' philosophy being manifested in the private school movement is a credit to Charleston County," he said. "We urge people in other communities to sit up and take notice of what can be accomplished."

Vacillating Virginia

North Carolinians like to refer to their state as a "valley of humility between two mountains of conceit." On the one side lies South Carolina and on the other Virginia, both steeped in the history of the plantation South. Virginia is not, geographically, in the Deep South. But on the school desegregaton issue Virginia—at first —aligned itself with South Carolina and other Deep South states. By 1964 Virginia had outdone North Carolina in token compliance, although more by necessity than by choice. Leading Virginia in its vacillations, or reflecting them as the case may be, was James Jackson Kilpatrick, successor to Douglas Southall Freeman as editor of the Richmond *News Leader*.

For a brief period after the May 17, 1954, Supreme Court decision Virginia flirted with the "token" approach that North Carolina adopted. This was fully in keeping with Kilpatrick's first editorial advice to the people of the state. "This is no time for rebellion," he cautioned. "It is not time for a weak surrender either. It is a time to sit tight, to think, to unite in a proposal that would win the Supreme Court's approval. . . . To bring the two races together in the social intimacy of the classroom will not come easily to the South. This newspaper, as its readers know, believes in segregated schools. We believe also in abiding by the law—abiding by *all* the law, including laws that may be devised consistent with the law laid down by the Supreme Court yesterday." The editorial continued: "We accept the Supreme Court's ruling. We do not accept it willingly, or cheerfully, or philosophically. We accept it because we have to. . . ."

Tokenism was not long in losing its attraction for Virginia, and the state became wedded to "massive resistance." Kilpatrick and the state changed together. In the fall of 1955 he wrote: ". . . the Supreme Court has determined in the field of racial relations, to repeal the Tenth Amendment to the Constitution, and to twist and distort the Fourteenth Amendment. The Court has chosen to ram down the South's throat the full bitter dose of its sociological ideas. Through a ruthless process of judicial oppression, the court is saying to the South: You will not conduct your public affairs as your people wish, but as we command; you will no longer exercise your judgment in maintaining public peace and order between the races, but henceforth will be governed in your most intimate relationships by judicial fiat. . . . By every lawful means that can be devised, this tyranny must be resisted, step by step and inch by inch, if the vitality of Southern civilization is to be preserved, and all that is best and finest in our culture is not to be lost in the indolence and degradation of a mixed society."

Soon after that the *News Leader* posed a question: "What we must ask ourselves as Virginians, as heirs to the philosophical inheritance of Jefferson and Madison, is whether any means exists by which this 'process of judicial legislation' may be brought to pause." And it gave its answer: "This is the right of interposition."

As the rediscoverer of "interposition"—the placing of the power of the state between its people and the federal government—Kilpatrick's voice was heard throughout his own state, and beyond. In a debate with Thurgood Marshall, general counsel of the NAACP Legal Defense and Educational Fund, in Newton, Massachusetts, in the fall of 1958, Kilpatrick expressed his credo: "We will fight state by state, county by county, city by city, school by school, and if necessary, room by room. . . . The white South proposes to resist compulsory integration of its schools by every device of legislation and litigation that ingenious men can contrive—and we can yet contrive quite a few."

But not enough, not in Virginia. In February, 1959, massive resistance crumbled in Virginia, and in the years that followed Negroes were admitted to schools with whites in growing numbers. By 1961 the *News Leader* was saying, "What we have learned in Virginia in the past year or so—in Richmond, Norfolk, Charlottesville and other communities—is that a certain level of desegregation is not, in fact, intolerable." But Kilpatrick did not give up. "Will the war ever end?" he asked. And his reply was: "No. For in a deep sense, it is merely a continuation of a ten-thousand-year conflict that began when a consciousness of race first filtered into the mind of man."

The Nonconformists

Most editors, whether in the compliance, token compliance or resistance states, expressed opinions that coincided with controlling public opinion in their localities. Some editors, however, took positions contrary to the thinking of the white majority. In a number of instances their deviation brought reprisals, or rewards, and in some cases both.

One of the first to pay the price for expressing his unorthodox convictions was John H. O'Dowd, executive editor of the Florence

(South Carolina) *Morning News.* On June 17, 1955, he said in an editorial: "Since the Supreme Court's publication of its implementation decree, the Southland has been feeding itself large doses of self-delusion and false hope. Politicians, writers, wishful thinkers and the unthinking have been telling our people that the court's decree can be defeated and will be defeated. The court's decree will not be defeated. South Carolina's people need to hear realism."

O'Dowd's readers responded with anonymous threatening letters and phone calls, cancellation of subscriptions and advertising and attempted physical violence against him. In a speech in May of 1956, he made a plea for "honest disagreement." "Our Southland is becoming a place where non-concurrence with the established orthodoxy is cause for rejection and social ostracism," he said. "When people cannot disagree in good faith, fear has replaced conviction and concern. . . ." A few months after he made his speech, he resigned and went to Chicago to work.

Ralph McGill of the Atlanta *Constitution* came as near to being an "integrationist" as any editor in the South. He could write from personal experience that the newspaperman in the Deep South who "produces critical opinion experiences an immediacy of thermal reaction. . . . A cross may be burned in his yard, or his windows broken by stones thrown in the night. He personally is pilloried, vigorously and libelously, by political demagogues."

Perhaps no newspaper suffered as great losses as did the *Arkansas Gazette,* which took its stand against Governor Faubus at Little Rock in 1957. J. N. Heiskell, editor and publisher, later told the Southern Newspaper Publishers Association: "It's like hell. . . . 1. You lose circulation. 2. You get abusive letters. 3. You get argued at. . . . But there comes a time when a newspaperman has to decide whether to follow his conscience or material considerations." Heiskell followed his conscience, and according to Harry Ashmore, executive editor of the paper, "had to watch the substance he had gathered for his family drain away under boycott and bitter, constant abuse—well over two million dollars irrevocably lost before circulation and advertising hit bottom and began the slow crawl back."

The Mississippi editor who stepped out of line did so at his peril. Hodding Carter of the *Delta Democrat-Times* at Greenville was hanged in effigy. J. Oliver Emmerich of the McComb *Enterprise-Journal* was assaulted on the street.

Mrs. Hazel Brannon Smith of the Lexington (Mississippi) *Advertiser* was an outspoken critic of the Citizens' Councils. In 1958 a group of local businessmen launched an opposition newspaper because, the UPI reported, "Mrs. Smith does not reflect the thinking of most of the white people of the county at a time when solidarity of opinion is needed to preserve the Southern way of life." Her paper lost most of its local advertising. Two years earlier her husband, who had been administrator of the Holmes County Hospital, had been fired, against the recommendation of the staff. To the hospital trustees he was too "controversial." Her newspaper office was bombed.

Ira B. Harkey, Jr., editor and publisher of the Pascagoula *Chronicle,* was a special target of the segregationists. His philosophy was that "the hateists must be taken by the shirtfront and have the facts of life rammed down their throats—figuratively, of course." Among these facts was that "the Negro is a human being . . . a radical idea in some parts of the South." In one editorial he wrote: "Christ was the greatest champion of the underdog the world has ever known. If he were to visit us here, now, by whose side would he stand, beside the brick-throwing, foul-mouthed, destroying eggers-on, or beside the trembling victim of their hate?" The Jackson County Citizens' Emergency Unit organized a campaign to drive the *Chronicle* out of business. Harkey sold his paper in 1963.

Mingled with the local brickbats thrown at the nonconformist editors were bouquets tossed from afar. The Pulitzer prizes, most coveted of all recognitions of journalistic achievement, suggest the flow of awards to Southern editors who expressed locally unpopular views about race and education. Six of the ten prizes awarded for editorial writing in the decade after the 1954 Court decision went to these editors: 1957, to Buford Boone of the Tuscaloosa (Alabama) *News;* 1958, to Harry Ashmore of the *Arkansas Gazette;* 1959, to Ralph McGill of the Atlanta *Constitution;* 1960, to Lenoir Chambers of the Norfolk *Virginian-Pilot;* 1963, to Ira Harkey of the

Pascagoula *Chronicle;* 1964, to Mrs. Hazel Brannon Smith of the Lexington *Advertiser*. In 1958 the *Arkansas Gazette* also received the Pulitzer prize for disinterested and meritorious public service and J. N. Heiskell received the first special award to be given by the Columbia University School of Journalism "for singular journalistic performance in the public interest."

The Influence of Facts

In their editorials newspapers make a deliberate effort to influence public opinion. But the facts that newspapers print in their news columns also influence public opinion. "Facts are the basis of reason, the only hope of a solution," Coleman A. Harwell of the Nashville *Tennessean,* said in his presidential report to the Associated Press Managing Editors in the fall of 1958. "A public that does not know the facts cannot act intelligently. A public that does not comprehend the facts is dangerous. That places a tremendous responsibility on newspapers."

Harwell spoke of school desegregation, of the problems it brought to a community and to a newspaper. He knew how explosive these problems could be. The previous fall the first Negroes had entered classrooms with whites in Nashville, and a desegregated school was bombed.

As a rule, newspaper editors subscribe to the principle that they should print "the facts, all the facts and nothing but the facts," subject to their judgment of news values and the limitations of space. In handling the run of the day's news, these judgments are made quickly and routinely.

In those places where the Supreme Court decision was accepted from the first with little or no opposition, the school desegregation story was regarded as routine. When Louisville desegregated its schools in 1956, Norman Isaacs of the *Times* said, "As far as we are concerned, we were just adding to the school reporter's beat."

South of the border states, however, editors viewed the approach of desegregation with degrees of apprehension varying with the fever of public reaction. Accordingly, they did not treat the story routinely but took whatever measures they deemed appropriate to control the news their papers printed. They were concerned about their responsibility to inform the public, but they also were concerned about law and order in their communities. This desire to maintain public peace often was the occasion for the use of unaccustomed caution in writing and displaying the news, and sometimes for the deliberate withholding of facts.

In Winston-Salem, North Carolina, plans for covering the start of school desegregation in 1957 were made in conferences attended by all the editors and reporters who would be directly involved. From these conferences emerged a statement of policy:

"Our first responsibility is to inform our readers of all events which are of interest and importance to them. The school segregation-desegregation story is news which must be reported.

"We also have a responsibility to aid in reaching satisfactory solutions to community problems. In this instance, we should try to make possible a calm, peaceful adjustment to the new situation brought about by the Supreme Court decision and to avoid the stimulation of passion and perhaps violence. . . .

"If incidents occur in connection with desegregation, we must report them as they happen. If there are mass meetings, or if delegations call on the school board, or if suits are filed, or if there is violence, we should report according to our judgment of news values and community responsibility.

"Whatever happens, we want to take particular pains to be accurate in our reporting and headline writing and to exercise restraint in our treatment of the news."

The statement spelled out in detail how the policy was to be executed—by reporters, photographers, copy readers, headline writers and editors. While the policy was to print the news, the procedure was far from routine.

Some editors took an active part, beyond what they printed in their newspapers, in planning community policy. With the advent of school desegregation in Dallas, Texas, in 1961, a group of white and Negro leaders met in the offices of the *Times Herald*. From this meeting came the committee of seven whites and seven Negroes who worked with the Dallas Citizens Council toward orderly change.

The Dallas newspapers helped the Citizens Council, composed of top businessmen, to prepare the community for peaceful acceptance of desegregation. According to Gladwin Hill of the *New York Times,* one of the main tenets of the Dallas plan was "to avoid publicity to prevent stirring up controversy." Editors of the Dallas papers flatly denied that they cooperated to the extent of suppressing the news. "It would have been difficult to cover the story more thoroughly than we did," said Tom J. Simmons of the *News.* Felix McKnight of the *Times Herald* said: "It is not true that Dallas newspapers suppressed newsworthy events during the long period of integration. . . . We published countless integration stories but we did not publish the inconsequential. If that be bad newspapering, I am guilty, but I feel gratified that we have not had a serious racial incident in this city."

The *Times Herald* won the Texas Associated Press Managing Editors award for community service in 1961. The citation read: "Its news reports, editorials and leadership had much to do with the peaceful beginning of integration in the Dallas schools. This was a fine example of the effectiveness of responsible journalism. . . . It followed a policy of playing down incidents which if sensationalized could have flared into violent racism."

In Memphis, the Tennessee metropolis on the bluffs of the Mississippi, the *Commercial Appeal* "consciously played down certain news on racial matters." Editor Frank Ahlgren explained his paper's policy and performance:

"In wartime we accept censorship and voluntary suppression of news. We do so not because we like it but because we would otherwise give aid and comfort to the enemy. In many cities today we are, in a sense, at war. Our enemies are all the extremists on both sides. . . .

"When Memphis began desegregation of the schools . . . the *Commercial Appeal* carried two little advance items. . . . On the morning of the event itself we carried no advance news whatever—

for fear that it would cause the extremists to turn out and endanger the peace. After the event we gave reasonable coverage to the developments, with some pictures.

"I must admit that as an editor evaluating news interest I have been remiss by normal journalistic standards. Yet it has seemed to me to be the responsible course . . . putting, you might say, the public interest above journalistic interests as traditionally interpreted."

In Memphis, as in Dallas, there was a biracial committee on which all the news media were represented. Ahlgren conceded that in Memphis the media joined in what "could doubtless be called news management."

The policies and practices in Winston-Salem, Dallas and Memphis were not identical, but basically they were the same. The newspapers adopted carefully considered special criteria for handling the school desegregation story. The editors placed a higher priority on their sense of responsibility for public order than upon their responsibility to give the public all the facts. In deciding what to print, they looked beyond the news to the effect that its publication would have on those who read it. What editors in these three cities did was representative of what many editors throughout the South were doing, with local variations.

Some editors, mostly in the Deep South, did not fear violence as much as they feared any breakdown in segregation. Ralph McGill charged that "certain Mississippi papers have encouraged violence, and several South Carolina newspapers have done the same thing"; he added that Southern newspapers had "failed pretty badly" in their handling of the school desegregation story. Ira Harkey said that some papers—he singled out those in Jackson, Mississippi—"are very rabid and prejudicial in their stands and actually added to the hate and confusion by slanting or distorting the news."

Not all the editors who regarded school desegregation as just another story were in the border states. Scattered through the South were editors who took the position that their newspapers should print the facts, no matter how the public might react.

As time passed, attitudes in the South began to soften. After school desegregation came to a community, it relaxed—not always, but usually—and some of the rawer emotions drained off. As the people relaxed, the editors of their local newspapers relaxed with them; and school desegregation was reported more nearly like any other important event.

C. A. McKnight, as executive director of Southern Education Reporting Service, in 1955 evaluated press treatment of school desegregation during the first year after the Supreme Court decision. He found that the story had received "minimum coverage" that "all too often has been unbalanced, and frequently distorted." In 1959, then editor of the Charlotte *Observer,* his assessment was that "the press North and South is doing a much more authoritative, complete and constructive job."

Toward the end of the decade the eruption of the Negro protest movement took the spotlight off school segregation in the South and turned it on every facet of race relations throughout the country. No longer was there a dearth of news about the race issue. The newspaper reader who wanted to keep abreast of all the news that was published faced a formidable task.

10.
The Clergy

Clergymen, like newspaper editors, are regarded as molders of public opinion. While editors greeted the Supreme Court opinion in the *School Segregation Cases* with a torrent of comment, most white Southern clergymen—Protestant, Catholic and Jewish—followed the first part of the Biblical injunction, "There is . . . a time to be silent and a time to speak."

In their silence the individual clergymen were not following the example of their denominational leaders. The central bodies of the major denominations endorsed the *Brown* decision, and most of them acted quickly.

The response was immediate from national organizations representing Protestant, Catholic and Jewish faiths. The decision came down on May 15, 1954. On May 18 the Catholic Interracial Council issued a statement that: "This is a logical step in the expansion and perfection of American democracy. The next step is the creation and practice of community educational patterns consistent with the spirit and intent of the court decision." The National Council of Churches on May 19 said, "The decision is a milestone in the achievement of human rights, another evidence of the endeavor to respect the dignity and worth of all men." The Synagogue Council of America welcomed the decision "with deep satisfaction."

The White Protestants

The South is predominantly Protestant. The Baptist, Methodist, Presbyterian and Episcopal churches, in that order, have the largest memberships. All of these denominations adopted statements of position on the Supreme Court opinion.

The Southern Baptist Convention recognized "the fact that this Supreme Court decision is in harmony with the constitutional guarantee of equal freedom to all citizens, and with the Christian principles of equal justice and love for all men." The Methodist General Conference observed that the decision necessitated "far-reaching and often difficult community adjustments"; the Conference called upon Methodists "to effect these adjustments in all good faith, with brotherliness and patience." The General Assembly of the Presbyterian Church in the United States (South) commended "the principle of the decision" to its members and urged them "to lend their assistance to those charged with the duty of implementing the decision." The General Convention of the Protestant Episcopal Church declared that "the Court's decision is just, right and necessary." The corresponding central bodies of other major denominations adopted similar statements of position.

These were first reactions. As time passed, the denominational bodies adopted stronger statements of policy. They tended generally to look beyond the question of school desegregation and to encompass the total relationship of the church to Negro Americans. Other influential groups could, and usually did, treat desegregation as a practical, secular question. The churches by their inherent nature were compelled to examine the moral, ethical, religious aspects of the issue.

The individual Southern white Protestant minister was torn by strong conflicting forces in establishing his role in the controversy. Most of the ministers served churches of the denominations that unequivocally had declared the justness of the Supreme Court decision by religious and democratic standards. Neither the ministers nor the congregations they served were bound by the policy statements of their denominations. So the minister had to reach a personal decision in the light of his own conscience and convictions and those of his congregation.

Whatever their personal beliefs, most ministers elected to remain aloof from the conflict. Few of them preached sermons forthrightly opposing segregation in the schools or on general principle. Those who did preach on the issue tended to allude to it briefly when speaking on some other subject. Fewer still took active part in school desegregation controversies in their local communities.

The Rev. John Morris, an Episcopal minister in Dillon, South Carolina, suggested the explanation when he said, "A clergyman should be a leader, but he shouldn't be so far ahead of his people that he's cut off from them. If I felt the schools here in Dillon should be integrated tomorrow—which I don't—but if I did, I would not be a minister here any more."

The Rev. Robert Collie, a Methodist minister of Kentwood, Louisiana, said, "I can preach my whole convictions—with the realization that the Bishop will have to find another place for me." Collie expressed doubt about the influence of clergymen in their communities. "Does anyone really believe that the community in general and the power structure in particular will reverently bow their heads in obedience if a pastor tells them what their attitudes and actions on a given course of action should be?" he asked. And he answered, "Our society just doesn't accord that kind of power to ministers; it hasn't since the time of the Puritans."

In different words the ministers were saying the same thing that Editor Mahaffey of Texarkana had said to describe his situation. The minister ran greater risks than the editor, however. The editor's audience was an entire community, to whom he had no direct responsibility; that is, the community could not fire him if it disliked his editorial opinions. But the Protestant minister usually was dependent upon his congregation for his job; in any event his effectiveness hinged upon his having the financial and moral support of his members.

No matter what the convictions of their minister might be, the members of almost any church shared the prevailing sentiment of their local community on segregation. The minister who stepped out of line did so at his peril. When the Rev. Robert Trotman of Lumpkin, Georgia, praised the Court decision as "just and Christian," his Baptist congregation requested his resignation. The Rev. Henry A. Buchanan, who served two rural Baptist churches near Shellman in Southwest Georgia, also was asked to resign when he spoke in favor of the decision. The Rev. John Lyles, pastor of a Presbyterian church at Marion, South Carolina, was dismissed after he collaborated with other ministers in putting together a book of essays, entitled *South Carolinians Speak,* expressing "moderate" views. The First Presbyterian Church of Columbus, Georgia, severed its pastoral ties with the Rev. Robert Blakely McNeill when he wrote an article for *Look* magazine in which he advocated "creative contacts" between whites and Negroes. In January, 1963, twenty-eight young Methodist ministers in Mississippi issued a statement condemning racial discrimination and opposing the closure of public schools to avoid desegregating them. Retaliation was swift and severe. The salaries of three were discontinued immediately. Another church withdrew the financial aid it was giving to one of the ministers who was attending college. Pressures on fifteen were so great that they resigned and moved to other states. An official of the Southern Regional Council commented, "In the South we have a new class of DP's—displaced parsons." He said that the Council had helped to relocate a number of ministers who had lost their churches for supporting the Supreme Court decision. The denominations also operated relocation projects.

Among the first places where violence met the move to desegregate the schools were Sturgis and Clay, Kentucky, in 1956. Two ministers, the Revs. C. Sumpter Logan and Theodore A. Braun, who lived near Sturgis, went there to investigate for themselves the reports they had been reading in the newspapers about mob action. They wrote in *Christian Century* that "no white church was making any attempt to interpret the crisis. . . . We found not one white pastor who knew a Negro pastor (there are several in Sturgis) with whom we might talk." They visited in the home of James Gordon, the Negro who had sought to have his children enrolled in white schools in Clay. For this, they said, "We too had become objects of mob anger."

The next fall brought Little Rock, where the forces tearing at the clergymen were revealed clearly. During the summer of 1957, when it was generally assumed that Central High School would desegregate quietly in September, the Little Rock Ministerial Association requested that its members speak from the pulpit to urge orderly conduct and respect for the law. A number of ministers did.

The ministers were not prepared for the actions taken by Governor Faubus. But on September 3, the day after the governor sent National Guardsmen to Central High School, fifteen of them issued a statement protesting the action. Another fifteen immediately countered with a statement supporting the governor and continued segregation.

Over the next three weeks—until September 23, when the National Guard was withdrawn and the mob took over—ministers from Little Rock and elsewhere in Arkansas published five separate statements deploring Faubus's actions. Most of these statements advocated the observance of law and order. On September 21, however, thirty-five Arkansas ministers (including eight from Little Rock) contended that segregation was improper for religious and ethical reasons.

On Sunday the 22nd, the day before Central High School was to reopen with no Guardsmen on duty, a number of Little Rock ministers held "Prayers for Peace" with their congregations. At the Henderson Methodist Church five Negroes sought to join in the prayers. They were turned away.

When Monday the 23rd arrived, the city's clergy was split. A few favored an all-out endorsement of desegregation on religious-ethical grounds. A far larger number, including Little Rock's most influential ministers, pleaded for compliance in the name of law and order. A third group, headed by the Rev. Wesley Pruden, a leading Citizens' Councilman, favored continued segregation. Pruden was affiliated with the Southern Baptist Convention; the others in his group were members of fundamentalist Baptist splinter sects.

After federal troops had checked mob action, the segregationist ministers became increasingly articulate. Pruden, speaking to the Citizens' Council, berated the "Communist Supreme Court." Missionary Baptists in North Little Rock sent a telegram to President Eisenhower protesting the "unholy invasion of the customs, rights and privileges of the citizens of Arkansas."

Early in October, the Right Rev. Robert Raymond Brown, Episcopal bishop of Arkansas, proposed that all denominations join in a Columbus Day prayer service dedicated to the restoration of law and order. The proposal was endorsed by President Eisenhower and opposed by Governor Faubus. The ministers who agreed to join in the Columbus Day services were labeled "race mixers" by the Citizens' Council and by the Mothers' League of Central High School.

On the night before the Columbus Day prayer services, twenty-four segregationist ministers held a prayer session of their own. It was well attended. The Columbus Day service of the following day was not well attended, and the prayers were cautious in tone. That tone is reflected in the words of the minister who said, "Good Christians can honestly disagree on the question of segregation or integration. But we can all join together in prayers for guidance, that peace may return to our city."

On the day of the prayer service Pruden published a quarter-page advertisement in the Arkansas *Democrat* in which he gave an affirmative answer to the question, "Can a Christian be a segregationist?" In the ad Pruden quoted the Rev. Robert G. Lee of Memphis, three times president of the Southern Baptist Convention, as favoring segregation. Lee immediately replied that he was not a segregationist and demanded a retraction. Pruden responded in another ad saying, "In my opinion Dr. Lee was mistakenly identified with that glorious band of Christian patriots who are standing courageously by the South in her hour of crisis."

In September, 1958, after Governor Faubus had closed the high schools in Little Rock to avoid desegregation, a group of Presbyterian ministers protested. The reaction caused Faubus to tell the press, "I am aware that a large number of ministers in the Presbyterian church have been effectively brain-washed."

A reporter asked, "By whom?"

Faubus replied, "By the leftwingers and the Communists."

A number of ministers, representing different denominations, demanded—unsuccessfully—that the governor apologize. After that, the ministry in Little Rock lapsed into silence.

Thomas F. Pettigrew and Ernest Q. Campbell, of the Harvard University Laboratory of Social Relations, made a study of the attitudes and actions of the clergy in the Little Rock crisis. They found that a majority of Little Rock ministers personally favored school desegregation, but only eight were outspoken on the subject. The eight were young (average age, thirty-six), relatively new to their pastorates (average, four years) and their churches were small (average, four hundred members) and not particularly influential in the community. None was engaged in a major fund-raising project at the time of the crisis. "In other words," said Pettigrew and Campbell, "the freer the minister from organizational restraints, the more likely he was to defend integration publicly. . . . Ministerial behavior in a crisis is less a matter of courage than it is a matter of pressures for money and members squelching principle."

"In Little Rock," they concluded, "neither of the two major clerical moves—the condemnation of Faubus and the peace prayers —declared segregation morally wrong. Yet moral judgments are the unique source of ministerial influence. . . . Notwithstanding the real restrictions placed on them in a tragic situation, the fact remains that the Little Rock ministry did not make the most efficient use of their influence."

Although most of the Southern ministers who opposed segregation kept their convictions to themselves, some carried their convictions beyond speech to action. At Mansfield, Texas, in 1956, the Rev. Donald W. Clark, an Episcopal rector from Fort Worth, urged the mob opposing desegregation to take a "Christian attitude." Texas Rangers rescued him from the mob's wrath.

That same fall in Clinton, Tennessee, the Rev. Paul Turner, pastor of the First Baptist Church, led six Negro children through the mob at the door of Clinton High School. A dozen men later assaulted him. After the beating of Turner, the people of the community defeated segregationist candidates for public office, and order returned to Clinton.

When two schools in New Orleans were desegregated in November, 1960, white students boycotted them. The first white child to break the complete boycott was Pamela Lynn Foreman, five-year-old daughter of the Rev. Lloyd Foreman, a Methodist minister. Each day the minister led his daughter through the crowd of screaming, cursing white mothers gathered around the school, and gradually other white parents joined him in escorting their children to and from school. Vandals damaged his home with rocks, bricks and red paint.

The climax to violent resistance to desegregation came at Oxford, Mississippi, in the fall of 1962 when James Meredith was admitted to the University of Mississippi. Before the rioting in which two men were killed and many injured, the ministers of Oxford had kept their counsel. In the midst of the outbreak one of them, the Rev. Duncan Gray, Jr., walked into the mob and tried to persuade the demonstrators to stop. He removed rocks and bottles from the hands of some. On the following Sunday he preached a sermon in which he said, "We must accept the fact that the color of a person's skin can no longer be a barrier to his admission to the University." He called Governor Ross Barnett "a living symbol of lawlessness." He received many abusive and threatening phone calls.

Gray was rector of St. Peter's Episcopal Church in Oxford and his father was the bishop of the Diocese of Mississippi. While he was the only clergyman who braved the wrath of the mob, ministers of the town joined in issuing a statement a few days later in which they declared that "obedience to the law and lawful authority is an essential part of the Christian life" and called for "acceptance of the action of the courts and wholehearted compliance." They set the next Sunday as a "time for repentance for our collective and individual guilt in the formation of the atmosphere which produced the strife."

Among Southern ministers who spoke out against segregation, some were shot at, threatened with bombings and beating, beaten and horse-whipped, assaulted with rocks and acid, or jailed. Assorted epithets were directed at them—from "do-gooders" and "meddlers" to "traitors to the Southern way of life" and "victims of Communist brain-washing." They received anonymous, often threatening and obscene phone calls; and slanderous rumors were circulated about them. Crosses were burned in their yards.

These circumstances perhaps explain why ministerial opposition to segregation, in the schools and elsewhere, was strongest in national church organizations and weakest in the local church. They also suggest the reasons why ministers on the firing line were bolder in groups than as individuals. The ministers of Little Rock, never very bold, were more forthright when they acted together than when alone. In a number of places groups of ministers openly gave their support to the Supreme Court decision and criticized efforts to evade it.

When the Virginia legislature passed the state's massive-resistance laws, sixty Richmond ministers issued a "statement of conviction" branding the laws as "neither democratic nor Christian." When Georgia adopted laws under which schools would be closed to avoid desegregating them, eighty Alabama ministers signed a "manifesto" declaring, "The public school system must not be destroyed. To sacrifice that system in order to avoid obedience to the decree of the Supreme Court would be to inflict tremendous loss upon multitudes of children." A year later 312 Atlanta clergymen signed a second manifesto that went far beyond the first. Similar statements came from clergymen in Columbus, Georgia; Dallas and Houston, Texas; Miami, Florida; Chattanooga, Tennessee; and other places.

When Mayor Beverly Briley of Nashville appointed a Human

Relations Committee in 1963, he pointedly omitted any white clergymen from its membership and gave as his reason that if the ministers had done their job the committee would be unnecessary. In an article describing Nashville as "the best city in the South for Negroes" *Jet* magazine said, "Most backward in racial progress are white preachers. . . . From the white churches there is almost utter silence." In May, 1964, white Nashville clergymen organized a march on City Hall to present to the mayor a statement urging "the integration of all grades in the public schools without further delay" and general desegregation of public facilities and employment. As the decade progressed, clergymen became more outspoken and active against racial discrimination.

While, particularly in the early years, the majority of the Protestant clergymen who opposed segregation trod softly on the sensitive subject, the defenders of segregation always feared these ministers' potential influence. In 1956 John Kasper, in a speech in Maryland, named the eight organizations he felt were primarily responsible for threatening the "Southern way of life." Five of the eight were religious organizations. In North Carolina, Dr. W. C. George, one of the philosophers of the segregationist movement and the first president of the Patriots of North Carolina, said, "The group most difficult to combat and the group most influential, perhaps, in bringing this evil upon us are the ministers." Speaking in New Orleans, Robert B. Patterson, Executive Secretary of the Citizens' Councils of America, urged Councilmen to infiltrate the churches and take the offensive against "the mixing of the races." Patterson continued, "By organizing within the churches, foes of integration could bring pressure on ministers to support segregation and change the position of state and national organizations which have endorsed the mixing of the races." The Citizens' Councils advocated the use of economic pressures to whip wavering clergymen into line. "Money talks and they all listen," was the slogan.

Segregationist Protestant Clergymen

The Southern white Protestant clergyman who favored segregation was not under the same restraints as those who opposed it. His views usually were those of his congregation, and he could ignore with impunity the contrary statements of policy of the highest official bodies of his denomination. He was voluble and active. Soon after the 1955 *Brown* decision, Spottswood W. Robinson III, one of the NAACP attorneys, said, "The worst obstacle we face in the fight to preserve segregated schools in the South is the white preacher."

The segregationist cleric was representative of the culture of which he was a part. Segregation was the tradition of his society, and he expressed the conviction that it was correct, not only socially but also theologically. In the Bible he found scriptural justification for his position. Most often cited was the first chapter of Genesis which says that "God created . . . every living creature . . . after their kind." Among the other passages quoted were Genesis 9:25 ("And he said, Cursed be Canaan; a servant of servants shall he be unto his brethren") and Joshua 9:23 ("Now therefore ye are cursed; and there shall none of you be freed from being bondmen, and hewers of wood and drawers of water for the house of my God").

The ministers who opposed segregation fired back other selections from the Bible to support their view. From the first chapter of Genesis they quoted, "So God created man in his own image." And from Acts 17:26, "And hath made of one blood all nations of men." And from Galatians 3:28, ". . . for ye are all one in Christ Jesus."

Regardless of interpretations of the Bible to the contrary, many devout Southern church members and their ministers maintained their belief in segregation. The Rev. Will Campbell of Nashville, Tennessee, a Baptist minister and director of the Committee of Southern Churchmen, is one of the most active clergymen in working against segregation. He wrote in his book *Race and the Renewal of the Church*: "In the eyes of the segregationist . . . the true defender of Christianity is he who would keep the races forever separate in the church and in society."

Running through the written and spoken statements of the segregationist ministers was the theme of maintaining racial purity and integrity. The Rev. J. Paul Barrett, Methodist, was the author of a pro-segregation pamphlet distributed by the States Rights Council of Georgia. In warning that racial intermarriage would be the result of school desegregation, he wrote, "A dove is as important and valuable as a quail but who wants them so mixed until you have neither?" The executive secretary of the council was the Rev. William T. Bodenhamer, a Baptist.

The Rev. Edward Brailsford Guerry, rector of St. John's Parish, John's Island, South Carolina, and son of a former bishop of the Episcopal Diocese of South Carolina, wrote in a similar vein. His article on "The Church and the Supreme Court Decision" was published in *The Living Church* in April, 1956. He said that "there are vast multitudes of both races . . . who believe that racial integrity for both races is God's will" and "cannot conscientiously accept the modern dogma that separation or segregation is per se unconstitutional or unChristian."

The Citizens' Councils gave wide distribution to a pamphlet by the Rev. G. T. Gillespie, a Presbyterian and for many years president of Belhaven College in Jackson, Mississippi, on "A Christian View on Segregation." The Rev. T. Robert Ingram, rector of St. Thomas's Episcopal Church in Houston, Texas, published a book called *Essays on Segregation.* There were many other articles, pamphlets and books developing the religious basis of segregation.

Some of the segregationist clerics joined forces to give more effective expression to their convictions. One such group called itself the Evangelical Christian Council. Its first public statement bore the signatures of fifty-three ministers, from Baptist, Methodist, Pentecostal and Assembly of God churches. They labeled "anything leading to racial amalgamation" as "a sin against almighty God." They declared, "We believe the races were created and separated by Jehovah God. . . . Each race should maintain its purity. . . . The integration of races in our schools to any extent presents grave moral, social, constitutional and political questions."

Clergymen became affiliated with lay organizations dedicated to maintaining segregation, notably the Citizens' Councils. The Editorial Advisory Board of the *Citizen*, official journal of the Citizens' Councils of America, included three ministers—the Rev. Henry J. Davis of Dundas, Virginia; the Rev. L. B. McCord of Sumter, South

Carolina; and the Rev. James P. Dees of Statesville, North Carolina. Davis was the head of the Council in Virginia. McCord had the distinction of being the superintendent of schools for Clarendon County, South Carolina, which the United States Supreme Court in 1954 ordered desegregated "with all deliberate speed." McCord responded by saying, "We have no plans to integrate our schools this year or any year in the future. Our way of life in Clarendon calls for separation of races and, come hell or high water, we plan to keep it that way." And they did.

Of all the segregationist clergymen, none was more voluble and active than the Rev. James Parker Dees, rector of Trinity Episcopal Church at Statesville, North Carolina. The late Judge John J. Parker of the United States Fourth Circuit Court of Appeals was his uncle. After graduating from the University of North Carolina in 1938, Dees went to work as a warehouse superintendent for the Atlantic Coast Line Railroad. It was not until he finished military service, in 1946, that he decided to prepare for the ministry. He served as rector of two small parishes in eastern North Carolina before going to Statesville in 1955. Until then his views on race had attracted no public attention. Soon after arriving in Statesville, he spoke to the Lions Club on the topic, "Is it Necessary for a Christian to Support Integration?"

In this speech Dees said, "I am unequivocally opposed to desegregation." He went on: "Do black birds intermingle with the blue birds? Does the redwing fly with the crows? Would it make sense for my Senior Warden to mix Black Angus cattle with his purebred Herefords? Common sense, knotty-headed common sense, cries out against it, 'No.'" He said that "the NAACP is the greatest enemy that the Negro people have" because it "is driving the Negro race to destruction." The Patriots of North Carolina, the state's leading pro-segregation organization, printed and distributed 190,000 copies of the speech.

With this publicizing of his views, Dees was in great demand as a speaker. He assumed leadership in organizations to preserve segregation. He was named president of the North Carolina Defenders of States Rights (successor to the defunct Patriots) and a member of the board of directors of the Federation for Constitutional Government. Early in 1959, when his election as president of the Defenders was announced, he issued a statement on the organization's purposes, in which he said: "We are concerned primarily with the preservation of racial segregation in our public schools. . . . The evidence is plain. We are now passing through the most critical time in the history of the human race, when the destruction of the white race through racial amalgamation is being carefully planned, when the Constitution of the United States is being rewritten by nine men on the Supreme Court, and when evidence of the Communist ideology is entering our society."

The vestry of his church asked Dees to concentrate more on his church duties and less on his outside interests, but they were powerless to do more than ask. Bishop Edwin A. Penick of the Diocese of North Carolina talked with Dees about his segregation activities but told a newspaper reporter, "I have never reprimanded him. . . . His statements are quite at variance with the position of the Episcopal Church. . . . But he is entitled to think as he pleases."

In the fall of 1963 Dees solved the problem for his bishop and those of his parishioners who disapproved his views and actions. He quit the Protestant Episcopal ministry to establish the Anglican Orthodox Church. In a statement of explanation he said: "I am getting out of the Church that I feel has departed from what I consider to have been its intellectual, spiritual and doctrinal heritage. I have had all that I can stand of its social, economic, and political program of socialism; of its pseudo-brotherhood; of its appeasement of the Communists; of its so-called civil rights; and of its rejection of much that I consider to be fundamental to the Biblical faith."

While the white Protestant clergyman who opposed segregation had his difficulties, his brothers of the cloth who upheld segregation also had their troubles. The segregationist ministers were out of step with the official positions of their denominations. They also were fighting against the rising tide of the movement to eliminate racial discrimination from the church and from national life.

277

The Catholics

The position of the Catholic church in the South was unlike that of the Protestant churches in several respects. Catholics were a minority, although a large one. There were as many Catholics in the region as there were Methodists, but only in Louisiana and Texas were there sizable concentrations of Catholics. Neither the clergy nor the laymen in the Catholic church had the freedom of thought and action characteristic of the Protestant denominations. The vast majority of Southern Protestant children were enrolled in public schools, but wherever there were enough Catholic children the church usually operated its own schools for them.

Despite these differences, the Catholic church in the South showed that it, like the Protestant clergy, was sensitive to local public opinion. The church opposed segregation. As a general rule, however, public opinion in an area was a determining factor in the timing of desegregation of Catholic schools there.

In the border states, desegregation of Catholic schools came either before or immediately after the 1954 Supreme Court decision in the public school cases. Archbishop Joseph E. Ritter desegregated the parochial schools of St. Louis in 1947; he warned parents that they would be "excommunicated if they presumed to interfere in the administrative office of their Bishop by having recourse to any authority outside the church." Between then and 1954 Catholic schools in the border states and the District of Columbia desegregated.

In some of the Southern states parochial schools were desegregated in 1954. Bishop Albert L. Fletcher of Arkansas, Bishop Vincent Waters of North Carolina and Bishop Peter L. Ireton of Virginia ordered an end to segregation in the Catholic schools of their states then. Archbishop Robert E. Lucey of San Antonio and Bishop William L. Adrian of Nashville opened the parochial schools of those cities to both races in 1954; the spread of desegregation to other Catholic schools in Texas and Tennessee tended to follow developments in the public schools. The first parochial schools in

Florida to desegregate were in Miami in 1960, after public school desegregation began there in 1959.

Desegregation in the Catholic schools began last in the Deep South, where the resistance was greatest. The change came to Georgia and Louisiana in 1962 and to South Carolina in 1963. (Tiny St. Anne's at Rock Hill, South Carolina, had admitted Negroes since 1954). At the end of the tenth school year after the Supreme Court decision, only in Alabama and Mississippi were the parochial schools still segregated.

In ordering the change, the diocesan prelates showed their concern about public opinion. The three bishops of Georgia and South Carolina announced through a joint pastoral letter early in 1961 that "Catholic pupils, regardless of color, will be admitted to Catholic schools as soon as this can be done with safety to the children and the schools." When Archbishop Paul J. Hallinan ordered segregation in the Atlanta archdiocese, he said, "We decided to move at this time to desegregated archdiocesan schools, first because it's right, and second, because an excellent climate of opinion and action already exists here." The Atlanta public schools had been desegregated the year before. In calling for desegregation in South Carolina, Bishop Francis H. Reh said, "We realize that this may be difficult, but Christ often calls upon us to act in difficult situations." A letter from Archbishop Thomas Toolen was read in all the churches of Alabama on April 26, 1964, in which he said, "After much prayer, consultation and advice, we have decided to integrate all the schools of our diocese in September. I know this will not meet with the approval of many of our people, but in justice and charity, this must be done."

Nowhere was the sensitivity of the church to public opinion better illustrated than in New Orleans, with a very large Catholic population. Archbishop Joseph Francis Rummel ordered an end to segregated churches in his diocese in 1953, and a year later gave indications that he was about to order the parochial schools desegregated. He did not issue the order until eight years later.

Before schools opened in the fall of 1954, the Right Rev. Henry C. Bezou, superintendent of Catholic schools, said that it would be impossible to desegregate them because of lack of facilities. The archbishop reassured his parishioners, many of whom vigorously opposed the change, that the parochial schools would not be desegregated "in advance of" the public schools of New Orleans. The next fall he said, "immediate integration would not be prudent or practical." In February, 1956, the archbishop, in a pastoral letter declared that "racial segregation is morally wrong and sinful," and it was assumed that he was on the point of ordering the desegregation of the diocesan schools.

Opponents to desegregation of the parochial schools organized an Association of Catholic Laymen, limiting membership to "persons of the Caucasian race who profess the faith of the Holy Roman Catholic Church." The president of the association was Emile Wagner, banker, attorney, prominent Catholic layman and member of the Orleans Parish school board. When the association ran a newspaper advertisement announcing its purpose and soliciting members, the archbishop ordered it dissolved and said that failure to comply would make its leaders "liable to the penalty of excommunication." The dissident Catholics obeyed the archbishop's order, but Wagner served notice that he intended to appeal his case to the Pope. He did send a formal appeal to the Pope, but it never was answered.

When desegregation began in the public schools of New Orleans in the fall of 1960, the Catholic schools remained segregated. Monsignor Bezou said that the parochial schools would "integrate only when public school integration has been effectively carried out." In August, 1961, he said that the Catholic schools would continue segregated and explained that "where you have less than a handful of children in the schools, it would be less than effective integration."

In the spring of 1962 the archbishop announced his decision that the Catholic schools would be desegregated in the fall. Before the bitter opposition to the move was quelled, three persons had been excommunicated. One of them was Leander Perez, a political leader in the state. Another was Jackson G. Ricau, executive secretary of the Citizens' Councils of South Louisiana, who had been executive secretary of the disbanded Association of Catholic Laymen. The third was Mrs. B. J. Gaillot, Jr., president of a group of segregationists who called themselves Save Our Nation (SON), Inc. Approximately 12,000 white students withdrew from the parochial schools during the first year of desegregation, white enrollment dropping from 48,000 in 1961–62 to 36,000 in 1962–63. Negro enrollment grew slightly, from 9,000 to 9,170. After that, enrollment by race was not announced for Orleans Parish.

All the parochial schools in the eleven parishes of the Archdiocese of New Orleans were desegregated in 1962. When five Negro pupils entered Our Lady of Good Harbor School at Buras, a complete boycott by white pupils took effect. Buras is in Plaquemines Parish, the political domain of Leander Perez. Just before the school was to reopen in September, 1963, gasoline was poured through vents on the roof, and the resulting explosion and fire severely damaged the building. The school was repaired; but it remained closed because the parish building inspector would not approve the work that had been done on it.

The Catholic clergy in the South took no leadership in promoting desegregation or preserving segregation in the public schools. As to the Catholic schools, in some instances they were desegregated before or at the same time as public schools. The general pattern was to gear change in the parochial schools to change in the public schools.

The Jews

The Jewish rabbi, like the Catholic priest, represents a minority religion in the South. Yet the Jews are far fewer in number and much more widely scattered than the Catholics. As individuals, the rabbis are more vulnerable to pressure than the priests. While the rabbis seldom took a leading role in the school desegregation struggle, when they did they almost always opposed segregation.

In a culture dominated by white Protestants, the rabbi was not in a position to be very effective in promoting change. Rabbi S. I. Goldstein has said that the rabbi must fill the role of goodwill ambassador to the gentile world. This discourages the espousal of unpopular causes. When rabbis took public part in the school desegregation controversy, it usually was in cooperation with those of other faiths. The rabbis of Little Rock participated in the "peace prayers" there, and it was a rabbi who suggested that they be held on Columbus Day as an appropriate time "to reiterate the principle of equality, justice and liberty on which the country was founded." Rabbi Julian Feibelman, in September of 1955, presented to the New Orleans school board a petition bearing 180 signatures of persons who called upon the board to comply with the Supreme Court decision.

However circumspect the rabbis were, segregationist organizations often displayed more than a tinge of anti-Semitism. In their speeches and publications they frequently described the Supreme Court decision as the product of a Jewish plot. Synagogues and Jewish community centers were subjected to bombings and vandalism. Jewish buildings were bombed in Atlanta, Jacksonville, Miami and Nashville, and bombings were attempted in Birmingham, Charlotte and Gastonia.

Occasionally a rabbi took the side of the segregationists. Rabbi Benjamin Schultz of Temple Beth Israel in Clarksdale, Mississippi, was one. In a speech to a local civic club a few weeks after James Meredith had entered Ole Miss, he said, "What America needs is more Mississippi, not less." He outlined the "Mississippi principles" which he said "could save America."

Rabbi Schultz was a rare exception. The Jewish clergy generally, although quietly, supported desegregation. The national Jewish organizations—the American Jewish Congress, the Synagogue Council of America and the Anti-Defamation League of B'nai B'rith—were actively aligned with the fight against segregation.

The Negro Protestants

Among one large group of Southern clergymen there was little division and wavering. The Negro Protestant ministers presented a strong, united front and gave leadership to the school desegregation movement and to the broader Negro protest against all forms of discrimination. The ministers marched in step with their denominations and their congregations.

The Negro clergymen put their beliefs into action. They filed desegregation suits. They joined and became leaders in groups working to remove racial barriers, and they formed some new organizations. Their churches became operations centers.

The Rev. Oliver Brown, of Topeka, Kansas, gave his name to the *School Segregation Cases*. He filed suit for admission of his daughter, Linda, to a school with whites. On May 25, 1964, the Supreme Court rounded out the decade with another key decision —in the case of *Griffin v. Prince Edward Board of Supervisors*. The Rev. Leslie Francis Griffin, president of the Prince Edward Christian Association and special consultant to the NAACP in the Virginia county, brought the suit on behalf of his son. In the decade between *Brown* and *Griffin* numerous other Negro ministers went to court to break the ground for their own and other children.

Some Negro ministers headed chapters of the NAACP. The Rev. J. F. Grimmett of Nashville was president of the NAACP in Tennessee. The Rev. Matthew C. McCollom was president of the Orangeburg, South Carolina, chapter. The Rev. Theodore Gibson, head of the Dade County, Florida, chapter, brought the suit that desegregated the schools of Miami. Alabama State Senator Sam Englehardt said at a "Black Monday" Citizens' Council rally on May 17, 1956, that "75 percent of the Negro preachers in the South are paid organizers of the National Association for the Advancement of Colored People."

Perhaps so. But some Negro ministers were critical of the NAACP. The Rev. H. H. Hume, president of the Mississippi Negro Baptist Convention charged that the NAACP "has fallen into bad hands, both nationally and locally." He described it as "an organization designed to kill off leaders who don't think like they think." There were even some Negro clergymen who championed segregation. One was the Rev. Dr. M. L. Young of Memphis, president of the Mutual Association of Colored People in the South. Dr. Young supported his position by saying, "The Bible is right regardless of the stand anyone else may take." And he added, "Negroes can't eat integration. They need jobs."

Negro ministers who held the views of Hume and Young were few. Most were in the vanguard of the Negro protest movement that the *Brown* decision sparked. Events produced new leaders, and new organizations. The Montgomery bus boycott of 1955 catapulted the Rev. Dr. Martin Luther King, Jr., to regional and national prominence. The Southern Christian Leadership Conference, which Dr. King headed, sought the desegregation of schools along with elimination of all racial restrictions. Joining King as executive director of SCLC was the Rev. Wyatt T. Walker of Petersburg, Virginia.

In Birmingham the Rev. Fred L. Shuttlesworth organized the Alabama Christian Movement for Human Rights. He filed a suit to desegregate Birmingham schools, and it went to the Supreme Court, where he lost when the Court upheld the state pupil placement act. But the way was paved for the suit that succeeded in 1963. The activities of Negro ministers subjected them to the risk of personal injury and their churches and homes to damage or destruction. Shuttlesworth's home was dynamited on Christmas night, 1956, and again on June 1, 1958. Five days after school desegregation began in Birmingham, the Sixteenth Street Baptist Church was dynamited, with four Negro girls being killed. During the decade Birmingham experienced more than forty incidents of dynamiting.

Another Negro minister who early was the victim of violence was the Rev. J. A. DeLaine of Lake City, South Carolina. He had helped to organize one of the cases—from Clarendon County, South Carolina—that the Supreme Court had decided in 1954. His church was gutted by fire in October, 1955, and his home earlier had been the target of oranges, rocks and bottles. He left the South.

Occasionally Negro ministers called attention to the inactivity and silence of the white clergymen who sympathized with their cause. The Rev. William L. Wilson of Spartanburg, South Carolina, said, "I am sometimes ashamed of my white colleagues. They tell me privately that segregation is wrong, but they will say nothing publicly." And Dr. King said, "If ever the white ministers of the South decide to declare in a united voice the truth of the gospel on the question of race, the transition from a segregated to an integrated society will be infinitely smoother."

11.

The Businessmen

Businessmen tend to shun controversy, because they feel that to become involved in it is bad for business. So it was that, during the period immediately following the Supreme Court decision in the *School Segregation Cases,* most businessmen sat on the sidelines, watching while others fought.

In the border states the resistance to compliance with the decision was so slight that the businessmen had no occasion to be concerned about it. In the Southern states, as school desegregation slowly spread, it became apparent in community after community that when controversy developed into public disorder and violence, it was bad for business, regardless of the businessmen's abstention.

At that stage businessmen began to act in their accustomed role as community leaders. They used their economic power, and they showed how effective it could be. In some places businessmen successfully exerted their influence to prevent disorder before it developed.

Citizens' Councils

There were exceptions to the general rule that businessmen steered clear of direct involvement in the school desegregation controversy until it was unavoidable. From the time the first Citizens' Council was formed in Indianola, Sunflower County, Mississippi, on July 11, 1954, businessmen were the backbone of this movement that was to become a potent expression of resistance to desegregation. The businessmen gave the Citizens' Council an aura of respectability. They also were in position to bring economic pressure against Negroes who stepped beyond the limits of the place in society to which Southern orthodoxy assigned them.

Economic pressure, however, had a disconcerting habit of backfiring on its users. Events in Orangeburg, South Carolina, location of a state college for Negroes, illustrate the point. Early in September, 1955, several petitions were circulated among Negroes in the city and surrounding rural area requesting the desegregation of schools. By the end of the month three Citizens' Councils had been formed in the county.

Negroes who signed the petitions and who worked for white men were fired. If they rented from white men, they were evicted. Merchants cut off credit, and some refused to make cash sales to Negroes who signed the petitions. Mayor R. H. Jennings of Orangeburg, the president of a bakery, the ice and fuel company and the local Coca-Cola bottling works, cut off supplies from three Negro merchants and the proprietor of a gas station. The Coble Dairy ceased deliveries to persons who signed the petition.

Orangeburg Negroes retaliated by identifying the merchants— there were twenty-three—who joined the Citizens' Council. The local Negroes, supported by the students of the college, boycotted the places of business operated by councilmen. They pointedly ceased patronizing the enterprises operated by Mayor Jennings and the Coble Dairy.

The Negroes and the businessmen were not long in learning that the boycott is a double-edged sword and that both edges are sharp. Something like a truce evolved, although it remained an uneasy one.

Throughout the decade economic retaliation, despite its dangers, continued to be used as a weapon by both sides in the fight about segregation. In addition to boycotts by Negroes against merchants identified as segregationists, there were many instances of boycotts by whites of local businesses because their proprietors favored desegregation.

Little Rock

Except where they were active in the Citizens' Councils, Southern businessmen seemed to have the attitude that school desegregation was not their problem. Little Rock and its aftermath began to change that. In Little Rock the business community did not anticipate trouble. The desegregation plan developed by Virgil Blossom had been in the works for at least two years, and the school superintendent was confident he had sold the plan to the community.

When Governor Faubus called out the National Guard to keep Negro children from entering Central High School in September of 1957, some businessmen voiced their opposition. The manager of a Little Rock department store wrote letters to the local papers urging moderation and compliance with the law. A competitor retaliated with an advertisement of rebuttal which, in net effect, was an invitation to boycott the letterwriter's store.

In October, after the federal troops had taken over, a group of twenty-four Little Rock businessmen and civic leaders signed a statement calling for peaceful compliance with the law. The same men, organized by several past presidents of the Little Rock Chamber of Commerce and including Superintendent Blossom and Congressman Brooks Hays, attempted to establish a bridge between Governor Faubus and the federal government over which a compromise solution could be negotiated. Nothing came of the effort.

Dr. Charles Carpenter of Little Rock, an industrial site engineer who was consultant for firms seeking Southern plant locations, said that the governor's action had cost Arkansas thousands of jobs. He added: "The quality of state government is an important factor to industrialists. When a governor flouts law and order it is an indication to them that the government is not a responsible one. . . . It means the loss of large, substantial industries which might otherwise have come to Arkansas." Governor Faubus labeled Dr. Carpenter a "Judas."

Winthrop Rockefeller, a member of the oil family, headed Governor Faubus's Arkansas Industrial Development Corporation. A month after the schools opened he described the situation as "tragic" and said that it would take at least six months just to assess "the damage that had been done."

A year later, when the governor had closed the Little Rock high schools, the damage was being assessed. In October, 1958, Frank Cottrell, manager of the Arkansas Chamber of Commerce, told the North Little Rock Rotary Club that industrial development in Little Rock had ground "practically to a standstill."

Soon after that the Little Rock Branch of the American Association of University Women conducted a survey of the effect that the school situation had on local business. Of the eighty-five businessmen interviewed, forty-four said they had been hurt by the school crisis, thirty-five said they were not affected, and six reported that their business improved.

The last group was made up largely of operators of long-distance moving vans and operators of filling stations who served the visitors who came to Little Rock to see Central High School. One of the van line executives explained, "I regret to say that to some extent our business has been bettered by the situation. We are moving families away from Little Rock faster than ever before. Incoming families are predominantly service personnel."

Seven of eight real-estate dealers interviewed reported they had been hurt badly by the racial unrest. One of them said, "It is going to take us years to repair the damage this man [Faubus] has done to our town. Just go up in Pulaski Heights and in nearly every block you'll see at least one house for sale. People don't want to live here if it means they have to send their children away to schools in other states."

One businessman complained: "The rest of the South tells us, 'Fight to the last ditch. We know that we can count on you. Don't be traitors!' And meanwhile cities like Nashville, Charlotte and Greensboro are making minimum adjustments to the situation and getting by. Nobody calls them traitors. I say to hell with it! Why should Little Rock bleed and die for Memphis, Vicksburg and Montgomery?"

As 1959 began, the Little Rock Chamber of Commerce gave serious attention to the school crisis. A poll of its members showed that a substantial majority favored reopening of the schools "on a controlled minimum plan of integration acceptable to the federal courts." The board of directors issued a statement of the Chamber's position in which it expressed the view that the Supreme Court decision was "erroneous" but that the decision, "however much we dislike it, is the declared law and is binding upon us."

That spring, when the three segregationists on the Little Rock school board dismissed forty-four teachers suspected of supporting the Supreme Court decision, the business community reacted. A group of prominent business leaders—Governor Faubus called them "the Cadillac brigade"—organized STOP (Stop This Outrageous Purge). In a recall election the segregationist members of the school board, who had the governor's active support, were unseated. After that, Governor Faubus began his strategic retreat, and schools reopened in September, 1959, desegregated.

The reopening of the schools did not break the industrial drought that began in Little Rock in the fall of 1957. From the beginning of the school crisis until February, 1961, Little Rock got no new major industry from outside, although its industrialization program had been booming through the summer of 1957. In the period 1950 through September, 1957, Little Rock averaged five new industrial plants a year. The high was eight in 1957.

In June, 1959, Governor Faubus, who regularly contested claims that business had been hurt in Arkansas, said, "None of the industrialists who have talked with me have expressed any concern with the school situation." Boyd Ridgeway, manager of the Little Rock Chamber of Commerce, replied, "They've discussed it with us. We've had only one real good prospect since the racial crisis erupted and they turned us down when the schools were closed." Everett Tucker, a member of the school board and the promoter of a thousand-acre industrial park in Little Rock, reported in 1960 that the only land he sold after the school crisis began was rights of ways for highways and a railway plus five acres to a Little Rock appliance dealer.

In February, 1961, Jacuzzi Bros., Inc., of Richmond, California, a manufacturer of pumps, announced it would build a $1.4 million plant at Little Rock and eventually would move its headquarters there. Since then the city has done well in its business and industrial development.

The situation in Little Rock when desegregation began contrasted sharply with that in Winston-Salem, where the first Negro also entered a white high school in September of 1957. In the North Carolina industrial city, the business leaders were in firm control. They held a private meeting in the spring and agreed among themselves that there wasn't "going to be any trouble" when desegregation began—and there wasn't.

One of the leaders present later described what happened. "Among us, we represent probably 95 percent of the financial resources of Forsyth County," he said. "We quietly passed the word that trouble here would be bad for business, and we weren't going to have any. We have this thing so well locked up that a cab driver couldn't get a gasoline credit card without our say-so."

New Orleans

As the school desegregation crisis developed in New Orleans in the fall of 1960, the city's businessmen ignored the warning of Little Rock, although there was every reason to anticipate trouble. Governor Jimmie Davis and the legislature had chosen a course of collision with the federal courts. But, except for some warnings regarding the economic losses that would accompany racial unrest and closing the public schools, the business community in New Orleans was inactive before the first Negroes were admitted on November 14 to formerly all-white schools.

In New Orleans the impact of the school crisis on local business was immediate and drastic. In November, the Christmas trade should have begun, but the manager of the Maison Blanche, a department store, told reporters, "Our sales were running about ten percent below a year ago, but they dropped this past week 20 to 30 percent." Surveys made by the *New York Times* and the *Wall Street Journal* reported department store sales in New Orleans were off 35 to 40 percent from November of 1959. One businessman said, "Canal Street merchants told me that their business for November—as of last Friday—was the worst in memory, even during the depression." I. Leon Sears, manager of Mertner's Clothing Store, located off Canal Street, said, "The past five weeks have been bad, but this week was even worse. Negroes are afraid to come downtown, and whites aren't out much either."

H. B. Lawrence, manager of Home Finance Service, told reporters, "Business has stopped cold." An advertising agency partner said, "My clients don't think it wise to spend lots of money now. They're very pessimistic over sales prospects for the coming year." Hotels and restaurants reported that business was off more than 20 percent. By late November hotel cancellations in New Orleans were running at a rate twice the national average.

On December 14, exactly a month after desegregation began, a group of 105 business and professional men placed an ad in the newspapers. Their statement said that Louisiana's legal position on segregation had become "untenable" and urged an end to "threats, defamation and resistance to those who administer our laws." They made clear their preference for segregation, and also for protesting the Supreme Court decision by legal means instead of street demonstrations.

The next day Mayor deLesseps S. Morrison asked the news media to observe a three-day moratorium on coverage of the protesting mothers who daily lined the walks surrounding the William

Frantz School. "Bad publicity," the mayor said, was hurting the tourist trade. Before schools opened the next fall, the New Orleans Chamber of Commerce called for the restoration of law and order. "Business climate," the statement observed, "greatly affects the economic development of our area, and when it is unfavorable it retards our economic development through loss of industry, trade and employment." A few days later thirty community leaders, many of them businessmen, issued a statement carried as a newspaper advertisement which, among other things, said, "Preservation of law and order in Louisiana requires compliance with the final decision of the Supreme Court; any other course would result in chaos."

As in Little Rock, the turbulence died away when the leadership of the community, a great part of it business leadership, made its influence felt. And in New Orleans, as in Little Rock, business leadership did not exert itself until experience proved that all-out resistance to school desegregation involved more than ideals. It also involved dollars.

Dallas and Atlanta

The businessmen in Dallas and Atlanta were the first to make effective use of the experience provided by Little Rock and New Orleans.

By early 1960 it was apparent that Dallas was going to lose its court fight to keep its public schools separate. At that time the members of the Dallas Citizens Council acted. This organization has no relationship to the segregationist Citizens' Council movement. It was organized to bring the Texas Centennial of 1936 to Dallas. Since that time it has continued in being as a behind-the-scenes civic organization of 250 top business, industrial and professional leaders. The members represent enterprises that pay 80 percent of the local taxes and employ most of the local labor force. C. A. Tatum, president of the Dallas Power and Light Co. and the Council's president in 1961, asked, "Who could have more of a stake in Dallas?" In this instance the stake was to avoid racial violence in the city. J. Erik

Jonsson, president of Texas Instruments, Inc., a large electronics firm, said, "Violence hurts everything and everybody. Little Rock has been hurt and if violence occurs in Dallas, we would be hurt the same way."

To avoid such hurt the Dallas Citizens Council early in 1960 appointed a seven-man committe headed by Tatum to prepare the city for peaceful desegregation. Operating behind the scenes and in cooperation with a seven-man committee of Negro leaders who represented some 125 separate organizations, Tatum's group undertook a massive public relations campaign.

The committee quietly enlisted the support of other major organizations in the community: the Dallas Bar Association, the Dallas County Medical Association, the Greater Dallas Council of Churches, the news media, the unions, the various civic clubs, the women's clubs, the fraternal organizations and the like.

"The program," Tatum explained, "does not advocate integration, it does not advocate segregation; it confines itself to the fact federal law decrees that the Dallas schools will desegregate and that the good citizen obeys the law. . . . What we have tried to do is stir into action that group of citizens who want to obey the law and behave properly. We also want to emphasize that arrest and punishment await those who react ignorantly or impulsively."

Using a film, "Dallas at the Crossroads," posters and a variety of leaflets and other publications, the organization harped on the contrast between peaceful compliance and what occurred in Little Rock and those other communities where the mobs took over. Through the churches alone 100,000 copies of a pamphlet entitled "Dallas at the Crossroads" were distributed. Employers in Dallas stuffed the pay envelopes of their employees with leaflets hammering on the theme "It must not happen here." Union leaders impressed upon their membership that their jobs were dependent on Dallas's continued prosperity.

While this preparatory barrage continued, the police in Dallas were trained to prevent trouble before it could begin. Dallas police identified the potential trouble-makers and kept a spot check on their activities.

On September 6, 1961, operating on a grade-a-year plan, the public schools of Dallas desegregated. There was no trouble.

Atlanta was under court order to begin school desegregation at the same time as Dallas. Atlanta businessmen, headed by Ivan Allen, then president of the Chamber of Commerce and later mayor, joined other community forces in a high-powered program of public preparation for desegregation. Unlike the Dallas program, the community preparation in Atlanta was conducted in the spotlight of continual publicity. Both programs, however, sought the same end. The result in each instance was the same. Like Dallas, Atlanta began to desegregate its public schools without incident.

Industrial Development

All the Southern states engaged in efforts to attract new industry, and racial discord was considered by most, although not all, to be detrimental to these efforts. Increasingly, businessmen expressed concern about the effect that "bad publicity" might have on the long-range economic development of their local community, their state and their region.

Time and again the nation's leading industrialists made statements indicating that there was reason for concern. In an interview Thomas J. Watson, president of International Business Machines, said, "We wouldn't make any new move into any particular area with racial fights of any kind. Our stockholders would think we were crazy." General Lucius Clay, a native of Georgia and president of Continental Can Co., spoke in Atlanta in June, 1961, to the Governor's Conference on Trade and Commerce. He told the businessmen in attendance: "Employes being transferred to Georgia worry about school conditions for their children. . . . Manufacturers worry about the conditions which could develop within their plants. . . . None of us wants to locate in areas where there is serious risk of conflict between local custom and federal law."

Even in the massive-resistance states the effect of racial strife on economic development ultimately caused businessmen to exert their influence for acceptance of orderly change. In the first several years after the Supreme Court decision, Virginia was a leader in the cause of massive resistance. Businessmen played a major role in steering Virginia away from massive resistance toward acceptance of some desegregation in the schools.

In the period 1951–53 Virginia added an average of 31,400 new industrial jobs to its economy each year. In the three-year period 1957–59, the period in which massive resistance ballooned and then collapsed, the average fell to 5,100 additional industrial jobs a year, one-sixth of what it had been.

The Virginia business community was slow to organize and to act. Until the fall of 1958, when public schools were closed in Front Royal, Charlottesville and Norfolk, the businessmen were inclined to leave the school issue to the politicians. Once, however, the schools were closed, the businessmen acted.

In Norfolk, headed by Paul Schweitzer, an industrialist who was chairman of the school board, the business community conducted an open campaign to preserve the public schools. In November, 1958, a group of business and industrial leaders of statewide prominence began to meet secretly. One month later this group—twenty-nine in all—had dinner with Governor Almond. The identities of the businessmen who attended the meeting remained a secret. It was an open secret, however, that these men let the governor know in no uncertain terms that Virginia was being seriously damaged. This quiet pressure from the state's business leadership was considered to be a major factor in Almond's decision early in 1959 to begin a planned retreat from massive resistance.

Of course, some new industry continued to move into even the most defiant states. In September, 1962, Governor Ross Barnett of Mississippi announced that Standard Oil of Kentucky had decided to locate a $125 million refinery at Pascagoula because Mississippi was "a symbol of successful segregation." William C. Smith, president of Standard Oil of Kentucky, explained, "We moved to Mississippi for strictly economic reasons."

Early in October of 1962, just after James Meredith had been installed at the University of Mississippi, U.S. Attorney General Robert Kennedy said in an interview: "I have been talking this week to the top executives of 40 important business firms whose central offices are not in the South, but who have branches and investments in Mississippi, and have asked them to use their influence, either by persuasion or by threatening to curtail their investments in Mississippi, but I doubt whether it will have much of an effect."

In Mississippi there was no significant break in the segregationist ranks, but business leaders did recognize the urgency of maintaining the public schools. In November, 1962, the Mississippi Economic Council and the State Chamber of Commerce announced a policy on school desegregation containing these points:

Public education is vital to Mississippi's future, and the public schools must be kept open.

Desegregation should be resisted by all legal and constitutional means, but violence and bloodshed have no place in Mississippi. No respectable citizen or public officer can directly or by implication condone such actions.

If at any point federal control of our schools is forced it should be endured as a temporary condition with the expectation that the nation will ultimately face reality in constitutional matters.

One of the most important of the business firms with branches in the South was the U.S. Steel Corporation. The company was criticized for not using its influence to quell the racial unrest in Birmingham in 1963. Roger Blough, chairman of the board, replied: ". . . For a corporation to attempt to exert any kind of economic compulsion to achieve a particular end in the social area seems to me to be quite beyond what a corporation should do and quite beyond what a corporation can do. . . . Any attempt by a private corporation like U.S. Steel to impose its views, its beliefs and its will upon the community by resorting to economic compulsion or coercion would be repugnant to our American constitutional concepts. . . . Even if U.S. Steel possessed such economic power—which it certainly does not—I would be unalterably opposed to its use in this fashion."

In the spring of 1963 Secretary of Commerce Luther Hodges at a news conference said that businessmen could play a key role in solving racial difficulties. They "can look at this thing a little bit more dispassionately than politicians who have to weigh their words," he added. As a former governor of North Carolina and before that a textile executive, Hodges was in a position to speak from personal experience both as a businessman and a politician.

About the time the secretary was holding his news conferences, businessmen throughout the South were taking a new interest in helping to solve racial conflicts. In city after city mayor's committees were being formed to settle school and other race questions by quiet negotiation rather than demonstrations. Businessmen were heavily represented on these committees.

Prior to Little Rock and New Orleans the role of the business community in the desegregation struggle was either passive or, in the case of the Citizen's Councils, actively on the side of maintaining segregation. By 1960–61 this attitude had begun to change, and the change accelerated during the remainder of the decade. The business leaders in the Southern states and in the major cities of the South no longer were willing to pay the price exacted by open race struggle.

12.
Organized Whites

Public opinion was a powerful force in shaping official action on school desegregation. Leaders charted courses that followed the line of prevailing sentiment among controlling groups. In the eleven Southern states the white people were in control.

Where desegregation was an issue of special interest, those with strong enough feelings joined with others of like mind in organizations, new and old, to promote their positions. The organizations fell roughly into three categories. One group upheld segregation and fought against any weakening of it. Another opposed segregation and directed its efforts towards removing racial barriers. The third was concerned primarily with preserving public education and public order.

For Segregation: The Citizens' Councils

Among the organizations favoring segregation, the Citizens' Councils took firmest root and had the most rapid and widespread growth. The seeds that produced the Council movement were a phrase, a speech, a book and a meeting.

Representative John Bell Williams, Congressman from Mississippi, supplied the phrase when he labeled the day of the *Brown* decision "Black Monday." State Circuit Judge Tom P. Brady picked up the words to set the tone of a speech. Brady expanded his remarks into a book, also entitled *Black Monday,* in which he recited his case for segregation: the "innate inferiority" of Negroes as a race; the social, cultural and health problems that the Negroes create; the necessity for preventing the destruction of the white race through miscegenation, or "mongrelization." The judge wrote that the Supreme Court decision was "socialistic" and that it was invalid because it ignored long-established legal precedents. He called for creation of a "third political force" (he favored the name Sons of the White Camelia) through which the white South could fight to preserve its way of life.

Robert B. "Tut" Patterson, a former captain of the Mississippi State football team, World War II paratrooper and operator of a large delta plantation, liked what Brady said and decided to do something about it. He asked fourteen leaders of the town of Indianola in Sunflower County to meet on the night of July 11, 1954, at the home of D. H. Hawkins, manager of a cotton compress. In the group were the mayor, the city attorney, the town banker, a dentist, a druggist, two automobile dealers, a planter, a farmer, a ginner, a farm implement dealer, a hardware dealer, Hawkins and Patterson. "Everybody of any standing was there," Patterson later said.

In calling the meeting, Patterson had kept in mind Judge Brady's advice, "This thing will die a-borning if lawless and reckless people are brought into it." This first Citizens' Council group adopted two basic policies: (1) to recruit its membership from the same community levels as the leading civic clubs and (2) to employ only "legal means" of resistance.

The movement mushroomed in Mississippi after the Indianola meeting. By the end of the year the Mississippi Association of Citizens' Councils counted 110 groups claiming 25,000 members. Patterson, as executive secretary of the association, was confident of success in achieving the Councils' aims. "This isn't just a delaying action," he said. "There won't be any integration in Mississippi. Not now, not 100 years from now, maybe not 6,000 years from now—maybe never."

In 1955 William J. Simmons organized the Citizens' Council in Jackson. He became an important member of Patterson's state organization. The creation of chapters in other states led to the formation of the Citizens' Councils of America, with Patterson as executive secretary and Simmons as editor of its official publication. "In no place has there been integration—even so-called 'token integration' —without the active support of white people in the community," Simmons said in an interview. "As long as people are strongly organized on the local level—as long, in other words, as the 'die-easys' are not in control—a community can withstand pressure from Washington regardless of what kind it is." The Councils sought to provide strong local organizations of white people who wanted to keep their own communities and the South segregated.

In Alabama State Senator Sam Englehardt was chief Council organizer. Herman Talmadge of Georgia in the summer of 1955 told a rally of about 6,000 at Selma how he would deal with the "scalawag" whites who did not stand up for segregation. "Don't admit them to your homes," he said. "Don't let them eat at your table. Don't let them trade at your store or filling station."

Emory Rogers, the attorney who represented the Summerton School District in the Clarendon County case, was the top Councilman in South Carolina. "We've got more members than Rotary or Lions because we've got both of them and some more too," he commented. State Senator William Rainach and Leander Perez ramrodded the movement in Louisiana. Amis Guthridge, the lawyer who urged defiance of federal authority at Hoxie and Little Rock, was a Council leader in Arkansas. During the period of peak membership (1956–59), some reports put the number of separate Councils as high as 600, with a combined membership of as many as 300,000. Most estimates were considerably lower, however.

In some Southern states organizations having goals compatible with those of the Citizens' Council developed under different names. Roy V. Harris, Georgia newspaper publisher and political figure, was president of the Georgia States' Rights Council and became president of the Association of Citizens' Councils of America. The Patriots of North Carolina gave way to the North Carolina Defenders of States' Rights. Tennessee had its Society for the Maintenance of Segregation and the Tennessee Federation for Constitutional Government. In Virginia there were the Virginia League and the Defenders of State Sovereignty and Individual Liberty. These and other organizations shared with the Councils the desire to create an image of respectability and legality, eschewing violence as a means of achieving their ends.

In his book Judge Brady proposed that as a last resort the white Southerner should use his position of strength in "a cold war and economic boycott" against troublemakers. In 1954 the official organizational plan of the Councils called for the creation of a legal committee "to anticipate moves by agitators [and] recommend application of economic pressure for trouble-makers." Arthur Clark, one of the charter members of the Indianola Council, said, "We propose to accomplish this [the removal of Negro trouble-makers] through the careful application of economic pressure upon those men who cannot be controlled otherwise."

In the face of severe criticism in the press, the Councils restated their policy on economic reprisal. Robert Patterson announced the new position when he said, "We do not recommend economic pressure. That's false propaganda from the press. But, of course, we don't denounce 'freedom of choice' in business arrangements. If employers fire their help, that's their business."

An incident in Yazoo City, Mississippi, in the summer of 1955 showed how the new policy worked. The Citizens' Council, "as a public service," publicized the names of fifty-three Negroes who signed a petition for desegregation of the city's schools. Medgar Evers of the NAACP described the results. "The petition signers became famous, in a way," he said. "Their names were printed in a newspaper ad. The Council also printed their names on a big placard, and this was posted in every store in town—even the bank. These people were blacklisted. They couldn't buy in local stores. The placards even were posted in cotton fields. With the awful spectre of Yazoo City before them, few Mississippi Negroes would sign a desegregation petition today." All but two of the signers withdrew their names from the Yazoo City petition. Similarly, names on school desegregation petitions melted away elsewhere in Mississippi and in other states.

While the immediate objective of the Council movement was to hold the line at home, the long-range strategy of its leaders was to project it into the mainstream of national conservatism. They voiced the conviction that time was on their side as the migration of Negroes from the South brought new race problems to the North and West. Patterson said, ". . . in the past ten years Mississippi has contributed 322,306 breeding-age Negroes to the economic and social structure of the Northern and border states. This contribution will do more to create an understanding of our Negro problem than all the written logic and dramatic presentations of fact would ever have done." U.S. Senator James O. Eastland of Mississippi expressed the Councilmen's confidence in the future when he said, "You'll remember that the Confederate army made 'a token capture' at Gettysburg. Some of Pickett's men reached the top of the ridge. But who won the battle? Since the decision of 1954 we've had token integration in a few places but the South has not yet been breached."

The Ku Klux Klan

Striving for respectability, the Citizens' Councils sought to distinguish themselves from the Ku Klux Klan. In their appeal to business and professional men, the Councils shunned lower-status whites. The once-powerful Klan welcomed those whom the Councils rejected.

After a resurgence in the 1920's the Klan had lapsed into quiesence and impotence. The remnant of the national Klan organization—the Invisible Empire, Knights of the Ku Klux Klan, with headquarters in Atlanta—officially disbanded in 1944 and in 1947 surrendered its charter. A few splinter groups survived, chief among them being Dr. Samuel J. Green's Association of Georgia Klans.

The *Brown* decision sparked a Klan revival. In most of the Southern states, organizers quickly took advantage of the situation. To the tunes of "Onward Christian Soldiers" and "The Old Rugged Cross," they rallied recruits under the banner of white supremacy. This dominant theme was heavily tinged with anti-Semitism and anti-Catholicism.

At the peak of the Klan revival, estimates of the number of klaverns, as the local units were called, ran as high as 500, with total membership of 50,000 to 100,000. The klaverns were affiliated with a dozen or so separate and competing Klans. The largest was the U.S. Klans, Knights of the Ku Klux Klan. Until his death in 1960, Eldon Lee Edwards, a paint sprayer in an Atlanta automobile assembly plant, was its Imperial Wizard. After the *Brown* decision, Edwards said, "The good niggers don't want this integration any more than we do. It is the NAACP that is trying to jam it down our throats, and it is backed by Jew money." Robert Lee "Wild Bill" Davidson of Macon, who was Grand Dragon of the Georgia Klan, succeeded Edwards as Imperial Wizard. "I believe in using any and all of the forces to preserve segregation," he said. "I'd believe in using a rattlesnake to preserve segregation, if that's necessary." Robert M. "Bobby" Shelton, rival Klan leader in Alabama, said, "The Klan doesn't want to break any laws, but it may have to bend a few." In his speeches he declared that the Klan would "take all measures necessary to preserve Alabama customs" and he predicted that "there is going to be a lot of bloodshed."

Wherever the Klan was active, it opposed desegregation of the schools. A speaker at a Klan rally in Monroe, North Carolina, in August, 1957, just before the first schools in the state were to desegregate voluntarily, said, "We can muster 50,000 men by the time schools begin to open this fall. We will not stand for integration, voluntary or any other kind." The Supreme Court decision on segregated schools gave the Klans their rebirth, but the school question served mainly as a springboard to a broad attack on Negroes, Jews and Catholics, all of whom Klansmen placed under the umbrella of Communism. Until fairly late in the decade, desegregation of schools was little more than a topic for debate in the states with the greatest Klan activity.

By the time the Negroes began to attend schools with whites in the South, the Klan again was on the decline. When he resigned in 1960 as Imperial Emperor of the Southern Knights of the Ku Klux Klan, Bill Hendrix of Florida, who left and re-entered the Klan several times, suggested explanations for its losses. In letters to Ralph McGill of the Atlanta *Constitution,* Hendrix wrote: ". . . 20 years ago when I joined the Klan I took an oath that I would obey and uphold the Constitution of the United States and its political sub-divisions. . . . I know that the Klan is going to get lawless. . . . If the loud-mouthed politicians of the South want to help, let them tell the people the truth—that the decisions of the Supreme Court have become law. . . . Integration is now the law of the land and a person can stop it only by violating the law. . . . So far as their grand dragons are concerned, they have about 50 that I know of. We used to give out badges to grand dragons to keep them from organizing each other. . . . There are now some eight Klan groups in Atlanta and Georgia and they are keeping busy fighting one another." Referring to claims by Georgia Klansmen that they had a "secret weapon," Hendrix said, "Any secret weapon they may have would be just another gimmet [sic] to get 10 or more dollars out of decent Georgia people."

What Hendrix said corroborated a 1958 report by Arnold Forster, civil rights director of the Anti-Defamation League of B'nai B'rith. Forster reported that the Klan was "operating in a piecemeal fashion without any real leadership or cohesive force" and was "ridden with factional rivalries and corruption." The report also said, "In virtually every Southern community the Klan has been identified as a tool of violence and lawlessness and as a movement that constitutes more of a police problem than anything else." In 1964 Governor Paul B. Johnson of Mississippi said, "The Klan claims that it does not indulge in violence. Its activities, however, indicate otherwise."

Klansmen were accused of many acts of intimidation and violence. The traditional burning cross was itself a warning to whites and Negroes who violated the Klan's code. Crosses burned regularly at public Klan ceremonials; they also lit the night skies at the homes of those whom the Klansmen considered transgressors and at other places such as schools and churches. Klansmen also were charged with bombings, burnings, beatings and other acts of violence.

As a rule no one paid much attention to the Klansmen except as objects of curiosity when they donned their robes and hoods, paraded in their regalia, burned their crosses or were suspected of responsibility for some incident of violence. The Klans did offer an outlet for vigorous pro-segregation views. Their fortunes fluctuated according to the stimulation of events. The passage of the Civil Rights Act of 1964 and the surge of civil rights activities that summer gave the Klans a new lease on life.

Men with Klan backgrounds formed other organizations with related purposes. Bill Hendrix tried his hand at launching two groups, one called White Brotherhood and the other the American Confederate Army. Jack Dempsey (not related to the boxer) of Augusta, Georgia, started the National Association for the Preservation of the White Race. Two former Klansmen of Griffin, Georgia, established the National Association for the Advancement and Preservation of the Majority of the White People, Inc. Talmadge Luttrell helped to set up Florida States' Rights, Inc.

The *Brown* decision spawned a wide array of organizations dedicated to the cause of preserving racial segregation in the South. The long list included the American Society for the Preservation of State Government and Racial Integrity, the Knights of the White Christians, the Southerners, the Southern Gentlemen, the Pro-Southerners League, the American States' Rights Association, the National States' Right Party, the Hermitage Crusade, the Grass Roots League, White America, Inc., the Caucasian League and many more. Most of them were local groups.

The white Southerners who organized to maintain segregation shared a common goal. They differed on the means by which they sought to attain it. Where their strength was great enough, as it was in many places, they created an atmosphere of fear that stifled the expression of views contrary to their own.

Against Segregation: The Southern Regional Council

A small minority of white Southerners openly and firmly supported school desegregation. The leading organization opposing segregation, not only in the schools but on general principle, was the interracial Southern Regional Council. Based in Atlanta, it emerged in 1944 as the successor to the Commission on Interracial Co-operation, which had worked since 1919 for understanding, friendship and cooperation between whites and Negroes.

Before the 1955 Supreme Court decision the SRC urged "joint fact-finding and planning by all elements of the community" in preparation for compliance. Later James McBride Dabbs of Mayesville, South Carolina, said as president of the organization, "The Council believes in moving as easily and as inexpensively as possible from the outmoded pattern of segregation to the coming pattern of desegregation. . . . If communication between whites and Negroes has suffered in the South since the May, 1954, Supreme Court decision . . . it may be of that variety of which the white South knows best, the paternalistic one-way communication from the white to the Negro. Often today, the Negro just isn't there to listen."

Late in 1959 the SRC called for efforts to "get the issue of school desegregation out of the courts and into the hands of responsible educators." The Council's statement referred to pupil placement plans as "a political device to evade or thwart desegregation." It added, "When placement is not guided by professional concern and criteria, but is designed to perpetuate racial separation, its use will only prolong the South's unrest."

Soon after that, Council Vice President Marion A. Wright, speaking in Nashville, Tennessee, condemned "token compliance" with the Supreme Court decision as indefensible in either law or morals. "Consider for a moment the application of this idea of token compliance to other laws," he said. "When driving, I will stop at only every tenth red light. I will pay only one-tenth of my income tax. As a draftee, I will serve only one-tenth of my induction period. I will observe only those parts of a business contract that are favorable to me. Such is token compliance. What is the result? Raw, naked anarchy. And what about its application in the realm of morals? I will bear false witness against my neighbor for only nine out of ten days—on the tenth day I will tell the truth. I will observe only one of the Ten Commandments. Only every tenth day will I love my neighbor as myself. Such is token morality. What is the result? Universal moral license and iniquity."

With New Orleans under court order to desegregate in 1960, the Council issued a report saying, "When desegregation breaches the Deep South, the myth of Southern ability to defy the law will have been fatally punctured; the consequences could be an emotional release in the upper South that would enable desegregation to move without the lash of law. If, on the other hand, the imminent crisis in New Orleans is not overcome, or even if New Orleans treads the bitter path of Little Rock between 1957–59, the prospects will be gloomy for the South and for national self-respect."

Throughout the decade the Council conducted research and information programs aimed at the elimination of racial segregation and discrimination in the South. Prior to 1954 it was a membership organization, but in that year it changed its structure. With a grant from the Fund for the Republic, it organized Human Relations Councils in the Southern states. The Southern Regional Council became a body of eighty members.

Until 1957, the state groups were an integral part of the parent organization. Then, according to plan, they became independent affiliates. The SRC continued to contribute financially to the state groups—but never more than half of their budgets and usually much less than half—and to serve them in an advisory capacity. In 1964 affiliates had full-time staffs in eight of the thirteen states in which the SRC operated. These eight states were Alabama, Arkansas, Florida, Georgia, North Carolina, South Carolina, Tennessee and Virginia. Dr. Leslie Dunbar, executive director of SRC, said in 1964, "Louisiana at one time had a council, but it was licked and it surrendered." The state councils had about one hundred local member groups.

The Dade County Council on Community Relations at Miami, Florida, was one of the more active local units. In the spring of 1955 it conducted an all-day seminar on human relations at the University of Miami. Dr. H. Franklin Williams, vice president of the university and moderator of a panel discussion, said, "I don't see why school boards should wait for legislative decisions. The sooner we begin the quicker the complications are over." Mrs. Marie Roberts, high school social science teacher and a panelist, said, "Community preparation and acceptance are vital if integration is to be achieved in an orderly manner." These statements were in effect the keynotes for the Council's program over the next few years.

To help pave the way for compliance with the Supreme Court decision, the Dade Council held neighborhood forums at which white and Negro speakers discussed the issued involved in school desegregation. On the third anniversary of the 1954 decision, the Dade group called on the County Board of Public Instruction "to discharge its responsibilities by announcing its plans for desegregation, including the time and manner in which this will be accomplished." In a statement the Council said: ". . . we have carefully examined the experiences of other communities which in the past three years have successfully desegregated their public schools. In each instance we have observed that successful desegregation is carefully correlated to careful planning, recognition of the responsibility of our schools to obey the law of the land as expressed by the Supreme Court and a further understanding that the longer it takes to initiate the actual process of desegregation the more difficult this action can become. . . . We believe we have had a sufficient time to examine the nature of this problem, to become aware of its proportions, and to recognize the need for immediate progress."

The Council on Community Relations was not alone in working for desegregation of Dade County schools. In the fall of 1956 more than six hundred teachers, parents, business and professional men and civic leaders held a Little White House Conference on Education. The conference voted "general agreement with the general principle of integration" and agreed that "the community as a whole has a definite responsibility in this problem." Early in 1958 the Community Planning Committee published a program of action for the county. The committee, composed of a number of organizations, spent six months studying the problem of school desegregation before issuing its report. It said, "There is general agreement that desegregation is inevitable, even among those who seek to delay it. No problem becomes easier to solve through inaction—and abundant evidence is at hand to demonstrate that this one becomes more and more difficult. The sooner we begin work at it the less difficult it will be. . . . Tension is greater before desegregation than after the process has begun. There are always anxieties about what will happen which are not borne out in practice. Segregation fosters misunderstandings and fails to provide a means for resolving differences, thus creating tension. Desegregation makes possible a truly democratic approach to problems which invariably meets the needs." When Dade County schools desegregated in 1959, the community quietly accepted the step.

Mississippi was the last of the states to start desegregation. The climate of white public opinion was overwhelmingly in favor of segregation, but in the spring of 1963 a group met at Tougaloo Southern Christian College near Jackson to organize a Mississippi Council on Human Relations. A statement issued after the meeting said that the group would be affiliated with the Southern Regional Council "because we intend to build in association with members of other Southern states a new way of life which will preserve what is of abiding value in our best traditions, purged of the poison of legalized segregation." The statement contained a "bill of particulars" of things that the organization would support and oppose. Among the things to be supported was: "Wise compliance with the spirit of the Supreme Court decision of 1954 within the living context of the situation in Mississippi through: voluntary removal of state and local laws enforcing segregation; prompt acceptance of qualified Negro applicants on the part of colleges and graduate schools; initiation, on the part of men of good will of both races within local communities, of plans for compliance in the lower schools, in advance of compulsory action by federal courts; and immediate representation by qualified Negroes on local and state boards of education where these posts are appointive." The group opposed "the attitudes and practices of the Citizens' Council of Mississippi in its domination of the political, economic and social structure of our state through propaganda, intimidation and reprisals." Within a short time Dr. A. D. Beittel, president of both Tougaloo and the new council, announced that the group had met in executive session and decided against affiliating with the Southern Regional Council. It also amended its bill of particulars by eliminating all of those things that it opposed. "We decided to take the positive, objective approach," Dr. Beittel explained.

Supporters of Desegregation in the Border States

In the border states, by contrast to the Southern states, opposition to desegregation was not very strong. Consequently there were few organizations working either for or against segregation. Some white groups did urge quick desegregation and pledged their support to boards of education in implementing plans of compliance with the Supreme Court decision. More often groups directed their attention to problems that arose after the schools desegregated.

The Parent-Teacher Associations took an active role in some of the states. The Maryland Congress of Parents and Teachers, at its annual convention in the fall of 1954 affirmed its obligation to abide by the decisions of the Supreme Court and voted to support the efforts of state and local boards of education to achieve school desegregation with a maximum of local control. The next spring the Inter-group Relations Committee of the P.T.A. Congress, functioning as a clearing house for information about desegregation, distributed kits of resource materials to county P.T.A. councils. The Executive Committee of the Montgomery County P.T.A. Council recommended to the County Board of Education that "public school integration at all levels of the school system throughout the county be put into effect at the start of the 1955 fall term and that the school construction budget be planned in terms of this policy." In the summer of 1956, following the first year of desegregation, the Montgomery County Council published a review of local P.T.A. actions in desegregated schools as a guide for future conduct. The review emphasized that each local P.T.A. should do what was "comfortable" when desegregation started in its school. It reported that P.T.A.'s at schools already desegregated "ranged all the way from doing nothing to intensive programs of preparation of continued efforts to assist their members and school officials to accomplish integration with maximum smoothness."

A group of forty to fifty residents of Louisville organized what they called "Parents in Our Block." They decided early in 1955 to use their personal influence in P.T.A.'s and other organizations to encourage calm discussion of school desegregation problems, to establish relationships with Negro leaders and to engage in person-to-person discussion with those worried or apprehensive about desegregation. The group met monthly in the home of a member.

In St. Louis the West End Community Conference was active in promoting interracial understanding, with emphasis on public schools. In 1961, when resegregation was developing on a rather large scale in St. Louis, the Conference warned that if the public schools in its area were allowed to become all-Negro much ground would have been lost in the effort to desegregate schools. It called for intelligent planning by community agencies to prevent resegregation.

Baltimore, like St. Louis, also faced the problem of resegregation late in the second half of the decade. There the League of Women Voters supported "active racial integration in our schools." In a statement the League said, "We have come to believe, having faced up to the issues, that this is far more than a legal or governmental question, that this is indeed a moral issue, and that the citizens of Baltimore and their school board must ask themselves the central question, 'What is right?' "

Throughout the region there were white people who spoke for desegregation. In the border states public opinion in general was on the side of compliance with the Supreme Court decision. In the

Southern states, and especially in the Deep South, the preponderance of vocal white opinion was on the side of segregation; only those with strong convictions and considerable courage openly opposed segregation.

For Public Schools

Where public schools closed, or were threatened with closure, white residents usually formed emergency organizations to reopen them or to keep them open. The members of these groups were not interested primarily in whether the schools were segregated or desegregated. Their purpose was to preserve public education, and they preferred desegregated schools to no schools.

Virginia was the first state in which there was a serious threat to close schools. Cases moving through the courts in 1958 would have required the desegregation of schools in Arlington, Charlottesville, Norfolk and Warren County that fall. Under the state's massive-resistance laws, the schools would be closed rather than desegregated.

Arlington was the first community to act. In June between six hundred and seven hundred people met to form the Arlington Organizing Committee to Preserve Public Schools. They elected O. Glenn Stahl, former president of the school board, as their chairman and adopted a three-point platform: "1. We are determined to pursue every legal means to keep the public schools open; 2. We are here concerned neither with perpetuating segregation in schools nor hastening integration; 3. We have faith in Arlington's ability to meet its public education problems." The effort to keep the schools open won the endorsement of other community groups, among them the Arlington Civic Federation, the Arlington League of Women Voters and twenty-six of the thirty-nine white P.T.A.'s in the county.

As it developed, the Arlington schools, because of a court delay, were not ordered to desegregate that fall, but schools in Charlottesville, Norfolk and Warren County were. Governor Almond closed the schools, and a group in each place followed the Arlington example by organizing a Committee for Public Schools. The Norfolk committee was especially active, and within a short time it had about sixty-five hundred members. The committee argued that unless the schools were reopened, the school system would be "crippled for a generation," the best teachers would leave, and the city's economic future would be "bleak." The Norfolk group filed a suit on behalf of white children for whom there was no public school, and in January, 1959, a federal court decided in their favor. Virginia's "massive resistance" collapsed, and the schools reopened.

In December of 1958 a meeting in Richmond resulted in the formation of the Virginia Committee for Public Schools. Representatives attended from fourteen cities and counties. The committee set up an office with a full-time staff and took an active part in helping to construct new laws to replace those declared unconstitutional. At its peak the committee had more than twenty-two thousand members.

Schools also closed in Little Rock, Arkansas, in September of 1958 by order of Governor Faubus. That same month about fifty women met at the home of Mrs. D. D. Terry, wife of a former congressman, to organize the Women's Emergency Committee to Open Our Schools. Mrs. Joe R. Brewer, daughter of a former mayor, was elected chairman. The group explained that it was neither for nor against desegregation, that it did not ask anyone to change his personal convictions. Since the district was under court order to desegregate, the committee in effect favored desegregation in order to achieve the reopening of the schools.

For Christmas that year members of the WEC enclosed a mimeographed letter with their cards. It began: "We know it will be a long time before the state of Arkansas can live down the shame and disgrace with which it is now viewed by the entire world. We thought you might like to learn that there is one group here dedicated to the principle of good public education with liberty and justice for all." With the reopening of schools in the fall of 1959, the committee turned its attention to other questions involving the schools. Five years after it began, it disbanded in the place where it started, at the home of Mrs. Terry.

Early in 1959, Florida legislators spoke of taking drastic action to preserve segregation. The Florida Congress of Parents and Teachers, at a legislative conference in Tallahassee, endorsed the principle that "free public schools must be maintained regardless of racial problems." X. L. Garrison, a delegate to the conference, said, "No student in Florida should be deprived for a year, a month or a day of his education." In a speech a short time later Mrs. Myron Blee, first vice president of the Congress, said at a district P.T.A. meeting, "You will have to ask yourselves and your legislators: 'What do they promise to give that is half so precious as our public schools? . . .' We are not taking a stand on integration or desegregation, whatever word you wish to use. That is left to the legislators and the administrative branch of education." The Board of Managers of the P.T.A. Congress issued a statement saying, "Our survival as a democratic, free and responsible people depends directly on a strong, free, effective public school system." The Florida Junior Chamber of Commerce voted its opposition to any move that would close public schools. No schools were closed in Florida.

In the spring of 1960 the Orleans Parish school board, faced with a court order to desegregate that fall, announced that it would conduct a poll to determine the choice of the people of New Orleans between compliance and closing the schools. This action prompted a group of civic leaders, men and women, to form an organization that they called Save Our Schools. Its purpose was to use "all legitimate means [to further] a statewide system of free public education and to offer support to all elected or appointed public officials in their efforts to continue free education." In a statement of its position the group said: 'The closing of public schools inevitably means an increase in juvenile delinquency, as thousands of youngsters are left to their own devices. It means loss of accreditation, loss of federal funds and the shifting of tax burdens to all the citizens of Louisiana. It means the sacrifice of the health-protecting services now available to public school children, such as physical examination, immunization and the school lunch program. It means economic stagnation, because new industries refuse to move into an area in which the public schools have been closed."

The stand by SOS attracted both opposition and support. The Citizens' Council of Greater New Orleans asked state and federal authorities to investigate the financial backing of the organization. The Louisiana State Citizens' Council named SOS in a newspaper advertisement charging that "several national organizations who have espoused total integration in the South" were behind the move to keep the schools open. SOS denied the charge; in all its activities it carefully refrained from advocating desgregation or endorsing the Supreme Court decision. Among the groups that joined in the campaign for public schools was another new organization called the Committee on Public Education. Whereas SOS was an organization of community leaders, COPE drew its members from the ranks of white parents of school children. The New Orleans Junior Chamber of Commerce and the Independent Women's Organization also backed the open-schools movement. The schools in New Orleans remained open, but white students boycotted the desegregated schools; and white parents, mostly mothers, picketed the schools and engaged in demonstrations outside them. With the start of a new term in the fall of 1961, the boycott relaxed to some extent, although many of the white pupils remained in private schools; and the demonstrations did not resume.

Anticipating the time when a school system in Georgia would be confronted with the necessity of complying with a court order to desegregate, a group of Georgians early in 1959 organized Help Our Public Education. Under the direction of a full-time coordinator, HOPE launched a statewide program to "champion children's rights to an education within the state of Georgia." The organization carefully avoided the issues of states' rights and segregation. About two thousand persons attended a meeting of the charter chapter in Atlanta, and other chapters soon were formed in Rome, Gainesville, Athens, Savannah and Macon. With a budget of $1,500 a month, HOPE named a group of attorneys to analyze school laws and court decisions, appointed a public information committee, promoted public discussions and debates on the school crisis, set up a speakers' bureau and distributed free printed material. As the crisis deepened, HOPE sponsored a "Save Our Schools Week" throughout the state in December of 1959. Late in 1960 it launched "Operation Last Chance" to win support for the recommendations of the Sibley

School Study Commission at the 1961 session of the legislature. When the legislature met, the state school-closing laws were repealed, and new local option, pupil placement and tuition grant laws were enacted. Joining HOPE in support of these measures were the United Churchwomen, Active Voters and the League of Women Voters.

After the passage of the "open schools" laws, HOPE decided that since "the way was cleared for peaceful compliance with the law" it still had a role to play "in keeping our schools open in an atmosphere of dignity and calm." The one thousand delegates to the state P.T.A. convention passed without a dissenting vote a resolution urging all local P.T.A.'s whose schools were ordered to desegregate to help bring about compliance peacefully and "with dignity."

Atlanta was the first city in Georgia ordered to desegregate its schools. With the assistance of HOPE, forty-six organizations in the summer of 1961 combined their forces to create "a climate of calm dignified acceptance of desegregation in the fall." The coordinated group was called Organizations Assisting Schools in September. Mrs. Philip G. Hammer, a leader in the Georgia League of Women Voters, was general chairman of OASIS. She said, "When schools re-open next September, every citizen will be familiar with the facts of desegregation and the role he can play in insuring responsible compliance with the law." To conduct its campaign OASIS divided its members into four groups: civic and service, religious, youth-serving and a speakers' bureau. Throughout the summer it conducted meetings and discussions. The start of desegregation in September was calm, and OASIS disbanded, its job completed. Within a few weeks the board of directors of HOPE decided to close its office but to be ready on a "standby basis" if needed. Mrs. Benson Downing, chairman, said, "Atlanta had given us a blueprint, and each community must be ready when the time comes to desegregate."

As the time approached for desegregation to begin in Alabama public schools, citizens groups in Birmingham and Mobile declared their support for law and order and open schools. The Birmingham group, headed by the Rev. H. Frank Ledford, called itself the Community Affairs Committee on Public Schools. In a statement it said,

"The first job of this committee is to support the school board as they carry out the difficult decisions they have been required to make under the court orders. . . . We sincerely believe that the thinking citizens of our beloved city are deeply concerned about this crisis. We also believe that they are determined to keep our schools open in an atmosphere of peace."

The Mobile organization, Alabamians Behind Local Education, drew criticism from Governor George Wallace and legislative leaders, who said that it was promoting desegregation. They threatened an investigation of it. Mrs. Hollis J. Wiseman, wife of a Mobile pediatrician and president of ABLE, replied that the governor was misinformed. She said that ABLE was "a Mobile organization led by responsible Mobilians" and would welcome an investigation, adding that none was necessary, since the group had proclaimed its objectives "as loudly and as clearly as our limited funds allowed." These objectives were, Mrs. Wiseman said, "open schools instead of no schools and a peaceful community instead of racial violence." No investigation was conducted. When ABLE was organized, Mrs. Wiseman, in a statement of its purpose, had said, "We don't want to argue the relative merits of segregation or desegregation. But we believe that each of us has an individual responsibility to let our local leadership and our fellow citizens know that we stand on the side of law, order and public schools." Governor Wallace sent his highway patrolmen to Birmingham and Mobile to prevent desegregation of the schools, but he yielded to federal authority, and there was no further trouble.

Mississippi was the only state to maintain complete segregation in its public schools for a full decade after the *Brown* decision. Four school systems were under court order to desegregate in September of 1964, however, and that summer an organization was formed to work for peaceful acceptance of the change. It was called Mississippians for Public Education, and its president was Mrs. Gordon G. Henderson of Jackson, wife of a political scientist at Millsaps College. In an ad in the Jackson newspapers the group said: "As parents, taxpayers and citizens, we wish to create the kind of community climate in which public education can flourish and grow in an atmosphere of good will within the framework of the law. . . . We sincerely urge that you leave the business of desegregation in the hands of the proper authorities—your local school board and city and county law enforcement officers. We invite responsible Mississippians to join with us in attaining this goal." Desegregation began in the state that fall without incident, and without closed schools.

Those Southern whites who were not actively engaged in the segregation-desegregation struggle kept their thoughts to themselves —until crisis threatened their local schools. In almost every community where schools closed or faced a serious possibility of being closed, white residents raised their voices in support of public education. They wanted the public schools kept open, even if they were desegregated. While they hardly could claim full credit, their influence was a factor in the achievement of this objective.

13.
The Negro Protest

Negroes acclaimed the *Brown* decision as a second Emancipation Proclamation. The Supreme Court ruling applied only to schools, but it held the promise of an end to "second-class citizenship." As the first bright glow of the promise faded, Negro disillusion and disappointment replaced hope, and militancy took the place of patience.

The victory in the *School Segregation Cases* belonged peculiarly to the National Association for the Advancement of Colored People and its Legal Defense and Educational Fund. The 1954 decision was the capstone of a series of victories for the NAACP and its approach to racial progress through litigation, negotiation and political action.

Until 1954 the NAACP was the unchallenged leader of Negro Americans in their aspirations to achieve full participation in the machinery and fruits of the nation's government and economy. The only other organizations with a claim to significant influence were the National Urban League and the Brotherhood of Sleeping Car Porters. The former's primary concern was the creation of greater employment opportunities by negotiation with white employers. The latter worked mainly toward elimination of discrimination in trade unionism. In 1954 the NAACP, the Urban League and the Sleeping Car Porters were the "Big Three" in race relations in the United States.

Following the *Brown* decision, and in the absence of quick, dramatic change, Negroes became restless and turned to more direct action to achieve their goals. Within a few years the "Big Three" grew into the "Big Six." From a bus boycott in Montgomery, Alabama, in 1955 emerged the Southern Christian Leadership Conference. Four college students in Greensboro, North Carolina, sat at a variety store lunch counter in 1960, stimulating demonstrations that resulted in the birth a few weeks later of the Student Nonviolent Coordinating Committee. The staging in 1961 of "freedom rides" through the South brought to the front the Congress of Racial Equality, relatively unknown during the almost twenty years of its prior existence. All of these organizations worked toward common goals. They disagreed on methods for attaining them.

The place of whites in the movement for Negro progress developed into an issue. The NAACP, the Urban League and CORE had strong traditions of interracial membership and cooperation. The Southern Christian Leadership Conference was all-Negro but received substantial white support. The Student Nonviolent Coordinating Committee was Negro-led, although it welcomed white participation in its activities. One Negro group was strictly segregationist. The Black Muslims preached that the Negro could expect no help from white men, who were said to be inherently evil.

The NAACP

Of the major organizations through which Negroes gave voice to their protest against inequality and discrimination, the NAACP was the oldest. Organized in 1909 by white liberals, its rallying cry through the years was "first-class citizenship for all." Its methods for achieving its goals, as described by Roy Wilkins, who served as executive secretary after Walter White's death in 1955, were "the courts and the legislature and the education of public opinion."

The only truly mass membership organization among the protest groups, the NAACP in 1964 claimed approximately half a million members in some fifteen hundred local chapters. Its annual budget was more than one million dollars, the greater part of which came from its members.

At the time of the *Brown* decision, the NAACP and its Legal Defense Fund could reflect with some satisfaction on previous victories won in the courts. In the area of voting rights, the courts had ruled against the "grandfather clause" and the "white primary" as devices to disfranchise Negroes. In the field of housing, the courts had banned zoning by race and the enforcement of racially restrictive covenants in real estate conveyances. As a result of another decision, the systematic, deliberate exclusion of Negroes from a jury placed its verdict in legal jeopardy. Before the *Brown* decision, the Supreme Court in effect already had declared segregation in tax-supported graduate and professional schools to be unconstitutional.

In the *School Segregation Cases* the Supreme Court for the first time held that segregation itself did not square with the Constitution. The NAACP and Negroes generally waited for the walls of segregation to crumble. Thurgood Marshall, chief counsel of the Legal Defense Fund, said soon after the decision that the NAACP was pledged to an all-out effort to "break down segregation in all forms."

The NAACP won more victories as the federal courts applied the principle of the *Brown* decision to other areas of public affairs. The courts ruled against segregation in public parks, in municipal transportation systems, in facilities attached to interstate transportation, in public housing, in hospitals constructed or operated with public funds, in motels built on land in urban renewal projects. In short, the courts banned segregation where there was public money or public control.

These victories marked progress toward the achievement of equal rights for Negroes. Still segregation persisted, and most Negroes could see little, if any, improvement in their personal circumstances. Early in 1957, Marshall, speaking at a meeting of the National Newspaper Publishers Association, said, "We are finding that this problem is not going to be solved in the courts alone. . . . It will be solved on the community level by voting and other means." Two years later he said, "It will take time to get complete integration, but we are willing to stay in the courts to do it." Observing that some Negroes wanted integration "on a silver platter," he added that "in a democracy you have to push for what you want within the law." By 1961 Marshall sounded more militant when he said, "I think that some people in this country consider integration as some form of charity to be spooned out at the will of the majority. We must make it clear that we are talking about our rights . . . and we want all of them and we want them now."

The changing tenor of Marshall's comments as time passed reflected his reactions to growing Negro criticism of the NAACP, its organization, its approach and its programs. Critics charged that the NAACP leadership was too much interested in status goals and too little interested in goals of the masses. They said that the NAACP, with its emphasis on legalism, was winning symbolic victories that had little meaning to the average Negro. They called for a shift to direct action.

Roy Wilkins responded to this criticism in an interview in the spring of 1963. He said: "Our policy reflects the dominant mood of the Negro today. That mood is one of impatience with the pace of desegregation, or, as we say, impatience with the speed with which the Negro comes into the status of full citizenship. It is a very great impatience, I think, spurred by the resistance to implementing the 1954 Supreme Court decision against segregated public schools. . . .

"I feel that the Negro had the right to conceive of that decision as getting rid of the doctrine of 'separate but equal' facilities for Negroes. That's what the decision said. The Negro was prepared for reasonable progress toward implementing the decision, provided it began and was in good faith. . . .

"Instead of that, resistance broke out—extreme resistance. Now the Negro sees—nine years after the Court decision, come May 17, 1963—still more than 2,000,000 Negro youngsters in segregated schools and school districts, having to fight every step of the way, county by county and school district by school district. Even where there is integration, it's only token. So some Negroes are coming to say: 'Why do you put so much stock in the courts? Who cares what the Supreme Court says, because it doesn't have any effect on me, anyway?'. . .

"I wasn't so naïve as to think the Court's decision would be self-enforcing. But I did believe that, with reasonable representations on the part of the Negro public as to what it wanted, and through conferences with school and public officials, plans would have been worked out for a steady implementation of the Court's ruling, even though at a relatively slow pace. This has not happened. And this is the reason why some Negroes may lend an ear to appeals for less diplomacy and more action. . . .

"Generally, the Negro wants the color line wiped out, because it restricts his rights and opportunities. That's his general objective. And, to be effective, this has got to be on more than just a token basis."

At its annual meeting in the summer of 1963, the NAACP formally adopted a change in policy. It endorsed direct-action methods. It gave greater freedom to its youth chapters. It empowered the national board to remove leaders of local chapters who remained too conservative.

The NAACP could point to instances in which it had engaged in direct action. It had looked mainly to the courts, however, to achieve civil rights objectives. Negroes expected tangible results from the *Brown* decision and other decisions that flowed from it. Disappointed, they turned to direct action to force change. Events caused the NAACP to shift its emphasis toward direct action in order to maintain its position of leadership in the Negro protest movement.

The Southern Christian Leadership Conference

The first of these events began in Montgomery, Alabama, on Thursday afternoon, December 1, 1955, when Mrs. Rosa Parks boarded a local transit bus. The seats were divided into a section at the rear for Negroes and one at the front for whites. Mrs. Parks sat on the front row of seats for Negroes. When the bus became crowded, the driver asked Mrs. Parks and three other Negroes to move toward the rear to make room for white passengers. She refused, was arrested and was taken to the police station to be booked on the charge of violating the bus segregation laws.

That night the Montgomery Negro community buzzed with indignation. The next night at a mass meeting the Negroes made plans to boycott the city bus system. Over the weekend the word spread, and on Monday morning the drivers had the buses to themselves as they made their rounds. Most of the bus patronage came from the city's fifty thousand Negroes. The "great walk" had started.

At her trial on Monday, Mrs. Parks was found guilty and was fined $10 and costs. That night five thousand Negroes jammed into the Holt Street Baptist Church for another mass meeting at which they formed the Montgomery Improvement Association. As their chairman they elected the Rev. Dr. Martin Luther King, Jr., pastor of the Dexter Avenue Baptist Church. The boycott continued under Dr. King's leadership. The NAACP filed a suit in federal district court, which on June 4, 1956, ruled that state laws and local ordinances requiring segregation on city bus lines were unconstitutional. On November 13 the United States Supreme Court affirmed the lower court's decision. Sitting where they pleased, Negroes began to ride the buses again.

The Montgomery bus boycott was a milestone in the civil rights movement. Spontaneous and indigenous, it joined the total Negro population of a city in a common cause. It showed how effectively Negroes could use their economic power. It introduced the technique of nonviolent protest. And, perhaps above all else, it gave the movement a new spiritual and symbolic leader, Martin Luther King, Jr.

Born in 1929 in Atlanta, King was the son of a Baptist minister. His grandfather and great-grandfather also were preachers. He was educated at Morehouse College, Crozer Theological Seminary and Boston University. After receiving his doctorate, he went to Montgomery and had been there about a year when asked to lead the bus boycott. Later, writing of this experience, he said that as a theological student "... I had almost despaired of the power of love in solving social problems. ... Then I came upon the life and teachings of Mahatma Gandhi. As I read his works I became deeply fascinated by his campaigns of nonviolent resistance. The whole Gandhian concept of *satyagraha* (*satya* is truth which equals love, and *graha* is force; *satyagraha* thus means truth-force or love-force) was profoundly significant to me. As I delved deeper into the philosophy of Gandhi my skepticism concerning the power of love gradually diminished, and I came to see for the first time that the Christian doctrine of love operating through the Gandhian method of nonviolence was one of the most potent weapons available to oppressed people in their struggle for freedom. ..."

The Montgomery bus boycott gave King an unexpected opportunity to test his theory. "When I went to Montgomery, Alabama, in 1954 I had not the slightest idea that I would later be involved in a crisis in which nonviolent resistance would be applicable," he said. "The Negro people of Montgomery, exhausted by the humiliating experiences that they had constantly faced on the buses, expressed in a massive act of non-cooperation their determination to be free. They came to see that it was ultimately more honorable to walk the streets in dignity than to ride the buses in humiliation. At the beginning of the protest the people called on me to serve as their spokesman. In accepting this responsibility my mind, consciously or unconsciously, was driven back to the Sermon on the Mount and the Gandhian method of nonviolent resistance. This principle became the guiding light of our movement. Christ furnished the spirit and the motivation while Gandhi furnished the method."

The example of Montgomery inspired similar bus boycotts in Birmingham and Tallahassee. Martin Luther King, Jr., immediately became a figure of national prominence in the civil rights movement. In 1957 he organized the Southern Christian Leadership Conference. At a meeting of the Montgomery Improvement Association on December 3, 1959, the fourth anniversary of its founding, King announced that he was moving to Atlanta. "For the past year," he explained, "the Southern Christian Leadership Conference has been pleading with me to give it the maximum of my time, since the time was ripe for expanded militant action across the South. After giving the request serious and prayerful consideration, I came to the conclusion that I had a moral obligation to give more of my time and energy to the whole South." On February 1, 1960, he returned to Atlanta to give himself a more convenient base for his activities as president of SCLC and to become associate pastor to his father at Ebenezer Baptist Church.

The Southern Christian Leadership Conference did not develop into a mass membership organization along the lines of the NAACP. Instead it has been a loose confederation of affiliates—some eighty-five of them—dominated by clergymen, most of whom are Baptists. Its chief asset has been Dr. King, whose eloquence and beliefs attracted wide support from both Negroes and whites. Following his success in Montgomery, King was in great demand as a speaker and as a leader in demonstrations.

As the philosopher of the Negro protest movement, Dr. King spoke from many rostrums across the country. In Charleston, West Virginia, just before his move to Atlanta, he said, "Although the removal of legal barriers against desegregation is an important need in the South, ultimately we seek integration, which is true inter-group, inter-personal living, where you sit on a bus—you sit together —not because the law says it but because it's natural, because it's right."

Preaching at Howard University on a Sunday morning in April of 1962, King said, "We have the bigoted white man baffled because he does not know how to cope with nonviolence. He is completely at the mercy of his conscience and knows better than we do that segregation is dead. The only thing that concerns the white Southerner now is how costly the funeral of segregation should be and when to hold the burial services. . . . If we as a race of people do nothing about it then nothing will be done, for the white man has shown, both in the North as well as the South, that time doesn't change his thinking, but action does."

For his work, including his words, Dr. King received the Nobel

Peace Prize in 1964. His emphasis on peaceful methods of forcing racial change brought criticism as well as honor. C. Eric Lincoln, Negro sociologist, said in an address at Brown University that King was "anathema" to the Negro masses, who thought of him as "a man who is financed by whites." Militant Negroes, Lincoln added, regarded King as "a man who has kept us from fighting" and looked upon his winning the Nobel Peace Prize "as a payoff for his keeping the peace."

The Student Nonviolent Coordinating Committee

The projects and demonstrations in which Dr. King participated often started independently of him and his organization. One that ranked in importance with the Montgomery bus boycott had its beginning in Greensboro, North Carolina, on February 1, 1960. At 4:30 P.M. on that day, four freshmen at North Carolina Agricultural and Technical College for Negroes entered a variety store and sat at the lunch counter until the store closed an hour later. They were not served, but unknowingly they had started a movement that was to spread like a brush fire fanned by a brisk wind.

The next morning seventy-five A. & T. students sat at the lunch counter. Two days later white students from the Woman's College of the University of North Carolina and Greensboro College and Negroes from Bennett College joined the A. & T. students. The "sitins" expanded to other stores, to other cities and to other states, as if by spontaneous combustion. Thousands of students soon were engaging in this new form of demonstration, and many of them were being arrested and jailed. Crowds of white segregationists gathered to taunt the demonstrators, to assault them, to pour ketchup over their heads.

One of the early demonstrators in Greensboro expressed the rationale of their action. "They sell us merchandise from other counters," she said. "If they sell us other merchandise, we say they should serve us at the lunch counter." The store operators hardly knew what to do. Most of the stores were affiliates of national chains, which were vulnerable to boycotts outside the South. Their first reaction was to take the position that each of their stores followed local custom. To avoid desegregating their lunch counters in the South, they closed them, or they removed the seats from the stools. But the pressure continued, and it brought capitulation from store after store in town after town.

The first students who sat at a lunch counter acted as individuals. They had been members of NAACP Youth Councils, but they did not represent the NAACP or any other organization. They had no conception of what they were starting. As the demonstrations and the opposition to them grew, the students turned to the established civil rights organizations for help and advice. The NAACP sent Herbert Wright, its youth secretary, to North Carolina. From the Congress of Racial Equality came Gordon Carey, field secretary, and a team of field workers headed by Len Holt.

The sit-in technique was not new. The NAACP had used it in Oklahoma and Kansas in 1958 and 1959. CORE originated from a sit-in at a Chicago restaurant in 1942. These were isolated incidents, however. The NAACP and CORE, especially the latter, instructed the students in behavior during demonstrations, and gave them a semblance of organization and leadership.

The movement waited for the appearance of Martin Luther King to take its ultimate form. King went to North Carolina to observe the demonstrations. Then he addressed a meeting of about one hundred students in the White Rock Baptist Church in Durham. "Let us not fear going to jail if the officials threaten us for standing up for our rights," he told them. "Maybe it will take this willingness to stay in jail to arouse the dozing conscience of our nation." The Durham meeting was the forerunner of one to be held April 15–17, Easter weekend, at Shaw University in Raleigh under the sponsorship of Dr. King's Southern Christian Leadership Conference. By then sit-ins had been staged in seventy-five cities in twelve states, and almost thirteen hundred students had been arrested.

More than two hundred delegates from fifty-two colleges and high schools in thirteen states gathered in Raleigh for the "Leadership Conference on Nonviolent Resistance," as it was called. Speaking before the students, but addressing his remarks to the white community, Dr. King said, "Do to us what you will and we will still love you. We will meet your physical force with soul force. You may bomb our homes and spit on our children and we will still love you. But be assured that we will wear you down with our capacity to suffer. . . ." The group divided into workshop committees, which later reported to the conference. The chairman of the "Jail vs. Bail" committee recommended that all students arrested remain in jail rather than be released on bail or pay fines. "This will show that arrest will not deter us," she said.

The culmination of the Raleigh meeting was the creation of the Student Nonviolent Coordinating Committee. The delegates adopted a statement of purpose, written by the Rev. James Lawson, who had been expelled from the Divinity School at Vanderbilt University for his role in the student demonstrations in Nashville. It said, in part, "We affirm the philosophical or religious ideal of nonviolence as the foundation of our purpose, the presupposition of our faith, and the manner of our action. . . . By appealing to the conscience and standing on the moral nature of human existence, nonviolence nurtures the atmosphere in which reconciliation and justice become actual possibilities."

Singing "We Shall Overcome," the students demonstrated through the spring and summer. The idea of "sitting in" at eating places found other expressions—kneel-ins at churches, wade-ins at beaches, swim-ins at pools, stand-ins at theaters. SNCC never had a large formal organizational structure, but thousands of students, white and Negro, participated in its activities. More than four thousand of the demonstrators were arrested. Going to jail became a badge of honor. Aaron Henry, president of the NAACP in Mississippi, said, "We will make these jails temples of freedom."

Within two years after the first sit-in, demonstrations had taken place in more than one hundred cities, and negotiations had been conducted in many others, with restaurants and theaters as the major targets. These efforts were successful in some two hundred cities. SNCC employed James Forman, a school teacher from Chicago, as its executive secretary and took a leading place among the established civil rights groups in the nation.

Harold Fleming, who in 1960 was executive director of the Southern Regional Council, called the sit-ins "the psychological turning point in race relations in the South." He said, "This is the first step to real change—when the whites realize that the Negroes just aren't having it any more." August Meier, associate professor of history at Morgan State College, termed the sit-ins "the really decisive break with the past." He gave three reasons for his judgment: "For one thing these sit-ins involved the use of nonviolent direct action on a massive, South-wide scale, never before attempted. Secondly, they involved tens of thousands of students, thousands of whom were arrested—an involvement of numbers of people heretofore inconceivable. Thirdly, it began a period . . . in which the spearhead of the civil rights struggle has come from the youth." Thurgood Marshall was asked at a North Carolina NAACP rally in the spring of 1960 why the student protest movement had spread so rapidly through the South. He replied that the young people were impatient with the slowness of court action in furthering equality, and he added, "And if you mean, are the young people impatient with me, the answer is yes."

The Congress of Racial Equality

Not only the young people were impatient. One group of adults who had been impatient for a long time were the members of the Congress of Racial Equality. Without attracting much attention nationally, CORE had engaged in nonviolent direct action since its organization in 1942 as an offshoot of the Fellowship of Reconciliation, a pacifistic, social-action organization of the Quakers.

From the automobile strikes of the 1930's CORE borrowed the idea of the "sitdown." At its inception CORE staged a sit-in at a Chicago restaurant. In 1946 the United States Supreme Court ruled in a case from Virginia that state laws requiring racial segregation of the races in interstate public transportation placed a burden on interstate commerce and were unconstitutional. CORE then staged a "journey of reconciliation" in the upper South to test the extent to which the Court's ruling was effective. Periodically such protests were made. CORE organized a sit-in at the lunch counter and in the cafeteria of a Charleston, West Virginia, department store in 1959. At that time Mrs. Elizabeth Gilmore, local chapter secretary, said, "Some of our actions may seem drastic, but you can't cure cancer with an aspirin."

When the student sit-ins began in 1960, CORE was little known in the South, but it was asked for help because of its previous experience with nonviolent protest techniques. Its membership was composed in the main of white liberals. It was very loosely organized, and had no paid field worker until 1956. The student movement gave CORE an opportunity to expand its activities, but still it remained in the background.

On February 1, 1961, the first anniversary of the sit-ins, James Farmer became national director of CORE. A former Methodist minister and one of the founders of CORE, Farmer moved to his new job from the NAACP national staff, where he was program director. Within a few months, CORE burst into headlines.

Shortly before Farmer changed jobs, the Supreme Court ruled in another transportation case from Virginia. Bruce Boynton, a Negro law student, was on a bus en route from Washington to Montgomery. When the bus stopped in Richmond, Boynton went to the white lunch counter in the terminal, was refused service, declined to move to the Negro counter and was arrested. On December 5, 1960, the Supreme Court held that a restaurant in an interstate bus terminal, although not owned by the bus company, must operate "without discrimination." Recalling CORE's test of the 1946 transportation decision, Farmer decided to test the new one in a similar manner. On April 28 he wrote a letter to President Kennedy informing him that CORE planned a "freedom ride" by bus from Washington to New Orleans to learn whether terminal facilities were available to Negroes as well as whites without discrimination, as the Supreme Court said they should be.

On May 4 seven Negro and six white "freedom riders" boarded a bus in Washington and headed south. In age they ranged from eighteen to sixty-one. For ten days they rode through Virginia, North Carolina, South Carolina and Georgia, with only minor incident.

In Atlanta the riders split into two groups, part taking a Trailways bus, and the others a Greyhound bus, and on May 14, a Sunday, they started toward Alabama.

A white mob met the buses at Anniston, would not permit the riders to get off and slashed the tires of the Greyhound bus. Six miles outside the town on the way to Birmingham, the tires went flat. From one of the cars in pursuit, someone threw an incendiary bomb into the bus, which burned. Some of the passengers were treated in an Anniston hospital for smoke inhalation, and then they went on to Birmingham in secrecy. The Trailways bus meanwhile had continued on the road to Birmingham. The U.S. Department of Justice notified Birmingham Police Commissioner Eugene (Bull) Connor that it had received reports of planned violence when the bus reached his city.

At the Birmingham terminal, a white mob attacked the disembarking riders. As Tom Lankford, a reporter on the scene for the Birmingham *News,* described it, "A giant of a man, bloody from slugging individuals while his gang held them, led the attackers, crazily swinging blackjacks and lengths of pipe; about eight of them pounded a white man and a Negro to the concrete floor of the bus station." The police station was two blocks from the bus station, but no police appeared until the violence subsided. Commissioner Connor expressed shock at what had happened, blamed it on "out-of-town meddlers" and said that his force was reduced because it was Mothers' Day. Governor John Patterson advised the riders to "get out of Alabama as quickly as possible." They did, flying to New Orleans.

Thus ended the first "freedom ride," but others quickly formed. One group of students rode from Nashville to Birmingham, where some were jailed, released and taken to the Tennessee line by police. The students quickly returned to Birmingham. There on Saturday morning, May 20, they left on a Greyhound bus for Montgomery.

Both President Kennedy and Attorney General Robert Kennedy tried unsuccessfully to talk with Governor Patterson to obtain his assurance of safe conduct for the riders. On Friday, John Seigenthaler, administrative assistant to Attorney General Kennedy, talked with the governor, who issued a statement saying, "We are going to do all we can to enforce the laws of the state on the highways and everywhere else, but we are not going to escort these agitators."

A crowd of angry whites met the riders at the Montgomery bus terminal, but no police were present. For the next four hours a melee took place in which both riders and bystanders were attacked indiscriminantly. Seigenthaler was among the victims. As he attempted to aid one of the young riders, he was struck, and he lay in semiconsciousness in the street for almost half an hour. Explaining the late arrival of city police on the scene, Montgomery Police Commissioner L. B. Sullivan said, "We respond to calls at the bus station just like any place else, but we have no intention of standing guard for a bunch of trouble makers coming into our city."

Attorney General Kennedy ordered U.S. marshals to Montgomery and sent Deputy Attorney General Byron White there to take charge of federal activities. On Sunday Martin Luther King flew from Chicago to Montgomery to address a mass meeting. Rioting broke out again. The governor declared martial law in the city, and ordered eight hundred National Guardsmen to duty. Three days later a convoy of highway patrolmen and Guardsmen escorted a busload of riders to the state line and surrendered them into the custody of Mississippi authorities. Upon their arrival in Jackson, the riders were arrested and jailed.

By this time the NAACP, SCLC and SNCC were involved in the freedom rides, which continued through the summer. The goal, and fate, of most of the riders was Jackson, Mississippi, and jail. About one thousand persons took part, and the cost ran around half a million dollars, largely to pay for fines and bail. The NAACP supplied most of the money.

The freedom rides accomplished their basic purpose. On September 22, 1961, the Interstate Commerce Commission issued a regulation prohibiting racial discrimination in the seating of passengers on interstate buses and in the use of terminal facilities. The freedom rides also placed CORE and James Farmer in the front ranks of the civil rights movement.

Until 1961 CORE had remained a small, predominantly white

organization. The freedom riders attracted many Negroes to it, so that at its annual convention in 1963 Negroes for the first time outnumbered whites among the delegates.

The Black Muslims

The overriding purpose of the Negro protest movement was to erase the color line from American life and thereby to elevate the position of the Negro. All of the major organizations involved sought to achieve this objective with the aid and cooperation of white Americans; all, that is, but one—The Lost-Found Nation of Islam in the Wilderness of North America, popularly known as the Black Muslims.

Perhaps the Muslims should not be regarded as a part of the same movement. The other groups sought integration of the Negro into full and equal citizenship with whites. The Muslims preached that the white man was the devil incarnate, from whom the Negro could expect no good; if Negroes were to improve their lot, they would have to do it themselves, by total separation from the white man, preferably in their own independent, all-black nation. Muslims advocated that the United States government give the land for this nation as a form of compensation for all the wrongs done to Negroes in the past.

The Black Muslims trace back to Wallace D. Fard, an itinerant peddler of unknown origins, who appeared in Detroit in 1930. He had a facile tongue, and soon he was attracting growing numbers of Detroit Negroes to meetings that he addressed. Fard told his followers that the "so-called Negro" did not exist, that he was a creation of the white man. The American black man, he said, really was a member of the "Lost-Found Nation of Islam" and the heir to a richer and older culture than the white man's.

In 1934 "Mr. Ferrad Mohammad," as he called himself, disappeared as mysteriously as he had appeared, and nothing more ever was heard of him. His chief lieutenant, Elijah Muhammad, assumed leadership of the sect. Then in his thirties, the new "Messenger of Allah" was the son and grandson of Baptist preachers. He was named Elijah Poole upon his birth in Sandersville, Georgia.

For years the Nation of Islam was an esoteric cult in the Detroit slums. When, in the mid-fifties, several Negro newspapers began to print a column by Elijah Muhammad, his following grew rapidly. In 1962 the sect was said to have members scattered through twenty-seven states, although the exact size of its membership was a closely guarded secret.

One of the principal temples was in Harlem, under the leadership of Malcolm X. Born Malcolm Little, he replaced his surname with "X" as do all Muslims, on the theory that their only known names were handed down to them from slavery, and those aren't their real names. Like many Muslims, Malcolm was converted to the sect while serving a prison sentence. Elijah Muhammad himself was imprisoned for four years during World War II upon conviction for sedition. Elijah was a small, frail man who spoke with a bad lisp. Malcolm, nicknamed "Big Red," was a large man of commanding presence and voice, and he became the leader's chief aide and principal spokesman. Later Malcolm split with Elijah and formed his own group.

The Muslims have a special appeal to the Negro in the big city slums. They offer him pride in his race and pride in himself as a person. The use of alcohol, tobacco and narcotics is forbidden, as are pork and other rich foods. Members are taught to dress well, to live within their means, to patronize businesses owned and operated by black men and, above all, to remain as separate from the white man as conditions of society permit.

By contrast to Martin Luther King's appeal for love and non-violence, Elijah Muhammad advocated "return to the Mosaic law of an eye for an eye and a tooth for a tooth." He asked, "What does it matter if ten million of us die? There will be seven million of us left, and they will enjoy justice and freedom." And Malcolm X said, "No white man really wants the black man to have his rights, or he'd have them." When asked whether being born in the United States didn't make him an American citizen, Malcolm replied, "Just because a cat has kittens in an oven, it doesn't make them biscuits."

The Black Muslims did not march in step with the other Negro organizations, but Muslim voices were raised in loud protest against what they considered to be injustices to Negroes. Moreover, many

Negroes listened and agreed with what they heard. The rise of the Muslims coincided with growing suspicion and criticism of whites within the organizations committed by policy to the nonviolent approach. Fear was expressed that the failure of peaceful protest to satisfy Negro demands might cause a turn toward violence.

Birmingham: 1963

As the sit-ins and freedom rides showed, demonstrators who considered themselves peaceful often were agitators in the eyes of others. Nonviolent protests sometimes provoked violent reactions, as was the case in Alabama in 1963.

Concerned about the impression that civil rights turmoil was creating, the Alabama Chamber of Commerce appointed a New Image Committee. On March 4, 1963, John A. Williamson, chairman of the committee, spoke in Birmingham. He said that his committee was dedicated to an "all-out drive to change what the nation thinks of us.

"The image is that of reaction, rebellion and riots, of bigotry, bias and backwardness, of high taxes, crooked politicians and trouble with a capital 'T,' " he said. "What are the words we hear? They are the words of raw hate and naked fear—blind hate and dumb fear. What are the feelings? Desperation and defiance on one side, and dismay and disgust on the other." He said that Birmingham's image was "grievously bad . . . because some of our political leaders have, in effect, volunteered Birmingham for the next big battle."

Martin Luther King, Jr., accepted the invitation. On April 3 he announced that Birmingham was to be the prime target of the Southern Christian Leadership Conference. Demonstrations began immediately and continued for weeks. Thousands of Negroes, including school children, participated in sit-ins, parades, picketing and boycotts. Police Commissioner Connor turned fire hoses and police dogs on the demonstrators. A news photograph of a police dog lunging at a young Negro man became a symbol of the protest movement.

King was jailed on a charge of parading without a permit, and on April 16 he released a letter to six white clergymen in response to their published statement criticizing the demonstrations. The "Letter from a Birmingham Jail" was reprinted widely. Excerpts from the letter follow:

"While confined here in the Birmingham City Jail, I came across your recent statement calling our present activities 'unwise and untimely.' . . . You deplore the demonstrations that are presently taking place in Birmingham. But I am sorry that your statement did not express a similar concern for the conditions that brought the demonstrations into being. . . . There can be no gainsaying of the fact that racial injustice engulfs this community. . . .

"You may well ask, 'Why direct action? Why sit-ins, marches, etc.? Isn't negotiation a better path?' You are exactly right in your call for negotiation. Indeed, this is the purpose of direct action. Nonviolent direct action seeks to create such a crisis and establish such creative tension that a community that has constantly refused to negotiate is forced to confront the issue. It seeks so to dramatize the issue that it can no longer be ignored. . . . The purpose of the direct action is to create a situation so crisis-packed that it will inevitably open the door to negotiation. . . .

"One of the basic points in your statement is that our acts are untimely. . . . We know through painful experience that freedom is never voluntarily given by the oppressor; it must be demanded by the oppressed. Frankly I have never yet engaged in a direct action movement that was 'well timed,' according to the timetable of those who have not suffered unduly from the disease of segregation. . . . We have waited for more than three hundred and forty years for our constitutional and God-given rights. The nations of Asia and Africa are moving with jet-like speed toward the goals of political independence, and we still creep at horse and buggy pace toward the gaining of a cup of coffee at a lunch counter. I guess it is easy for those who have never felt the stinging darts of segregation to say wait. . . .

"You express a great deal of anxiety over our willingness to break laws. . . . One may well ask, 'How can you advocate breaking some laws and obeying others?' The answer is found in the fact that there are two types of laws: There are *just* laws and there are *unjust* laws. I would be the first to advocate obeying just laws. One has not only a legal but moral responsibility to obey just laws. . . . In no sense do I advocate evading or defying the law as the rabid segregationist would do. This would lead to anarchy. One who breaks an unjust law must do it *openly, lovingly* (not hatefully, as the white mothers did in New Orleans when they were seen on television screaming 'nigger, nigger, nigger') and with a willingness to accept the penalty. I submit that an individual who breaks a law that conscience tells him is unjust, and willingly accepts the penalty by staying in jail to arouse the conscience of the community over its injustice, is in reality expressing the very highest respect for law. . . .

"One day the South will know that when these disinherited children of God sat down at lunch counters they were in reality standing up for the best in the American dream and the most sacred values in our Judeo-Christian heritage, and thus carrying our whole nation back to great wells of democracy which were dug deep by the founding fathers in the formulation of the Constitution and the Declaration of Independence. . . ."

After eight days King left jail on bond. On May 10, white business and civic leaders reached an agreement with Negro leaders on the terms of a truce. It called for desegregation of lunch counters, restrooms, sitting rooms and drinking fountains in the big downtown stores in planned stages within ninety days; employment and upgrading of Negroes by the stores on a nondiscriminatory basis; release on bond or personal recognizance of all persons arrested during the demonstrations; and appointment of a biracial committee to provide a "channel of communications" and to determine a timetable for school desegregation.

Local and state political leaders were not parties to the agreement. Birmingham Mayor Arthur J. Hanes called the white negotiators "a bunch of quisling, gutless traitors." Governor George C. Wallace said, "I, as governor, will not be a party to any such meeting to compromise on the issues of segregation." Early on Sunday morning, May 12, two bombs ripped apart the home of the Rev. A. D. King, younger brother of Martin Luther King, Jr. A short time later two more bombs exploded at the A. G. Gaston Motel, headquarters for the demonstrations. Thousands of Negroes gathered at the scenes of the blasts, and a weekend of wild rioting followed. More than one thousand city and state police officers were sent to the riot area. The federal government moved three thousand troops to bases near Birmingham for use if they were needed and prepared to federalize the National Guard, but order was restored without troops. Demonstrations continued in Birmingham, but events in other places temporarily diverted attention from the city.

The Birmingham demonstrations and rioting in the spring of 1963 had a heavy impact in Washington. The Kennedy administration acted with new vigor in the civil rights field. President Kennedy, who had sent a civil rights message to Congress in February, followed it in June with a second one advocating passage of a stronger law than he previously had recommended.

Soon after school started in the fall, racial violence returned to Birmingham. After the collapse of resistance by Governor Wallace, five Negro children on Tuesday, September 10, entered previously white schools. During the remainder of the week, white students and adults engaged in demonstrations and rioting, and some whites boycotted the schools.

At 10:25 A.M. on Sunday, September 15, a dynamite bomb exploded in a stairwell outside the Sixteenth Street Baptist Church, which had served as a rallying point for Negro demonstrations. The explosion killed four Negro girls attending Sunday school and injured twenty-three other persons. In the rioting that followed, a policeman accidentally killed a Negro boy, and a group of white boys shot and killed another Negro boy who was riding his bicycle. Within a few hours city and state police had the situation under control.

President Kennedy expressed "a deep sense of outrage and grief" but added that if the bombing could awaken Birmingham and Alabama to "the folly of racial injustice and hatred and violence, then it is not too late for all concerned to unite in steps toward peaceful progress before more lives are lost." The President sent Kenneth C. Royall, former Secretary of the Army, and Earl H. Blaik, former Army football coach, to Birmingham as his special envoys to confer with white and Negro leaders.

Martin Luther King blamed Governor Wallace for the deaths. "It was segregation that killed them," he said. "Wallace created the climate that made it possible for someone to plant that bomb." King called for a resumption of demonstrations, but two other Negro leaders rebuked him. Arthur D. Shores, an attorney whose home had been bombed several times, and A. G. Gaston, millionaire businessman whose motel had been bombed, opposed "additional outside interference" while Royall and Blaik were trying to "bring the leaders of the . . . community together with a view to solving our problem."

Governor Wallace rejected King's accusation. "The Supreme Court and the administration in Washington and the agitators who come into this state" were responsible, the governor said. He called the bombing a "dastardly act by a demented fool who does not love either the white or black people of Alabama" and the bomber someone who "has universal hatred in his heart." The church bombing was the only one of more than forty in Birmingham in which anyone was killed. One effect of these and other acts of violence was to stoke the fires of the Negro protest movement.

The March on Washington

The most massive of all civil rights demonstrations was peaceful. On August 28, 1963, more than 200,000 persons, about one-third of them white, marched from the Washington Monument to the Lincoln Memorial to show their support for strong new civil rights legislation. Their slogan was "Jobs and Freedom."

Almost a quarter-century earlier—in 1941—A. Philip Randolph had planned a march on the nation's capital, but that march did not materialize. President Franklin D. Roosevelt removed the reason for it when he signed an executive order forbidding racial discrimination in employment under contracts with the federal government.

In 1963 Randolph revived his idea for a march on Washington. All of the major civil rights groups cooperated in making and executing plans for the largest rally of its kind ever held. Their purpose was to impress upon the administration and Congress the necessity for action on civil rights. Leaders of the march met with members of Congress before the demonstration and with President Kennedy and Vice President Johnson afterward.

Authorities in Washington feared disorder and made elaborate plans to control it, but none of any consequence developed. Police urged the marchers not to bring automobiles into the demonstration area. They came in buses, trains and planes; on bicycles, scooters and motorcycles; and on foot. The occasion was both festive and solemn. As the crowds gathered, groups formed on the grass around the base of the monument and sang and clapped and exchanged experiences. Many carried placards.

The march was scheduled to begin at 11:30 A.M., with its ten leaders in the vanguard. Some of the marchers jumped the gun, moved ahead of the leaders and started the march about ten minutes early. Someone commented that it was symbolic of the civil rights movement for the rank and file of Negroes to want to go faster than their leaders. Randolph parried, "Don't worry, we've been in this position many times in the past. We've been forced to run to keep ahead." One of the marchers was quoted as saying, "We don't need no leaders. We know the way to go."

The vast throng spread from the Lincoln Memorial, around the Reflecting Pool, toward the Washington Monument in the background. Some of them cooled their feet in the pool while they listened to a program of entertainment. Then came the speeches, intended to inspire the marchers and to challenge the nation.

The speech that made the deepest impression was Dr. King's. "Five score years ago," he began, "a great American, in whose symbolic shadow we stand, signed the Emancipation Proclamation. This momentous decree came as a great beacon light of hope to millions of Negro slaves who had been seared in the flames of withering injustice. It came as a joyous daybreak to end the long night of captivity.

"But one hundred years later, we must face the tragic fact that the Negro is still not free. One hundred years later, the life of the

Negro is still sadly crippled by the manacles of segregation and the chains of discrimination. One hundred years later, the Negro lives on a lonely island of poverty in the midst of a vast ocean of material prosperity. One hundred years later, the Negro is still languished in the corners of American society and finds himself an exile in his own land. So we come here today to dramatize an appalling condition."

While Dr. King was eloquent, other speakers hit harder, and none more so than young John Lewis, chairman of the Student Nonviolent Coordinating Committee. What Lewis did not say attracted more attention than what he did say. The Most Reverend Patrick J. O'Boyle, Catholic archbishop of Washington, who pronounced the invocation, refused to participate unless Lewis deleted a section of his prepared remarks. The omitted part said, "We will not wait for the President, the Justice Department, nor the Congress, but we will take matters in our own hands and create a source of power, outside of any national structure, that could and would assure us a victory."

When the demonstration ended, the leaders went to the White House to meet with the President and Vice President. Following this meeting, President Kennedy issued a statement in which he said, "The cause of 20 million Negroes has been advanced by the program conducted so appropriately before the nation's shrine to the Great Emancipator, but even more significant is the contribution to all mankind."

The march on Washington gave new impetus and unity to the civil rights movement, but it did not spur Congressional action. The heads of seven Negro action groups formed a Council for United Civil Rights Leadership. After President Kennedy's assassination, some members of the council suggested a moratorium on demonstrations during the period of transition to the Johnson administration. Others rejected the proposal outright.

Demonstrations continued in the months ahead. Dr. King led a campaign for desegregation in St. Augustine, Florida. Civil rights groups joined to form the Council of Federated Organizations to conduct a drive for the registration of Negro voters in Mississippi. College students from all over the country flocked to the state for the summer to help. On June 21 two white students from New York and a local Negro youth disappeared near Philadelphia, Mississippi, where police had detained them on a charge of speeding. The search for them continued for six weeks, until their bodies were found buried under an earthen dam.

The first anniversary of the march on Washington was approaching when Congress passed the Civil Rights Act of 1964. The bill went to the White House on the night of July 2, and three hours later President Johnson signed it into law.

"A Time of Testing"

"This act is a challenge to all of us to go to work in our states and communities, in our homes and in our hearts, to eliminate the last vestiges of injustice in America," the President said as he signed the act. Then he added, "My fellow citizens, we have come to a time of testing."

On that same day in Kansas City, CORE opened its annual convention, and James Farmer quickly took up the President's challenge. "We have a responsibility now to test this bill in every place of public accommodation, North and South," he said in his keynote address. "Voluntary integration has not worked in this country, and this state and every state must be prepared to enforce its laws if that voluntary integration is not forthcoming." The Civil Rights Act of 1964 "is no magic carpet that's going to take us to the promised land," he concluded.

Martin Luther King said that SCLS would test the act in two stages, which he described as "Operation Dialogue" and "Operation Implementation." The first stage would be devoted to obtaining pledges of voluntary compliance. In the second stage, recalcitrant towns and cities could expect "dramatic moves," he warned. At a civil rights rally in Chicago a few days before the bill passed, King told the seventy thousand who filled Soldier Field, "It is necessary to move vigorously. . . . We must continue to engage in demonstrations, boycotts, rent strikes and to use all the resources at our disposal to get rid of these conditions."

The NAACP was more cautious than CORE and SCLC. Roy Wilkins charged that Farmer and King were trying to beat the NAACP to the draw in announcing plans to test the Civil Rights Act. "We don't consider that we are in a race to make the first announcement," he said. "We ought to use every bit of the wisdom we can muster in taking advantage of this bill. . . . We ought to be smart rather than loud."

Negroes and their leaders openly disagreed on the best methods for achieving "first-class citizenship." They were in general agreement on basic goals, however, and they found greater strength in unity as they worked together toward their objectives. Dr. King spoke for all when he said, "We have a long way to go."

14.

An End and a Beginning

The *Brown* decision of 1954 and the Civil Rights Act of 1964 were milestones along the road that American Negroes traveled toward equality as citizens. The Supreme Court clearly enunciated the principle that separation of the races by force of law did not square with the Constitution. Ten years later Congress embodied this principle in federal statute.

The judicial declaration of the principle and its enactment into statutory law did not, however, establish it in the lives of those most immediately and directly affected—Southern Negroes. The Court's ruling and the act of Congress pointed the direction of the future.

Robert L. Carter, general counsel of the NAACP, in 1963 commented, "Before 1954 the civil rights struggle was chiefly a lawyer's battle. . . . But lawyers cannot implement decisions. Implementation rests with the will of the people." Carter had in mind all the people, Negro as well as white. Earlier U.S. Attorney General William P. Rogers observed, "If you have everybody in the state against you, there's not much you can do with law enforcement." Rogers referred to the controlling white majority in the Southern states.

The will of the white people varied from state to state and from place to place within a state. In the border states there was little resistance to compliance with the *Brown* decision. In the eleven Southern states the will to comply was missing, and few Negro children were admitted to schools with white children.

The degree of compliance related to several major factors. One was geography. Resistance stiffened with proximity to the Deep South. Another was the proportion of Negroes in the population. Resistance was greatest where the ratio of Negroes to whites was highest. Opposition also was stronger in rural than in urban areas.

The white people of the South who looked to leaders in public and private life to pilot them through the rocky rapids of social change most often saw their own image reflected, as if in a mirror. Those who occupied positions of leadership usually marched with the people, not ahead of them.

The passage of the Civil Rights Act of 1964 brought from U.S. Attorney General Robert F. Kennedy a comment on the "vacuum of leadership" that followed the *Brown* decision. "What happened after that decision?" he asked. "What was the reaction of responsible national and community leaders? Where were the pulpit, the press, the public officials? The answer is that they were silent. There was a vacuum of leadership from responsible sources until, finally, leadership was provided by demagogues and mobs. Their slogans were 'segregation forever' and 'massive resistance' and their philosophy was not respect for law, but intimidation. We got what we deserved. After all, when a whole generation and a whole region are told that a Supreme Court decision is unconstitutional and that it need not be obeyed, how could we expect that the mortar of public respect would be added to the brick of law?"

Time and events brought changes in attitudes among white Southerners and their leaders. They found that when desegregation no longer could be avoided, it could be controlled. When faced with the choice between desegregated schools and no public schools, they chose desegregation except in a few instances. Once Negroes entered schools with whites, the fires of public passion burned lower. Although desegregation was not desired, its inevitability was accepted.

The magnitude of the change depends on how it is measured. The number of Negro children attending schools with white children ten years after the *Brown* decision was small relative to the total of Negro school-age children in the South. But the change was great when viewed against the deep-rooted customs and traditions of a society that had been segregated for more than three hundred years.

The attitudes of Negroes partially accounted for the gradualness with which desegregation spread. While some Negroes fought militantly for desegregated schools in a desegregated society, most Negroes took no active part in the struggle. Whatever their reasons —fear of reprisals, the oppression of the past, or indifference—the vast majority of Negroes in the South made no attempt to exercise the right to a desegregated education that the *Brown* decision gave them. As late as 1963, Louis L. Redding, Negro lawyer of Wilmington, Delaware, who had led the fight for desegregation in his state, said, "The principal barrier we have in this state today to complete public school integration is the lethargy, the apathy, the indifference . . . of the Negroes who would be benefited in taking advantage of the opportunity that is legally theirs." In 1960 Roy Wilkins, executive secretary of the NAACP, had deplored "the spineless attitude of some Negroes who are afraid to stand up and be counted for freedom." The more solidly entrenched segregation was in a community, the more reluctant the local Negroes were to challenge it.

As the flush of the *Brown* victory wore off, and as more and more Negroes attended biracial schools, the realization dawned that the desegregation of schools was not the panacea that many had hoped and thought it would be. Segregation barriers fell in compliance with the decision, but the practical situations of most Negroes were little changed. The achievement of desegregation was a mechanical, legalistic process. Desegregation sowed seeds of opportunity that would be slow in germinating and growing to maturity.

In the years that followed the *Brown* decision, the Supreme Court's opinion was pitted against public opinion in the South. At first public opinion appeared to be stronger than the Court's opinion. Even some federal judges gave more weight to local sentiment than they did to the ruling of the nation's highest court. By 1964, however, there no longer could be any hope that the courts would permit separation of the races in the public schools by force of law or by action of any official public body.

Although the period of legal testing of the *Brown* decision might be regarded as ended, the basic problems that produced the decision remained largely unsolved. On the tenth anniversary of the decision, Burke Marshall, assistant U.S. attorney general in charge of civil rights, said, "In terms of what they—the Negroes—want and what they're entitled to, it's really just a beginning."

The *Brown* decision cleared the way for the movement of Negro Americans toward full equality of citizenship. It laid the foundation on which full equality under the law could be built. The Civil Rights Act of 1964 added part of the framework. When the structure would be completed was unpredictable. But a start had been made, and work continued toward the goal of creating a society in which the eyes of the law would be color blind.

Appendix: The Pace of Change

The preceding chapters have told the story of the people who wrought and fought the change that the *Brown* decision sparked. The statistics on school desegregation help to bring the story into sharper focus and to reveal the pattern and the pace of change.

Since 1954 Southern Education Reporting Service has compiled the available figures on enrollment by race in the public schools and colleges of the Southern and border states. Variations among the states in their methods of keeping records make absolutely accurate and complete tabulations impossible to obtain. Some states do not record the race of students, but reasonably close estimates can be made.

Ten years after the Supreme Court decision more than half of all Negro pupils in the District of Columbia and the border states of Delaware, Maryland, West Virginia, Kentucky, Missouri and Oklahoma were attending biracial schools. About one in 45 Negro children in Virginia, North Carolina, Tennessee, Arkansas, Texas and Florida was enrolled in a school with white children. In the Deep South states—South Carolina, Georgia, Alabama, Mississippi and Louisiana—the ratio dropped to approximately one in 750.

In the tenth year after the decision, almost 316,000, or 9.3 percent, of the 3,400,000 Negro school children in the 17-state region attended desegregated schools. The vast majority—281,000—were in the six border states and the District of Columbia, where 54.8 percent of the 514,000 Negroes were in biracial schools. In the 11 states of the old Confederacy, 34,110, or 1.18 percent of the 2,900,000 Negro children of school age were enrolled in schools with whites. More than 90 percent of the Negroes admitted to racially mixed schools in the Southern states were in the six states surrounding the Deep South.

In 1963–64 there were 3,028 biracial school districts (that is, districts in which both white and Negro school children lived) in the 17 Southern and border states. Of the biracial districts 1,161 had desegregated their schools, either by admitting both races to the same schools or by adopting policies that permitted both races to attend. Closer analysis gives greater meaning to the figures for each of the three major subdivisions of the region.

The Border Area

In all of the border states, school systems moved quickly to desegregate. In the first year after the 1954 decision, 156 border school districts desegregated. Within two years 70 percent of the districts had complied. Midway through the decade almost 80 percent of biracial school districts had desegregated, and 45 percent of Negro children were in schools with whites. In the tenth school year fewer than 10 percent of school districts remained segregated, but 45 percent of Negro children attended segregated schools.

Ten years after the decision only 55 of the 772 biracial school districts in the border area remained segregated. All districts were desegregated, at least in policy, in Delaware, Maryland and West Virginia. The District of Columbia had desegregated immediately. In Kentucky only 2 of its 165 biracial districts remained segregated; in Missouri, 9 of 212; in Oklahoma, 44 of 241.

Most of the school districts in the border states desegregated voluntarily. The one major exception was Delaware, which was required by court order to desegregate all of its schools in 1961; at the time only 11 of the 86 school districts in the state had adopted policies of desegregation. In Maryland

and Missouri the process was entirely voluntary, and in the remaining border states only 18 districts acted under court order.

Desegregation began in the cities. The rural areas were slower to change. In 1963–64 very nearly all of the 7,500 Negro pupils in Wilmington attended biracial schools, but almost half of the Negro school children in Delaware still attended all-Negro schools. Four in every 5 Negroes attending biracial schools in Kentucky were in Louisville. In Maryland 8 in 10 Negroes in schools with whites were in Baltimore. One-third of all Oklahoma Negroes attending biracial schools were in Oklahoma City and Tulsa. Neither Missouri nor West Virginia keeps racial statistics, but the pattern of urban-rural differences also applied in those states.

Even in the desegregated urban centers, the number of schools attended entirely or predominantly by children of one race was large and tended to grow. Population movements were mainly responsible. White families moved to the suburbs, and Negro families took their places in the central cities. Place of residence was a major factor in determining which school a child would attend. In most cities children, regardless of their race, were assigned to their neighborhood school. In some cities children were given a choice of schools to attend, and usually they chose their neighborhood school. Thus a school in a Negro neighborhood generally was all-Negro or predominantly Negro.

The District of Columbia desegregated its school system in 1954, and assigned pupils to neighborhood schools. In 1954 about one-fourth of total school enrollment was white. Ten years later fewer than one-seventh of public school pupils were white. After two years of desegregation 97 percent of Negro pupils were enrolled in schools with whites. At the end of ten years not quite 84 percent of Negroes were in biracial schools. During the decade the number of white pupils declined steadily, from about 39,000 in 1954 to fewer than 20,000 in 1964. At the same time the number of Negro pupils was climbing from about 69,000 to almost 118,000. These circumstances have produced a trend toward resegregation in District schools.

The city of Baltimore also desegregated in 1954, and retained its policy of giving pupils a free choice of a school to attend. In the first year less than 3 percent of the Negro pupils elected to attend schools with whites, and in the second year just over 7 percent. After seven years more than two-thirds of Negro pupils were in all-Negro schools. In August, 1961, Dr. Houston R. Jackson, a Negro and assistant superintendent of Baltimore schools, commented that more Negro pupils were "in essentially segregated situations than when segregation was compulsory." During the decade the number of white pupils in the city's schools declined by 7,000, while the number of Negro pupils increased by almost 54,000. The relative proportions of whites to Negroes very nearly reversed. At the beginning of the decade 62 percent of all pupils in the city system were whites, and at the end 57 percent were Negroes. In the 1963–64 school year 62 percent of the Negro students were in biracial schools, but many of the schools had just a few white students.

Other large cities in the border area had experiences similar to those of Washington and Baltimore. This resegregation in the cities combined with resistance in the rural areas kept almost half of the Negro children of the border states in segregated schools in 1964. Yet at the decade's end seven of every eight Negro children attending schools with whites in the entire region were in the border area. Only 15 percent of the Negro children enrolled in the region's schools lived in this section but they comprised more than 89 percent of all Negro children in schools with whites.

The Token Tier

In the ring of six states around the Deep South, school desegregation began in the years between 1954 and 1959, and in all but Virginia the process began voluntarily. In every instance the start was faltering, and the brakes were kept on to hold forward movement to the slowest possible pace.

Texas started first and moved fastest. Friona, a small West Texas town, admitted two Negro pupils to a school with whites in 1953. The next desegregation came in the fall of 1955, when 73 districts admitted more than 2,600 Negroes to formerly white schools. By the end of the decade 264 of the 900 biracial districts in the state had enrolled about 18,000 Negroes in schools with whites. Of the state's 326,000 Negro pupils, 19 in every 20 remained in a segregated school. Almost all of the desegregation in Texas was confined to the western part of the state. In the 1963–64 school year Texas accounted for about 60 percent of the desegregated school districts and more than half of the Negroes attending biracial schools in all eleven Southern states.

Arkansas was next to start after Texas. In 1954 both Charleston and Fayetteville desegregated voluntarily, followed in 1955 by Bentonville and Hoxie and in 1956 by Hot Springs. So, before Governor Faubus defied the federal courts in Little Rock in 1957, five Arkansas school systems already had desegregated. And in 1957 Fort Smith and Van Buren desegregated voluntarily without incident. At the end of the decade 13 of Arkansas' 228 biracial school districts had admitted 366 of the state's 112,000 Negro school children to formerly white schools.

Desegregation came to Tennessee in 1955, when the city of Oak Ridge, then federally-operated, voluntarily opened all its schools to Negroes. By 1960 only seven of the state's 143 biracial districts had desegregated. Beginning in 1961, the pace of change quickened. In 1963–64 the number of desegregated districts had reached 45, but only 4,500 of the state's 165,000 Negro school children were in schools with whites.

North Carolina followed Tennessee into the desegregated ranks. In 1957 eleven Negroes voluntarily were admitted to schools with whites in Charlotte, Greensboro and Winston-Salem. Desegregation spread slowly in the state during the next four years; in 1961 eleven school districts admitted 203 Negroes to biracial schools. By 1963–64 the number of desegregated districts had jumped to 40, and more than 1,800 of the 346,000 Negroes in the state's 171 school districts were in schools with whites.

Florida and Virginia experienced their first desegregation in 1959. In the next five years 16 of Florida's 67 school districts desegregated, and in 1963–64 they admitted 3,650 of the state's 238,000 Negro pupils to biracial schools. Virginia actually preceded Florida, having admitted Negroes to schools with whites in 4 districts in February, 1959, when its policy of "massive resistance" collapsed under attack in the federal courts. Once started, desegregation expanded relatively rapidly so that by the end of the decade 55 of Virginia's 128 biracial districts enrolled more than 3,700 Negro pupils in formerly all-white schools. Virginia had about 230,000 Negro school children.

Except in Texas the number of Negro children attending desegregated schools in the "token compliance" states was very small through the first seven years of the decade. Omitting Texas, the five remaining states had about 800 Negroes in biracial schools in 1960–61. These five states then had almost 1,000,000 Negro children in their public schools. During the next three years the number of Negroes in biracial schools in the five states grew to 14,000, and the total Negro enrollment to about 1,090,000. At the decade's end some 32,000 of 1,417,000 Negro children were attending desegregated schools in 433 of the six states' 1,636 biracial school districts. The token states had about 42 percent of the Negro enrollment in the 17-state region and 10 percent of the Negroes in desegregated schools. All but 53 districts, or 12 percent of the 433 that desegregated in the section, acted voluntarily.

The Deep South

The Deep South hardly had made a beginning toward desegregation when the decade ended. The border and token states accounted for 99.4 percent of all the Negro children in biracial schools in the tenth year following the Supreme Court decision.

In the five Deep South states, slightly more than 2,000 of the 1,477,000 Negro schoolchildren attended schools with whites. This figure is inflated, because it includes 1,439 Negro pupils in a New Orleans school attended by a single white child. The number of Negroes in formerly all-white schools in the Deep South at the end of the decade was 582, or about one in 2,400.

In the three states of Alabama, Mississippi and South Carolina 30 Negroes attended schools with whites; actually, all of them were in Alabama and South Carolina. Mississippi alone maintained complete segregation in its public schools throughout the decade. Alabama and South Carolina held the line until the tenth year, when they admitted 21 and 9 Negroes respectively to desegregated schools.

All five of the Deep South states kept their public schools segregated for six full years after the Supreme Court declared segregated schools unconstitutional. The first to yield to the federal courts was Louisiana. Four Negro first-graders entered formerly white New Orleans schools in November of 1960. Georgia followed in 1961, when eight Negro high school students were admitted to Atlanta schools. At the decade's end, only 11 of the 620 biracial school districts in the section had begun to desegregate, and all but two—both in Georgia—had acted under court order.

The Public Colleges

The pattern of desegregation in the public colleges and universities of the region loosely fit that of the schools, but the pace generally was faster. In each of the 17 states desegregation began in the colleges before it started in the public schools. Once inaugurated, it spread more quickly through the state systems of higher education than in the public schools. The border states took the lead, followed in turn by the token and Deep South states.

With the exception of Florida, all of the border and token states had made a beginning toward desegregation of their colleges before 1954. Delaware, Maryland, West Virginia and Arkansas were the only states in the region to take the initiative voluntarily. But when the courts required the admission of Negroes to one formerly all-white college in a state, the policy of desegregation was extended voluntarily to others. In the Deep South no state voluntarily began desegregation in its colleges, and only in Georgia was any white public institution opened to Negroes without a court order.

In the first academic year after the Supreme Court decision, almost half of the colleges in the border states desegregated. One year later 80 percent had biracial admission policies, and by 1961 the process was complete. During the first eight years after the decision, almost one-half of the colleges in the token states desegregated, and in the next two years the number increased substantially. At the end of the decade three-fourths of the colleges in the token states admitted both races, and in Arkansas, North Carolina and Tennessee all colleges were desegregated. Ten years after *Brown* less than one-third of the colleges in the Deep South had desegregated, and half of these were in Georgia and Louisiana. Of the 17-state region's 292 tax-supported colleges 203, or 70 percent, were desegregated in 1963–64. The decision to desegregate had been made voluntarily by 85 percent of them, and by 90 percent of those outside the Deep South.

The number of Negroes actually attending colleges with whites more precisely indicates the extent of desegregation than does the enumeration of colleges with biracial admission policies. Ten years after the Supreme Court's 1954 decision all the Negroes enrolled in public colleges in the border states attended biracial colleges, almost 60 percent in the token states and less than 10 percent in the Deep South. Included in the biracial colleges are predominantly Negro colleges attended by whites.

When the extent of desegregation is measured by the number of Negroes attending predominantly white colleges, the results are substantially different. In the border states in 1963–64 only 41 percent of Negro college students were in predominantly white institutions, 11 percent in the token states and 3 percent in the Deep South. A few unusual situations in some of the states put the sectional figures in a somewhat different light.

In the border states, Delaware and Maryland more nearly fit the Southern pattern. Only 20 of the 653 Negro students in Delaware attended predominantly white colleges, or 3 percent; in Maryland 848 of 2,493 Negro students, or 19 percent. West Virginia State was unique in being the only formerly all-Negro college that became predominantly white. Almost 80 percent of West Virginia Negro students were in predominantly white colleges, but 75 percent of the total were at West Virginia State. Of the 12,300 Negro students in the border states 5,100 were in predominantly white colleges.

The token states had the greatest number of Negro students, 34,700, of whom 3,700 were in predominantly white colleges and 20,000 in biracial colleges. No Negro college in Arkansas, Florida and Virginia enrolled white students. Arkansas and Virginia in 1964 each had 46 Negro students in formerly white colleges; in Florida almost 1,000 of its 5,000 Negro students were in predominantly white colleges. North Carolina had 250 Negroes in its previously white colleges and 7,700 in biracial colleges; in Tennessee the comparable figures were 400 and 4,600; in Texas, 2,000 and 6,600.

In the Deep South Louisiana offers the one exception to the pattern. Louisiana State University desegregated under court order in 1950, and in 1964 the state had 850 Negro students in seven of its predominantly white institutions, ranking sixth among the 17 states in this respect. Louisiana accounted for 95 percent of all the Negroes attending predominantly white colleges in the Deep South. The state's 10,300 Negro students were 40 percent of the 26,400 in the five states. Outside Louisiana only 47 Negroes attended formerly white colleges in the Deep South when the 1963–64 academic year ended—35 in Georgia, 6 each in Alabama and South Carolina and none in Missisippi.

The District of Columbia was in a unique situation. In 1954 it had only two tax-supported colleges, one for whites and one for Negroes. Immediately after the Supreme Court decision, the two colleges were merged. The single institution, the District of Columbia Teachers College, became predominantly Negro. In 1963–64 it had 1,438 students, of whom only 153 were white.

The Private Colleges

Records for the private colleges are incomplete and unofficial. Southern Education Reporting Service has kept a tabulation of their admission policies, but no figures on enrollment by race are available for the private institutions in the region.

The principle of the *Brown* decision applied only to public schools and colleges, so that desegregation by the private colleges and universities was in every case voluntary. Even so, by the end of the decade more than 80 percent of the 147 private colleges in the border area had adopted biracial admission policies. The same was true of 54 percent of the 189 private colleges in the token states and 24 percent of 102 in the Deep South. Of the

438 private colleges in the whole region, 246, or 56 percent, were desegregated in 1964.

In the region almost three-fourths of the private colleges were church-related. In each of the three divisions the percentage of desegregated colleges was higher among church-related than among other private institutions. In the border states 74 percent of the secular and 86 percent of the church-related colleges had desegregated by 1964; for the token states the percentages were 39 and 59; and for the Deep South, 15 and 26.

The pattern of desegregation in the private colleges corresponded roughly to that for the public ones. The greatest change took place in the border states and the least in the Deep South, with the token states in the middle. In each of the three sections a smaller proportion of private than public colleges desegregated, but the private institutions were not under the spur of legal compulsion.

Legislation and Litigation

In the volume of laws they passed, the legislators of the 17 states reflected the varying attitudes shown by the statistics on public school and college desegregation. During the decade the legislatures of the border states passed 26 laws dealing directly or indirectly with school segregation and desegregation. In the token states 154 laws were enacted; and in the Deep South, 291. The total for the region was 471.

Legislative activity in the token area correlated with the degree of resistance to desegregation within the respective states. Virginia resisted most vigorously and accumulated 56 laws. Arkansas was close behind with 44, followed by Florida with 21; Tennessee, 13; North Carolina, 11; and Texas, 9.

Louisiana passed 131 laws to take a commanding lead in the legislative sweepstakes. Among the other Deep South states, Georgia came second with 50, followed by Mississippi with 40 and Alabama and South Carolina with 25 each. Louisiana accounted for 45 percent of the Deep South's legislative output and 28 percent of that for the 17-state region. The Deep South enacted 62 percent of the region's laws; the token states, 32 percent; and the border states, 6 percent.

The two peaks of legislative activity came in 1956 and in 1960. During 1954 only 10 laws were passed. The Supreme Court handed down its implementation decision in May of 1955, but most of the state legislatures had adjourned, and only 30 laws were passed that year. But in 1956 the Southern states began to build their defenses against the impact of the decision and passed 96 laws. The process continued into 1957, when 66 laws were passed. In 1960 desegregation began in Louisiana, and the state legislature went into a frenzy of activity, passing 80 laws that year; other states passed 13 laws, giving the year a total of 93. In the last year of the decade only nine laws were passed, fewest for any year.

While the numbers of laws passed were indicative of the relative efforts of the states to evade or avoid compliance with the Supreme Court decision, the numbers of lawsuits filed suggests the relative amount of effort applied to bring the states into compliance.

In the entire region 404 lawsuits were filed during the decade in school desegregation cases. According to the general pattern, fewest suits—21 percent of the total—were brought in the border states, where compliance was generally quick and voluntary. But the token and Deep South states reversed the positions they might have been expected to occupy. More than half the region's lawsuits were filed in the token states, and just over one-quarter of them in the Deep South.

The reasons for this reversal were strategic. Whereas the border states escaped court action because they complied voluntarily, the token states were reluctant to comply and attempted to hold their compliance to a minimum. Suits were filed against school boards in the token states to force a beginning of desegregation and to accelerate it and remove obstacles to it after it had begun. The chances of success in promoting desegregation through court action were greater in the token states than in the Deep South because resistance was weaker in the former. The token states were reluctant to comply, but the Deep South was determined not to comply. The Deep South's defenses were hardest to breach, and so they were avoided while the attack centered on the token states.

Virginia was under the heaviest bombardment in the courts, 54 suits having been filed in that state. Next came Louisiana and Texas, with 42 each; North Carolina, 37; Arkansas, 33; and Florida, 28. Almost 60 percent of all the suits filed in the region were in these six states. All were token states except Louisiana, which invited lawsuits by its intensive legislative activity.

Every form of statistical measurement of desegregation in education reflects the predominant attitudes of the people in each state and each section of the region. The pace of change was fastest in the border states. The token states moved very slowly by comparison. The Deep South states hardly had crossed the starting line when the decade ended.

TABLE 1. PUBLIC SCHOOL DESEGREGATION, MAY, 1964

	School Districts			Enrollment		Enrollment in Desegregated Districts		Negroes in Schools with Whites	
	Total	With Negroes and Whites	Desegregated	White	Negro	White	Negro	No.	per cent†
Alabama	114	114	4	539,996**	287,414*	106,199**	70,896**	21	.007
Arkansas	415	228	13	328,023**	112,012**	66,752	18,643	366	.327
Florida	67	67	16	964,241*	237,871*	669,375	130,667	3,650	1.53
Georgia	197	181	4	689,323	337,534	95,731	77,599	177	.052
Louisiana	67	67	2	460,589**	301,433**	68,700	79,077	1,814	.602
Mississippi	150	150	0	304,226**	291,971**	0	0	0	0
North Carolina	171	171	40	820,900*	347,063*	367,764*	133,164*	1,865	.537
South Carolina	108	108	1	368,496*	258,955*	3,108	9,539	10	.004
Tennessee	154	143	45	687,902*	164,940*	380,321	120,447	4,486	2.72
Texas	1,421	899	263	2,045,499	326,409*	1,300,000*	200,000*	18,000*	5.52
Virginia	130	128	55	710,176	228,961	486,231	145,658	3,721	1.63
SOUTH	2,994	2,256	443	7,919,371	2,894,563	3,544,181	985,690	34,110	1.18
Delaware	86	86	86	78,730	18,066	68,321	13,976	10,209	56.5
District of Columbia	1	1	1	19,803	117,915	19,803	117,915	98,813	83.8
Kentucky	204	165	163	611,126*	54,874*	492,701*	54,874*	29,855	54.4
Maryland	24	23	23	540,667	160,946	535,691	160,946	76,906	47.8
Missouri	1,597	212*	203*	793,000*	95,000*	NA	90,000*	40,000*	42.1
Oklahoma	1,160	241	197	541,125*	43,875*	324,023*	35,596*	12,289*	28.0
West Virginia	55	44	44	417,595*	23,449*	417,595*	23,449	13,659*	58.2
BORDER	3,127	772	717	3,002,046	514,125	1,858,134††	496,756	281,731	54.8
REGION	6,121	3,028	1,160	10,921,417	3,408,688	5,402,315††	1,482,446	315,841	9.3

* Estimated.   ** 1962-63.   † No. of Negroes in schools with whites, compared to total Negro enrollment.
†† Missouri not included.   SOURCE: Southern Education Reporting Service.

TABLE 2. SCHOOL DESEGREGATION, 1954-64
GRADES KINDERGARTEN-12 IN 17 SOUTHERN AND BORDER STATES AND D.C.

		School Districts		Enrollment		Enrollment in Desegregated Districts		Negroes in Schools with Whites	
		Total	With Negroes and Whites	Deseg-regated	White	Negro	White	Negro	No.	per-cent†
1954-55	South	4,355	3,337	3	6,105,378	2,315,062	NA	NA	23	.001
	Border	6,214	907	156	2,438,611	323,752	NA	NA	NA	NA
	Region	10,569	4,244	159	8,543,989	2,638,814	NA	NA	NA	NA
1955-56	South	4,204	2,909	78	6,349,790	2,417,798	419,670*	21,299*	2,782	.115
	Border	5,654	912	329	2,470,787	324,539	NA	251,247	NA	NA
	Region	9,858	3,821	407	8,820,577	2,742,337	NA	272,546	NA	NA
1956-57	South	4,055	2,885	110	6,478,796	2,437,893	524,539	26,285	3,514	.144
	Border	5,642	810	573	2,645,015	360,408	1,323,405‡	298,989	106,878§	NA
	Region	9,697	3,695	683	9,123,811	2,798,301	1,847,944‡	325,274	110,392§	NA
1957-58	South	3,047	2,090	137	6,770,710	2,538,554	638,842	51,949	3,829	.151
	Border	5,467	813	621	2,656,865	385,397	1,313,919‡	325,337	127,677‡	NA
	Region	8,514	2,903	758	9,427,575	2,923,951	1,952,761‡	377,286	131,506‡	NA
1958-59	South	3,227	2,095	144	6,938,867	2,609,447	752,357	85,494	3,456	.132
	Border	4,647	780	596	2,711,653	398,971	1,509,156‡	361,528	142,352‡	NA
	Region	7,874	2,875	740	9,650,520	3,008,418	2,261,513‡	447,022	145,808‡	NA

1959-60 South	3,164	2,095	153	7,225,977	2,636,320	1,000,997	148,391	4,216	.160
Border	3,852	756	602	2,777,822	420,943	1,550,024‡	372,022	191,114	45.4
Region	7,016	2,851	755	10,003,799	3,057,263	2,551,021‡	520,413	195,330	6.4
1960-61 South	3,115	2,095	172	7,358,920	2,660,438	1,449,040	305,167	4,308	.162
Border	3,548	744	611	2,824,798	436,429	1,657,090‡	400,996	212,895	49.0
Region	6,663	2,839	783	10,183,718	3,096,867	3,106,130‡	706,163	217,203	7.0
1961-62 South	3,063	2,265	214	7,549,251	2,792,186	1,922,545	486,698	6,725	.241
Border	3,307	782	698	2,856,477	457,402	1,661,282‡	431,419	240,226	52.5
Region	6,370	3,047	912	10,405,728	3,249,588	3,583,827‡	918,117	246,951	7.6
1962-63 South	3,038	2,279	277	7,739,629	2,842,315	2,742,728	644,764	12,868	.453
Border	3,160	775	702	2,915,921	486,016	2,023,419	451,870	251,797	51.8
Region	6,198	3,054	979	10,655,550	3,328,331	4,766,147	1,096,634	264,665	8.0
1963-64 South	2,994	2,256	443	7,919,371	2,894,563	3,544,181	985,690	34,110	1.18
Border	3,127	772	717	3,002,046	514,125	1,858,134‡	496,756	281,731	54.8
Region	6,121	3,028	1,160	10,921,417	3,408,688	5,402,315‡	1,482,446	315,841	9.3

* Estimated. † Negroes in schools with whites compared to total Negro enrollment. ‡ Missouri not included.
§ Missouri and West Virginia not included. NA Not Available. SOURCE: Southern Education Reporting Service.

TABLE 3. DESEGREGATED PUBLIC COLLEGES AND UNIVERSITIES: PREDOMINANTLY WHITE—PREDOMINANTLY NEGRO

	Pre-1954	1954-55	1955-56	1956-57	1957-58	1958-59	1959-60	1960-61	1961-62	1962-63	1963-64	Total Schools
	PW-PN	PW-PN	PW-PN	PW-PN	PW-PN	PW-PN	PW-PN	PW-PN	PW-PN	PW-PN	PW-PN	PW-PN
Alabama			1-0	1-0	1-0	1-0	1-0	1-0	1-0	1-1	3-1	7-2
Arkansas	1-0	1-0	7-1*	7-1*	7-1*	7-1*	7-1*	7-1*	7-1*	7-1*	7-1*	7-1
Florida						1-0	1-0	3-0	5-1	9-1	10-2	20-13
Georgia								1-0	2-0	6-0	7-1	16-3
Louisiana	1-0	4-0	4-0	4-0	4-0	5-0	5-0	5-0	5-0	5-0	6-0	10-3
Mississippi										1-0	1-0	19-6
North Carolina	2-0	2-0	2-0	3-0	4-1	4-1	4-1	4-1	6-1	8-1	11-6*	11-6
South Carolina										1-0	2-0	5-1
Tennessee	1-0	1-0	1-0	3-1	5-1	5-1	6-1*	6-1*	6-1*	6-1*	6-1*	6-1
Texas	7-0	9-0	14-1	21-2	23-2	23-2	25-2	26-2	29-2	39-2	40-3	50-4
Virginia	5-0	5-0	5-0	5-0	5-0	5-0	5-0	5-0	6-0	8-0	9-0	19-2
SOUTH	17-0	22-0	34-2	44-4	49-5	51-5	54-5	58-5	67-6	91-7	102-15	170-42
Delaware	1-0	1-1*	1-1*	1-1*	1-1*	1-1*	1-1*	1-1*	1-1*	1-1*	1-1*	1-1
Dist. of Columbia		1-1*	0-1**	0-1*	0-1*	0-1*	0-1*	0-1*	0-1*	0-1*	0-1*	0-1
Kentucky	3-0	3-1	4-1	7-1*	7-1*	7-1*	7-1*	7-1*	7-1*	7-1*	7-1*	7-1
Maryland	2-2	3-2	8-4	8-4	12-4	14-4	14-4	14-4	16-4*	16-4*	16-4*	16-4
Missouri	2-0	11-1	12-1	12-1	12-1	13-1*	13-1*	13-1*	13-1*	13-1*	14-1*	14-1
Oklahoma	1-0	2-0	18-1	21-1	22-1*	22-1*	22-1*	22-1*	22-1*	22-1*	22-1*	22-1
West Virginia	1-0	10-1*	10-1*	10-1*	10-1*	10-1*	10-1*	10-1*	10-1*	10-1*	10-1*	10-1
BORDER	10-2	31-7	53-10	59-10	64-10	67-10	67-10	67-10	69-10*	69-10*	70-10	70-10
REGION	27-2	53-7	87-12	103-14	113-15	118-15	121-15	125-15	136-16	160-17	172-25	240-52

*Indicates all public colleges and universities desegregated.

**Two schools merged.

SOURCE: *Southern Education Reporting Service.*

Legislation	Ala.	Ark.	Del.	D.C.*	Fla.	Ga.	Ky.	La.	Md.	Miss.	Mo.	N.C.	Okla.	S.C.	Tenn.	Tex.	Va.	W.Va.
Anti-NAACP/Barratry	X	X			X	X	X	X	X	X		X	X	X	X	X	X	X
Closure of Schools Permitted	X	X			X	X	X	X	X	X		X	X	X	X	X	X	X
Compulsory Attendance Amended or Repealed	X	X			X	X	X	X	X	X		X	X	X	X	X	X	X
Emergency Powers to Officials					X	X		X	X	X				X	X	X	X	
Freedom of Choice—Seg./Deseg.	X	X			X	X	X	X	X	X		X	X	X	X	X	X	X
Human Rights Commissions			X	X			X		X		X		X		**			X
Interposition/Protest	X	X			X	X		X	X	X		X		X	X	X	X	
Legal Defense Authorized	X	X			X	X		X	X	X				X	X	X	X	
Limitations of Federal Powers Proposed	X	X			X	X		X		X					X	X		
Private Schools: Authorized/Encouraged	X				X	X		X									X	
Property Sold/Leased to	X	X			X	X		X	X	X				X	X		X	X
Pupil Assignment	X	X			X	X		X	X	X		X		X	X	X	X	X
Racial Designations: Removed	X										X	X			X		X	X
Required					X			X						X	X		X	
Scholarships Out-of-State	X	X	X		X	X	X	X	X	X		X	X	X	X	X	X	X
Segregation by Sex	X				X			X							X	X		
Segregation Committees	X	**			X	X		X	X	X		X	X	X	X	**	X	
Sovereignty Commissions	X	X				X		X		X							X	
State Constitutional Provision for Public Schools Removed	X													X				
Teachers: Tenure/Removal	X				X			X				X		X	X		X	
Protected in Private Schools	X																X	
Tuition Grants to Schools/Students	X	X			X	X		X		X		X	X	X	X		X	X
Withheld Aid to Deseg. Schools	X				X			X		X				X		X	X	X

* D.C. Board of Commissioners.   ** *Appointed without legislation.*   NOTE: *The table indicates types of legislation passed, not the number. One bill often included several features; several bills might duplicate each other. Several laws included have been held unconstitutional or been repealed.*   SOURCE: *Southern Education Reporting Service.*

Index